Theoretical Sociology

To the memory of my dear friend, Clara Dean, who in 1969 began typing all my manuscripts and who, at age 85, retired in 2010 from typing, only to die in 2012. I will forever be grateful to her friendship and incredible competence for over forty years in getting my manuscripts ready for publication.

Theoretical Sociology

A Concise Introduction to Twelve Sociological Theories

Jonathan H. Turner

University of California, Riverside

Los Angeles | London | New Delhi
Singapore | Washington DC

Los Angeles | London | New Delhi
Singapore | Washington DC

FOR INFORMATION:

SAGE Publications, Inc.
2455 Teller Road
Thousand Oaks, California 91320
E-mail: order@sagepub.com

SAGE Publications Ltd.
1 Oliver's Yard
55 City Road
London EC1Y 1SP
United Kingdom

SAGE Publications India Pvt. Ltd.
B 1/I 1 Mohan Cooperative Industrial Area
Mathura Road, New Delhi 110 044
India

SAGE Publications Asia-Pacific Pte. Ltd.
3 Church Street
#10-04 Samsung Hub
Singapore 049483

Copyright © 2014 by SAGE Publications, Inc.

Printed in the United States of America

Library of Congress Cataloging-in-Publication Data

A catalog record of this book is available from the Library of Congress.

9781452203478

This book is printed on acid-free paper.

Acquisitions Editor: Diane McDaniel
Editorial Assistant: Lauren Johnson
Production Editor: Eric Garner
Copy Editor: Lana Todorovic-Arndt
Typesetter: C&M Digitals (P) Ltd.
Proofreader: Jennifer Gritt
Indexer: Diggs Publication Services, Inc.
Cover Designer: Gail Buschman
Marketing Manager: Erica DeLuca

13 14 15 16 17 10 9 8 7 6 5 4 3 2 1

Brief Contents

Detailed Contents

About the Author

Jonathan H. Turner (PhD, Cornell University) is Distinguished Professor of sociology at the University of California, Riverside and University Professor for the University of California. The leading authority on sociological theory, Dr. Turner is the author of 38 influential books, which have been published in twelve different languages, as well as the author of many research articles in numerous journals and books.

Preface

There is surprisingly little consensus among sociologist about what theory is and what it is supposed to do for sociological analysis. For some, theory represents the way that science explains the empirical world. For others, it is simply an orienting perspective that can be used to describe events. For still others, theory is to be normative, advocating social arrangements that reduce oppression and inequality. All of these views of theory have been present since sociology's beginnings, and the arguments and debates among those holding one or the other of these views can become, to say the least, quite contentious. So, in writing a short introduction to sociological theory, it is difficult to know where to begin and end, given the controversy. I have sidestepped the controversy by outlining diverse approaches within twelve broad theoretical traditions. In some, scientific explanation is the dominant view; in others, a more descriptive view prevails; in still others, a critical view of the role of theorizing dominates; and in a few, two or all three visions of what theory should be can be found. My biases are toward scientific theorizing, where abstract laws and models that explain how the social universe operates are preferred. Yet, I have given fair coverage to the alternative approaches because, like it or not, they are part of what is called sociological theory today.

I have written many long books on theory, but I have tried something new here. I have—at least for me—written a short book that is still comprehensive but that highlights the key elements of a particular theoretical perspective and some of the important theorists working within a perspective. The goal has been to create a handbook that packs a lot of information into a small space, especially compared to the other large books on theory that I have written in the past. I originally thought of titling the book *Lectures on Theoretical Traditions* because the chapters have drawn upon my lecture notes, but I have also pulled important elements from my larger and longer books. The result, I hope, is a book that is useful in many different ways, such as a concise introduction to the range of theorizing in sociology, a convenient review of theory for those brushing upon on sociological theorizing, a source of lectures for instructors, and a quick guide to those who do not know much about sociological theory and are just curious about what it is.

It was fun to write this book, and moreover, it was good for me—champion of theoretical tomes—to summarize in an abbreviated but a still robust manner.

Jonathan Turner
Murrieta, California
USA

CHAPTER 1

Theoretical Sociology Today

Controversy Over What Theoretical Sociology Can or Should Be

Sociology emerged as an explicit discipline in the early 1800s, although people have always thought about the universe around them, including the social universe of their own creation. Auguste Comte,[1] the titular founder of sociology, preferred the name social physics for the new discipline because, during his time, the notion of "physics" had not been usurped by the current discipline using this name. Physics back then meant "to study the nature of"; therefore, *social physics* was to be a scientific discipline devoted to studying the nature of the social universe created by people's behaviors, interactions, and patterns of social organization. For Comte, explanations in science are developed through theory, and thus, sociological theory was to be the vehicle by which explanations of the social universe were to be achieved—just as is the case in physics and biology.

Since the label, *social physics*, had already been used by a Belgian statistician, Comte had to adopt the Latin-Greek hybrid label of *sociology*—a name that he did not like but had to accept. From the very beginning, the view of sociology as an explanatory science, like any natural science, was questioned by many. Today, many still do not believe that sociology can be a natural science, and hence, theoretical sociology cannot offer explanations like those in the "hard" sciences. For these critics, humans have the capacity to change the very nature of their universe, with the result that there can be no universal laws about social dynamics like those in physics or even biology. Moreover, so much of what happens in history is by chance events converging to produce unpredictable outcomes. And so, at best, sociological theory can describe for a time the social universe, but as this universe changes its fundamental character, old theories must give ways to new theories, which will also eventually become obsolete as humans remake their universe.

For others, whether or not sociology can be a science, it must first of all be critical of social conditions where oppression and inequality prevail. Sociology should emphasize unjust social conditions and propose liberating alternatives; and for many who make this argument, the scientific pretension of some in the discipline is part of the problem—a theme that has existed in sociology from its first moments as a new discipline.

---

[1]Auguste Comte, *The Positive Philosophy of Auguste Comte*, three volumes. Condensed and translated by H. Martineau (London: George Bell and Sons, 1896, originally published in serial form in French between 1830 and 1842).

For still others, theoretical sociology should be seen as conceptual schemes that allow sociologists to describe important social processes, at least for a time until these processes change fundamentally. Sociology provides, in essence, a set of eyeglasses for seeing reality and, equally significant, for understanding this reality at a given time and place.

There are many variants on these views of what theoretical sociology can, and should, be. Given this lack of consensus—and indeed, outright hostility among some epistemological camps—it becomes difficult to know what to include in a book on theory, and particularly in a short book like this one. My biases, as are well known, lean toward a view of theory as scientific, but I would be foolish to assume that others all feel the same way. As a result, I have written this book to emphasize that theoretical sociology has a set of theoretical perspectives—some scientific, others less so; some descriptive, others explanatory; some critical, others value-neutral— that have been developed over the last two centuries of sociological theorizing. I have done my best to summarize these perspectives fairly and in as much detail as a short book will allow.[2]

For each perspective, I first seek to examine its origins in classical sociology. Then, I review its basic structure and line of argumentation. And finally, I offer examples of variations in how theorists have used a particular theoretical perspective and orientation. Thus, I try to pack a great deal of material into relatively short number of pages, but not to the point of making the book too dense. I offer a concise but not, I trust, a dense introduction to theoretical sociology.

Violating the Law of Small Numbers

There are eleven chapters after this one, and thus, it might seem that this book reviews this many distinctive theoretical approaches—which might be true except for the fact that there are variants of these perspectives that are often quite different. The result is that the number of perspectives examined is much greater than the twelve that are advertised in the subtitle of this book, which always imposes the problem of "small numbers." Any intellectual field can probably have fewer than seven major perspectives that everyone can grasp,[3] and so once we go beyond seven, the intellectual landscape becomes cognitively more complex. So, from the start, we are at twelve perspectives, but once we see the sometimes dramatic variations within a perspective, we have easily doubled the total number of distinctive approaches in the field of theoretical sociology.

Despite the cognitive overload of having many variants of what I see as the twelve basic approaches outlined in the next chapters, this complexity must be accepted because it is the state of sociological theory today. Depending upon one's preferences, some of the theoretical orientations examined in these chapters are not essential, whereas for others, they are. Clearly, some approaches are more widespread than others, and yet some of the less practiced approaches are among sociology's oldest perspectives or, alternatively, some of the newest perspectives promise to become increasingly prominent over the next decades. I have, therefore, had to make some judgments about what I think is most prominent today; others might make up a somewhat different

---

[2]I have also written very detailed reviews of theoretical sociology. See, for example, Jonathan H. Turner, *Contemporary Sociological Theory* (Thousand Oaks, CA: Sage, 2012) and *Theoretical Sociology: 1830 to the Present* (Thousand Oaks, CA: Sage, 2012).

[3]Randall Collins, *The Sociology of Philosophies* (Cambridge, MA: Harvard University Press, 1998).

list but, in the end, I do not think that our lists would be so different because, despite the complexity of theoretical sociology, there is a core set of approaches that continue to dominate the field.

When I entered the field of sociology almost fifty years ago, textbooks on theory listed many perspectives, which I found confusing because, as I looked at the field in the 1960s, only a few approaches really dominated. Still, texts had lots of historical detail, and the result was many more perspectives than I can review here on these pages. When I wrote my first text on sociological theory,[4] I reduced the number of contemporary perspectives down to four basic approaches: functional, conflict, exchange, and interactionist theory. One can still find this list organizing introductory textbook descriptions of theoretical sociology today. While I knew that I had chosen the most dominant approaches in the field, I also suspected that this small number of recognizable perspectives would not last, and I was correct. They began to differentiate and elaborate, and once we add some of those that I had not included, the actual number of approaches was much greater than was evident almost forty years ago in that first book, titled *The Structure of Sociological Theory*. What changed theoretical sociology was further breakdown over the consensus of what theory is, can be, or should be, coupled with the comeback of approaches that had been left for dead.

Without consensus over epistemology, the criterion of science could no longer be used to sort out dominant perspectives. Furthermore, with the resurrection of older approaches, such as evolutionary theory, the number of theoretical approaches began to grow and, as variants within perspectives were successfully added, sociology finds itself almost back to where I started in the 1960s—with perhaps too many approaches. But this is the reality of the day, and I have tried to do my best to capture this variety without overwhelming the reader with too many fine-grained distinctions. For the goal of this book is to be concise and to offer a broad overview of theoretical sociology as it is currently practiced in the discipline.

Issues That All Theorists Must Resolve for Themselves

Over that last five decades, I have often been dismayed by the controversies in theoretical sociology. Debate can be intense among protagonists, and unfortunately, because the debate is over epistemologies and often moralities as well, it never ends. I would encourage all who read this book not to get bogged down in these issues that cannot be resolved, except by personal preferences of theorists. Certain questions need to be answered by each theorist, and depending on the answers given, different scholars will pursue different theoretical approaches. What are the basic questions? There are surprisingly few.

Can Sociology Be a Science?

This is probably the most fundamental question. Depending upon the answer, the kind of theorists that a scholar becomes will vary. My views were not always as strong as they are today. I recall in graduate school that there were great debates among students on whether or

---

[4]Jonathan H. Turner, *The Structure of Sociological Theory* (Homewood, IL: Dorsey Press, 1974). There were seven editions of this book, mostly published by Wadsworth Publishing when the book then went out of print in 2012.

not sociology could be a science. I had no strong views at the time, but over the years, I have decidedly come down on the side of trying to make sociology a hard science. Others have gone the exact opposite route. Several of my (still) good friends from graduate school were once as rabid as I am now about the prospects for a natural science of society; today, we are in opposite camps but, thankfully, we can live with each other's differences in epistemological faith. But, anyone who becomes a theorist must make a decision on this fundamental question. Even in reading the pages of this book as, perhaps, a beginner in theory, you may find yourself starting to think about this question; and the more you pursue sociology, and theoretical sociology in particular, the more salient this question becomes.

Should Sociology Be Critical, Moral?

Critical sociologies and scientific sociology are often viewed as opposites, but such need not be the case. Most people who become sociologists often begin by being drawn to a discipline because it studies problems in societies and, it would appear, seeks to do something about these problems. I was certainly drawn to sociology for this reason, and I was not alone in the 1960s, which was a watershed period of protest and realignment of Western societies around the world. Critical theorists are normative, and moral; they search out oppressive conditions; they analyze their root causes and effects; and they demand that these conditions be eliminated. One can be a scientist and pursue this agenda, as I have done for many years—less in my actually sociology and more in my personal life. But critical theorizing demands the value neutrality of scientists, where the goal is to understand as much as to condemn social conditions. Critical theorists often argue that, by not taking a critical and moral stance, the scientists end up implicitly supporting the oppressive status quo. I do not accept this judgment, but many do; and so, at some point, scholars have to make decisions about where their inner critical theorists will reside, and whether or not these inner critical theorists will be subordinate to a more dominant value-neutral scientist. Early in my career, I gave much more free rein to my inner critical theorist; today, I keep it bottled up when I do science, letting it out when I am done doing scientific analysis. Others do just the opposite, and still others let the two battle it out.

Whatever the decision, it has to be made, perhaps not so much as a conscious decision, as was my case, but as an emerging preference where one just prefers one side or the other. I decided in the mid-1970s that my sociology would be a better sociology and, moreover, a more useful sociology if I began by holding in check my moral biases and, instead, devoted my time to figuring out how the social world operates, without passing moral judgments. With such knowledge, I would be in a better position to propose viable solutions to real world problems. Again, others do not accept this, seeing it as a "cop-out," but the important point is that you have to make a decision or let these two inner demons fight it out for control of how you do sociology.

What Is the Most Important Approach to Sociological Analysis?

This question is less disturbing because it does not have to be answered early in a career, and indeed, it can be answered in different ways at varying points in a sociological career.

I started out as a committed symbolic interactionist (see Chapter 5), and then switched to other perspectives, primarily functionalism (Chapter 2) and conflict theory (Chapter 3). But over the years, I have found just about every theoretical perspective useful, and so, now I am so eclectic that I could not categorize myself by any of the perspectives examined in the chapters to follow. My goal is to figure out how the social universe operates, and I am willing to beg, borrow, or steal an idea from any perspective that allows me to achieve this goal. Indeed, I spend much of my time integrating theories.

Still, when we first start out, some approaches are typically more appealing than others. And often, people stay with this initial decision for their entire careers. One has to start somewhere, and picking an approach that is appealing is one way to begin. But, I found myself intrigued by almost every new approach that I learned over the decades, even ones that I initially did not like (but later saw merit in); for others, maybe just a couple of perspectives will do it for a career. Reading the theories outlined in this volume will probably lead readers to prefer one or two over the others, and this is a good place to begin developing one's sociological imagination.

What Level of Analysis Is Most Important?

The answer to this question is much like the one above: you may start out at the micro level of interpersonal processes, but then move to more meso- or macro-level phenomena. Some scholars never leave where they start out. For example, many symbolic interactionists stay at the more micro level; conflicts theorists and functionalists might stay at the macro level. Yet, others begin to see that we need to understand all the levels, and so, they begin to theorize about all levels of social reality.

Social reality unfolds at three levels: (1) the face-to-face interpersonal level; (2) the macro level of societies, inter-societal systems, institutions (e.g., economy, polity, law, kinships, religion, science, etc.), and stratification; and (3) the meso level of corporate units (groups, organizations, communities) and categoric units (membership in social categories like class, ethnicity, gender). Some argue that one or the other of these levels is more "primary" than the others in the sense that one level yields more understanding than the other two. I have called those who make this argument micro and macro chauvinists because they assume that social reality can only be understood by focusing on the micro or macro levels of reality. There also could be meso-level chauvinists. Being a chauvinist in this sense is not necessarily bad because, by studying one level and seeking how far one can take explanations, it often yields important insights, although I would argue that at some point, further understanding cannot be gained without shifting levels of analysis.

Early sociology was decidedly macro in its interests in trying to understand the big transformations to societies that came with modernity. More recently, theorizing in sociology often has a more micro bias. Again, as a starting point, one needs to jump into reality at one of these levels—just to get started being a sociologist. I found the micro level fascinating as an undergraduate, but when I got to graduate school and was exposed to macro sociology, I found this level of reality just as fascinating. I spent half my career being primarily a macro-level theorists, but the second half has involved a great deal of micro-level theorizing on emotions and interpersonal processes. And most important, to me at least, is that I have tried to integrate all three levels of theorizing into a more general theory.[5] My view is that sociologists should not dismiss any of these three levels, no matter what one's preferences are. A preference for a particular level does not mean that only this level matters; they all matter if we are to understand social reality, and the best theories seek to integrate explanations across more than one level.

So, the answer to the question on levels of analysis can be almost anything, as long as it does not lead to intolerance. My experience has been that sociology majors tend to refer the micro level—say, as outlined in Chapters 6 and 7—but such is not always the case. You should try to answer the question when you are finished with the book and see where your preferences lie, at least for the present.

Conclusion

We all must accept the empirical fact that sociology is a very diverse discipline. It is the broadest of the social sciences, covering the entire spectrum of human behavior, interaction, and organization; moreover, it attracts people with very different orientations. It should not be surprising that sociologist argue a lot because they develop different preferences over epistemology, morality, and substantive inquiry into social reality. The theories in this book reflect these differences. The diverse perspectives reviewed in the pages should be viewed as different sets of eyeglasses. Each perspective allows you to see some social processes much better than others, but none allows you to see everything. You will need many other sets of eyeglasses to capture a fuller image of social reality; and so, by the time that these pages are finished, you will have more than a dozen prescription lenses for seeing and making sense of the social universe. I would recommend that you hang onto these prescriptions and, in fact, keep adding to you collection of eyeglasses.

---

[5]Jonathan H. Turner, *Theoretical Principles of Sociology*, three volumes (New York: Springer, 2010–2012).

CHAPTER 2

Functional Theorizing

The Beginnings of Functionalism

Auguste Comte's Advocacy

By the early decades of the nineteenth century, the time was right for a new discipline committed to the systemic study of the social world. As noted in the last chapter, Auguste Comte put a name to an accumulating body of theorizing about the nature and dynamics of societies, calling this discipline by the Latin-Greek hybrid name of *sociology*, or the study of the social.[1] Comte had preferred the name *social physics*, by which he meant to study the fundamental nature of the social universe. But, to Comte's dismay, he discovered that the name had already been taken by a Belgian statistician, and so, he was reluctantly forced to use the label "sociology."

Comte was well aware that the nineteenth century would be the "century of biology" because the idea of evolution was in the air, but he also recognized that the most successful of the sciences—what eventually became known as "physics"—represented the appropriate model of how science should formulate theories. Biology could provide the metaphor as well as the entry point for legitimating the new science of society, while physics could provide the template for how sociological laws are to be formulated and tested.

Comte's Use of Biology

In trying to justify sociology, Comte constructed his infamous "hierarchy of the sciences" to argue that the last and most complex science to emerge in the new era of what he termed *positivism*, or theoretically driven science, would be sociology. Sociology was now in the process of arising from biology and, in so doing, would complete the hierarchy with, not surprisingly, sociology being at the top. Indeed, in a fit of modesty, he termed sociology "the queen science." Biology was to be the study of organisms, while the new, emerging sociology was to be the study of *social* organisms, or the analysis of the structured patterns of relations among organisms. In making his case for sociology, Comte began to analogize that society is a more complex organism. As a complex organism, societies are ultimately built *not* from individual human organisms but, rather, from another social organism—families—which, in societies, were the

---

[1]Auguste Comte, *The Positive Philosophy of Auguste Comte*, three volumes. Condensed and translated by H. Marinteau (London: George Bell and Sons, 1896, originally published in serial form in French between 1830 and 1842).

functional equivalent of cells in biological organisms. He went on to assert that all other parts—groups, organizations, communities, and other social structures—were ultimately elaborations of the family as the most fundamental part of societies. And so, societies as social organisms could be distinguished from biological organisms by the fact they were built from social organisms that were linked together by common culture and political authority.

From this "organismic analogy," sociology's first theoretical perspective was forged, although Comte did not take this analogy theory very far. He divided sociology into *statics* (structural properties of the social) and *dynamics* (processes creating, sustaining, and changing the properties and relations among these properties making up the social organism). This image of a social organism suggested a particular mode of analysis, and this approach eventually became known as *functionalism* or, at times, as *structural functionalism*.

The essence of functionalism is to visualize particular social structures as having effects on the viability of the social organism in its environment. Just as the heart, lungs, stomach, or any structure in an individual organism has a "function" for sustaining the body, so the "body social" or society can be analyzed by discovering the functions of particular social structures. What typified the societies over the course of history was their growth in their size and complexity; and thus, like individual organisms, the evolutionary trend is toward increased complexity of organisms and social organisms. Furthermore, like individual organisms, social organisms become more complex as they grow or, in more modern language, *differentiated* into increasingly diverse social units that make up the whole. Each of these units can be examined by the functions they serve for sustaining societies.

Another element of functional analysis was positing a series of needs or requisites that *must be met* if a society or any social system is to persist in its environment. As we will see, subsequent functionalists began to construct lists of multiple requisites or, alternatively, one master system need and then analyze any social structure in terms of meeting a particular system requisite. For Comte, there was one basic need among all social systems that grow and become more complex: the need for *social integration*, or the coordination, regulation, and control of differentiated system parts. Societies that cannot meet this inclusive requisite will reveal increased potential for social "pathologies," whereas those that can develop (a) mechanisms of mutual interdependence among system part, (b) centers of power for political control and regulation of system parts, and (c) cultural codes common to all differentiated social units, would be the most likely to meet the requisite for social integration. Comte's basic model is outlined in Figure 2.1.

As simple as this model appears, it contains many of the elements that define sociology, not only in the past but also today. Still, Comte only hinted at functional theory, viewing this theory as arising from biology, and moreover, in one of his many pretentious moments, Comte felt that the development of scientific sociology would be able to guide the future development of biology. Yet, even though actual theorizing by Comte is rather spotty, he gave the discipline its first self-conscious agenda. But, he also did more: he offered a vision for how theory should be developed in sociology.

Comte's Use of Early Physics

Comte was a champion of a natural science view of what sociology could be. Like any science, sociology can develop *explanatory laws* about the properties and dynamics of the social world, and the best of these laws would be those that are about timeless and fundamental processes that

Figure 2.1   Comte's Implicit Model of Social Statics

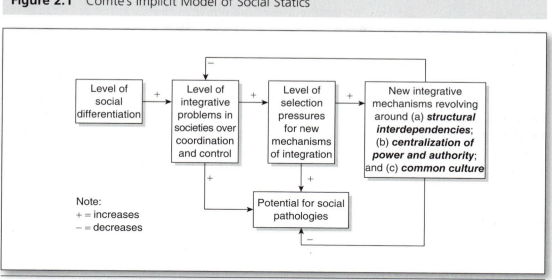

Source: Turner, Jonathan. (2012). *The Emergence of Sociology Theory,* Figure 3.1, p. 49. SAGE Publications, Inc.

always occur when humans organize themselves into social systems. This was the image of science in the era after Newton's formulation of the law of gravity that was thought, at the time, capable of explaining many of the properties and dynamics of the cosmos. The same, Comte argued, was possible for the social universe; explanation would come from articulating abstract laws about the dynamics of fundamental properties of a cosmos composed of social systems.

This advocacy was controversial in Comte's time, and as we shall see in later chapters, it remains controversial to the present day and, no doubt, well into the future of the discipline. His vision for theory was a series of abstract laws that, much like those in physics, could explain why the fundamental properties of the social universe exist in the first place and, then, how these properties operate. So, from the model in Figure 2.1, he clearly advocated that three of the fundamental properties of the social universe are (a) structural interdependencies among differentiated units, (b) centers of power and authority, and (c) cultural systems that regulate the actions of individuals and the social units. These three properties of the social universe have evolved because they were needed, and once they exist, their dynamics revolve around increasing system-level coordination, control, and integration among differentiated subsystems in society. Thus, for Comte, the substance of sociology was pulled from an analogy to biology—the study of social organisms and their evolution toward increasing differentiation—but the explanatory methodology came from physics.

Herbert Spencer's Functionalism

Herbert Spencer was one of the most prolific and well-known scholars of the nineteenth century, whose star began to fall in the early decades of the twentieth century and could never be fully reignited to its earlier brightness. Indeed, contemporary sociologists are often rather hostile to Spencer, frequently without ever having read very much, if any, of his work. Spencer was a philosopher who embarked on a project that he labeled Synthetic Philosophy. To say that this project was ambitious is an understatement because his goal was to subsume ethics, physics, psychology, biology, and sociology under some basic laws of the universe, loosely "deduced" from the laws of physics as they had been articulated at the midpoint of the nineteenth century. This law was to explain the evolution of all domains of the universe from simple to more complex forms.[2] In laying out his grand Synthetic Philosophy to subscribers of his work, Spencer wrote a short summary of his theoretical principles, two major treatises on ethics, and multi-volume works on psychology, biology, and sociology.[3] He wrote *Principles of Biology*[4] before he began to write *Principles of Sociology*[5] in 1873, which came out in serial form to subscribers to his Synthetic Philosophy. As installments of these serial publication of his ideas accumulated into a volume, they were bound, eventually producing the three volumes of *Principles of Sociology* that are still available today and that, in the decades between 1874 and 1994, were among the most read books ever written by a sociologist (this is why so many copies are available today).[6] This sequence in Spencer's treatise on psychology and biology was no coincidence because he was following—through he denied it—in Comte's footsteps, but with considerably more detail and sophistication.

Spencer's Theoretical Methodology

Like Comte, Spencer had a natural science view of what sociology should and could be. The notion of "principles" appears in most of his major works because he felt that he had isolated the fundamental properties of the social, biological, psychological, physical, and ethical universes, with specific sets of volumes developing highly abstract principles or laws loosely "derived" from the physics of his time about the operative dynamics of each of these universes (see footnote 2 below for the basics of this "law").

In the case of sociology, the three volumes of *Principles of Sociology* are filled with abstract laws about a wide range of social phenomena, copiously illustrated with data from biology and vast amounts of data on societies of the past and present at all stages of development from preliterate to modern industrial forms of social organization. These data were published in the separate volumes of what he labeled *Descriptive Sociology*—a monumental achievement that, like so much of Spencer's work, have fallen in obscurity.[7] These principles were interwoven, in

---

[2]Here is one of Spencer's statements on his general law of evolution:

> ". . . an integration of matter and concomitant dissipation of motion, during which the matter passes from an indefinite incoherent homogeneity to a definite coherent heterogeneity; and during which the retained motion undergoes a parallel transformation." P. 343, *First Principles* (see note 3).

[3]Herbert Spencer, *First Principles* (New York: A. L. Burt, 1880, originally published in 1862); *Social Statics: Or, the Conditions Essential to Human Happiness Specified, and the First of Them Developed* (New York: Appleton-Century Crofts, 1888, originally published in 1850–1851); *The Principles of Psychology*, 3 volumes (New York: Appleton-Century-Crofts, 1880, originally published in 1885).

[4]Herbert Spencer, *The Principles of Biology*, 3 volumes (New York: Appleton-Century-Crofts, 1864–1867).

[5]Herbert Spencer, *The Principles of Sociology*, 3 volumes (New York: Appleton-Century-Crofts, 1895, originally initiated in 1874).

[6]For a more recent republication of this great work, see *The Principles of Sociology*, 4 volumes (New Brunswick, NJ: Transaction Publishers, 2002) with, for it is worth, a long introduction by me.

[7]Herbert Spencer, *Descriptive Sociology, or Groups of Facts* was initiated in 1873 and finished after Spencer's death, with the last volume coming out in 1934. See my and Alexandra Maryanski's review of the logic of *Descriptive Sociology* in "Sociology's Lost Human Relations Area Files," *Sociological Perspectives* 31 (1988): pp. 19–34.

both his biology and sociology, into an organismic emphasis. For biology, it was the study of *individual organisms*, whereas sociology was the study of what he labeled *superorganisms*, or the "organization of organisms" into societies. Moreover, anticipating the effort to reconnect biology and sociology in the present era (see Chapters 11 and 12), Spencer felt that *any* species of animals that organizes into a society is a superorganism worthy of sociological analysis.

Spencer's Organismic Analogy

Spencer wrote a rather defensive essay about "reasons" for "dissenting from A. Comte," but it is clear that he took Comte's ideas and simply developed them further.[8] Probably Spencer's most famous passages to the mind of contemporary sociology are on the comparison of the superorganic with the organic, where the similarities or "parallels in principles of organization" between individual and superorganisms were listed along with differences between societies and organisms. These analogies constitute only a few pages in a work that is over 2,000 pages long, and yet, this is about all that theorists in the contemporary era know about Spencer—an obvious sign that he is no longer read extensively. Nonetheless, his ideas have endured, even if their influence on present-day theory is not fully recognized.

Similarities between the organic and superorganic include:[9] both can be distinguished from inorganic matter because the organic and superorganic grow and develop; in both, growth is accompanied by increases in complexity or differentiation of structure; in both, an increase in the number of distinctive functions occurs with the differentiation of structure; both reveal interdependencies among diverse parts, with change in one affecting the structure of other parts; in both, each part of the whole is either an micro superorganism in itself (e.g., family, groups, organization) or a living part (e.g., cells, organs) within an organism; and in both, the life of the whole can be destroyed, but the parts will live on for a while.

There are, however, some distinctive differences between superorganisms and organisms: The degree of connectedness and proximity of parts is greater in organisms than superorganisms; the nature of communication is vastly different because communication in organisms occurs through "molecular waves passing through various channels," whereas in superorganisms, communication occurs via cultural symbols organized into languages; and there are vast differences in consciousness and thought in organisms and superorganisms, with all units in superorganisms possessing capacities for consciousness, reasoning, and decision making, while only one part (the brain) is capable of consciousness in organisms.

The Four Functional Requisites

The organismic analogy in Spencer's work is only important because it follows on his great treatise on *Principles of Biology*, where individual organisms were seen as having fundamental requisites that must be met to sustain life. Like organisms, superorganisms reveal structures that integrate diverse parts, and moreover, superorganisms and organisms reveal basic functional needs or requisites that must be met to ensure their viability in an environment.

---

[8]Herbert Spencer, *Reasons for Dissenting From the Philosophy of M. Comte and Other Essays* (reprinted in Berkeley, CA: Glendessary, 1968).

[9]Spencer, *Principles of Sociology*, volume 1, p. 448.

The result of this emphasis is that Spencer posited three general functional requisites for superorganisms that have correspondence to similar requisites for organisms. In reality, there are four requisites because Spencer divides one into two halves. The four requisites are listed and defined in Table 2.1.

Table 2.1   Spencer's List of Functional Requisites in Superorganisms

1. **Production** revolving around the gathering of resources and their conversion into usable resources for sustaining a population (operation)

2. **Reproduction**: Structures for creating new members of the population and for sustaining as well as creating the social structures and cultures organizing their activities (operation)

3. **Regulation**: The consolidation of power and authority as well as cultural symbols (e.g., ideologies and beliefs) to control and coordinate individual and corporate units' activities

4. **Distribution**:
   a. The development of *infrastructures* for moving persons, information, and resources in geographical space
   b. The development of mechanisms for *exchanges* of resources among individuals and corporate units in a population

Thus, superorganism must meet needs for (1) *operation*, or (a) *production* of substance that sustains the superorganism and (b) *reproduction* of both the individual organisms (i.e., people) and the social structures and culture of superorganisms that organizes people's activities; (2) *regulation*, or the capacity to coordinate and control people and the structures organizing their lives by the consolidation of power and the development of cultural systems of values, beliefs, norms, and laws; and (3) *distribution* or the movement of people, resources, and information about the territories and structures of superorganisms.[10] As noted and emphasized in Table 2.1, I have broken the requisite of *operation* (also termed the "sustaining system") down into its separate requisites, thereby producing the four total functional requisites listed in Table 2.1: production, reproduction, regulation, and distribution.

Spencer's basic argument is that as populations grow, the superorganism or society organizing the activities of all its members will differentiate new kinds of structures and associated cultural systems. This differentiation will occur on what he often termed the basic *axes* of production, reproduction, regulation, and distribution since these are what is essential for sustaining the viability of a superorganism. For example, as populations grow, there are pressures to produce more food to sustain the larger population, with the result that structures within the economy differentiate. With population growth and differentiation, there are new problems of making sure that individuals are capable of participating in the new and diverse structures and their cultures, thus leading to the differentiation of ever-more education structures to ensure reproduction of the new structures. With growth, problems of coordination of diverse types of actors in diverse types of social structures increase, as do problems of poten-

---

[10]Spencer, *Principles of Sociology*, volume 1, pp. 498–548.

tial conflict as the degree of stratification increases or as do problems of deviance as cultural controls weaken, thereby leading to the evolution of polity and law as social control mechanisms and alterations in the cultural systems that are used to regulate conduct. And with growth, problems of distributing resources, people, and information increase, causing the development of new distributive infrastructures (roads, ports, canals, etc.) and distributive mechanisms for exchanging resources (e.g., new, more differentiated markets).

For Spencer, then, theory must first explain the dynamics of population growth and differentiation, which represented an application of his general law borrowed from physics (see footnote 2 on p. 10). In general, population growth will cause differentiation in order to supply the necessary "structural support" for the larger "social mass." As noted above, differentiation occurs in a clear pattern along each of the four axes that correspond to the functional requisites summarized in Table 2.1. All other theoretical principles in Spencer's *Principles of Sociology* are devoted to explaining patterns of development and change in institutional systems that evolve along these four axes, especially the consolidation of power and its relation to stratification and inequality that also increase with differentiation of institutional systems. For, just as institutional systems differentiate, so do the number of classes and social strata in a society; and these new strata always pose problems of regulation and thus encourage more consolidation and centralization of power, along with ideologies legitimating this mobilization of power. Thus, Spencer was a conflict theorist (see next chapter) as much as a functionalist, but it is his functionalism that has exerted the most influence in sociology.

Emile Durkheim's Functional Analysis

Emile Durkheim borrowed much from Spencer. Like Spencer, he emphasized the basic relationship between population growth and structural differentiation. In contrast to Spencer, however, Durkheim argued that this transformation from simple to complex posed *one* master requisite for societal survival: the need for *integration* among differentiation actors.[11] Like Comte, he posited pathological forms of differentiation in this transition from simple to complex societies, but he also assumed that over time the proper mechanisms of integration would eventually evolve. Unlike Spencer and more like Comte, Durkheim emphasized the importance of cultural systems as a unifying force, especially the evolution of the institution of law to coordinate and control relations within and between social units. He recognized that cultural values—or general moral standards of right and wrong—become more abstract and "enfeebled" if they are to have relevance for all actors pursuing diverse goals and interests in highly differentiated social systems. Thus, the problem in complex social systems became one of backfilling more specific cultural rules and beliefs, derived from highly abstract values, into all of the differentiated spheres of institutional activity in complex societies. In this way, the morality of a society as expressed in its values could be made salient and relevant to actors operating in diverse social worlds created by structural differentiation.[12]

---

[11]Emile Durkheim, *The Division of Labor in Society* (New York: Free Press, 1947, originally published in French in 1893).

[12]Durkheim's idea was that values have to become very generalized and, in so doing, they thus cannot provide sufficient or precise regulation of actions by themselves. They can only provide powerful moral premises, but these must be translated into more specific premises and rules for the basic domains of institutional activity—e.g., economy, polity, kinship, religion, law, education, etc.

Later in his career as Durkheim turned to the study of religion,[13] Durkheim began to emphasize the importance of society-wide symbols marked by totems that would personify the whole society and to which its members must give ritual observance so as to increase their emotional attachments not only to local groupings but also to solidarity across the entire society. In this way the master requisite for integration could be realized in highly differentiated societies. This analysis of cultural dynamics, without their functionalist trappings, has influenced a great many other theoretical traditions in sociology, as we see in many chapters in this short review of theoretical sociology. But for my present purposes, it is Durkheim who extended Comte's ideas and brought to functionalism a conceptualization of culture as critical to meeting the requisite of integration in complex social systems.

The Basic Elements of Early Functional Theories

By the time of Durkheim's death in the second decade of the twentieth century, functionalism was dead in sociology, but as I examine shortly, anthropologists picked it up, keeping it alive until the mid-twentieth century. At this point, functionalism would rise from the dead and, surprisingly, become the dominant theoretical perspective in sociology, at least for a relatively short time. At the early death or abandonment of functionalism by sociologists, the basic contours of functionalism were clearly evident, and perhaps I should pause to list its key elements:

1. Social systems are composed of interrelated parts.

2. These systems reveal both internal and external problems of adaptation to their environments that must be resolved if the system is to endure. These problems can come from

    A. External changes in the physical and bio-ecological environment of a society

    B. External relations with other populations

    C. Internal environments generated by the growth and differentiation of societies

3. Whether from external or internal sources, these problems of survival and adaptation can be visualized as system "needs" or "requisites" that must be met; depending upon the theorists, these requisites are typically seen to revolve around such adaptive problems as

    A. *Integration* within and among differentiated units of

        1. Diverse institutional systems (e.g., economy, family, government, religion, etc.)

        2. Diverse classes and strata created by the stratification of inequalities in resource distributions

    B. *Coordination and control* of differentiated actors through the

        1. Consolidation and use of power and law as social control mechanisms

        2. Development of common symbol systems and totems marking the sanctity of the entire social system and toward which emotion-arousing rituals are performed

        3. Development of new mechanisms of structural interdependence that connect differentiated units

---

[13]Emile Durkheim, *The Elementary Forms of the Religious Life* (New York: Free Press, 1947, originally published in French in 1912).

C. *Production* of necessary resources to support members of the population, especially population's and society's growth

D. *Reproduction* of members and the new, more complex social units organizing their activities evolve with system growth

E. *Distribution* of resources, individuals, and social structural units, cultural symbols and information to more differentiated social units and across the expanded territories of a system as it grows

4. Understanding of social systems as a whole and their constituent parts is only possible by analyzing the need(s) or requisite(s) of the system that any given part of a society meets.

The Transition Into Modern Functionalism

Functional approaches to explaining the social universe were not abandoned in sociology because of their defects, which were many, but because of their emphasis on evolution (see Chapter 11). All functional schemes were couched in an evolutionary framework, emphasizing the movement of societies from simple to complex forms. There was always an Enlightenment commentary by white Europeans about such evolution from simple to more complex societies as representing "progress" and "advancement." Unfortunately, this commentary on progress tended to see all those societies below the European industrial endpoint of evolution as somehow inferior, not just in their structure and culture but also in the biology of the human organisms that inhabited them. The labels "savage" and "primitive" were often used to describe non-industrial societies and their members. The not so subtle racism in many of these portrays of preliterate societies eventually produced profound backlash, especially when Social Darwinism advocating a world of the "survival of the fittest" emerged to justify the abuse of "inferior" peoples as a "natural part" of the evolutionary process. Ironically, Darwin never phrased his ideas about natural selection in these terms. Rather, the phrase—"survival of the fittest"—is Spencer's, uttered in *Social Statics* in 1850,[14] nine years before Darwin's *On the Origins of Species* was published. The result was to stigmatize Spencer more than Darwin but, more fundamentally, to stigmatize evolutionary models of progressive evolution in general. And as these often rather racist models were thrown out, the baby in this bathwater—functionalism—was also discarded. But it did not die; it found new and nurturing home in anthropology, where it prospered as a theory. It was so successful that by the midpoint of the last century, sociologists brought functionalism back it its original home, making it the dominant theoretical orientation in sociology for a decade or so, before its many problems were used to mount a devastating critique of functionalism as a flawed mode of theorizing in general. The result was that, once again, functionalism appeared to die, but instead, it morphed into a more acceptable guise where the notions of "function" and "functional requisites" were downplayed, if not hidden from view—thus making it more acceptable to larger audiences of social scientists.

Anthropological Functionalism

The demise of evolutionary stage models, which anthropologists helped create because they provided the data on preliterate societies, was generally accepted in anthropology

---

[14]Spencer, *Social Statics* (see note 3 for full citation).

but, in contrast to sociology, the functionalism was *not* thrown out with the evolutionary bathwater. The reason for the retention of functionalism is that anthropologists doing fieldwork in preliterate societies confronted a problem: How could they explain the existence of particular structures and cultural practices among preliterate populations? These populations do not have a written history, and so, even with oral traditions (which were highly mythologized), researchers could not trace the history of an important structure (e.g., kinship system) or practice (e.g., religious ritual or belief), with the result that it was hard to explain *why* preliterate populations had built such structures or come to engage in certain practices.

Functionalism provided an answer: examine how the structure or practice operates to meet certain functional needs of the social whole organizing the members of a population. By being able to posit the function that a structure or a practice performed for maintaining the viability of a preliterate society, the sense having explained that structure was achieved. This has always been the comforting thing about functionalism; it gives the sense that one has answered the big questions about a society—what allows it to survive?—and this is the reason that anthropologists adopted functionalist modes of explanation. In addition, it is also the reason that functionalism refuses to die despite its near-death experiences in the twentieth century. It asks and tries to answer an interesting question—perhaps the most interesting question—about societies. Two anthropologists in particular—both icons of mid-twentieth century anthropology—adopted functional strategies that mirrored Spencer's and Durkheim's respective approaches.

The Functionalism of Bronislaw Malinowski

Much like Spencer, Malinowski posited multiple functional requisites for different system levels in societies, as Spencer had done in *Principles of Biology* and *Principles of Sociology*. Unlike Spencer, however, Malinowski posited different survival requisites for each system level in his theory: organisms, social structure, and culture.[15] Table 2.2 summarizes the requisites for just the structural and cultural systems of a society.

For the social structural level of human social organization, the requisites posited by Malinowski look much like Spencer's: production and distribution, social control and regulation, reproduction through education, and consolidation of power and authority. Thus, those populations that can develop institutional systems that produce and distribute sufficient resources to sustain and reproduce system members and that regulate and coordinate action through authority are more likely to survive. If we add to this list the requisites enumerated by Malinowski for the cultural system level, then we can complete Spencer's list of requisites and add those integrative requisites deemed critical by Durkheim. And as will become very evident shortly, the combined lists anticipated the functional needs posited by the most famous modern-era functionalist—Talcott Parsons.

---

[15]Bronislaw Malinowski, "Anthropology," *Encyclopedia Britannica*, supplemental volume 1 (London, 1936); *A Scientific Theory of Culture* (Chapel Hill, NC: University of North Carolina Press, 1944); *Magic, Science, and Religion and Other Essays* (New York: Free Press, 1948).

Table 2.2   Malinowski's Conception Requisites for System Levels

---

Requisites for the Cultural or Symbolic System Level

1. Requisite for systems of symbols that provide information necessary for adaptation of a population to its environment

2. Requisite for systems of symbols that provide a sense of control over a population's destiny and over change events

3. Requisite for systems of symbols that provide members of a population with a sense of a "communal rhythm" in their daily lives and activities

Requisites for the Structural (Instrumental) System Level

1. Requisite for production and distribution of consumer goods to sustain a population

2. Requisite for social control of behavior and its regulation

3. Requisite for education of people in traditions and skills

4. Requisite for the organization and execution of (power) authority relations

---

The Functionalism of A. R. Radcliffe-Brown

In his analysis of kinship systems among pre-literates,[16] A. R. Radcliffe-Brown argued that the problems of functionalism—to be addressed later—can be obviated by three steps. One, recognize that any society must meet some minimal level of integration among its parts. Two, understand that the term function refers to those "necessary conditions for a societies existence" which can be seen, *a la* Durkheim, as the necessity for *integration*. And three, in each society, look for features that can be shown to contribute to the maintenance of integration. The goal of explanation, therefore, is to describe these features and outline how they contribute to integration; once this task is completed, these features are "explained"—at least by the logic of functionalism.

These two theories and others carried functionalism in anthropology to the mid-century when the sociologists, Talcott Parsons and colleagues, began to develop their own functional schemes alongside those of anthropologists who continued to develop functional explanations well past the century's midpoint.[17] Why the sudden interests by sociological theorists in functionalism? Functionalism came back into sociology because, while the decades between 1900 and 1950 were not bereft of any theorizing, there was clearly a lack of general theories[18] that sought to explain large

---

[16]A. R. Radcliffe-Brown, "Structure and Function in Primitive Society," *American Anthropologist* 37 (July–September 1937): pp. 31–50; *Structure and Function in Primitive Society* (New York: Free Press, 1952).

[17]See, for example, Walter Goldschmidt, *Comparative Functionalism* (Berkeley, CA: University of California Press, 1966).

[18]There was not a complete lack of general theory. For example, urban ecology was an ongoing perspective, as was human ecology. Scholars like Pitirim Sorokin wrote large theoretical treatises, although these did not endure in the sociological imagination. Still, a few scholars are now trying to revive Sorokin's ideas (e.g., Vicent Jeffries). Also, work in the tradition of George Herbert Mead on interaction processes continued but really did not break out as a distinct theoretical perspective until the 1950s.

segments of the social world. There was almost a theoretical vacuum, and with the repression of Marxist theory and scholarship (see next chapter) during the McCarthy era in America, functional theory was sucked into this vacuum and, for a brief time, became dominant, almost by default because there were no compelling alternatives for analyzing societies as a whole.

Contemporary-Era Functional Theories

Talcott Parsons' "Action Theory" as an Illustration

It is difficult to over-estimate the influence of Talcott Parsons on sociological theory in the contemporary era—even now when his approach has seemingly passed into relative obscurity. Parsons began his climb to fame in 1937 when he opened his first big book with a famous quote that he borrowed: "Who now reads Spencer?"[19] Today, we might ask the same question about Parsons, but much like Spencer, Parsons still exerts a very large influence on theorizing; we do not see it because few read Parsons' major works and, perhaps more significantly, many of Parsons' ideas have simply been absorbed into mainstream sociology without the functionalist trappings.

After his first big book, it was thirteen years before Parsons' wrote his first functionalist book, *The Social System*.[20] Parsons' functionalism erupted in a very brief three-year period between 1950 and 1953,[21] where the basic scheme was put forth, often in rather difficult prose. The general theory is, in many ways, a re-blending of Spencer's, Durkheim's, and Malinowski's ideas. First, he posits four basic functional requisites—really five because one is subdivided into two in the scheme outlined in Table 2.3.

Table 2.3 Parsons' Four (Really Five) Requisites for All Action Systems

1. **Adaptation:** The requisite for securing resources from the environment, converting them into useable substances and produce, and distributing them to members of the population

2. **Goal Attainment:** The requisite for setting goals for the system as a whole and for mobilizing resources to meet these goals

3. **Integration:** The requisite for coordinating relations and actions of all actors—collective and individual—in a system

4. **Pattern Maintenance and Tension Management:** The requisites for (a) sustaining and reproducing social units—both individual and collective—in a system and (b) managing tensions that arise within and between individual and collective units in a system

---

[19]Talcott Parsons, *The Structure of Social Action* (New York: McGraw-Hill, 1937); the most recent paperback edition (New York: Free Press, 1968).

[20]Talcott Parsons, *The Social System* (New York: Free Press, 1951).

[21]Talcott Parsons and Edward Shils were elaborated in *Toward a General Theory of Action* (New York: Harper & Row, 1951); Talcott Parsons, Robert F. Bales, and Edward A. Shils, *Working Papers in the Theory of Action* (Glencoe, IL: Free Press, 1953).

Second, he begins to see distinctive system levels: the (1) personality, (2) social, (3) cultural, and (4) organismic (later to become the *behavioral*) systems. Each of these systems levels meets one of the more the more inclusive action systems four functional needs for *adaptation, goal attainment, integration,* or *latency.* These functions of each action system for the overall action system are summarized in Figure 2.2.

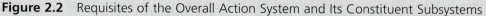

Figure 2.2   Requisites of the Overall Action System and Its Constituent Subsystems

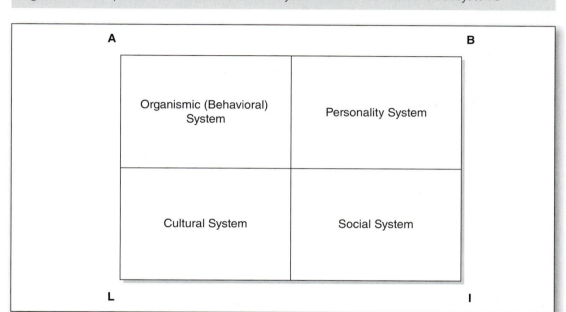

With this relatively simple conceptual edifice, Parsons began an almost forty-year elaboration of the scheme. One of the most important elaborations was the creation of a graphic way of conceptualizing the four requisites as sectors in a box with four divisions, denoted at the corners by *A* for adaptation, *G* for goal attainment, *I* for integration, and *L* for latency (subdivided into *pattern maintenance* and *tension management*). In Parsons' view, placing a structural feature of a society in the proper box in the AGIL scheme, such as its core institutional systems, would represent an explanation of these systems. For example, Figure 2.2 offers a view of an AGIL box for the overall action system, while Figure 2.3 presents an example of a societal-level social system (a social system in the overall action system that meets the integrative requisites in the overall action system). In Figure 2.3, placed within the four sectors are core institutional systems of a society, thus indicating the requisite that each institution fulfills.

Another elaboration, with Neil J. Smelser, involved an examination of the resources, conceptualized as *generalized media of exchange,* that flow through a society.[22] *Generalized media* are the resources that actors use for conducting transactions within a functional sector—that is,

---

[22]Talcott Parsons and Neil J. Smelser, *Economy and Society* (New York: Free Press, 1956). These requisites are the same as those enumerated by Malinowski.

Figure 2.3   Functions of Key Institutional Domains in a Societal Social System and Their Interchanges

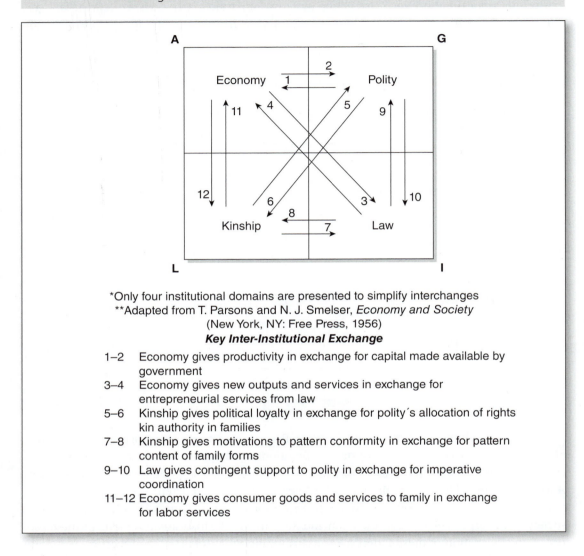

*Only four institutional domains are presented to simplify interchanges
**Adapted from T. Parsons and N. J. Smelser, *Economy and Society*
(New York, NY: Free Press, 1956)

Key Inter-Institutional Exchange

1–2   Economy gives productivity in exchange for capital made available by government

3–4   Economy gives new outputs and services in exchange for entrepreneurial services from law

5–6   Kinship gives political loyalty in exchange for polity´s allocation of rights kin authority in families

7–8   Kinship gives motivations to pattern conformity in exchange for pattern content of family forms

9–10 Law gives contingent support to polity in exchange for imperative coordination

11–12 Economy gives consumer goods and services to family in exchange for labor services

one of the four boxes labeled A, G, I, and L in Figure 2.3 emphasizing core institutions for the societal social system. When actors from different sectors—and in this case, from differentiated institutional domains like economy, polity, law, family, and religion in the societal social system—interact, they often exchange their symbolic medium for that of another sector. For instance, the medium of *love/loyalty* in the family is given to polity as loyalty and commitment to the polity's right to make decisions in a society (thus giving legitimacy to polity) in exchange for family authority, or the right of families to govern their internal affairs without extensive intrusion by polity. Or, to look at the exchange between economy and family, working members of families receive *money* from the economy for commitments (as a form of *love/loyalty*) to work hard in economic roles. The full list of the generalized symbolic media and the nature of exchanges of these media is provided in Figure 2.3. In this kind of analysis, Parsons and Smelser felt that they had been able to understand "the glue" that binds actors in mutual relations of interdependencies within and between differentiated institutional domains.

Generalized symbolic media have a number of special qualities:[23] (1) they are often the terms of discourse and talk; (2) they often carry moral overtones and become the basis for ideologies governing what is right and wrong within an institutional system; and (3) they are also valued resources in their own right that are distributed within institutions and between institutions. Thus, by discovering the location of an institution in the AGIL box, one first learns what requisite an institution functions to meet. Then, by examining the generalized symbolic media developed within an institutional domain within a given functional sector— that is, A, G, I, or L—it becomes possible to see the terms of discourse, exchange, and ideological formation among actors in an institutional domain, thereby integrating actions within the domain. And finally, by tracing out the exchanges of media across institutional domains, one learns a great deal about the dynamics occurring among actors in differentiated domains, and especially those dynamics that integrate diverse domains into a more cohesive society.

Parsons argued that, for any social system—a group, an organization, a community—the analysis above for a societal system can also be performed for these subsystems in a society. *All* social systems at whatever level of social organization become differentiated into four basic sectors (or as Spencer argued, axes)—whether roles in a group, offices and divisions within organization, or as neighborhoods and sectors of a city. The actors in these sectors tend to use at least some of these symbolic media evident at the institutional level, and moreover, they exchange these media.

Parsons began to develop his scheme to emphasize sectors within sectors. For example, take a business corporation as an organization within the economy, which is located in the A sector of a societal social system, as is illustrated in Figure 2.4. The organization, like the whole society, can be conceptualized in terms of A, G, I, and L, and hence, it can be divided into these four sectors as is done in Figure 2.4. The administration is the G or goal attainment sector for the organization, and it too can be divided into four additional sectors where different offices in the administration meet AGIL requisites. For example, the CEO's office meeting goal attainment requisites and thus is placed in the G sector of the organization; the human relations department might be seen as meeting pattern maintenance requisite in the L sector of the business corporation; the legal department might be seen as meeting integrative needs of a business; and perhaps the accounting and payroll office can be seen as the adaptive sector of the goal attainment section of the business because it brings in resources to the administrative offices of a business. Each one of these sub-offices meets an AGIL requisite in a business organization that is part of the G sector of an economy that, in turn, is located in the A sector of a societal social system, and these have exchange relations with each other using different generalized media. If this kind of analysis seems to get too complicated, it is; and this was part of the reason for Parsonian action theory's demise. Over the years, it became an ever-more complex category system with sectors within sectors exchanging within and between different levels of sectors.

---

[23]Parsons' writings on this topic are incomplete, but see "On the Concept of Political Power," *Proceedings of the American Philosophical Society* 107 (1963): pp. 232–262; "On the Concept of Influence," *Public Opinion Quarterly* 27 (Spring 1963): pp. 37–62; and "Some Problems of General Theory," in *Theoretical Sociology: Perspectives and Developments,* eds. J. C. McKinney and E. A. Tiryakian (New York: Appleton-Century-Crofts, 1970), pp. 28–68. See also Talcott Parsons and Gerald M. Platt, *The American University* (Cambridge, MA: Harvard University Press, 1975).

Figure 2.4 Systems and Subsystems With the Social Action Systems

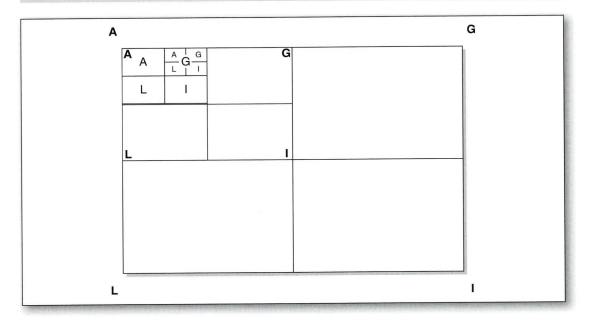

There are many fascinating ideas developed in Parsons' scheme, which cannot be summarized in this brief analysis, but let me close with the final push that Parsons made in elaborating the scheme[24]—a push which, ironically, is reminiscent of Herbert Spencer's overall Synthetic Philosophy, indicating that even if no one else read Spencer in 1937, Parsons certainly had. Parsons began to conceptualize four action systems (see Figure 2.5)—i.e., cultural, social, psychological, and organismic (later behavioral)—into what he called a cybernetic *hierarchy of control*. In this hierarchy of control, the higher is an action system, the more it regulates the system below it with informational controls. Thus, the highest in information action system is the cultural system and it regulates with information the other three in the hierarchy. Conversely, the lower is a system in the hierarchy, the more it provides the energy to those systems higher in the hierarchy. Hence, the organismic system provides the energy to all other action systems. For the psychological action system it provides energy for individuals to play roles in status locations in the social system; and for the cultural systems, it provides energy via the psychological and social action systems provide the energy to build symbol systems that, reciprocally, will regulate the social, psychological, and organismic system. With sufficient energy, then, the cultural system provides the informational direction to the social system (beliefs, ideologies, values, and norms), the psychological system (targets for commitments, morality), and even the organismic system (e.g., physiological changes of stress from, for example, the moral codes producing guilt at the personality system level that, in turn, affect physiological well-being). Figure 2.5 illustrates the cybernetic hierarchy where information in one system regulates the energy mobilized in the system below it in the hierarchy and where the energy mobilized in one system drives the mobilization of energy in the system above it.

---

[24]Talcott Parsons, *Action Theory and the Human Condition* (New York: Free Press, 1978).

Figure 2.5 Parsons' Conception of the Cybernetic Hierarchy of Control

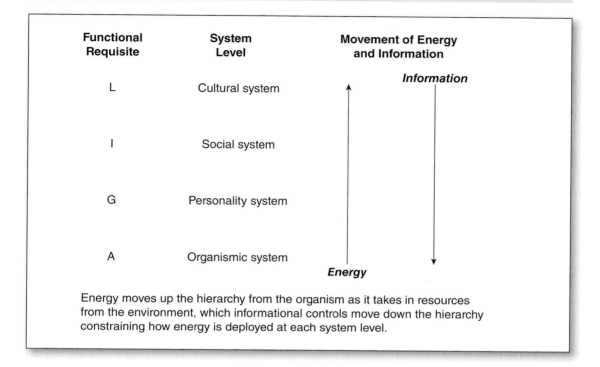

Energy moves up the hierarchy from the organism as it takes in resources from the environment, which informational controls move down the hierarchy constraining how energy is deployed at each system level.

Parsons sought to portray old theoretical ideas using this hierarchy. For example, Karl Marx's notion of *alienation* can be considered a breakdown between the personality and social system, where there is insufficient energy to play roles in status locations within the social system. Or, Durkheim's analysis of *anomie* as a "lack of regulation" can be viewed as insufficient information provided by the cultural system for regulating actions of individuals as they attempt to play roles in the social system. Yet, this is explanation by classification or finding the place in a scheme of a particular phenomenon and then assuming that this discovery of the proper place constitutes an explanation in the scientific sense. Most science, however, seeks to explain phenomena by models of the key processes of a universe and/or by abstract principles outlining their dynamics.

The final elaboration of the scheme, developed shortly before Parsons' death, involved the conceptualization of a scheme for the entire universe—ethnical, biological, organismic, and action. Figure 2.6 outlines this argument. As is evident, the action systems are the integrative system for the overall action system of the entire universe. The organic system had to be taken away as an action system (replaced by the *behavioral system*) because the *organic system* in this more general analysis of the human condition sets goals, and thus meets requisites for **G**oal attainment for all the other basic systems of the universe. And so, the behavioral system was introduced into the action system to replace the organismic system that had moved to a more prominent place in the general systems of the entire universe. The *physico-chemical system* is the **A**daptive system for the overall universe because it ultimately provides the resource necessary to fuel the other systems, and the *telic* system concerned with consideration of ultimate meanings is the **L**atency subsystem of the overall universe, as seen from the perspective of action systems in the **I** sector. This is certainly

Figure 2.6 Parsons' Conception of the Human Condition and Its Subsystems

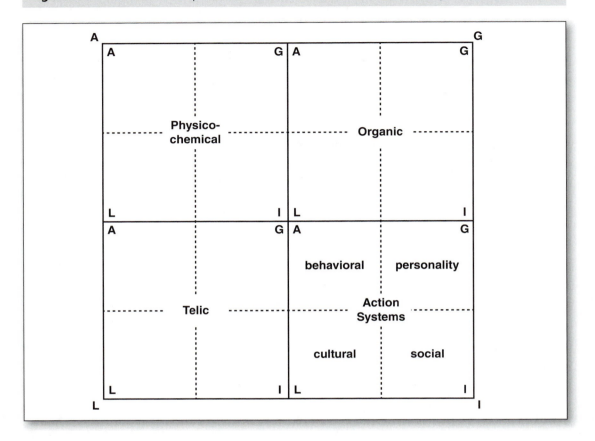

grand theory, or now more of a philosophy than a precise explanation of phenomena. And, it certainly is a grand category system, but the intent was the same as Spencer's Synthetic Philosophy: to "explain" the entire universe, from the human perspective, with an underlying set of theoretical ideas. The difference, and it is a big difference, is that Spencer would explain ethics (Parsons' *telic system*), biology (Parsons' *organic and behavioral systems*), psychology (Parsons' *psychological action system*), and sociology (Parsons' *social action system*) with principles and laws. In contrast, Parsons explained with categories and systems of categories. The result was very different looking functional theories, even though Parsons seems to begin with Spencer's original ideas of production and distribution (Adaptation in Parsons), regulation (Goal attainment in Parsons), coordination (Integration in Parsons), and reproduction (pattern maintenance portion of Latency in Parsons). But Spencer sought particular principles about the dynamics of differentiation along these four axes, whereas Parsons kept elaborating categories—only the most critical of which have been reviewed here.

The Downfall, Once Again, of Functionalism

The downfall of functionalism occurred primarily in the United States. European theorists had a number of traditions that competed with functionalism, with the consequence that functionalism was not as dominant there as it was in the United States. Still, even though the critique against functionalism began with European conflict theorists,[25] European functional analysis persisted— unlike what happened in the United States where functionalism virtually disappeared. For example, Richard Münch[26] has carried forth the AGIL Parsonian program into the twenty-first century, and before his death, Niklas Luhmann[27] who developed a less complicated program positing one functional requisite—the need to reduce complexity inherent in temporal, cultural, and material dimensions of the social universe. Moreover, Luhmann as one of the most important European theorists carried forth Parsons' emphasis on generalized symbolic media of institutional domains and performed some highly detailed analyses of their operation in various domains. This kind of theorizing still exists and is read, but in the United States, functionalism as a recognizable theory went underground in the constant barrage of criticisms.

As is discussed below, the criticisms of functionalism were (1) logical in that functional explanation tended to turn into illegitimate teleologies and tautologies, (2) substantive in that functionalism was viewed as a conservative ideology underemphasizing inequality and conflict and overemphasizing forces maintaining the status quo, and (3) explanatory in the overemphasis on analytical categories as opposed to models and principles explaining dynamic processes. Let me turn to each and very briefly review the issues, before closing with the state of functional theorizing today.

(1) Logical Problems in Functional Explanations[28]

The two big problems consistently brought up by philosophers of science and logicians were (a) illegitimate teleologies and (b) tautologies. An *illegitimate teleology* occurs when an end state or outcome of a process is viewed as causing the processes that brought about this end state, *without* specifying the mechanisms by which this reversal of means-end causality occurs. A legitimate teleology would be one where these mechanisms are specified. For example, we can imagine a social system with specific goals or end states working to achieve these by allocating resources and using them to construct structural and cultural systems that ensure that goals are first achieved and then sustained. In contrast to such legitimate teleologies, functional explanations often describe the outcome of a social structural or cultural system for meeting a particular functional requisite without detailing *how this structure came about* and just *how it operates* to have a certain outcome with respect to posited functional needs. Here the end state—a functional need or requisite—mysteriously causes a social structure, say an institutional system, to evolve without specifying how and through what processes or by what mechanisms the end has cause the means to the end state.

---

[25]For example, Ralf Dahrendorf, "Out of Utopia: Toward a Reorganization of Sociological Analysis," *American Journal of Sociology* 64 (1958): pp. 125–135.

[26]For the best of these efforts, see Richard Münch's work: *Theory of Action: Towards a New Synthesis Going Beyond Parsons* (London: Routledge, 1988); *Die Struktur der Modene* (Frankfurt am Main: Suhrkamp, 1984).

[27]Niklas Luhmann, *The Differentiation of Society*, trans. S. Holmes and C. Larmore (New York: Columbia University Press, 1982); see also his *Systems Theory* (Stanford, CA: Stanford University Press, 1995).

[28]Robert K. Merton, "Manifest and Latent Functions," in his *Social Theory and Social Structure* (New York: Free Press), pp. 45–61. See also Merton's "Discussion of Parsons' 'The Position of Sociological Theory," *American Sociological Review* 13 (1948): pp. 164–168. For a more comprehensive review and critique of functional theorizing, see Jonathan Turner and Alexandra Maryanski's, *Functionalism* (Menlo Park, CA: Benjamin-Cummings, 1979).

A *tautology* is circular reasoning. Many functional theories reveal circular reasoning and, hence, are tautologous. For example, many theories posit that a given structure is meeting a particular requisite and thus is promoting the survival of the social system. How do we know that such is the case? Because the system is surviving, and hence, the structure in question must be promoting survival. One can see a circularity here because the fact that a system is surviving is taken to affirm that functional need is being met; institution X exists in this system; therefore it must be meeting this need; how do we know? Because the system is surviving. What is being explained, if anything, by such circular reasoning is not clear.

(2) Substantive Problems With Functional Explanations[29]

Far more devastating to functionalism in the 1960s was criticism from the re-awakening of conflict and critical theories in the United States. The critique took many forms but, in essence, conflict theorists argued that Parsons in particular and, hence, functionalism in general, overemphasize how structures and processes *maintain* societies; in so doing, the forces of social transformation—especially inequality, stratification, and conflict—that *change* societies are not given sufficient attention. In functionalism compared to conflict theories, needs are being met by existing social structures (because, otherwise, the system would to be surviving); by constantly emphasizing this connection among social structures, requisites, and system survival, functionalism was seen, in essence, to be a conservative ideology legitimating the way things are and, moreover, from its beginnings with Comte and later Durkheim, seeing deviance, conflict, and tension as dysfunctional or pathological rather than as normal dynamics in highly differentiated social systems. This attack mortally wounded functionalism because, in part, it was true. Yet, the attack, like most polemics, was often overdone to the point of distortion of Parsons' functionalism. Moreover, the attack on the substance emphasis of functionalism resonated with the times, where conflict and dramatic social and cultural change in Western societies was occurring in the 1960s. In this context, functional theories were perceived as not being able to explain obvious sources of change, and the result was for new generations of theorists and sociologists to abandon functionalism and, indeed, view it in highly hostile—if not sometimes unfair—terms. Parsons as a person was seen as reactionary and conservative, when in fact, he was a very liberal person politically (who had stood publicly against Senator Joseph McCarthy's paranoid attack on the political left in America, especially in higher education). Even more unfairly, critiques of Parsons' theory went beyond intellectual criticism to criticisms of functionalists individuals as persons, or even human beings—ironically re-creating a rather McCarthyesque intellectual climate from the political left in the 1960s and 1970s.

(3) Deficient Methods of Explanation[30]

The final line of criticisms could perhaps be examined under (1) above on logical problems, but it is useful to separate it out. Parsons truly believed that if you could find the place of an empirical event, process, or structure in his category system, you had explained this event, process, or structure. In fact, all that is really accomplished is to classify but not explain. An explanation requires

---

[29]See Dahrendorf, "Out of Utopia" (cited in note 25).

[30]See Turner and Maryanski, *Functionalism*, for details (cited in note 28).

that a theory have principles and models outlining *dynamic processes* that always occur when humans behave, interact, and organize; Parsons presented categories and linkages among categories without very much analysis of the underlying processes that drive sociocultural formations. The result is that the explanatory category system in Parsons action theory became needlessly complex because ever-more categories and categories within categories were added in an effort to explain more of social reality. The original architecture of the AGIL scheme boxed (pun intended) any action theorist in because, once committed to categorization in boxes, there were few other options for explaining the social universe.

In contrast to Parsons' strategy of explanation, Herbert Spencer had used his categories to emphasize the domains of reality most in need of explanation with abstract principles; categories were the starting point of explanation, not the end point. Thus, Spencer's categorization system of needs or requisites was simple and only the beginning of theorizing. The actual explanations in Spencer's work, and to a lesser extent Durkheim's as well, come from abstract laws and principles highlighting dynamic processes, although these principles in Durkheim are more implicit when compared to Spencer's theories. In my view, this is by far the most damaging criticism of functionalism, especially that practiced by Parsons, and yet, it is the least mentioned.

The end result was, as I have emphasized, the virtual disappearance of functional analysis in sociology in the United States by 1990, if not a decade earlier. Yet, functionalism still asked and tried to answer an important question: What must occur if a society is to remain internally integrated and meet other problems of adaptation in a given environment? This is a question that will always intrigue those interested in understanding the social universe, and it is the guiding question of all functional theories. Is it possible, perhaps, to answer this question with many of the ideas developed in functional theories, without falling into the logical and substantive traps so emphasized by critics? I think that there is, and so in closing this chapter, let me outline how functional analysis can be saved and produce true explanatory theories.

Conclusion: Can Functionalism Be Saved?

The answer is clearly affirmative because Spencer's and Durkheim's functional approaches provided theoretical explanations of key social processes. And so, the route to the full salvation of functionalism is to adopt the explanatory methods proposed by Comte, Spencer, and Durkheim, while getting rid of the notion of functional needs and requisites, at least in the form emphasized in most functional theories. Radcliffe–Brown came closest to understanding what had to happen with functional analysis if it was to be a viable mode of explanation, but in the end, his analysis was illegitimately teleological and full of tautologies. However, his view of needs as "necessary conditions for existence" came close to what I propose.

What is required is to view social systems as subject to *selection pressures* that arise from (a) their external environments and (b) their internal environments as growth and differentiation produce many new logistical problems that, in turn, generate selection pressures on actors in social systems.[31] These pressures become manifest in *fundamental forces* of the social universe that, like

---

[31]See my *Macrodynamics: Toward a Theory on the Organization of Populations* (Newark, NJ: Rutgers University Press, 1995), and more recently, my *Theoretical Principles of Sociology, Volume 1 on Macrodynamics* (New York: Springer, 2010).

gravity in physics or natural selection in biology, push on actors to build new kinds of social structures and attendant cultural systems along just a few axes or paths. The social universe, like the physical and biological, is constructed around underlying forces that generate selection pressures on individual and collective actors in social systems, forcing these actors to build new kinds of social structures in response to these pressures, or die and suffer the disintegrative consequences.

Traditional functional analysis short-circuited the analysis of forces and selection pressures and simply posited a list of functional requisites and social structures meeting these requisites. The same kind of attenuated argument occurs in physiology and medicine when talking in shorthand. For example, we often hear physiologists emphasize that the function of the lungs is to aerate the cells and remove carbon dioxide from the body (and other things as well; I am keeping the example simple). This alone does not explain the origins of lungs and why they came into existence, just as associating a social structure with a functional need does not explain how this social structure came about. What is left implicit in the physiological account of the lungs, however, is the well-understood evolutionary argument: in the distant past, as organisms got larger, there were selection pressures for new ways to and distribute air and remove waste products among larger organisms. Natural selection and the other forces of evolution (mutation, gene flow, and genetic drift) worked over time to produce lungs and vessels for circulating blood through the bodies of larger organisms, and these organisms were more likely to survive and reproduce. And, over time, new species of organisms were generated by the increased fitness made possible by a pump (the heart) pushing blood full of air through veins and capillaries that allow for aeration and discharge of waste products. The details of this kind of explanation are not so important as their logic: an explanation is given about the processes and mechanisms (forces of natural selection on variations over long periods of time) by which selection pressures for a better circulation system have generated new adaptive systems in new species of organisms. This simple redirection of functional explanations removes the tautology and illegitimate teleology.

This logic can also be inserted into functionalist explanation in sociology. Human populations find themselves under pressures to reorganize or die. And, in the past, many populations probably were not able to do develop new social structures and cultural systems in response to these selection pressures, causing population disintegration from within or conquest from without by a better organized population. Under selection pressures, then, actors seek to create new kinds of structures, whether through borrowing from other societies, innovation, or trial and error. If they are successful in creating a structure that mitigates these selection pressures, the new structures will be retained in a society and, not only this, copied by others, thus leading to the differentiation (a kind of sociocultural speciation). If we go back to early functional arguments, they were implicitly invoking this logic. For example, Spencer who addressed the issue of how circulation systems develop simply brought this idea over as the *distributive* need of a population; and moreover, he invoked a selectionist argument: as populations grow, their members are under pressure to find new ways to distribute resources, people, and information, or face the disintegrative consequences. If they are successful in meeting these pressures, they will have caused the differentiation of a new set of structures and perhaps new elements of culture as well.

Unlike blind natural selection on the phenotypes and underling genotypes of organisms, superorganisms have consciousness, goals, and purposes at all levels of organization toward which they can mobilize resources. They do not have to wait for random mutations or selection on tail ends of a distribution for new traits; instead, unlike organisms without agency, individuals and the units organizing their activities can innovate, borrow, and engage in trial and error; and if successful in mitigating a problem like distribution, the innovation will be copied and spread across a population very rapidly.

In fact, Comte, Spencer, and Durkheim had many of the elements in their theories that are necessary. In Figure 2.7, I conceptualize population processes as they generate selection pressures along just a few critical axes that are fundamental to superorganisms as a form of biotic reality: production, reproduction, regulation (through power and culture), and distribution. These are not so much functional needs as fundamental forces that are inherent in intelligent life-creating superorganisms *through which* selection pressures are channeled, causing actors with agential capacities to develop new kinds of sociocultural formations, or suffer the disintegrative consequences of failure to do so. Comte, Spencer, and Durkheim all had a kind of ecological model (see Chapter 4) as much as a functionalist theory implicit in their conception of how requisites listed earlier push on actors and cause sociocultural speciation of superorganism.

They recognized that population growth was probably the primal driving force in the evolution of superorganism because growth generates the selection pressures inhering in production, reproduction, regulation, and distribution as forces of the superorganismic realm of the biotic universe. Thus, selection pressures are channeled through the fundamental forces that allow for the creation, persistence, and evolution of superorganisms. History is the graveyard of failures of societies whose members could not respond adequately to these pressures, just as the history of organisms is the graveyard of extinct species. But, some species of organisms and superorganisms find ways to meet these selection pressures, at least for a time, because they have developed adequate responses to pressures for new forms of production, reproduction, regulation, and distribution. And for superorganisms, pressures also come from the internal organization of societies as they get more complex. Differentiation per se, as emphasized by Comte, Spencer, and Durkheim, generates selection pressures from integration (or what I see as elements of regulation and distribution as forces). Differentiation that increases inequality and stratification generates massive pressures for new forms of regulation, as was emphasized by Spencer. Use of power to solve problems of regulation often generates new internal pressures that come from inequality of power as it is used to increase inequality in the distribution of resources and, hence, the level stratification. Increases in production generate new selection pressures through distribution and regulation as forces and, eventually, reproduction. The complexity of superorganisms thus generates a continual flow of selection pressures, and it is for this reason that societies evolve, by fits and starts, toward more complexity. Also, as more complex societies evolve, they typically wipe out less complex ones in war, conquest, colonization, organic and superorganic genocide, and other destructive processes. So the environment of a superorganism is not just the bio-ecology of the biotic universe, but the ecology of the sociocultural universe when superorganisms compete, fight, and annihilate one another, and this was the process emphasized by Spencer's famous phrase, "survival of the fittest." Warfare had, Spencer believed, been one of the driving forces of history in a kind of Darwinian struggle among species of superorganisms. The larger and more complex societies generally win wars, and with each conquest, a simpler society is eliminated, colonized, or absorbed into the more complex society, thereby ratcheting up the level modal of differentiation in the superorganic realm. So, population size and growth are one source of selection pressures; another source is Darwinian conflict and warfare; and still another source is the logistical loads that come with differentiation itself.

Figure 2.7 Turner's Conception of Macrodynamic Forces and Selection Pressures on Populations

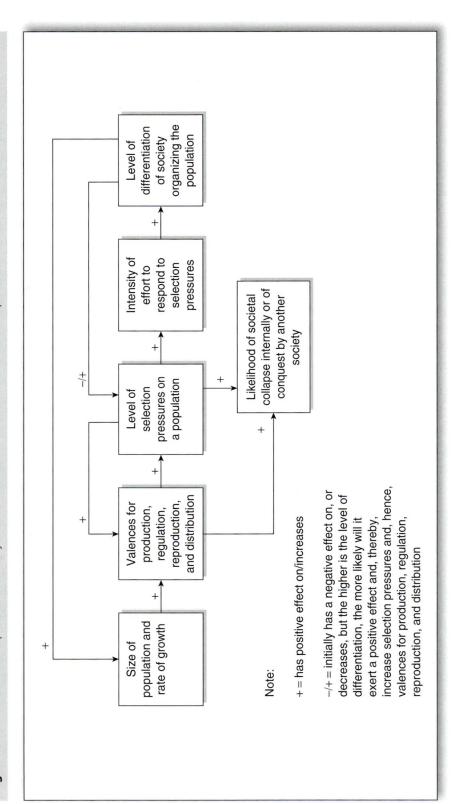

Note:

+ = has positive effect on/increases

–/+ = initially has a negative effect on, or decreases, but the higher is the level of differentiation, the more likely will it exert a positive effect and, thereby, increase selection pressures and, hence, valences for production, regulation, reproduction, and distribution

So, it does become possible to answer the question that has always made functionalism intriguing, once we lose the notion of requisites and make a subtle, but fundamental, shift in emphasis toward forces that are basic to the organization of superorganisms. These superorganisms, like all organisms in the biotic realm, are subject to selection pressures from a variety of sources, but unlike most organisms, superorganisms among humans can use consciousness at all levels of the social order in the superorganism's constituent parts to engage responses to these selection pressures, and thereby create new species of superorganisms in relatively short periods of historical time as opposed to the longer periods of time needed for much organismic evolution.

The vision of functionalism is retained but now with more acceptable theoretical tools borrowed from biology and ecology for use in the study of superorganisms whose parts—persons, groups, organizations, classes, institutions—all evidence capacities for agencies and hence the ability to respond to selection pressures and remake themselves into new sociocultural formations. Moreover, this form of analysis does not sugarcoat inequality, stratification, and conflict; these are endemic to superorganisms as they grow and differentiate; and they are one of many sources of selection pressures on these superorganisms.

CHAPTER 3

Conflict Theorizing

I n virtually all social systems, resources are distributed unequally. Some get more of whatever is valued than others—whether money, power and authority, honor and prestige, health, knowledge, or any resource. Inequality almost always generates some tension between those who have abundant resources and those who have comparatively few resources, and this tension will, under specific conditions, lead to conflict between the advantaged and disadvantaged. This basic fact of social life was recognized by the early figures in sociology, particularly Herbert Spencer, Karl Marx, Max Weber, and Georg Simmel, but each approached the topic of conflict in somewhat different ways.

Early Conflict Theories in Sociology

Herbert Spencer's Theory of Conflict

Spencer's work on conflict is rarely acknowledged because he is so identified with the rise of functionalist theory, which, in the modern era, has been heavily criticized by conflict theorists. Yet, Spencer emphasized some fundamental relationships among power, inequality, threat, and conflict.[1] For Spencer, as societies grow and become more complex, they experience selection pressures for increased regulation and control of the larger, more differentiated population. In response to these selection pressures, power is consolidated and, to varying degrees, centralized into the hands of relatively few actors. As power is mobilized and centralized, it is used to extract resources from other actors, thereby increasing the level of inequality in a society. In turn, inequality generates tension or what Spencer saw as "internal threats" to the social order. The ironical consequence is that in order to deal with this perceived threat, more power is consolidated, and the greater is the threat, the more likely is power to become more centralized, which in turn leads political actors and their allies to usurp more resources to finance the increased needs for social control.

Societies can get locked into this escalating cycle of using power to extract resources, thereby generating inequality and threat, which requires elites to use even more power and extraction of resources to quell the threat. In the long run, societies locked into this cycle will eventually generate

---

[1]Herbert Spencer, *The Principles of Sociology*, three volumes (New York: Appleton-Century-Crofts, 1895, original published in serial form beginning in 1874), vol. 1, pp. 479–558 and vol. 2, part V, pp. 229–643.

conditions for open conflict among strata in a society. Spencer also developed a more geo-political theory that intersects with these internal dynamics in societies.[2] Spencer argued that the evolution of society involved increased growth in the size of the population and their organization into ever-more diverse activities. Much of this size and differentiation had historically been the outcome of war, as more productive, powerful, and organized societies conquered less productive, powerful, and organized societies. Typically, the conquered society was incorporated into the more powerful society in some manner, thereby increasing the size and complexity of the new composite society. This increase in size and complexity, especially of the resentful and culturally diverse members of the conquered population, increased problems of regulation and social control. These problems had historically led to the consolidation and centralization of power to deal with the threat posed by members of the conquered society, thus setting off the cycle of consolidation and centralization of power, usurpation of resources to support social control by polity, increased inequality, escalating resentment of those subject to control by polity, and increased potential for conflict. Thus, while warfare had increased the size and complexity of societies over the long course of human evolution, it had also set into motion the dynamics of conflict within societies.

Karl Marx's Theory of Conflict

Karl Marx has been the most influential theorist of the classical era on contemporary conflict theorizing.[3] His influence has been multifold: first, he produced a general theory of inequality and conflict; second, he infused the analysis of conflict with a political agenda for creating a new kind of society (communism); and third, he offered a view of history[4] as successive epochs of conflict between those who own and control the means of production in a society and those subject to the power of these owners of the means of production. Thus, Marx's analysis of conflict had many dimensions; here I will emphasize the basic theory of conflict, saving for the chapter on critical theories his more ideological and political agenda.

Marx saw his primary goal as exposing the contradictions in capitalist modes of production that would, in turn, usher in a revolution in the name of communism. For Marx, capitalism is an economic system where those who own the means of production seek to make profits from the goods that they sell in competitive markets. In this capitalist system, workers become yet one more commodity that must sell itself to capitalists under unfavorable conditions (high supply of labor relative to demand for such labor). For capitalists to make profits, it is necessary that they pay labor as little as possible and sell their outputs for as high as is possible in a market. Marx made the assumption that the value of commodities is the *labor time* involved in producing them. The key to profits, then, is for capitalists to sell products for well above the labor time involved in making them; thus, Marx's measure of *exploitation of labor* was the difference between what they paid labor and the prices fetched for goods in markets. The greater this difference between paid labor and prices, the greater would be the exploitation of

---

[2]Ibid., vol. 2, part V.

[3]Karl Marx and Friedrich Engels, *The Communist Manifesto* (New York: International Publishers, 1971, originally published in1848).

[4]Ibid., pp. 87–96; Karl Marx, "Preface" to *A Contribution to the Critique of Political Economy* (New York: International Publishers, 1970).

labor. The contradiction in this system is that the production of a good is "social"—i.e., collectively organized—whereas the profits are usurped for the sole benefit of capitalists.

This system, Marx argued, is not inherently stable and will, in the end, sow the seeds for the revolution by labor or *proletariat* against capitalists or *bourgeoisie*. One source of instability is the very fact that capitalist must compete against each other in markets, which forces them to lower prices to point where profits become difficult. As production decreases and workers lose their jobs, they become a pool of restive reserve labor and, hence, a potential force in revolution against capitalists. As workers are thrown out of work, they cannot purchase goods, thereby lessening demand in markets and, hence, profits for capitalists. Capitalists seek to get around this *falling rate of profit* by using new technologies in production that allow them to lower prices, but these technologies are soon copied by competitors with the result that even more workers are displaced and thus unable to purchase goods in markets. In the end, this strategy lowers profits in markets because even more workers do not have resources to purchase goods made by capitalists. As some capitalists lose out in this competition, they too are pushed into the proletariat, and over time, Marx saw a society as polarizing into two hostile camps: the restive *proletariat* and the surviving *bourgeoisie*.

In addition to the inherent dynamics of capitalism to cycle increasingly into deeper and deeper recessions, capitalists are forced to act in ways that, eventually, prove self-destructive:[5] They must assemble labor in urban areas to work in factories where the proletariat can communicate their common grieves. They are forced to educate at least some workers so that they can read and communicate through media, thereby extending the range of communication of grievances. They are forced to disrupt daily routines of labor by laying off workers periodically and, later, hiring them back, thus shocking workers into some awareness of the contradiction between their interests for a steady income and capitalists' desire to maximize profits by keeping labor costs down. Capitalists also increase the sense of deprivation among workers as they are pushed from jobs to the reserve labor pool, thus further increasing their awareness of their interests relative to those of capitalists. They must make workers appendages to machines and thus alienate them because workers lose the ability to determine what they make with their labor, how they make it, and to whom they sell the productions of their labor.

Previous historical epochs, such as feudalism and slavery, revealed their own contradictions, but these in capitalism were the last ones because the new communist society would not evidence these contradictions—clearly a fatal mistake in Marx's political theory. In this analysis of capitalism, however, is a more general theory of conflict, once we raise the level of abstraction to include all societies, or even all social systems. The elements of this theory include: (a) Those who control production also are able to control the political system in a society and the ideologies that are used to justify their control. (b) This control of the means of economic and ideological production, as well as the polity, allows them to exploit workers and thereby gain wealth. (c) When power is used to extract wealth from others, those who gain and lose wealth reveal a fundamental conflict in their interests. (d) This conflict of interests will, under key conditions, enable subordinates in the class system built around exploitation to become increasingly aware of their interests in changing the system while arousing them emotionally to incur the risks of doing so. (e) The ecological concentration of subordinates, disruption of their routines, alienation from their basic need to control their productive activities, education, and literacy as it allows for extended networks of communication of grievances will together all increase subordinates' awareness of their true interests in changing the system.

---

[5]Ibid., p. 22.

(f) Leaders and ideological spokespersons will inevitably emerge under (e) above, and these leaders will charge up grievances, arouse emotions, focus subordinates on their true interests, and facilitate organization and mobilization of subordinates into a revolutionary force that overthrows elites (in Marx's case, the bourgeoisie) and ushers in a new type of society.

It is impossible to fully disentangle Marx's own ideology from this theory, and indeed, Marx would never have wanted the theory and his ideology to be separated. Still, the theory offered by Marx specifies some general conditions that increase the likelihood of conflict between super- and subordinates in almost any kind of social system. Thus, Marx went a long way in outlining the fundamental conditions by which inequality and conflicts of interests inhering in inequality lead to conflict and change in social systems. Before laying these out more explicitly, we also need to incorporate the criticisms of Max Weber and Georg Simmel—the other two German conflict theorists of the classical era of theorizing.

Max Weber's Conflict Theory

Unlike Marx, Max Weber did not see conflict as inevitable or even as the driving force of history. For Weber, conflict occurred under particular historical conditions and was far from inevitable. Nonetheless, Weber's theory is surprisingly similar to Marx's, once it is extracted from the rich historical detail in his analysis of what he termed "domination." What emerges in this exercise is a clear analytical theory of conflict processes.[6] For Weber, subordinates in a system of stratification will be more likely to pursue conflict with superordinates when they withdraw legitimacy from political authority. Thus, for Weber, the critical conditions that start the process of conflict are those affecting the withdrawal of legitimacy from superordinates by subordinates. These conditions include: (1) Membership in social class (life chances in markets and economy), party (house of power or polity), and status groups (rights to prestige and honor) are *correlated with each other*; those high or low in one of these dimensions of stratification are high and low in the other two. (2) High *levels of discontinuity* in the degrees of inequality within social hierarchies built around class, party, and status; that is, there are large gaps between those at high positions and those in middle positions, with large differences between the latter and those in lower positions with respect to class location, access to power, and capacity to command respect. And, (3) low rates of mobility up and, also, down these hierarchies, thereby decreasing chances for those low in the system of stratification from bettering their station in life.

Even when these conditions causing loss of legitimacy by polity are in place, Weber did not see revolutionary conflict as inevitable. Only if by chance *charismatic leaders* can emerge and mobilize the resentments of subordinates will the chances of conflict increase significantly. If a revolution occurs and is successful, a new problem emerges: the qualities of charismatic leaders are typically not the qualities for organizing and administering a new system, and thus, a crisis will inevitably occur among the winners in conflict. They must ensure a *routinization of charisma* whereby new leaders emerge to administer the new polity and, in the end, set up a new system of domination, which may set off once again a new round of conflict mobilization. Moreover, in contrast to Marx, Weber did not see capitalist societies as ripe for conflict because of the spread of what he viewed as "rational-legal" domination in which law and bureaucracy increasing cage people in dispassionate social structures. For Weber, rational-legal authority decreased the likelihood for revolution; in

---

[6]Max Weber, *Economy and Society* (Berkeley, CA: University of California Press, 1968), pp. 302–310, 927–935.

contrast, only in more traditional patterns of domination (as evident in feudal societies) is there likely to be society-wide revolutionary conflict. Yet, despite Weber's lifelong "silent dialogue" and disagreement with Marx, the conditions enumerated above increase the possibility for conflict and, therefore, can be blended with those of Marx to significantly extend the general theory of conflict developed in the classical era.

Georg Simmel's Conflict Theory

Georg Simmel disagreed with Marx about the conflict-producing effects of capitalism, but he also disagreed with Weber on rationalization. For Simmel, market-driven societies provide individuals with choices about what they purchase and how they live their lives, thereby increasing their sense of value and well-being.[7] True, market societies are more impersonal and perhaps cut-throat. Yet, they are also much more free and allow individuals to chose their group affiliations rather than be bound by them and the traditional authority inherent in pre-capitalist groups. Moreover, people have choices in markets to secure resources that match their individual needs.

Given this view of modernity, Simmel's theory of conflict tends to focus on the integrative or "positive" effects of conflict rather on the disintegrative consequences of conflict. Simmel argued that conflict will have integrative effects on a society when the conflicts are *frequent* as well as low in intensity and in violence. Such conflicts release tensions and are more readily managed by law and polity. These kinds of conflicts are the most likely in societies revealing high levels of structural interdependence among potential conflict parties; once interdependencies are high, actors have an interest in normatively regularizing conflict rather than letting it break rewarding interdependencies.

For Simmel, conflict can also have integrative consequences for the parties to a conflict. Conflict increases the sense of group boundaries, centralization of authority, decreased tolerance for deviance and dissent that, in turn, increases group solidarity. Conflict can also lead to coalition formation, as successful groups are drawn into the conflict by forming alliances with the original parties of a conflict. All of these outcomes promote some degree of integration in the larger social system. However, conflicts are not always integrative. If the parties to a conflict have high degrees of emotional involvement to a conflict—often an outcome of the enhanced group solidarity of parties to a conflict—it can become violent and malintegrative. Moreover, the level of violence to a conflict will increase when moralized so that the conflict is over fundamental values and ethics. Under these conditions, parties to a conflict will often not be able to compromise, and given their emotional involvement in the conflict, violence and intensity will increase, and they will increase the potential for disintegration. Indeed, Marx's theory would predict that these more disintegrative processes would always be part of societal-level conflict, whereas Simmel only indicated that this was a possibility, although the high levels of *structural interdependence* that typify market-driven capitalist societies mitigate against this polarization and value-infusion to conflict. Still, Simmel's ideas can, I believe, be rather easily blended into both Weber's and Marx's formulation of conflict processes; and so, by the modern era of theorizing in sociology, there existed a sophisticated body of theoretical principles on conflict dynamics that could be expanded upon to create a more robust theory of conflict dynamics.

---

[7]Georg Simmel, *Conflict and the Web of Group Affiliations* (New York: Free Press, 1951); see also his "The Sociology of Conflict," *American Journal of Sociology* 9 (1903–1904): pp. 490–525.

Contemporary Conflict Theories

Conflict theorizing continued in Europe for most of the twentieth century. In the United States, however, the Cold War between the United States and the Soviet Union limited such theorizing. Given Marx's association with communism, coupled with the anti-communist politics of the McCarthy Era in the 1950s, Marx's ideas were soft peddled in the United States, keeping this kind of theorizing at bay. There were, however, analyses of specific types of conflict—say, ethnic conflict or conflict among societies—but the conflict theories that had been built up in Europe around the tensions arising from inequalities were not highly visible. With the end of the McCarthy Era and the rise of the protests around the world of the 1960s, conflict theory reemerged in the United States. Conflict theory gained traction by criticizing functional theorizing as being too concerned with the status quo and functional integration (see Chapter 2). This critique became relentless and eventually dethroned functional theory as the dominant theoretical perspective in sociology in the United States.

Once this critique of functional theory proved successful, there was a rush to rebrand a wide variety of theoretical approaches as conflict theories. And the words "power" and "conflict" could be found in many works that, at best, were only marginally conflict oriented. So, as might be expected when a mode of work has been excluded if not persecuted, conflict theory often became as extreme on the side of viewing *everything* as being inherently conflictual, as functional theorizing seemed to see all phenomena as integrative. Still, despite these excesses, the new conflict theories extended the ideas of the early masters of the classical era into several distinctive conflict approaches. The first of these was a more analytical conflict theory that raised the level of abstraction so that the ideas of the masters could be seen as more generic and universal.

Analytical Conflict Theories

Ralf Dahrendorf's Conflict Theory

Not surprisingly, the early European conflict tradition was brought to the United States by European-origin theorists, some of whom had migrated to the United States from Nazi Germany and others who remained in Europe. Ralf Dahrendorf, a German sociologists, was probably the most important of these figures because it was his devastating critique of functionalism[8] that initiated its fall, but perhaps more important was his willingness to make Marx's theory highly abstract, while adding necessary correctives to the theory that were provided by Weber and Simmel. Dahrendorf began his theory by shifting the unit of analysis to what he termed *imperatively coordinated associations*, or ICAs, which could be any social system—from a group through an organization to a whole society—in which inequalities of authority were used to coordinate the actions of actors.[9] Inequality was thus about inequalities of power and authority, and the theory followed Marx's logic by trying to explain how super- and subordinate groups in ICAs would become organized to pursue conflict of varying degrees of intensity and violence. Figure 3.1 outlines Dahrendorf's argument in general terms.

---

[8]Ralf Dahrendorf, "Out of Utopia: Toward a Reorganization of Sociological Analysis," *American Journal of Sociology* 64 (1958): pp. 125–135.

[9]Ralf Dahrendorf, "Toward a Theory of Social Conflict," *Journal of Conflict Resolution* 2 (1958): pp. 170–183; *Class and Class Conflict in Industrial Societies* (Stanford, CA: Stanford University Press, 1969).

Figure 3.1 Dahrendorf's Dialectical Model of Conflict in Imperatively Coordinated Association (ICA)

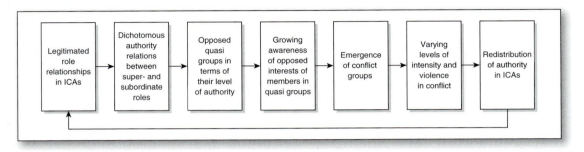

Like Marx and Weber, Dahrendorf views any social system, or ICA, as revealing patterns of legitimated authority, which tends to be somewhat dichotomous. This dichotomy sets up a basic conflict of interest or "opposed quasi groups" between superordinates and subordinates in the hierarchy of authority. Like Marx, Dahrendorf does not feel the need to explain how variations in authority arise; instead, these are built in assumptions about all social systems in general, with the theory beginning with the conditions increasing the growing awareness of members in opposed quasi groups, especially subordinate groups, of their true interests in forming a coherent group to engage in conflict against superordinates. The conditions that increase awareness of interests are basically the same as those enumerated by Marx but couched at a more abstract level: (a) *technical conditions* that allow for the emergence of leaders and the formulation of an idea system or charter for the quasi group; (b) *political conditions* that keep those in authority from having the power to prevent early mobilization of subordinates; and (c) *social conditions* that allow quasi groups to recruit new members and to articulate and circulate their grievances to potential recruits to a conflict group. Borrowing from Weber, Dahrendorf hypothesizes that the more these conditions are met, and the more inequalities in authority are correlated with other inequalities in the distribution of resources (e.g., money, honor, prestige), the more *intense* will the conflict between super- and subordinates be, with "intensity" defined as the level of emotional involvement of the conflict parties. Dahrendorf then borrows a corrective from Simmel to correct Marx's hypothesis: the less the technical, political, and social conditions are realized, the more *violent* will be the conflict. This corrective is inserted here because Marx had assumed that the more the proletariat became organized as a class "for themselves," the more violent would the conflict become, whereas empirically, violence seems to occur in the earlier stages of organization of a conflict group, where leadership and ideologies are in flux and only beginning to crystallize. During these early phases of conflict, individuals become emotionally aroused but without clear focus and direction. Other conditions also increase violence, including sudden increases in subordinates' sense of relative deprivation and failure to form regulatory agreements between the conflict parties. Violent conflict, when it occurs, will tend to increase the rate of structural change in an ICA, whereas conflicts that are intense will increase the degree of structural change.

Lewis A. Coser's Conflict Theory

Another German sociologists, Lewis Coser, who migrated to the United States developed a more functional-looking theory by drawing ideas from Georg Simmel. Going against the more

Marxian critique of functionalism, Coser said conflict theory did not emphasize the integrative consequences of conflict, whereas functionalism did not sufficiently stress the disintegrative effects of conflict. He placed a pox on both perspectives (conflict theories and functionalism) and used Simmel's basic ideas to formulate what he saw as a more balanced theory.[10]

The causes of conflict for Coser revolve around the withdrawal of legitimacy by subordinates in a system of inequality—phrased more in the manner of Weber than Simmel at this point. The Weberian imagery continues with Coser seeing the withdrawal of legitimacy as increasing when there are few channels for redressing grievances and when there are low rates of mobility from subordinate to superordinate positions in a society. The chances of conflict being initiated by subordinates increase with sudden increases in their sense of deprivation. The violence of the conflict will increase when conflict is over "nonrealistic" issues (values, morality) and when conflict endures over time and becomes moralized by the parties. In contrast, the conflict will be less violent when it is over "realistic issues" that allow for compromises and thus allow each party to achieve some of its goals. Conflicts vary by duration, with the duration increasing when the goals of conflict parties are expansive rather than focused, when consensus over goals among factions in conflict parties is low, and when parties to the conflict cannot easily determine their adversaries' symbolic points of victory or defeat. Conversely, conflict will be shortened when parties realize that complete attainment of their respective goals is not possible, which increases with near equal power between parties and clarity of what constitutes defeat or victory, and when leaders can persuade followers to terminate the conflict, which increases with centralization of power and integration within each party to a conflict.

Finally, like Simmel, Coser presents hypotheses on the functions of conflict for the parties to the conflict and for the more inclusive system in which the conflict occurs. When conflict is violent and intense, it will generate for each party to the conflict clear-cut group boundaries, centralization power and decision-making authority, and ideological solidarity among the members of the respective conflict groups. Yet, these conditions are likely to cause suppression of dissent that, over the long run, will increase tensions within each party to the conflict and, in the long run, intra-group conflict. The more differentiated (complex) and functionally interdependent are the units in a system, the more likely is conflict among such units to be frequent and of low degrees of violence and intensity. The more these conditions are met, the more likely are conflicts to increase the level of innovation and creativity among conflict groups, release hostilities before they accumulate and become too intense, promote efforts at normative regulation of conflict, and increase the number of associative coalitions for both parties to the conflict. And, to the extent that conflict can realize the conditions listed above, the greater will be the level of integration of the more inclusive system in which conflict occurs, and the more likely is this system to adapt to its external environment.

---

[10]Lewis A. Coser, *The Functions of Social Conflict* (London: Free Press, 1956), "Some Social Functions of Violence," *Annals of the American Academy of Political and Social Science* 364 (1960); "Some Functions of Deviant Behavior and Normative Flexibility," *American Journal of Sociology* 68 (1962): pp. 172–181; and "The Functions of Dissent," in *The Dynamics of Dissent* (New York: Grune & Stratton, 1968), pp. 158–170. Other prominent works with less revealing titles but critical substance include "Social Conflict and the Theory of Social Change," *British Journal of Sociology* 8 (1957): pp. 197–207; "Violence and the Social Structure," in *Science and Psychoanalysis*, ed. J. Masserman, vol. 7 (New York: Grune & Stratton, 1963), pp. 30–42. These and other essays are collected in Coser's *Continuities in the Study of Social Conflict* (New York, Free Press, 1967).

Jonathan Turner's Synthesis

Some years ago after reviewing the theories of Dahrendorf and Coser, I made an effort to synthesize them, and in so doing, my effort also provided for a blending of Marx's, Weber's, and Simmel's respective theories.[11] By keeping the theory at a high level of abstraction—that is, concepts and propositions are at a high level of generalization—a basic theory of conflict processes is evident. Conflict unfolds over time in systems of inequality, and there appear to be several basic steps or phases that lead up to the conflict that eventually emerges. In Figure 3.2, I outline one plausible sequence of phases of conflict, drawing from the insights of the conflict theorists examined thus far. Time flows from left to right in the diagram, with the arrows representing directions of causality. Arrows flowing from right to left represent reverse causal affects, where outcomes feed back and affect the very processes that cause these outcomes. The signs on the arrows indicate their effect—whether positive, negative, or in one case, curvilinear in which the effect is initially positive but eventually turns negative. By tracing the flow of causality, and reverse causality, we can get a sense for how the classical theorists (Marx, Weber, and Simmel) and early modern theorists (Dahrendorf and Coser) viewed the process of conflict.

Conflict occurs in an existing social system composed of interrelated units that reveals inequality in the distribution of resources (see left side of figure). These should be seen as variable states of interrelatedness and inequality—that is, they vary by degrees. The greater is the level of inequality, the more likely is conflict—at least in the long run—because inequalities set into motion certain dynamics that are difficult to arrest, once they get started. Weber and later Coser probably had it right when they emphasized that subordinates in this system of inequality first begin to withdraw legitimacy when (a) there is superimposition of rewards and deprivations with those high and low in their possession of one valued resource that predicts their receipt of other valued resources; (b) there are few channels for addressing grievances about inequalities; and (c) there are few opportunities for upward mobility on resource hierarchies. The converse of these conditions decreases the chances that legitimacy will be withdrawn from those in power and those in other key resource-distributing institutional domains (e.g., economy, polity, law, religion). That is, lower levels of inequality, channels for addressing grievances, and possibilities for upward mobility will generally work against withdrawal of legitimacy. Yet, when conditions promote the withdrawal of legitimacy, subordinates become ever-more aware of the fact that their interests are not the same as those who hold power; subordinates begin to see that their interests stand in opposition to those hording resources. As the middle portions of the figure document, awareness of interests feeds back and makes subordinates even more likely to withdraw legitimacy in a cycle that can escalate rapidly as awareness of interests and withdrawal of legitimacy feed off each other.

As this awareness increases, individuals also become more emotionally aroused—expressing anger and frustration at inequities of those who control resources. This mix among the beginnings of withdrawal of legitimacy, the increasing of a conflict of interest between subordinates and superordinates stand in conflict, and the emotional arousal over inequities can, together, all cause periodic outburst of anger in local contexts, such as neighborhoods, workplaces, and

---

[11]See my "A Strategy for Reformulating the Dialectical and Functional Theories of Conflict," *Social Forces* (1975), pp. 433–444. For more recent updates of this theory see, *Theoretical Principles of Sociology, Volume 1 on Macrodynamics* (New York: Springer, 2010), pp. 153–285; and *Theoretical Principles of Sociology, Volume 3 on Mesodynamics* (New York: Springer, 2010), pp. 337–372.

Figure 3.2 Turner's Synthetic Model of Conflict Processes

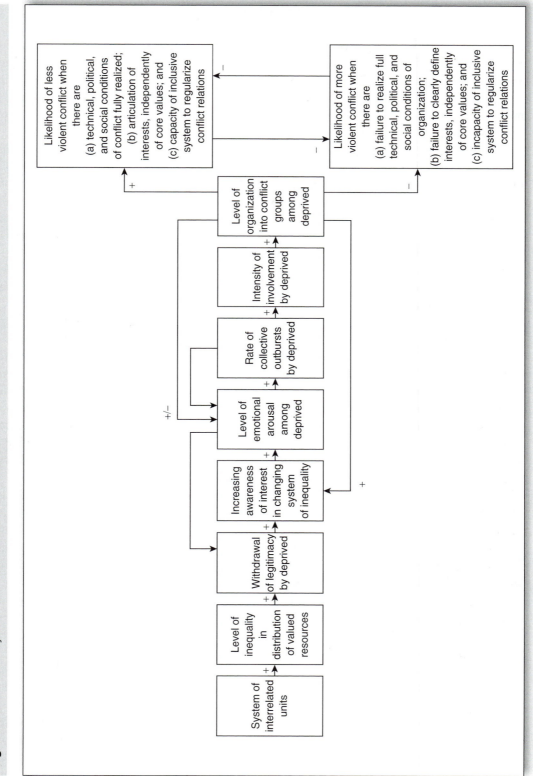

public places. If these outbursts are repressed by the forces of social control (e.g., police and military), emotional arousal increases that much more, and this heightened emotion feeds back to increase awareness, leading to further withdrawal of legitimacy and more intense emotional arousal. Leaders of protests also begin to articulate a more coherent ideology, but these leaders are often, among themselves, in conflict or, at least, competition with each other for the attention of subordinates—thus creating a flood of anti-establishment rhetoric that has yet to fully sort itself out. But, the intensity of involvement of subordinates will typically increase, and moreover, others will begin to be pulled into the opposition that is building.

Here, Dahrendorf's more abstract portrayal of the *technical, political, social* conditions of organization becomes important. The flow of the conflict between subordinates and superordinates will vary depending upon the extent to which (a) leaders can articulate a coherent ideology justifying, framing, and focusing the goals of subordinates, (b) polity and law or those in authority are willing to make concessions, and (c) subordinates can recruit new members and other resources, such as money, organizational skills, and new symbols that can be incorporated into the emerging organization for conflict and the ideology justifying mobilization for conflict.

It is at this point that the other German theories—that is, those theories developed by Weber, Simmel, Dahrendorf, and to a lesser extent, Coser—deviate from Marx. Marx felt that the more the technical, political, and social conditions could be met, the more intense and violent the conflict would be, but other theorists recognized that violent conflict tends to occur in earlier stages when these conditions are not fully met. For example, the early years of union organization in the United States were often violent, but as unions became broader, more accepted, and given rights by government and law, their actions became more strategic with some willingness to compromise with employers. However, when ideologies are first emerging and leadership is in flux, emotions are aroused but not yet focused on a clear strategic path. As a result, violence becomes more likely. But, when the conditions of organization are realized, violence declines and conflict becomes more strategic. Moreover, as both Simmel and Coser recognized, when a social system reveals high levels of interdependencies, actors become more motivated to regulate potential conflicts because these conflicts will disrupt the system in ways that harm all actors.

The structure of the larger social unit thus has effects on the degree to which the technical, political, and social conditions are met. Highly stratified systems reveal very large gaps in inequalities (as Weber emphasized) and levels of structural interdependencies among all actors are not so high; the result is that superordinates are more likely to repress conflict by limiting subordinates chances of meeting the technical, political, and social conditions. Ironically, in so doing, superordinates set themselves up for more intense and potentially violent conflict down the road, as emotions among subordinates accumulate. As Spencer emphasized, social control is costly to superordinates, and in order to engage in extensive social control, superordinates must tax subordinates and often elites as well, which only increases inequalities and resentments fueling conflict mobilization by subordinates.

If, however, conflicts can be frequent and of low intensity, then they will release tensions and generally lead to regulation of conflict by law that gives rights to subordinates to protest and limits the rights of superordinates to continuously usurp the resources of non-elites. This response to conflict is more likely in systems that reveal high levels of structural interdependence. Moreover, if subordinates perceive that they have opportunities for mobility and that they have at least some valued resources, they become less likely to incur the risks of conflict. And, if conflict occurs, it will tend to be focused on specific issues and not involve a broad and diffuse de-legitimation of superordinates in all domains of the society or any social system in which conflict occurs. Thus, there can be conflict over wages in the economy, without de-legitimating the economy or other institutions; there may be conflict over health care, educational opportunities, religious freedom, etc., but these conflicts are focused and do not become an attack on *all* institutional domains in a society. And, as long as there are mechanisms in place—such as an arena of politics in which issues can be openly debated, a legal system that is capable of responding to integrative problems, and a polity willing to make strategic concessions, then violence can be avoided. As a result, structural and cultural changes will be more evolutionary than revolutionary. If, however, these conditions do not exist, then conflict, when it does occur, can be violent and highly disruptive to a social system. The last boxes in Figure 3.2 outline these two basic outcomes of conflict, which depend upon the structure of the more inclusive social units within which conflict occurs.

Figure 3.2 thus summarizes the state of formal and analytical conflict theorizing by the end of the twentieth century. Alongside of the more abstract theories were other types of analytical theories that should be briefly reviewed. One set of theories revolved around comparative analysis of conflicts in the past to see what generalizations they yield.

Historical-Comparative Conflict Theories

Over the last five decades, a large body of historical work within sociology has focused on "revolutions" and conflicts within societies.[12] These theories emphasize the mobilization of both the masses of subordinates and elites against the state or polity. The collapse of the state can thus be the result of elites' dissatisfaction with polity, and if elites are joined by the masses, then the challenges to the state are that much greater. Thus, elite mobilization and mass mobilization of non-elites can individually or in tandem cause the state to collapse. However, the state must be in a weakened position, typically because of fiscal crises of the state whose leaders have squandered their wealth on consumption or, even worse, engaged in wars with other states, which inevitably drain the coffers of the state.

Much of this work in historical sociology has a Weberian feel in that it sees conflicts as events that take place under particular historical conditions. The theories produced in this tradition tend to have a somewhat ambivalent attitude—as did Weber—about whether general historical conditions causing conflict and state collapse can be specified or, alternatively, conflicts are unique historical events tied to the conditions of a particular time or place. Yet, from the work of these historical-comparative sociologists come some general ideas about conflict dynamics, which can be seen as part of a general theory of conflict dynamics in societies. The various theories focus on somewhat different problems, but at their core, they all seek to specify the conditions that generate change from conflict between subordinates in a system of inequality against those controlling the state. But, they also recognize that often it is challenges by elites to the analytical tradition summarized above, and they also recognize that conditions weakening the state are critical to understanding

---

[12]Barrington Moore, *Social Origins Of Dictatorship and Democracy: Lord and Peasant in the Making of the Modern World* (Boston: Beacon, 1966); Jeffrey Paige, *Agrarian Revolution: Social Movements and Export Agriculture in the Underdeveloped World* (New York: Free Press, 1975); Charles Tilly, *From Mobilization to Revolution* (Reading, MA: Addison-Wesley, 1978); Charles Tilly, *European Revolutions, 1492–1992* (Oxford, UK, and Cambridge, MA: Blackwell, 1993); Theda Skocpol, *States and Social Revolutions: A Comparative Analysis of France, Russia, and China* (New York: Cambridge University Press, 1979); Jack Goldstone, *Revolution and Rebellion in the Early Modern World* (Berkeley: University of California Press, 1991).

when revolutionary conflicts will occur and be successful, or fail. Much historical-comparative theorizing is on more agrarian societies, whether those of the feudal past or in the modern era, and so they offer an interesting comparison to many analytical theories that draw their inspiration from modern societies, even as they seek to develop theories that explain conflict in all types of societies.

Conditions of Non-Elite Mobilization for Conflict

Let me begin by enumerating the conditions in various theories that increase the likelihood that non-elites or subordinates in a system of inequality will mobilize for conflict. These conditions are, as will be evident, similar to those outlined by the analytical theories summarized above. Later, I will examine the conditions that weaken the state so that conflict has a chance of being successful, followed by the conditions under which elites also rebel against the state.

The conditions increasing the likelihood of subordinate mobilization for conflict in agrarian societies include: (a) concentration in physical space so that they can communicate their grievances and (b) increasing solidarity among subordinates that increases with: (i) sense of threat about what elites might do, (ii) avoidance of competition with each other so as to not divide their interests, (iii) weakening of traditional relations with elites (e.g., breakdown of feudal obligations of nobility to peasants on their estates), (iv) perceptions of exploitation by elites, (v) autonomy from direct supervision by elites and their managers, (vi) receptiveness to radical, change-oriented ideologies, (vii) perceptions that elites no longer provide useful resources, and (viii) perceptions that elites and the state are weak.

These conditions promoting mobilization are, however, potentially checked and countered by conditions that weaken the resolve of subordinates to mobilize. These include: (a) ecological dispersion so that communication is difficult, especially in non-media societies and among people who are not literate, and (b) forces that work against subordinate solidarity, including (i) dependence of subordinates on elites for necessary resources, (ii) lack of resources with which to mobilize against elites, (iii) constraints of powerful local communities locked into long-standing traditions of inequality, (iv) opportunities among subordinates for upward social mobility, and (v) competition among fellow subordinates for resources, which increase with introduction of labor markets.

Conditions Weakening State Power

Several interrelated forces weaken the state's capacity to exert social control over both elites and non-elites, thereby creating what some have called a "revolutionary" situation. These include: (a) demographic forces, such as (i) population growth and increasing demands for resources from the state by both elites and non-elites, (ii) price inflation created by population growth and increased demand in markets for basic resources, (iii) younger age cohorts (accompanying population growth) who are more prone to conflict, (iv) rural immiseration created by rural population growth, and (v) migration of younger age cohorts to urban areas where they can more effectively communicate their grievances and mobilize for conflict; (b) fiscal forces as a result of (i) population growth and shortages in resources, (ii) inefficient and abusive tax collection procedures that arouse antagonism of both elites and non-elites, (iii) efforts to implement new revenue collection mechanisms that arouse resentments of elites and non-elites, (iv) high demands of elites for patronage from state, (v) military expenditures for geopolitical activities, and (vi) high expenditures for internal social control of restive population; and (c) political forces, including (i) decreased coercive and administrative power as a consequence of fiscal forces, (ii) incapacity to make strategic concessions to elites and non-elites because of fiscal forces and/or rigidity of system of political control, (iii) geo-political engagements that erode fiscal position of state and, with loss of prestige in the geo-political system (from loss of a war), (iv) erode the state's legitimacy in the eyes of elites and non-elites, and (v) relative autonomy of military from control by political elites.

Conditions Increasing Likelihood of Elite Mobilization

Elites do not always remain loyal to the state when (a) their demands for patronage cannot be met because of fiscal crises or expansion of the number of elites (from population growth), (b) elites have strong social networks independent of those with elites in the state, (c) elites fear losing their privilege with increasing fiscal problems of the state, and (d) elites experience a sense of threat because (i) their dependence on the state for wealth is threatened when the state is under fiscal crisis, (ii) their upward mobility is threatened by the inability of the state to open opportunities and bestow patronage, and (iii) social reforms to meet fiscal crises or to meet demands of non-elites threaten their traditional bases of wealth, power, and prestige.

To the extent that all of these three sets of conditions—mobilization by subordinates, threats to elite privilege, and fiscal crises confronting the weakened state—can work independently or in conjunction to produce revolutionary conflict in societies. When all three sets work in concert, then state breakdown and change in the structure of a society are inevitable. While many of these conditions are tied to agrarian patterns of social organization, it is not too difficult to make them more general and applicable to other types of societal formations. For example, industrial elites can be threatened by the actions of the state, and if such is the case, they may mobilize for political conflict through financing of political campaigns or through lobbying. Such conflicts will not generally be violent but they are political conflicts generated by the same forces as in agrarian societies. Thus, even with a certain amount of historical specificity, the ideas that various historical-comparative theories can be converted to more abstract statements that make them more analytical and general. Moreover, historical-comparative sociology emphasizes something that, rather surprisingly, is not stressed in analytical conflict theories: the power of the state and centers of political control in societies. When this power is strong, revolutionary conflict is not likely to be successful; rather, only when the state is weakened by fiscal crises generated from a variety of sources will mobilization by non-elites or elites be effective in changing the structure of societies.

Randall Collins' Conflict Theorizing

Randall Collins has been one of the most productive theorists of the modern era.[13] His early works were highly analytical, drawing inspiration from Max Weber but stated as a series of abstract laws. Collins' later works are decidedly more micro in focus, bringing into conflict theory ideas from Emile Durkheim's later works on religion and from Irving Goffman's dramaturgy (see Chapter 7). As his work became more micro, it has emphasized the importance of emotions in forging solidarity among individuals engaged in conflict. Let's begin with the early neo-Weberian theorizing.

---

[13]Randall Collins, *Conflict Sociology: Toward an Explanatory Science* (New York: Academic, 1975).

Early Neo-Weberian Theorizing on Conflict

Collins' work has always had a historical-comparative emphasis, which understandably drew him to Weber whose work is historical, but unlike Weber and most historical-comparative thinkers, he has been willing to develop propositions that are abstract and transcend any particular society or historical epoch. Even as his later work reduced the emphasis on propositions, it remained highly analytical in trying to uncover the micro dynamics operating in all conflict situations.

In his *Conflict Sociology*, the subtitle "Toward an Explanatory Science" reveals his commitment to developing a science of conflict processes. In this book, he moves from the micro basis of conflict to ever more macro levels of conflict. Conflict is inherent in social organization at all levels because social reality evidences inequalities in the distribution of valued resources, particularly power, material well-being, and prestige (a very Weberian view of stratification). The theory seeks to develop propositions on conflict at different levels of social organization—from face-to-face encounters through organizations and social categories such as gender to societies and inter-societal formations.

At the micro level, individuals pay close attention to the inequalities of resources among individuals, adjusting their conduct to present the proper demeanor for their resources while giving the appropriate level of deference to others' resources. The more similar people's respective resources, the more likely are interactions to be more relaxed, whereas when larger inequalities exist, interactions will be stiff, highly ritualized, and short-term. When there are high degrees of inequality and when others are co-present and can observe what occurs, deference will be emitted in a highly explicit manner, as would be the case, for example, of lower-ranking military personnel briskly saluting a higher-ranking office when on the military base where monitoring is high or people at the workplace giving high deference to their superiors.

From these interactions, class cultures emerged, and these cultures reflect the extent to which individuals have been order-givers or order-takers over the course of the many face-to-face encounters that constitute daily life. Those who have had power and could give orders are more likely to initiate and control talk, to have positive self-feelings, to identify with the goals of groups and organization, and to experience positive emotions that, in turn, give them confidence in future encounters. Conversely, those who have less power and authority across the various types of situations in which they have previously interacted will experience less of these attributes, and perhaps even negative emotions like anger.

In organizations, control systems reflect the level and type of resources—material, coercive, and symbolic—that are distributed among offices and individuals and the configurations of these resources used to control others. When control is sought through heavy use of coercion, those subject to this coercive control will try to escape, fight back, or if escape is not possible, to comply with sluggish conformity. The more control is sought through the use of material resources as incentives (e.g., salary increases), the more individuals develop acquisitive orientations and self-interested and strategic behaviors. And the more control relies upon symbolic resources, the more individuals will be subject to indoctrination, to requests to participate in organizational rituals and ceremonies, and be rewarded for conformity with the norms and the cultural ideology of the organization.

The more those in authority rely upon coercive and material incentive resources, however, the more those with authority will have to rely upon surveillance of conformity to directives. And, the more surveillance is employed, the greater will be the level of *alienation* of those subject to this surveillance. As a consequence, the higher will be the ratio of supervisory to nonsupervisory personnel, and the more conformity to norms will be evident in only highly visible situations. In contrast, the more symbolic resources are used to administer the organization, the more will be the emphasis on standardized rules and commitments to the goals of the organization, which in turn will decrease reliance on levels of authority and negative sanctions.

Collins sees societies as ultimately built from what he terms *interaction rituals* emitted in face-to-face encounters; these rituals are the basic building blocks of all societies—from groups to organizations to societies to geo-political inter-societal systems. The dynamics of organizations outlined above are especially important because larger scale structures are built from organizations; furthermore, among the most important of these macrostructures is the economy and the state. The size and scale of political organization in a society is related to the productive capacity of the economy and its levels of technology, access to resources, efficiency of organization, and size of the population in a society. And, as the economy becomes more productive, the state can use taxes on this productivity to become larger. In addition, the more likely will the state engage in geo-political activities and, as a result, control larger territories, thereby increasing not only the size of territories to be governed but also the number of people who must be controlled. Under these conditions, it is more likely that coercive force (e.g., armies) will be used and that centers of power will be dispersed across the territory to be controlled. At the same time, the state will make efforts at symbolic unification within and among social units regulated by the state.

Power always generates some tensions, with the stability of the state related to its level of wealth, its degree of organization, and its ability to resolve periodic crises. As Weber and many historical-comparative sociologists have emphasized, the state is also a player in a larger geopolitical arena, with the stability of the state and its legitimation often dependent upon its success in this arena. States will often seek to conquer other states and build up empires as a distinctive type of geo-political formation. As Spencer argued (although Collins does not use Spencer but, instead, Max Weber), the more a state consolidates coercive power in the form of armies, the more likely will it try to use this power to conquer another state. And, the more a state has what Collins terms a *marchland advantage* (or the absence of enemies on many of its borders due to geographical obstacles like mountains and oceans), the more this state can move out from its home base, up to the point where it (a) loses its marchland advantage and encounters more enemies at its borders, (b) encounters another marchland state in a showdown war, and (c) exceeds its capacity to regulate and control the larger population spread out in geographical space, far from the empire's capital city.[14] The result will be the loss of a showdown war, erosion of its borders under constant assault from enemies, or internal collapse due to inadequate resources to control restive populations.

The Durkheimian Shift in Collins' Conflict Theorizing

Collins was always interested in the emotional payoffs of interactions for individuals, and when these are assessed in the context of conflict, then emotions affect the solidarity of members of social units engaged in conflict. Collins increasingly visualized individuals as motivated to enhance their positive emotional energy and to augment their cultural capital which,

---

[14]See Randall Collins, *Weberian Sociological Theory* (Cambridge, England: Cambridge University Press, 1986), pp. 167–212; "Long-Term Social Change and the Territorial Power of States," in his *Sociology Since Midcentury: Essays in Theory Cumulation* (New York: Academic, 1981).

in turn, would allow them to receive deference and honor. Interaction rituals had always been a focus of his micro theory, and in recent years, he expanded the model of interaction rituals to include the processes outlined in Figure 3.3, which lays out the forces in play.[15]

Durkheim had described how co-presence of individuals leads to talk and interaction, which generate an emotional mood, a sense of "effervescence" that seems to come from "outside" individuals. These emotions lead individuals to symbolize them as an external force whose power must be "worshiped." As individuals feel this need to acknowledge this seeming power, they begin to create totems symbolizing this power and to enact rituals directed at the power symbolized by totems. Collins takes this basic insight and develops a more refined model. By following the model in Figure 3.3 from left to right, plus noting the reverse causal effects (arrows from right to left) of outcomes of processes feeding back and affecting the operation of these processes, one can get a feeling for how emotions are aroused to the point where individuals experience high solidarity, experience an increase in *positive emotions*, and build up what Collins terms *particularistic cultural capital* (e.g., memories, feelings, experiences that are shared by group members). As emotions and cultural capital build up, individuals feel a need to mark the solidarity with symbols—names, words, phrases, clothing, badges, and other markers of group membership.

In the context of conflict, these are the necessary processes to build up solidarities in conflict groups and organizations, thus making the conflict more intense and involving. Thus, the variables in earlier models that simply denote increased emotional arousal are now filled in with more details on how this arousal *process* operates. Without this level of emotional arousal and its symbolization, conflict groups cannot be effective and hold together, but with group solidarity, they can more effectively confront other conflict groups. For Collins, this model of emotional arousal is also applicable *to all other forms of non-conflict organization*; indeed, groups, organizations, societies, and even inter-societal systems will not hold together without these interaction ritual dynamics operating at the micro level. The emotions generated in interaction rituals are, in essence, the glue that binds individuals in larger social units together and that keeps individuals motivated to participate in the activities of social units, whether these be conflict with another social unit pursuing non-conflict goals.

The New Theory of Micro-Level Violence[16]

Most interactions involve the phases of the interaction ritual outlined in Figure 3.3, but the potential for violence stands out in the neurologically hardwired propensity for humans to experience positive emotional energy in interactional rituals. The emotional field for individuals under situations of potential violence generates powerful fear emotions, creating enormous confrontational tension between the phases of positive emotional arousal associated with interaction rituals and the fear response to violence. Even when individuals are motivated to engage in conflict, it is difficult to "pull the trigger" and engage in violent acts. Most conflict situations fail to become violent, or they degenerate into posturing but never fully engaging violence because of this confrontational tension. Even when one party becomes violent, this violence is

[15]Randall Collins, *Interaction Ritual Chains* (Princeton, NJ: Princeton University Press, 2004).

[16]Randall Collins, *Violence: A Micro-sociological Theory* (Princeton, NJ: Princeton University Press 2008).

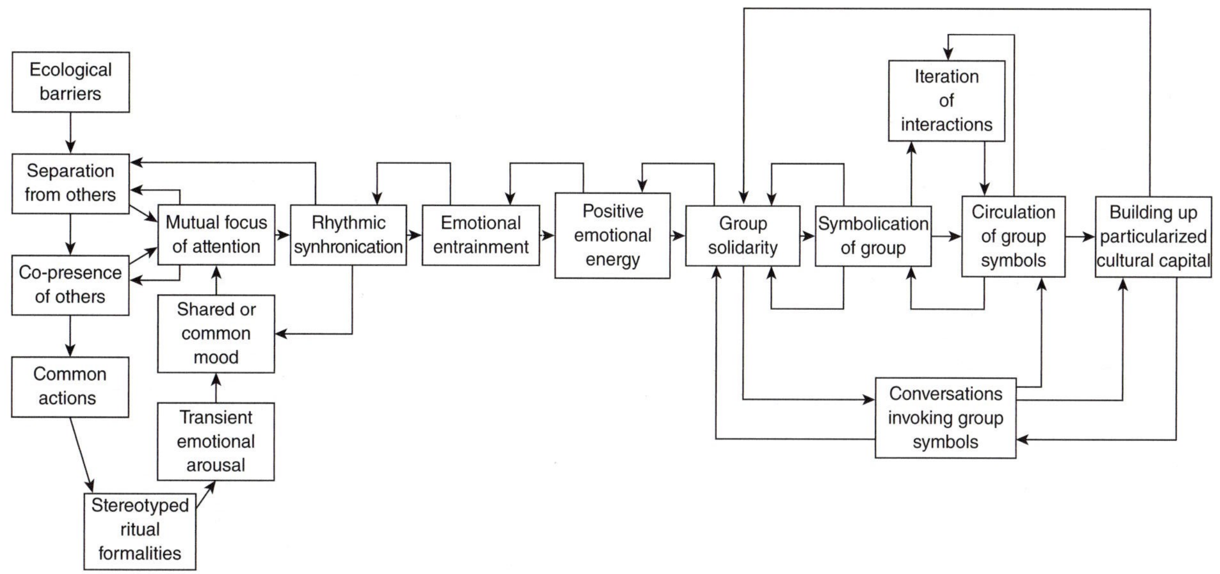

Figure 3.3 Collins' Elaborated Model of Interaction Rituals

often not reciprocated. And, in collective violence, when organized groupings engage in violence, as in the case of war or a riot, most individuals do not actively participate in the violence. Instead, people hold back and often dance around in the background. What forces, then, enable individuals to overcome the power of confrontational tension?

Collins' theory thus seeks to outline some of the conditions that answer this question. One answer, and perhaps the most important, is that the interaction rituals modeled in Figure 3.3 are used to mobilize actors to commit violence. When used to promote conflict, the stages of interaction rituals are dedicated to charging up positive emotional energy for committing violence against an enemy. Emotional entrainment, effervescence, positive emotional energy, solidarity, group symbols, and particularized cultural capital are all focused on "the enemy" and the positive emotional energy that will come from their harm or defeat. This use of interaction rituals is most effective if the enemy is some distance away, as is often the case in military confrontations where the protagonists do not see each as individuals. Armies, terrorist cells, and groups organized for violence all use the phases of the interaction ritual, practicing and routinizing violence by invoking symbols (flags, badges, and memories unique to the group) and powering up positive emotions for engaging in violence as an act promoting the ideals of the conflict group.

Thus, for violence to occur and to work on a mass level, one or both protagonists must collectively overcome their confrontation tensions. Humans have learned over the millennia how to do this: by usurping interactional ritual dynamics and using them to charge up positive emotions and the symbols of group solidarity for the purpose of violence. Yet, even then, not everyone participates, and many are fearful because fear is humans' most powerful, hardwired emotion, and it is difficult to override this emotion, even with the power of interaction rituals.

Neo-Marxian Theories of Conflict

Analytical conflict theorists separate Marx's ideas explaining conflict from his views that conflict *should be used to* undo patterns of oppression and exploitation.[17] There is always an element of *praxis*, or theory-driven action in the name of social good, in all of Marx's and modern Marxists theorizing. We will see this critical stance from Marx in Chapter 10 on critical theories on modernity, but it also pervades some more analytical efforts to develop explanatory theories. What is sometimes called *analytical Marxism* seeks to develop explanatory theories that recognize the failings of Marx's theory to predict the "revolution by the proletariat" and the conditions of contemporary capitalist society that have worked against

---

[17]For example, Perry Anderson, *Considerations on Western Marxism* (London: New Left Review, 1976); Michael Buraway, *The Politics of Production* (London: Verso, 1985); Sam Bowles and Herbert Gintis, *Democracy and Capitalism* (New York: Basic Books, 1986); G. A. Cohen, *History of Labor and Freedom: Themes from Marx* (Oxford: Clarendon, 1988) and *Karl Marx's Theory of History: A Defense* (Princeton, NJ: Princeton University Press, 1978); John Elster, *Making Sense of Marx* (Cambridge: Cambridge University Press, 1978); Barry Hindess and Paul Q. Hirst, *Capital and Capitalism Today* (London: Routledge, 1977); Claus Offe, *Disorganized Capitalism: Contemporary Transformations of Work and Politics* (Cambridge: Cambridge University Press, 1985); Adam Przeworski, *Capitalism and Social Democracy* (Cambridge: Cambridge University Press, 1985); John A. Roemer, *A General Theory of Exploitation and Class* (Cambridge, MA: Harvard University Press, 1982) and *Analytical Foundations of Marxian Economic Theory* (Cambridge: Cambridge University Press, 1981); and Michael Burawoy and Erik Olin Wright, "Sociological Marxism," in *Handbook of Sociological Theory*, ed. J. H. Turner (Kluwer Academic/Plenum, 2001), pp. 459–486; Erik Olin Wright, "What Is Analytical Marxism?" *Socialist Review* 19 (1989).

this predicted revolution. Other analytical Marxists have shifted the unit of analysis from societies to systems of societies, seeing the dynamics outlined by Marx as more likely to occur at the global level where the lack of an effective world-level central state enables the contradictions of capitalism to play themselves out and usher in the socialists revolution on a global scale. There still is much concern with *praxis* in both these types of analytical theories, but what makes them analytical is that they take the task of explaining conflict dynamics in less ideological terms, especially when compared to critical theorists examined in Chapter 10.

Analytical Marxism: Erik Olin Wright

The most well-known analytical Marxist in the United States is Erik Olin Wright. He has devoted his career to trying to understand why Marx's predictions about revolution went wrong and, most recently, to offer guidelines for creating what he has chosen to call "real utopias" that make peace between capitalism and collectivism.[18] Wright has collected hard data that expose the micro reality of class dynamics. When viewed from the macro level, people's class position seems clear, but when examined empirically, people's class location and interests present a more complex picture. One complication is that there is not a simple linkage between jobs in the means of production (i.e., economy) and class position; in addition, once this fact is realized, the neat relations between individuals material interests, their lived experiences in their daily lives, and their collective capacities to organize for conflict do not follow Marx's macro-level theory.

This conclusion can be illustrated by what Wright terms "the problem of the middle classes."[19] Marx predicted that capitalist society would polarize into two basic classes: the *bourgeoisie* who own and manage the means of production and the *proletariat* who must be exploited and give the surplus value of their labor as profits to capitalists (see earlier discussion on Marx). One problem immediately evident is that capitalist societies have proliferated rather than reduced the number of classes; there is a large mass in the middle between the rich and poor whose class locations are ambiguous and highly porous as people shuffle around in various middle classes during their lifetimes. When jobs do not point to clear material interests and when most people in a capitalist society are somewhere in the middle of the class structure rather that at the top and bottom, the lived experiences and collective potential of classes deviates from what Marx envisioned.

There are related problems with Marx's predictions. One is that individuals can have contradictory class locations. People can have varying configurations of owning the means of their production, selling their labor, and purchasing the labor of others. This becomes particularly evident if families are the unit of analysis where one adult is blue collar and another is white collar; what, then, would be the class location of the family in such a situation? It would be contradictory in Marx's sense, but more fundamentally, the lived experiences of individuals and

---

[18]Erik Olin Wright, *Envisioning Real Utopias* (London: Verso, 2010).

[19]Erik Olin Wright, "Class Analysis, History and Emancipation," *New Left Review* 202 (1993): pp. 15–35; Erik Olin Wright, "Rethinking, Once Again, the Concept of Class Structure," in *The Debate on Classes*, ed. E. O. Wright (London: Verso, 1989), p. 269; Erik Olin Wright, *Class, Crisis and the State* (London: Verso, 1978), *Class Structure and Income Distribution* (New York: Academic, 1979), and *Classes* (London: Verso, 1985); Erik Olin Wright and Luca Perrone, "Marxist Class Categories and Income Inequality," *American Sociological Review* 42 (1977): pp. 32–55; "The Comparative Project on Class Structures and Class Consciousness: An Overview," *Acta Sociologica* 32 (1989): pp. 3–22.

their potential for collective mobilization do not correspond to Marx's vision. Another problem is that highly skilled labor can sell itself in labor markets at great advantages and can thus collect "rents" (extra income) because of the value of their labor. It is hard for these professional and skilled workers to see themselves as exploited. Still another problem is mediated class relations where one family member performs household duties, while the other works at a job outside the family. What is the class position of the family member performing household duties? Still another problem not predicted by Marx is that a significant proportion of workers are employed by government, which makes their exploitation by capitalists difficult to visualize. Moreover, government employees as well as those working in non-governmental organizations may be able to purchase stock with their incomes or through their retirement programs, which makes them both workers and owners of the means of production. Still another problem in Marx's is the dispersion of ownership of the means of production through stocks such that no one person or family can be considered the bourgeoisie; in fact, workers and their pension funds are often the largest stock holder of a capitalist firm.

Wright has employed a number of analytical gambits to preserve the notions in Marx about exploitation as measured by surplus value extracted from the wages of workers. None of these has been highly successful, but the concern with overcoming the abuses of capitalist forms of production has persisted. The most recent effort in his book, *Envisioning Real Utopias*,[20] Wright appears to have relaxed his effort to sustain Marxian orthodoxy and simply outlined the harms of capitalism, while laying out potential trajectories by which these harms can be reduced and mitigated through the reconstruction of the economy and polity. Equally significant, he assesses the likelihood of various trajectories actually coming about, given the structure of capitalism and democratic forms of government; in so doing, he offers not only real utopias but more realistic utopias.

Wright's model is outlined in Figure 3.4, where the potential trajectories in the transformation from capitalism to socialism are outlined. Capitalism creates social harms through four different mechanisms of social reproduction of harmful social relations. One mechanism is coercion involving "imposing various kinds of punishments for making . . . challenges (to the system)." Coercion can come from the state or non-state actors that use coercion or the threat of coercion to keep people from mobilizing for conflict and change in the system of social relations. Another mechanism is institutional rules, or accepted rules of the game, that make challenges to the system of relations difficult to pursue. A third mechanisms is ideological, or more broadly, cultural that, as Marx argued, is controlled by those with power to manipulate the media and to control reproductive structures like education to generate commitments of individuals to the norms, beliefs, and ideologies of capitalism and, thereby, prevent individuals from challenging the system. The fourth mechanism listed in Figure 3.4 is material interests of individuals, which become tied up in the success of capitalism, and thereby keeps people realizing that their true interests may lie in not supporting the capitalist system and, in fact, reside in participating in actions that cause its demise. Such dependence of people's interest on the existing system of relations will make individuals fearful of challenging the system and thus keep them from considering their real interests in changing the exploitive system. Indeed, they remain committed to the very system that exploits them.

---

[20]Wright, *Envisioning Real Utopias* (cited in note 18).

Figure 3.4 Wright's Envisioning of the Path to Transformative Change

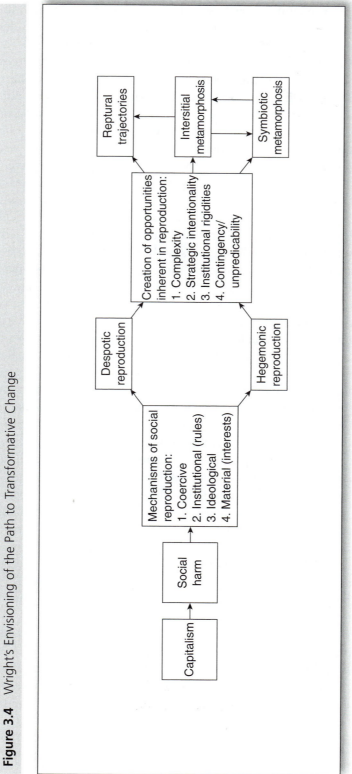

These mechanisms operate in various configurations depending upon the society in question. From these potential configurations, two basic kinds of social reproduction emerge: (1) *despotic reproduction*, which relies upon coercion and institutional rules, and (2) *hegemonic reproduction*, which draws people willingly through ideology and misperceptions of material interests into commitments to the system of exploitation. Still, even the most powerful of systems of exploitation will reveal limits, gaps, weaknesses that provide potential opportunities for transformative change. These are listed in Figure 3.4 under *complexity, strategic intentionality, institutional rigidities*, and *contingency/unpredictability*, and they open up three potential trajectories for transformative change: *ruptural, interstitial metamorphosis*, and *symbiotic metamorphosis*. One source of opportunities for transformative change resides in the complexity of capitalist societies. Complex system always have cleavages, conflicts of interest, contradictions, needs for trade-offs, power use, and other forces that make people aware of problems in the larger system and potentially motivated to change the system. Another source of opportunities inheres in strategic intentionality of actions designed to reproduce the system but, ironically, exposes problems in the system. Strategic behaviors are often made by arrogant actors who generate more problems than they solve; decisions can be made because of biases or inadequate information that, once again, create new problems; and all decisions and actions in complex systems can produce unanticipated consequences that expose problems in the system. Thus, explicit actions to reproduce the harmful system often end up exposing its problems that lead individuals to question the system and potentially take action to transform it. A third source of opportunity resides in institutional rigidities whereby older patterns of reproduction generate tensions but are difficult to change because of path dependencies, powerful ideologies, and investments by powerful actors. As these rigidities keep the system of reproduction form adjusting, individuals become increasingly aware of problems in the system and perhaps motivated to make transformative changes in this system. And, the fourth source of opportunities is the unpredictability of actions, even when powerful reproductive forces are in play. One change in the system can have unanticipated consequences and suddenly have unpredictable effects on other systems, thereby opening people's eyes to real problems that need to be addressed in transformative ways.

Even as Wright begins to map out new paths to transformation of capitalist systems, he still adheres to the basic Marxian view that systems of exploitation reveal contradictions that will be exposed, leading people to seek out new patterns of social relations. The path may be somewhat different than path conceptualized by Marx, but the basic relationship between exploitation, contradictions, and transformative change remains. Indeed, Wright emphasizes that many "of the predictions of historical materialism have in fact been borne out by the actual history of capitalism."[21]

Finally, Wright outlines the three trajectories to some form of socialism; interestingly, he rejects two of the trajectories as unrealistic. *Ruptural trajectories* are closest to standard Marxism and depend upon people recognizing the contradictions and harms of capitalism and becoming committed to a socialist alternative, something that has yet to occur in capitalist systems because of the power of reproductive forces in capitalism. *Interstitial*

---

[21]Ibid., p. 301.

trajectories gain momentum by finding spaces, holes, and cracks in the institutional structure by various local action groups, but their power to change the structure of capitalism is doubtful. Thus, only the last trajectory—*symbiotic metamorphosis*—is realistic and, hence, the real utopian alternative to present-day capitalism. Here compromises are made between the interests of capital and those of the working population.

Symbiotic metamorphosis is a bottom-up action that seeks to empower people while resolving problems that capitalist have faced. Change is evolutionary and involves a class compromise that balances the interests of labor and the general citizenry with goals of capitalists. Several key spheres of activity are critical for this class compromise. First are the sphere of exchange and the dynamics of markets where the population meets capitalists. There must be real compromises in this sphere between the interests of non-elite and non-capitalist classes and capitalists. Second is the sphere of production in which the relations between labor in firms and capital must be more balanced, with conflicts between the two involving negotiations among actors who are more equal. And third is the sphere of politics, where class compromises in the formation and implementation of state policies increasingly meet the interests of both the state and members of non-elite classes. Wright conducts a thought experiment in which the relative power of capital to realize its interests and classes to develop associational power is assessed. When capital's power is high, the associational interests of labor are high, and vice versa. At either extreme, Wright argues, are zones of "unattainability," and thus, it is the middle ground where both parties can realize some of their interests that are most viable. The United States is, Wright argues, on one side of this zone, favoring capital or class associational interests, whereas a society like Sweden is on the other side of this zone. Thus, the implication is that the United States needs to move toward the Swedish side where the interests of capital and non-elite classes are more equally balanced so that each side is able to meet many of its goals.

Thus, by the end, *Envisioning Real Utopias* is heavily ideological, but also analytical in that the power of present-day capitalist institutions is recognized as an impediment to a full revolution; rather, evolution to a more balanced form of capitalism where the interests of non-elites have as much influence on policies as elites is far more realistic and perhaps an even viable alternative to the harmful extremes of capitalism. However, thus far only very small societies of around six million people have been able to achieve this balance (e.g., Sweden, Denmark, and Norway); and so, it is not so clear that a society like the United States with over 310 million people can become more like these small, highly homogeneous societies.

World Systems Conflict Theorizing

Like both Spencer and Weber, world systems theorizing examines conflict dynamics among societies rather than among social classes within a society. The approach has many Weberian elements, but the underlying logic is often more Marxists and, at times, a thinly veiled ideology arguing that the revolution will occur at a global level when the contradictions of capitalism become fully exposed. There are not many different efforts to develop theories of world system dynamics,[22] but I will focus on the first scheme that gained wide attention in general theoretical circles.[23]

Emmanuel Wallerstein provided the first comprehensive theoretical scheme for analyzing world system dynamics, although many others have also contributed to theorizing on these inter-societal processes. In Wallerstein's and most theorists' scheme, emphasis is on the stratification among societies, with those societies with power and high levels of production having the capacity to exploit less developed societies by taking their raw resources at heavily discounted prices. Thus, replacing capitalists/bourgeoisie and workers/proletarians, world systems theories see capitalist societies using their market advantages and the dependence of less developed societies on capital to exploit weaker societies in ways that sustain their underdevelopment. Coupled with the ability to use their coercive power to take resources, less developed societies are always at a disadvantage in this inter-societal system of exploitation.

In Wallerstein's scheme, there are three levels of societies in this system of societal stratification: (1) *core* nations with the most coercive power and productive economies, (2) *peripheral* societies that are not well developed economically but which have valued resources, and (3) *semi-peripheral* nations that stand between the core and peripheral nations and that are often used as intermediaries in the core's exploitation of the periphery.

Before capitalism emerged and began to spread, the most common form of inter-societal system was a world empire, which is an empire created by military conquest of other nations. Conquest of another population allows for the extraction of surplus wealth to support the privilege and coercive forces of the dominant society. Collins' analytical theory, examined earlier, provides a list of some of the conditions affecting the size, reach, and stability of such empires, as does Wallerstein and many other theorists in the world system's tradition. This kind of world-level stratification is highly exploitive because the conquered have no real capacity to bargain with their conquerors, but the system is, in the long run, unstable because geo-political empires tend to expand beyond their logistical capacity to control territory and to repress potential revolt by those who are exploited.

With capitalism, another kind of world system began to evolve, Wallerstein argues; and this is a *geo-economic system*. A geo-economic system is built around three levels of societal formation: a *core*, *periphery*, and *semi-periphery* involving social relations based on differences in power and productivity of the core relative to the periphery and semi-periphery. Alongside of this geo-political dimension of the emerging world economy are markets in which resources

---

[22]For an early view on world system dynamics see John Atkinson Hobson, *Capitalism and Imperialism in South Africa* (London: Contemporary Review, 1900); *The Conditions of Industrial Peace* (New York: Macmillan, 1927); *Confessions of an Economic Heretic* (London: G. Allen and Unwin, 1938); *The Economics of Distribution* (London: Macmillan, 1900).

[23]Immanuel Wallerstein, *The Modern World System*, 3 volumes (New York: Academic, 1974, 1980, 1989) will be my main source, but earlier work by scholars such as Andre Gunder Frank on "dependency theory" anticipated much of what Wallerstein was to argue: Underdeveloped societies, especially those in Latin America, could not go through the stages to modernization because they were economically dependent on advanced economies, and this dependency and the corresponding exploitation by advanced industrial powers kept them from becoming fully industrialized and modern. See for example, Frank's *Capitalism and Underdevelopment in Latin America* (New York: Monthly Review Press, 1967). See also his later work, *Dependent Accumulation* (New York: Monthly Review Press, 1979). Also, historians such as Fernand Braudel had conducted analyses of world-system processes (for his overview see *Civilization and Capitalism*, 3 volumes (New York: Harper & Row, 1964).

are exchanged for capital investments by the core in peripheral and semi-peripheral nations at very unfair and, indeed, exploitive trade in expanding world-level markets. The core nations often compete with each other, but collectively, they exploit less-developed nations, extracting raw resources at cheap rates, and then often sending finished goods back to peripheral societies at high costs.

The world economy, however, is not stable in several senses. One is that the member societies of the core can change over time, as was the case when Spain and Portugal gave way to new core nations like the United States, Japan, and more recently, China and potentially India. There is, then, "upward mobility" to the core, typically from semi-peripheral. The emergence of world-level markets is thought by many world-systems theorists to generate the conditions for a transition to socialism. In world-level markets without external regulation by a world-level polity (which currently does not exist) or legal system (only in its infancy), the contradictions and self-destructive dynamics of capitalism will play out, generating crises that eventually lead to world socialism. It is this hope and prospect that has led world systems theories to devote considerable effort to understanding the cycles of capitalism within and between nations as they create constant waves of crises, which are seen as eventually leading to a socialist mobilization on a global scale.

Thus, the utopian dream of Marxism lives on in yet another form, beyond the efforts of analytical Marxists like Erik Olin Wright. World systems theorist make an interesting case for the transformative dynamics of Marx's analysis of the transition from capitalism to socialism, although there is relatively little evidence indicating that market crises on a global scale will actually lead to mobilization of members in diverse societies in pursuit of socialism.[24]

Conclusion

As is evident in this chapter, conflict theorizing has gone in many different directions since the foundational works of Spencer, Weber, Simmel, and Marx. Today, relatively few proclaim that they are "conflict theorists" because the analysis of conflict is now so well embedded in virtually all dimensions of sociological analysis that it is no longer an intellectual crusade against functionalism, which long ago, went underground only to resurface in non-functionalist disguises. The same is true of conflict theory; it is no longer needed as a foil for attaching a virtually non-extant functionalism, and the result has been the dramatic expansion of theorizing about conflict processes by many different labels. Still there is a core to conflict analyses, which can be summarized, in conclusion, as a series of basic assumptions about what is important in sociological analysis.

---

[24]For more recent view on world system dynamics building on Wallerstein, see Christopher Chase-Dunn and Peter Grimes, "World-Systems Analysis," *Annual Review of Sociology* 21 (1995): pp. 387–417; Albert J. Bergesen, ed., *Studies of the Modern World System* (New York: Academic Press, 1980); Christopher Chase-Dunn and T. D. Hall's edited collection of essays on *Core/Periphery Relations in Precapitalist Worlds* (Boulder, CO: Westview, 1991) as well as their coauthored, *Rise and Demise: Comparing World Systems* (Boulder, CO: Westview Press, 1997); Andre Gunder Frank and B. K. Gills, eds., *The World System: Five Hundred Years or Five Thousand?* (London: Routledge, 1993); Christopher Chase-Dunn, *Global Formation* (Cambridge, UK: Blackwell, 1989); Volker Bornschier and Christopher Chase-Dunn, *Transnational Corporations and Underdevelopment* (New York: Praeger, 1985).

1. All social systems—from groups through organization, communities, societies, and inter-societal formations—evidence inequalities in the distribution of valued resources.

2. These inequalities generate conflicts of interests among (a) those actors who have resources and the capacity to extract them from other actors and (b) those actors who have fewer resources and who are often the victims of exploitive relations with those actors who have the power to exploit.

3. The stratification of resource distributions generates more than a conflict of interests; it generates conditions that lead subordinates in the system to mobilize for conflict with superordinates in the system, with the likelihood of mobilization increasing when

    A. Subordinates become aware of their conflict of interests with superordinates, which increases with

       1. Disruption of subordinates' routine activities

       2. Increases in the sense of deprivation among subordinates

       3. Communication among subordinates about the common grievances

       4. Emergence of leaders to frame issues and develop beliefs about the nature of exploitation and the need to do something about it

       5. The withdrawal of legitimacy from the rights of superordinates to extract resources and to control reproduction of the culture sustaining exploitive social relations

       6. Emotional arousal of individuals, which increases under the conditions listed above and which makes subordinates willing to incur the costs of mobilizing for conflict

    B. Mobilization for conflict becomes more likely when the conditions under 3-A above exist and when subordinates can secure resources, including

       1. Demographic resources or members in conflict groups and organizations within and between societies

       2. Fiscal resources to support the administration of conflict actions

       3. Organizational resources to structure mobilization of members for conflict and to focus strategic actions of conflict groups and organizations

       4. Ideological resources that can legitimate the action of conflict groups and organizations, while de-legitimating superordinates in the system of inequality and stratification

       5. Emotional resources that arouse resentments that can generate commitments of individuals to engage in strategic actions against superordinates

4. The level of violence and intensity of conflict between superordinates and subordinates is influenced by

    A. The degree to which subordinates can secure resources, with violence in conflict increasing in early phases of conflict listed under 3-A and 3-B above, and decreasing with high levels of the resources listed under 3-B above

B. The structure and culture of the more inclusive system in which there is a conflict between subordinates and superordinates, with

   1. The likelihood of violent conflict increasing when

      a. Subordinates have some autonomy from superordinates

      b. Subordinates are not wholly dependent upon superordinates

      c. Subordinates have little to lose in initiating conflict

      d. Subordinates sense of deprivations suddenly escalate

      e. Superordinates capacities for social control are weak

   2. The likelihood of strategic and regularized conflict increasing with

      a. High levels of structural interdependences among all actors in the system, including superordinates and subordinates

      b. High rates of upward mobility by subordinates

      c. An arena of politics in which conflicts of interest can be debated and resolved politically

      f. A polity able to absorb conflicts by changing policies and forging compromises

      g. A legal system capable of absorbing conflicts of interest through enactment of new laws

      h. High rates of lower-intensity conflict

5. Conflict can occur at many different levels of social organization, from micro encounters through groups, organizations, and classes to systems of societies.

  A. At the micro level, conflict must overcome fears of potential participants, which can be mitigated when interaction rituals are dedicated to charging up positive emotions and group symbols in order to mobilize persons to pursue conflict against an enemy

  B. Conflict between organizations and social strata is most likely to follow the dynamics listed under 1 to 4 above

  C. Inter-societal conflict is most likely to occur when

   1. One society has a size, productive, and coercive advantage over another society

   2. One society has a marchland advantage over its neighbors

   3. Societies become stratified into a core of higher productivity, higher power core nations begin to compete with each other and/or begin to lose their capacity to exploit peripheral and semi-peripheral societies by (a) extracting their resources at favorable prices in world-level markets and (b) using their coercive power to sustain these exploitive practices.

CHAPTER 4

Ecological Theorizing

Early Ecological Thinking in Sociology

In the early 1850s,[1] Herbert Spencer saw a social universe where the "survival of the fittest" is one of the governing principles of societal evolution. In this utterance, Spencer introduced some nine years before the publication of Darwin's *On the Origins of Species*[2] an idea that comes close to the notion of natural selection. In Spencer's view, societal evolution had been driven by larger, more productive, and better organized societies winning wars against smaller, less productive, and organized societies;[3] the more fit society would survive the war, often absorbing the less fit and, thereby, ratcheting up the complexity of societies. The social universe could thus be conceptualized as an ecological system where *superorganisms* (i.e., societies) could be viewed to be in competition with each other for resources, with the more organized society prevailing in this competition.

Some twenty years later, Emile Durkheim also developed an ecological view of societal evolution, but in his case, he borrowed explicitly from Darwin.[4] Just as Darwin argued that speciation is the result of natural selection on variants of life forms that promoted adaptation, so specialization (same Latin root as speciation) of individuals and collective actors in a society is driven by selection processes. As societies become more materially dense and concentrated in space, competition among individuals and social units inevitably ensues, with the more fit individuals and corporate units surviving and the less fit finding a new resource niche and, in so doing, specializing in a new way.

Thus, Spencer and Durkheim recognized that social differentiation is very much an ecological process of social units seeking resources in various niches. As niches became more densely populated, the rate of competition among these units would increase, and from this competition come

---

[1]Herbert Spencer, *Social Statics, Or the Conditions Essential to Human Happiness Specified, and the First of Them Developed* (New York: Appleton-Century-Crofts, 1988, originally published in 1850–1851).

[2]Charles Darwin, *On the Origins of Species* (London: Murray, 1980, originally published in 1859).

[3]Herbert Spencer, *The Principles of Sociology*, 3 volumes (New York: Appleton-Century-Crofts, 1895, originally published in serial form starting 1874).

[4]Emile Durkheim, *The Division of Labor in Society* (New York: Free Press, 1947, originally published in French in 1993), pp. 262–263.

increases in the degree of social speciation or differentiation among units. The general model underlying early sociologically oriented ecology looked something like that in Figure 4.1.[5]

As Darwin emphasized, the level of material density of organisms seeking resources in a resource niche will increase the level of competition, but the level of material density is lessened by the total number of resources and the amount of space or territory where these resources are distributed. Thus, the level of resources and the amount of space will decrease material density, but if the population is large and continues to grow, then material density will eventually rise and set off competition for resources. With competition comes selection among social units, with those most fit and able to secure resources surviving in a niche and those that cannot dying off or, alternatively, moving to less dense resource niches. The result is increased differentiation, specialization, and "social speciation" among units in a population that, in turn, increases the complexity of the larger social system organizing a population.

Both Spencer and Durkheim viewed the process of societal evolution as the differentiation or social speciation within and between societies; furthermore, both had a selectionist argument whereby competition for resources drives differentiation. Spencer tended to emphasize competition *among* societies, whereas Durkheim stressed competition *within* societies. And, moreover, Spencer recognized that societies and individuals sometimes die in this competition, whereas Durkheim had a more benign view that individuals and corporate units would seek resources in new niches if they could not compete in a particular niche inhabited by more fit actors.

And so, just as the field of ecology developed within biology, so it prospered in sociology during the twentieth century. The ideas of Spencer and Durkheim, and particularly Durkheim, were blended with ideas from biologically oriented ecology as a field of inquiry to produce several types of ecological analysis within sociology. These ecological theories have never dominated sociology, but they have been persistently present from the turn into the twentieth century to the present; and with the recent revival of biologically oriented theories in sociology and the social sciences more generally (see Chapter 12), ecological analysis has found new currency.

Contemporary Ecological Theorizing in Sociology

Urban Ecological Analysis

At the University of Chicago, sociologists began to use the city of Chicago as a field of study on urban processes, and one of the dynamics that interested these scholars is the utilization of space by different actors.[6] They developed a number of specific models of urban growth and development, all of which were hampered by reliance on one city, but the underlying theoretical

---

[5]Adapted from Jonathan H. Turner and Alexandra Maryanski, *On the Origins of Societies by Natural Selection* (Boulder, CO: Paradigm Press, 2008).

[6]For examples of early Chicago School ecologists, see Ernest W. Burgess, "The Growth of the City," in *An Introduction to the Science of Sociology*, ed. R. E. Park and E. W. Burgess. (Chicago, IL: University of Chicago Press, 1921; Chauncy D. Harris and Edward L. Ullman, "The Nature of Cities," *Annals of the American Academy of Political and Social Science* (1945): pp. 789–796; Homer Hoyt, *The Structure and Growth of Residential Neighborhoods in American Cities* (Washington, DC: Federal Housing Authority, 1939).

Figure 4.1 Durkheim's and Spencer's Early Model of Ecological Processes

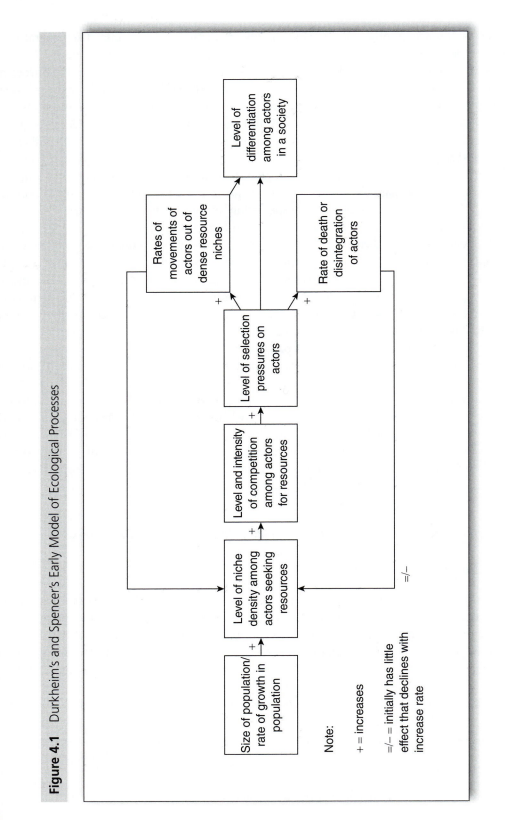

argument was sound. Their emphasis was on explaining why cities revealed different zones and regions populated by different types of actors—e.g., families, government, religion, schools, businesses of various types, etc. Their explanation was theoretical and, in general terms, along the lines outlined in the model presented in Figure 4.2.[7] Actors have varying amounts of money and other resources, such as power and influence, at their disposal; as they seek a key resource—e.g., geographical space in a city—they use these resources to locate themselves. The existence of a real estate market institutionalizes competition over price; and so, those with the most monetary resources will be more fit than those who are not and can therefore settle in the areas that they most prefer. Also, power and authority are like money in the sense that this resource can be used to exert influence on where to settle. For example, government can use its power to settle into particular areas that even those with money cannot occupy. The result of this competition for urban space, then, leads to the differentiation of cities by districts and neighborhoods dominated by particular types of actors and their activities. And like speciation in general, this differentiation of space is the result of density of actors, competition for resources, selection of the most fit, and differentiation of urban space by actors with varying degrees of resources or fitness to command particular areas of cities.

Figure 4.2   Early Model of Urban Ecology

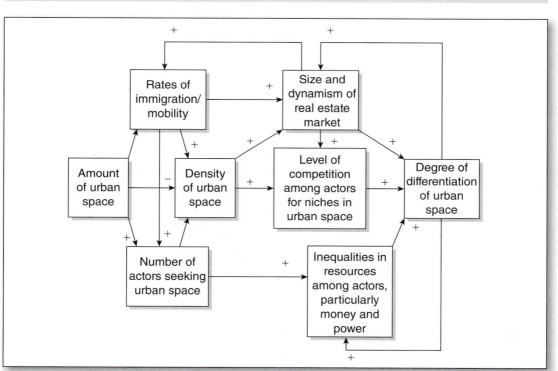

---

[7]Adapted from Jonathan H. Turner, "The Assembling of Human Populations: Toward a Synthesis of Ecological and Geopolitical Theories," *Advances in Human Ecology* 3 (1994): pp. 65–91 and *Macrodynamics: Toward Theory on the Organization of Human Populations* (New Brunswick: Rutgers University Press, 1995).

More recent urban ecological theories similarly seek to explain urban processes but extend the analysis beyond the internal differentiation of core cities like Chicago. They also seek to understand broader urban trends, especially the differentiation of types of cities and trends in the process of urbanization. As is outlined in Figure 4.3,[8] they have simply expanded the ecology of urban areas to include the processes of growth and differentiation among the topics denoted in this figure. As is evident in Figure 4.3, emphasis in urban ecology is on the forces increasing the size and density of settlement, the extent and rate of geographical expansion of settlements, and the overall level of "agglomeration," which is a catchphrase denoting the degree to which diverse urban settlements constitute a large metropolitan region composed of a central city, surrounded by more suburban settlements.

As with most ecological theories, population size and rate of growth are key forces, as are the level of economic production and the level of transportation and communication technologies. Production tends to pull individuals into urban areas in search of jobs, while the transportation and communication technologies facilitate movement to, or at least contact with, emerging urban centers. The level of distribution also becomes an important force because it encourages development of transportation technologies, while acting as a stimulus to increase production. Together, these forces increase the scale of the material (roads, ports, airports, trains, etc.) and administrative (bureaucratic) infrastructure in a society; and the greater this scale, the more individuals are pulled into urban areas as workers in businesses and factories, as incumbents in administrative bureaucracies of government, as workers in schools, religious organizations, and other types of organizations—e.g., sports, medicine, arts, recreation, etc.—in various institutional domains that service individuals, especially large numbers of individuals in urban areas. Once urban areas are growing, they serve as magnates to immigration from rural areas, other urban centers, and other societies. And, as these dynamics are unleashed, urban areas continue to grow by segmenting suburban areas around the original core city.

Development of communication technologies allows for remote urban areas to emerge because individuals can work through "telecommuting," which can decrease immigration, although the existence of material and administrative infrastructures in larger cities will still exert their pull on immigrants. Yet, when these infrastructures are developed in areas more remote from existing urban areas, they draw people from existing urban centers, thus decreasing the rate of agglomeration. The result is that new settlements away from established cities can emerge in societies with higher communication and transportation technologies, thus generating a polycentric system of settlements. The old principle that size of communities decreases the further removed are these settlements from core urban areas probably must be revised to take account of growing settlements far from core cities, but this growth does not obviate the basic principle. A related principle is that the flow of resources across settlements affects their integration; in addition, this flow of resources increases with the development of transportation infrastructures and, particularly important,

---

[8]In particular, the model summarizes ideas from Parker W. Frisbie, "Theory and Research in Urban Ecology," in *Sociological Theory and Research: A Critical Approach*, ed. H. M. Blalock (New York: Free Press, 1980); Parker W. Frisbie and John D. Kasarda, "Spatial Processes," in *Handbook of Sociology*, ed. N. J. Smelser (Newbury Park, CA: Sage, 1988); Mark Gottdiener, *The Social Production of Urban Space* (Austin: University of Texas Press, 1985); Amos H. Hawley, *Urban Society: An Ecological Approach* (New York: Ronald, 1981); John D. Kasarda, "The Theory of Ecological Expansion: An Empirical Test," *Social Forces* 51 (1972): pp. 165–175; C. Clark, "Urban Population Densities," *Journal of the Royal Statistical Society*, series A, 114 (1951): pp. 490–496; B. J. L. Berry and John D. Kasarda, *Contemporary Urban Ecology* (New York: Macmillan, 1977).

Figure 4.3 The Abstracted Urban Ecology Model

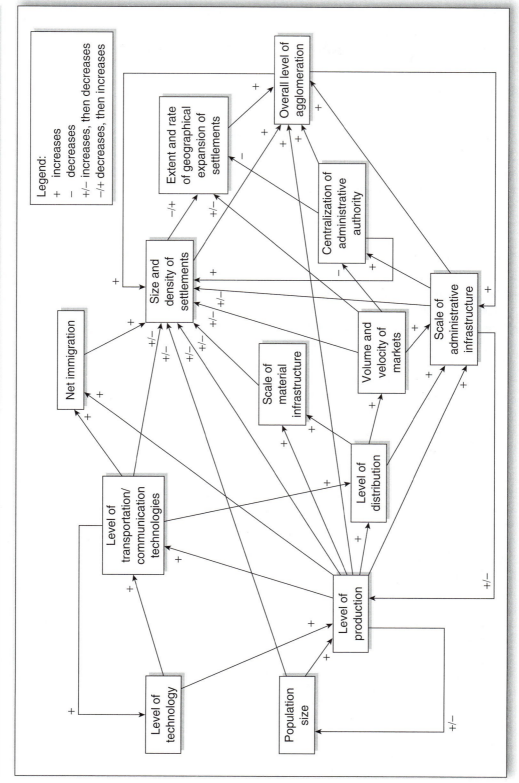

Legend:
+ increases
− decreases
+/− increases, then decreases
−/+ decreases, then increases

dynamic markets. Settlements connected by markets accelerate the flow of information, goods, services, and virtually any resource or product across urban areas, thereby integrating these to an ever-increasing degree.

Organizational Ecological Analysis

Over the last forty years, organizational ecology has supplanted urban ecology as the most prevalent form of ecological theorizing in sociology.[9] The students[10] of Amos Hawley[11] who was the last link to the Chicago School urban ecologies began to expand ecological analysis to populations of organizations seeking resources in their environment. A population of organizations is a set of organizations seeking the same set of resources in a particular resource niche. For example, automobile companies operate in the same resource niche composed of those who buy cars and trucks; newspapers operate in a niche composed of subscribers; universities and colleges operate in several niches, including the pool of students seeking education and the research funds available from government, foundations, and economic actors. The goal of ecological analysis of populations of organizations is to understand why the number of organizations in a niche grows and why, at some point, many organizations in the niche begin to fail.

The core of the organizational ecology model begins with the number of organizations in a niche relative to the level of available resources in this niche. As the number of organizations in a niche increases, the niche becomes more densely populated; and as density increases, so does competition among organizations in the niche. Competition increases the level and rate of selection on organizations within the population, and as both competition and selection increase, rates of organizational failure also increase, up to the point where density in the niche declines and thereby allows for existing organizations in the niche to survive, at least for a time. In Figure 4.4, these core elements in the organizational ecology model flow left to right across the middle of the figure. Let me now fill in the details of the model.[12]

---

[9]For some general overviews of research and theory on organizational ecology, see Glenn R. Carroll, ed., *Ecological Models of Organizations* (Cambridge, MA: Ballinger, 1988) and "Organizational Ecology," *Annual Review of Sociology* 10 (1984): pp. 71–93; Jitendra V. Singh and Charles J. Lumsden, "Theory and Research in Organizational Ecology," *Annual Review of Sociology* 16 (1990): pp. 161–195.

[10]Michael T. Hannan and John Freeman, "The Population Ecology of Organizations," *American Journal of Sociology* 82 (1977): pp. 929–964.

[11]Amos Hawley was the last generation of Chicago School urban ecologists, and when he moved to the University of North Carolina at Chapel Hill, Chicago School urban ecology declined, while growing at North Carolina, where Hawley taught John H. Freeman and Michael T. Hannan, who as graduate students began to conceptualize organizational ecology.

[12]This figure is closest to the Hannan and Freeman model. For representative works by Hannan and Freeman, see "Structural Inertia and Organizational Change," *American Sociological Review* 49 (1984): pp. 149–164; "The Ecology of Organizational Founding: American Labor Unions 1836–1985," *American Journal of Sociology* 92 (1987): pp. 910–943; "The Ecology of Organizational Mortality: American Labor Unions," *American Journal of Sociology* 94 (1988): pp. 25–52; *Organizational Ecology* (Cambridge, MA: Harvard University Press, 1989). See also M. T. Hannan, "Ecologies of Organizations: Diversity and Identity," *Journal of Economic Perspectives* 19 (2005): pp. 51–70; M. T. Hannan, L. Pólos, and G. R. Carroll, *Logics of Organization Theory: Audiences, Codes, and Ecologies* (Princeton University Press, 2007); M. T. Hannan and G. R. Carroll, *Dynamics of Organizational Populations: Density, Legitimation, and Competition* (New York: Oxford University Press, 1992).

Figure 4.4 The Generational Organizational Ecology Model

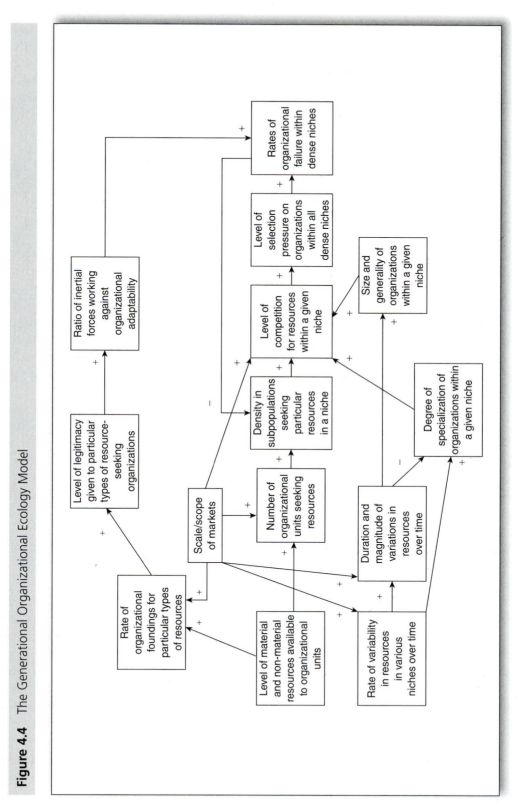

One set of forces affecting these organizational dynamics is the level of resources in a niche. In general, large-scale markets create many resource niches because these markets respond to full diversity of consumer demands; thus, the greater the scale and scope of markets, the greater will be the number of potential resource niches and the level of resources in each of these niches. High levels of resources in a niche encourage growth in the number of organizations seeking resources in these; and the greater the number of niches present in a society, the greater will be the diversity in types of organizations seeking resources in these differentiated niches. But, as ever-more organizations enter niches, eventually there will be too many organizations in the niche, with the result that density, competition, and selection on organizations increase, thereby increasing rates of organizational failure of those that cannot be successful in the competition. Organizations may survive if, as Durkheim suggested, they can move to another, adjacent niche where density is much lower. For example, as K-Mart and Walmart entered the niche for general retailers offering a wide range of consumer goods, the classic "department store" came under intense competition, with the result that many of these stores such as Wards and Woolworths went out of business, while still others like Sears struggle, as does K-Mart, which ironically started the invasion of this niche, only to find that it could not easily compete with new players such as Walmart, Target, and other general merchandisers. Other stores such as Penny's, which used to look very much like Sears, moved to a new niche, somewhat more upscale and emphasizing soft goods (basically clothing and just a few hard goods like furniture). The best example of too much niche density is the decline in the number of automobile companies over the last seventy years, with brands such as Packard, Nash, Studebaker, Mercury, Oldsmobile, Saturn, Pontiac, Plymouth, and the like dying out, while others such as Saab remain on life support.

Aside from the total level of resources in a niche, the rate of variability in the level of resources and the magnitude and length in the up and down cycles of resource variability also influence the life and death of organizations in a population. High variability encourages more specialized organizations to enter niches because they can often more effectively compete with general retailers, although if the magnitude of variation is great and the time of the down cycle long, smaller, more specialized retailers often cannot survive, whereas larger ones can ride the downturn out because they may be in other niches that are not in a down cycle. These forces are arrayed across the bottom of the model in Figure 4.4.

The number of organizations entering niches is as important as the volume, variability, and magnitude of resource variability. For the number of organizations entering a niche has large effects on the level of resources available in this niche because the level of density and competition increases. Again, markets kick off increases in the number of organizations in a niche because if one organization can be successful, others will soon follow founding organizations in a niche, often copying their structure because of the success of these founding organizations. As the number of organizations in a niche begins to increase with higher rates of founding, organizations of a given type gain legitimacy, and their structure is copied even more. As more organizations copy each other, a kind of inertia develops, and organizations can become rigid in their structures and cultures. For example, the American automobile companies before the invasion of cars from foreign manufacturers in the 1960s and 1970s had become rather inefficient and bloated, but more importantly, rigid to the point of almost dying off because they could not compete on price and reliability of their products with imports from Asia and Europe. These kinds of inertial tendencies give something for selection to work on, because the inability to change social structures and organizational cultures rapidly means that companies become less and less fit in the niche where competition is heating up. The result is that selection removes them from the niche. These forces are outlined across the top of Figure 4.4.

While companies selling goods in markets are prototypical populations of organization, churches, schools, government agencies, political parties, charities, foundations, and other kinds of service organizations requiring resources in niches, they are subject to these same ecological pressures of density, competition, selection, and death as business organizations in dynamic markets. Markets institutionalize competition over price relative to quality of productions and services; and so, once density begins to rise in a niche, market forces will, like natural selection in the biotic world, remove those organizations (as opposed to organisms in the biotic universe) that cannot adjust to these selection pressures by changing their structure or by migrating to a less-dense resource niche.

In fact, as societies in general differentiate and markets expand into almost every arena of social life, ecological dynamics become increasingly prominent. Each point of differentiation can represent the boundaries of a niche, and each organization within the boundaries defining differentiation can be subject to ecological forces revolving around density, competition, and selection. This is obvious in manufacturing and perhaps basic services, but these forces operate in almost every sphere of social life—religious, artistic, educational, scientific, health care, political, etc. Even kinship is created by individuals meeting in a marriage market. Thus, as the critical theorists examined in Chapter 10 are likely to bemoan, no sphere of life is immune to competition and selection in modern societies, which means that an ecological perspective is a most useful tool in explaining the dynamics of organizations in resource niches.

Macro-Level Ecological Theorizing in Sociology

The adaptation of Spencer's and Durkheim's ideas on ecological processes moved the unit of analysis in ecological theorizing down to the meso level. Organizations and communities are meso-level structures that stand between macro-level societal and institutional analysis, on the one side, and micro-level analysis of face-to-face processes in encounters, on other. Recently, various scholars have sought to take ecological back to macro level,[13] examining whole societies in terms of ecological forces and dynamics—much like Spencer and Durkheim had done. The work of Amos Hawley will serve as a useful exemplar because he carried Chicago School urban ecology into the modern era of theorizing, mentored the founders of organizational ecology, and then, in the 1980s, moved ecological theorizing back to the macro or societal level of social organization.

---

[13]Amos H. Hawley, *Human Ecology: A Theory of Community Structure* (New York: Ronald, 1950). Other works leading up to this shift to the macro level include the following: Amos H. Hawley, "The Logic of Macrosociology," *Annual Review of Sociology* 18 (1992): pp. 1–14; "Human Ecology," in *International Encyclopedia of the Social Sciences*, ed. D. C. Sills (New York: Crowell, Collier and Macmillan, 1968); *Urban Society: An Ecological Approach* (New York: Ronald, 1971 and 1981); "Human Ecology: Persistence and Change," *American Behavioral Scientist* 24 (January 3, 1981): pp. 423–444; "Human Ecological and Marxian Theories," *American Journal of Sociology* 89 (1984): pp. 904–917; "Ecology and Population," *Science* 179 (March 1973): pp. 1196–1201; "Cumulative Change in Theory and History," *American Sociological Review* 43 (1978): pp. 787–797; "Spatial Aspects of Populations: An Overview," in *Social Demography*, eds. K. W. Taueber, L. L. Bumpass, and J. A. Sweet (New York: Academic, 1978); "Sociological Human Ecology: Past, Present and Future," in *Sociological Human Ecology*, eds. M. Micklin and H. M. Choldin (Boulder, CO: Westview, 1980).

For Hawley, societies exist in physical, social, and biological environments to which they must adapt. Societies do so by forming systems of interdependence among members of a population and the social units organizing their activities. The underlying dynamics of integration of system parts revolve around the growth of the population and then differentiation of this population and the units organizing their activities, up the limits imposed by technologies. In particular, Hawley emphasizes that three classes of technology enable the building of facilities and infrastructures for (1) communications, (2) transportation, and (3) production. Once growth and differentiation exceed the capacities of technologies, growth stops until the population acquires more information and knowledge that can be translated into technologies for building up infrastructures for communication, transportation, and production.

As societies differentiate, there is a corresponding functional differentiation of the units of social organization. Those units engaged in what Hawley terms *key function* or the mediation between the society and its social, biological, or physical environments have greater effects on other functional sectors of a society because other functional sectors of a society only gain access to the environment via those engaged in key functions. For example, the economy and polity are almost always engaged in key functions with the environment of a society and, for this reason, exert the most influence on the operation of other institutions. As a result, the system of interdependencies that have been built up within a society revolve around connections among structures with those engaged in key functions. For, it is through institutional domains involved in key functions that the energy, materials, and information necessary for adaptation are received by a society and are used in a society's adaptive outputs to the environment. The more a key function mediates relations to the environment, then, the more power it has over other functional sectors and the more it constraints the development of other structures in a society. The more differentiated are key functions, the greater will be the proportion of social structures related to the environment via connections to key functions; and the more stable are these connections to key functions, the more likely will the cultural systems in a society correspond to the functional order created by key functions.

Social change occurs as the exposure of a society to what Hawley terms its *ecumenical environment*, or the social environment composed of other societies. Whatever the nature of the connection, new information will come into a society—whether via diffusion of ideas, conquest, or migration patterns—and this new information will alter technologies involved in production, transportation, and communication. If this technology lowers *mobility costs* or the time, energy, money, people, and materials involved in moving resources about a population, the more a system can grow and differentiate, up to the point where mobility costs increase to a point exceeding technologies and infrastructures. Thus, much like Spencer, Hawley sees societal complexity as very much related to distribution processes as these are affected by mobility costs, and structures that bring these costs down will cause growth, differentiation, and increased adaptation of a society to its environment. Thus, lowered mobility costs allow a society to expand its territory, to increase the size of its population, to develop new kinds of social units organizing people activities, to elaborate political systems, to develop new kinds of markets, and to develop more expanded and extensive networks among social units. All of these effects of lowered mobility costs increase differentiation around key functions, while at the same time integrating these units. In turn, the more a differentiated society that is able to integrate diverse social units, the more it can adapt to its physical, biological, and ecumenical environments. Yet, as size and differentiation increase, so do selection pressures for integration of these units and, moreover, for new technologies to lower mobility costs further and, thereby, to expand production.

Hawley's theory is not fully developed, but it is clear what he is trying to communicate. When a society is viewed as an adaptive system to the environment, the differentiation and integration of subunits in this system will be heavily influenced by those structures involved in key functions or direct contact with the environment. Integration will occur around structures as they come to depend upon the resources secured by subunits engaged in key functions. But, the productive capacity and infrastructures for communication and transportation will always place an upper limit on how big, differentiated, and integrated a population can become. And so, without new inputs of information into the system from its environment, societies will reach an equilibrium point. But new information—however acquired—will likely to be used to lower mobility costs and to increase production—thus setting off another round of growth, differentiation, and integration until the limits of technology are reached. For example, as the societies of nineteenth-century Europe acquired industrial technologies, these could be used to expand production; furthermore, with expanded production, it was necessary to distribute goods, information, and people, which in turn, led to the use of technologies to reduce mobility costs. Once these costs were reduced (by trains and steam ships, for example), the scale of societies could increase, until the limits of current technologies were reached, which set off selection pressures for the acquisition of more technologies that could reduce mobility costs through new kinds of markets, transportation systems, and communication systems. And so, the Industrial Revolution would eventually be followed by the Information Revolution in order to lower mobility costs of information, materials, and people—all leading to the growth and differentiation of post-industrial societies but also setting off the expansion of a true world system among the societies that was only possible with increases in the infrastructures for production, transportation, and communication at lower costs. None of this exponential growth in the size and complexities of societies and systems of societies could have occurred without development of communications and transportations infrastructures linked to a new production system—which is the basic point of Hawley's macro-level theory of societal ecology.

Conclusion

Ecological theorizing has thus come full circle—from macro to meso analysis and then back up to the macro level. Actually, ecological theorizing also moved down to the micro level of interpersonal behavior when theorists such as Irving Goffman began to emphasize effects of situation ecology—space, props, use-spaces, partitions, and other physical features of the micro environment. His work will be examined in Chapter 7 on dramaturgy, but it is important to realize that a more ecological perspective has not only been around for more than a century, but also, it has been taken to all level of social organization.

For the present, we should close with a list of the basic assumptions and postulates of ecological analysis in sociology:

1. The social universe is composed of resource niches in which actors, both individuals and collective, seek to sustain themselves.

2. Basic Darwinian principles operate for actors in resource niches, including

   A. Density increases as the number of actors seeking resources in a given niche increases, with the number of actors in a nice increasing when

      1. The success of early niche seekers leads to the legitimation of the organizational form of these early inhabitants of a niche

      2. Other organizations begin to copy the structure and cultural of early inhabitants of a niche that have been successful

   B. Increases in niche density will increase competition among actors for resources; and the greater the density and the more intense the competition, then two outcomes are most likely:

      1. Some organizational forms will die.

      2. Other organizational forms will seek new niches by changing their goals and perhaps their culture and organizational structure.

   C. As migration from a niche or death of less fit organizations increases, density declines, and after a dramatic fall off of actors in a niche, new actors can begin to re-enter the niche

3. At the societal level of social organization, the society as a whole seeks to adapt to its environment, consisting of biophysical and sociocultural elements.

4. A society will grow when it has the productive capacity to support its members and when transportation and communication technologies lead to the development of infrastructures that lower mobility costs of moving resources, people, and information about a society.

5. The internal dynamics of societies not only follow the paths outlined in 1 and 2A-C above, but the relation of subunits in a society to those engaged in key functions—or interchanges with the environment—determines the rate of growth and the level as well as pattern of differentiation in a society, which will increase with extensive networks in units connected to those engaged in key functions and with the development of technologies used in infrastructures reducing mobility costs.

CHAPTER 5

Exchange Theorizing

The Reluctance to Embrace Utilitarianism and Behaviorism

Early Distrust of Utilitarian Economics

In 1776, Adam Smith published *The Wealth of Nations*[1] where he explained the basic laws of supply and demand in markets of the emerging industrial capitalist system that dominates the world today. Smith's most famous argument was that the price of a commodity or service is related to its supply relative to the market demand—a line of thought that contradicted Marx's futile effort to link the value of commodities to the labor power needed to produce these commodities. Adam Smith himself had toyed with the labor theory of value and concluded that it was not workable, but Marx needed the concept to have an operational definition of exploitation: capitalists make profits by extracting the surplus labor value contained in commodities by simply paying workers less than a commodity is worth (in labor time), hence generating profits and wealth for capitalists.

Probably more fundamental to sociological theory in the long run was Smith's effort to develop a general theory of human behavior as motivated by self-interest in maximizing utility of rewards received from actions, once the costs in pursuing these rewards were deducted. When individuals all behave in this self-interested way, there emerges an "invisible hand of order" in free and open marketplaces that mysteriously sustains social order. To Sociologists, this line of reasoning seemed to be rather fanciful, and so, for almost 140 years, sociologists did not buy into Smith's reasoning and its subsequent reformulation in neo-classical economics. Too many assumptions were simply not true: people do not always try to maximize their utilities; they rarely have complete information to do so, even if they want to maximize their pay-offs; people are not rational in calculating costs and rewards; people make decision and choices in their actions based on all kinds of internal and external forces—emotions, needs, constraints imposed by beliefs, norms, values, power, and social structures. And so the criticisms went.

Interestingly, Smith's other great work, *The Theory of Moral Sentiments*,[2] was more acceptable to early sociologists. Indeed, Smith proposed the basic sociological problem that dominated

---

[1]Adam Smith, *An Inquiry into the Nature and Causes of the Wealth of Nations* (Indianapolis: Liberty Fund, 1981, originally published in 1775–1776).

[2]Adam Smith, *The Theory of Moral Sentiments* (Indianapolis: Liberty Fund, 1974, originally published in 1759, and later revised in light of the questions raised in *The Wealth of Nations*).

nineteenth-century sociology, especially in France: With the differentiation of society, people no longer live in similar worlds due to specialization of their activities; and so, it can be asked: what force is to hold them together so as to constitute an integrated society? One answer is the "invisible hand," which was just that, invisible, and hardly a very convincing explanation of social order. As articulated in *The Theory of Moral Sentiments*, the other integrative force is common sentiments or commitments to culture even among people living their daily lives in somewhat different social worlds—an idea that certainly resonated for Auguste Comte and Emile Durkheim.

Yet, as economics developed over the next 150 years, and particularly so in America, Smith's basic idea of humans as rational decision makers seeking to at least make profits, if not maximize their profits or utilities (rewards) less costs and investments in receiving these utilities, came to dominate economic thinking. And for much of this time, sociologists rejected neo-classical economics as too simplistic, limiting, and just plain wrong. By the midpoint of the twentieth century, however, sociologists began to incorporate the ideas of neo-classical economics into sociological theories, but with many modifications. By the 1960s, a new kind of theorizing was emerging—an approach labeled *exchange theory*. And today, this is one of the dominant forms of theorizing in sociology. As sociologists adopted utilitarian ideas, they dropped many of the extreme assumptions and emphasized that people seek utilities under many kinds of constraints—social, structural, cultural, motivational—and they are not always highly rational or determined to maximize profits. Utilitarianism became more acceptable because sociologists also began to adopt ideas from another extreme theoretical argument: behaviorism.

The Rise and Initial Rejection of Behaviorism

Exchange theory also emerged from what might initially seem like a rather unlikely source: a school of thought that eventually became known as *behaviorism*. We all know about Ivan Petrovich Pavlov's[3] (1849–1936) famous experiments with dogs where he discovered by accident that when his footsteps followed by his turning on the light on his back porch when feeding dogs (being used in experiments on salivation), the dogs soon associated the light with being fed and began exhibiting feeding behaviors. Of course, people had no doubt also noted such "conditioned responses" in their pets and animals for millennia, but Pavlov understood the broader implications of such conditioning for humans. After some agonizing over using knowledge about conditioned responses to control people, Pavlov overcame his fears and began to study conditioned responses. He discovered some of the basic tenets of behaviorism: a stimulus consistently associated with given physiological response will elicit that response when presented to subjects; these conditioned responses can be extinguished when the gratifications or rewards associated with the stimulus are withdrawn over repeated trials; stimuli similar to those involved in a conditioned response can also elicit the conditioned response; stimuli that increasingly differ from that used in a conditioned response will increasingly be unable to elicit this response. These principles can explain much human behavior, he felt, and equally important, they can be used to manipulate and control people—a concern that Pavlov never abandoned. In fact, one of the early American behaviorists left academia to pursue a very successful career in advertising to convince people of the reward

---

[3]Ivan Petrovich Pavlov, *Letters on Conditioned Reflexes*, 3rd edition, trans. W. H. Gantt (New York: International Publishers, 1928).

value of cigarettes, particularly a once very popular brand called Lucky Strikes. Indeed, to this day I can recite the advertising anagram, LSMFT, or Lucky Strikes Means Fine Tobacco, which I learned sixty years ago at the age of ten (from bombardment of commercials on the radio and, later, television), even though I have never smoked cigarettes.

At Harvard University, a psychologist named Edward Thorndike[4] was also conducting experiments in which he placed kittens in a puzzle box and recorded their behaviors as they learned to escape through the mazes in the box through trial and error. With each trial, the conditioned response of escaping took less and less time. As he watched them learn the escape route, Thorndike discovered some of the very same responses revealed in Pavlov's experiment: behaviors in situations that produce gratifications (in his case, escape from confinement in the puzzle box filled with mazes and many dead ends) will be repeated in similar situations; situation-response connections harden with repetitions and practice; and the connection between situation and response will weaken when a practice is discontinued, usually because the response does not bring the expected reward. People are like all other animals because they are driven by these concerns with securing rewards and avoiding punishments. Behaviors are thus learned or conditioned because of the reward value that they bring to individuals. By phrasing the argument of behaviorists in this way, we can begin to see how they converge with those from utilitarian theory, but with what became a huge difference.

As behaviorism developed within psychology in the United States in the first half of the twentieth century, it came under the spell of a very restrictive methodological assertion: It is not possible to observe human thought and cognition, and theory can only be about what is observable and, hence, measurable. So, for early behaviorists such as John B. Watson and, more importantly, B. F. Skinner at Harvard,[5] it is only possible to observe the external situation and responses of animals to this situation. Theories, therefore, can only be about situation and observable behaviors, which eliminated thought, emotion, and decision making from the behaviorists' theoretical agenda. Skinner and generations of students conducted experiments in what was termed the Skinner Box in which the behavioral responses of animals', mostly pigeons and mice, were manipulated under varying stimulus conditions, revealing the same laws of behavior originally articulated by Pavlov and Thorndike. Yet in fact, the experiments in the Skinner Box were rigged in a way that brought in some unobservable cognitive and emotional processes. The animals were deprived of food or water before entering the box and were rewarded by getting small doses of water and food. Thus, if the animal did what the experimenters wanted, it would press a bar in the Skinner Box and get some food or water as a reward. Thus, sneaking in the backdoor of the Skinner Box were some assumptions, quite reasonable but not wholly observable: hungry or thirsty pigeons (as measure by the length of their deprivation) will find food or water rewarding, and thus, they will engage in those behaviors that bring rewards; and the greater their hunger and thirst, the more valuable are food and water considered to be, and hence, the more likely would they be to perform behaviors that brought these rewards. Only if the conditioned behaviors in a situation suddenly do not bring rewards will the reward-seeking behaviors previously conditioned become, over time, fully "extinguished." Moreover, Skinner even anthropomorphized, again probably

---

[4]Edward Lee Thorndike, *The Elements of Psychology* (New York: Seiler, 1905).

[5]B. F. Skinner, *The Behavior of Organisms* (New York: Appleton-Century, 1938).

correctly, that when Pigeons do not receive an expected reward because of past conditioning, they appeared to become "angry," aggressively dancing around the Skinner Box and often striking or attacking the bar that will no longer bring them expected rewards. Once again, then, cognitive and emotional processes—expectations for rewards, emotions injustice at not receiving an expected reward, and attributions as to why rewards were not forthcoming (it was the bar's fault)—walked through the back door of experiments that supposedly only theorized about what could be directly observed.

As sociologists began to adopt behaviorists' ideas, they brought in the processes emphasized by neo-classical economists: people make decisions based on evaluations of the costs and investments required to receive rewards or utilities from particular kinds of behavior. Indeed, the process of making decisions and performing calculations is at the core of all behavior among humans; thus, to understand human behavior, it is important to know what is rewarding to an individual and what kinds of calculations occur with respect to rewards, costs, investments, information, justice, and other processes involved in decision making. Once the methodological straitjacket of behaviorism was taken off, behaviorism and utilitarianism suddenly looked more alike; and if more sociological content about the structure and culture of situations could be brought into theorizing, sociologists began to believe that these approaches could explain not only behavior and social interaction among humans, but also the emergence of culture and social structure. Many sociologists were still very skeptical, but the merger between behaviorism and utilitarianism into exchange theory broke the intellectual blockade that had existed for almost eighty years. Not fully recognized, however, is the fact that early sociologists had already adopted exchange theoretic ideas, but this adoption was hidden by their conceptual vocabulary.

Early Exchange Theories in Classical Sociology

Marx's Implicit Exchange Theory

The basic ideas of the exchange theoretic tradition were evident in Marx's theory.[6] Marx stressed that those who control scarce and valued resources are in a position to control and exploit those who do not have equally desired or scarce resources to exchange; those without highly valued or scarce resources will be at a disadvantage when exchanging with those holding valued resources. To put more substantive meat on this generalization, capitalists have jobs and workers are willing to work in these jobs, but the jobs are scarce and workers are not. Hence, capitalists now have power over workers and will be in a position to exploit them; yet, as resource holders press their advantage, they will eventually invite counter-mobilization by those being exploited by their dependency on those with power. These exploited individuals eventually begin to see how unjust their exchanges with capitalists are, and as this sense of injustice increases, they become more willing to incur the cost and risks associated with mobilization against those with power (much like the pigeon in the Skinner Box). Marx's theory can thus be seen as an exchange theory, but in conflict-theoretical clothing.

---

[6]Karl Marx, *Capital: A Critical Analysis of Capitalist Production*, vol. 1 (New York: International Publishers, 1967).

Simmel's Exchange Theory

Georg Simmel also offered exchange ideas, even as he criticized Marx:[7] The more valuable the resources held by an actor and the more scarce these resources the more will other actors be attracted to this resource-holding actor. But if the resources of these actors are valuable, then actors holding these valued resources gain power, especially if actors do not have alternative sources for these valued resources. However, when exchanges are seen as unfair because those with power give too little while demanding so much from their exchange partners, the dependent actors will feel exploited and begin to find the injustice as too great of a cost to endure. Thus, from basic ideas about exchange come very familiar sociological topics revolving the dynamics of power and conflict. One might even consider conflict theory a variant of exchange theory, or perhaps, vice versa.

The Persisting Reluctance

Yet, despite their suggestiveness, sociologists remained reluctant to incorporate the ideas of either utilitarianism or behaviorist psychology, although George Herbert Mead[8] as the founder of symbolic interactionism (see next chapter) understood the relevance of both traditions to understanding human behavior as driven by efforts to adapt to the social environment. He rejected strict behaviorism because it dogmatically asserted that one could only study observable phenomena— that is, an observable stimulus and an observable response associated with this stimulus. One must, behaviorists argued, stay out of the black box of human cognition and thinking because these are not observable. For Mead, however, the mental processes of human actors are behavior and must be studied, despite the difficulty of direct observation. And, these behaviors are learned or conditioned by the reward value they have for facilitating growing infants' adjustment and adaptation to ongoing social contexts. In fact, what makes humans so unique is the amount of thinking about self and its relationship to the external world. Thus, for Mead, behaviorism refuses to study the most important behaviors for human beings.

Still, sociologists were slow to adopt *any* aspect of behaviorism because of its methodological rigidity, just as they were not willing to embrace utilitarian arguments that humans are always rational and that they always seek to maximize their utilities in every situation. But, at least utilitarianism emphasized that people think and make decisions, and the processes by which they do so should be studied in terms of their utility for humans as they seek to adapt to the social world.

By the midpoint of the last century, sociologists began to blend the two approaches together, making thinking, decision making, emotional arousal, justice, and other "mental" processes part of behaviorism, while de-emphasizing somewhat the idea that people always seek to maximize utilities—although some contemporary exchange theories maintain this assumption. Moreover, they began to rediscover the underlying ideas of how exchange relations generate power, exploitation, and conflict that Marx and Simmel emphasized. The result was a dramatic flowering of exchange theories in the second half of the twentieth century. And so, a set of assumptions about exchange processes was beginning to make its way into mainstream sociological theory in the last decades of the twentieth century. These assumptions included the following:

---

[7]Georg Simmel, *The Philosophy of Money*, trans. Tom Bottomore and David Frisby (Boston: Routledge, 1990).

[8]George Herbert Mead, *Mind, Self, and Society* (Chicago, IL: University of Chicago Press, 1934).

1. The actions of individuals and collective actors are driven by needs for rewards or utilities.

2. The more rewarding or the more utilities to be gained from social relationships, the more likely are individuals and collective actors to pursue lines of conduct and action that secure these rewards.

3. Individuals assess the reward value of alternative lines of behavior and choose the alternative that offers the most, if not maximal, reward.

4. The more valuable are the rewards received by individuals, the more likely are these individuals to pursue conduct allowing them to receive these valuable rewards, now and in the future.

5. Individuals will implicitly or explicitly calculate the *costs* (alternative sources of rewards forgone or resources that must be given up) and the *investments* (accumulated costs) in pursuing a line of conduct, and they will always seek to make a *profit* in the resources received. A profit is the value of the resources received, less the costs and investments to get them, and those lines of conduct that yield the most profit are the most likely to be pursued.

6. The more of a reward of a given type has been received in the recent past, the more will an individual's preferences for this reward decline, and the less valuable to an actor will this reward become. In psychology, this is the principle of "satiation," whereas in economics, it is described as "marginal utility"; still, the dynamic is the same for both perspectives: The more of a reward that a person gets, the less valuable it becomes, or the less utility it has for actors.

7. Individuals and collective actors thus exchange resources, giving up some as costs to receive resources from others; and most resources in human interaction are intrinsic (e.g., affection, approval, prestige and honor, liking, self-verification), although some are also extrinsic (e.g., money, power).

8. Individuals and collective actors assess the "fairness" and "justice" of the resources that they received relative to their costs and investments, and they can invoke a number of different comparison points or standards for making this justice calculation. (For instance, they may invoke general cultural norms specifying what is fair; they may compare their rewards with those actors incurring equivalent costs and investments; they may use a sense of the rewards that they could have received in an alternative exchange; or they may invoke as a comparison point the rewards that they expected to receive relative to the rewards that they actually received.)

9. When payoffs to a person or collective actor fall below any of the several comparison points that can be invoked to assess the fairness, individuals (and individuals making decisions for collective actors) will experience negative emotions and seek to renegotiate the exchange; they may pursue any number of strategies in these renegotiations, including punishing (and thus incurring costs on) those who have failed to provide a fair and just reward or, alternatively, seeking new exchange partners who will provide a fairer level of reward.

Contemporary Exchange Theories

Present-day exchange theories often use the vocabulary of economics or behaviorist psychology, but they are in essence embracing the same phenomena: the dynamics by which people exchange resources and the effects of exchanges on social structures and culture, and vice versa. This blending of vocabularies is also the result of relaxing the extremes of behaviorism (the taboo about entering the black box of human cognition) and utilitarianism (actors are always rational decision makers who always seek to maximize utilities).

Basic Exchange Processes

Types of Rewards, Costs, and Value

All modern exchange theories in sociology study interaction, which is conceived to involve the exchange of resources between two or more actors. The resources exchanged can be extrinsic (e.g., money) and more often intrinsic (affection, friendship, solidarity, assistance, information, or anything that other find valuable and rewarding to a person). Interaction and the social structures that are built up by interaction or that constrain interaction are ultimately viable because people exchange resources that they find valuable. People create social structures to secure valued resources or to avoid punishments or costs, and social structures only remain viable if they provide at least some rewards to individuals. When structures consistently impose punishments or fail to provide expected reward, conflict becomes more likely.

Types of Exchange

Exchange can be of several basic types:[9] (1) *Negotiated exchanges* where individuals, in essence, bargain over the resources to be given and received; these negotiations can be very active, as when a person buys a car at a dealer, but in most interactions, the exchange processes are more subtle and low-key. (2) *Reciprocal exchanges* are sequential exchanges of resources where one party gives a valued resource to another—as in gift-giving—with the expectation that this generosity will be reciprocated by the unilateral giving of a gift back to the person who has bestowed a gift upon another. (3) *Productive exchanges* where individuals must coordinate their actions by giving resources to each other in order to complete a task and where the exact contribution of any one party is difficult to determine because of the "jointness" of the activity. (4) *Generalized exchanges* in which individuals do not directly negotiate, reciprocate, or productively exchange with each other, but rather, one party provides resources to another who then exchanges with yet another in what can become a fairly protracted one way movement of resources, but with the original giver of resources ultimately receiving payoffs from someone in the chain of exchanges who has received them from someone else. In such generalized exchanges, resources flow in a circle, although this circle need not be completely closed.

---

[9]Edward J. Lawler, "An Affect Theory of Social Exchange," *American Journal of Sociology* 107 (2001): pp. 321–352.

Motivational Forces Driving Exchanges

Actors, whether individuals or collective units (e.g., groups, organizations, even whole societies) always assess their resources relative to those of others, seeing what resources are available, which resources are most valuable, what alternatives sources are available for valued resources, and what must be given up to get a particular resource.[10] Thus, actors evaluate the potential rewards to be achieved by a given line of activity against the costs (alternative rewards forgone) and investments (accumulated costs) that must be given up or incurred to receive a reward. They also calculate the likelihood that the reward will be forthcoming or the probability of getting a reward for the costs and investments spent and incurred. Individuals are assessing alternative sources for rewards, if they can be found, because if multiple actors possess a reward, it will generally cost less to get the reward. If, however, only one actor controls a valued reward and if this actor has multiple resources for the rewards from dependent actors or does not value these dependent actor's resources highly, then it will be more costly for dependent actors to receive the desired reward. Moreover, when actors become dependent upon an actor holding a monopoly over a valued resource, these actors can expect that the actor monopolizing a reward will exert power over them and demand higher payments of whatever resources these actors have to exchange. Power is thus inherent in all exchanges, although if there are multiple sources for all rewards by all actors engaged in exchanges, these actors will have more equal power and, as a result, power-use will decline and actors will develop positive sentiments toward each other because they each receive valued rewards at what is perceived a fair cost. And the more exchanges are seen as fair and positive sentiments develop, the more likely will actors' relations reveal commitments to each other and high solidarity.

In contrast, if rewards are seen as unfair because those holding monopolies use their power to demand ever-more resources from dependent actors, these dependent actors will actively seek to reduce the power of the advantaged actor, using a variety of strategies:[11] (a) seeking to find alternatives for the valued resource from other actors, thereby reducing the advantage of the holder of a monopoly over a resource; (b) seeking to provide new resources that are more valuable to the holder of the monopoly, thus decreasing power differences between actors; (c) seeking to cut off the alternative sources of the resources that dependent actors are giving the monopolistic resource-holder, thereby making the this power-user more dependent for resources on those who have been exploited; (d) forming alliances with these other actors, thereby becoming a new single actor that can withhold resources from the actor that previously had a monopoly, thereby generating more equal power because now the holder of the monopoly no longer has alternative sources for rewards that it values, thereby giving the coalition equal power to the previous holder of the monopoly; (e) attempting to coerce or punish actors that abuse their monopolies through power-use against dependent actors; (f) doing without the valued reward controlled by a monopolistic and power-using resource holder. Thus, there are strategies that actors will generally pursue if they find themselves dependent upon other actors for valued resources. Most of these strategies involve trying to rebalance the exchange by reducing the monopoly of control by one actor or by increasing the value of the resources given to the holder of a valued resource by dependent actors.

---

[10]George C. Homans championed this conception of motivation; see, for example, the early work of George C. Homans: *Social Behavior: Its Elementary Forms* (New York: Harcourt Brace Jovanovich, 1961; second edition in 1972).

[11]Richard Emerson, "Power-Dependence Relations: Two Experiments," *Sociometry* 27 (September 1964): pp. 282–298.

Culture almost always influences these strategic actors and the calculations made by actors as they deal with power-use by another actor. There are almost always calculations about whether or not a given level of exchange of resources is fair or just. These calculations always involve invoking several comparison points.[12] One comparison point is the moral codes and norms in a culture that establish criteria for evaluating exchanges as just and fair. Another comparison point might be the expectations that a person had upon entering an exchange, which for some reason were not realized. Yet another comparison point might be the past rate of exchange of resources that had previously prevailed but was suddenly altered by one actor. Still another comparison point might be a person's perception (often a misperception) of the resources they would receive in alternative exchange relations (to which they may not have actual access). Exchange behavior is thus almost always *moralized*, and when individuals feel that the exchanges are not fair by invoking a comparison point, they become angry like Skinner's pigeons and, moreover, they may also be willing to mobilize others in a similar position and pursue conflict, just as Marx had hoped the proletariat would do against the bourgeoisie.

Exchange Processes of Inequality and Power

One of the first early modern exchange theories was proposed by Peter M. Blau[13] in the mid-1960s. In his approach, Blau outlined several basic processes that typify all exchanges at the micro level of exchanges among individuals and at the more macro level of exchanges among organizations and larger-scale corporate units. He saw the following processes as inherent in all exchange:

1. *Attraction* between actors because of the resources that they possess. Attraction occurs among individuals because they have been socialized into a common culture and, hence, value similar resources. Moreover, individuals also develop understandings about which resources are more valuable, both extrinsically and intrinsically.

2. The beginnings of *an exchange of resources*, which is almost always regulated by norms of "fair exchange" as well as by cultural prohibitions and by norms of fair exchange for individual actors and, for corporate actors, by external political authority and by formal laws

3. *Competition for power* between exchange partners as they engage in displays of the qualities of their resources through impression management, while seeking to devalue the resources of actual or potential exchange partners. Individuals do this through interpersonal displays, while corporate units advertise and market the value of their resources *vis-à-vis* potential exchange partners.

---

[12]Jonathan H. Turner, "The Structural Base of Resource Distribution," in *Handbook of Social Resource Theory*, eds. Kjell Tornblom and Ali Kazemi (New York: Springer, 2013).

[13]Peter M. Blau's major exchange work is *Exchange and Power in Social Life* (New York: Wiley, 1964). This formal and expanded statement on his exchange perspective was anticipated in earlier works. For example, see Peter M. Blau, "A Theory of Social Integration," *American Journal of Sociology* 65 (May 1960): pp. 545–556; "Interaction: Social Exchange," in *International Encyclopedia of the Social Sciences*, vol. 7 (New York: Macmillan, 1968), pp. 452–458; and Peter M. Blau, *The Dynamics of Bureaucracy*, 1st and 2nd eds. (Chicago: University of Chicago Press, 1955, 1963).

4. Differentiation between actors by virtue of who wins the competition for power, with the actor possessing the more valued resources having claims for

   A. *Honor* and *prestige* at a minimum and, if resources are more unequally valued and one party is more dependent than the other then one party can claim

   B. *Power* or the right of the party with the more valuable resources to tell what the more dependent actors must do

5. Contradictory strains for

   A. *Integration* of the inequalities in power by virtue of dependent actors' (1) acceptance and legitimation of the differences in the respective value of their resources relative to another actor and (2) subordinates' willingness to sanction negatively other who protest the exchange and bestowal of prestige and power to actors holding the more valued resources, and

   B. *Conflict* of dependent actors against superordinates actors, especially when (1) the imbalance in exchanges of resources violates norms of fair exchange and previous patterns of reciprocity, (2) subordinates experience their frustration and sense of injustice collectively because they are in propinquity and can communicate their grievances, (3) subordinates can develop ideologies expressing their sense of injustice that in turn arouse emotions, (4) subordinates can organize collectively and oppose those with power, (5) subordinates can develop a sense of solidarity and sense that their cause is not only justified but noble, and (6) develop a sense that opposition as an end in itself and as morally necessary.

Thus, exchanges that violate norms of fair exchange will, as Marx argued, set into motion conflict processes as strains for opposition build in intensity. Indeed, Blau has simply rephrased Marx's argument more abstractly, but the basic processes are those that Marx outlined for relations between the bourgeoisie and proletariat. In making the argument more abstract, Blau is able to apply it to both micro and macro situations. Whether it is tension and conflict in an office or a mass mobilization of a class of people in society, the same basic dynamics are in play. When inequalities are accepted and legitimated, conflict becomes unlikely because all actors believe that, despite inequalities, they are receiving a fair share of resources, given the less value attached to the resources they have to offer those holding more valued resources.

I should also note that another exchange theory, which is more actively researched today than Blau's theory, was also developed in the 1960s by Richard Emerson.[14] In contrast to Blau's theory, this approach by Emerson is actively pursued today by several generations of researchers and theorists. Emerson captured the basic idea in power differences among exchange partners with the simple formula:

---

[14]Emerson's perspective is best stated in his "Exchange Theory, Part I: A Psychological Basis for Social Exchange" and "Exchange Theory, Part II: Exchange Relations and Network Structures," in *Sociological Theories in Progress*, eds. J. Berger, M. Zelditch, and B. Anderson (New York: Houghton Mifflin, 1972), pp. 38–87. Earlier empirical work that provided the initial impetus to, or the empirical support of, this theoretical perspective includes "Power-Dependence Relations," *American Sociological Review* 17 (February 1962): pp. 31–41; John F. Stolte and Richard M. Emerson, "Structural Inequality: Position and Power in Network Structures," in *Behavioral Theory in Sociology*, ed. R. Hamblin (New Brunswick, NJ: Transaction Books, 1977). Other more conceptual works include "Operant Psychology and Exchange Theory," in *Behavioral Sociology*, eds. R. Burgess and D. Bushell (New York: Columbia University Press, 1969), and "Social Exchange Theory," in *Annual Review of Sociology*, eds. A. Inkeles and N. Smelser, vol. 2 (1976), pp. 335–362.

$P_{ab} = D_{ba}$, or to translate: the *Power* of actor A over actor B (whether and individual or corporate unit) is a function of the *Dependence* of actor B on A for valued resources.

Like Marx and Blau, Emerson then makes some additional assumptions (derived from behaviorist roots) that actors with power will generally press their advantage by demanding more from dependent actors if the latter want to receive the valued resources that they possess. He called these highly unequal exchanges of resources a *unilateral monopoly* because one actor, say A_1, controls resources that other actors $B_{1,2,3,4,...n}$ all want but have only *once place* to go in order to get these resources: actor A_1. Emerson argued that all such unilateral monopolies are unstable and will, in his words, activate *balancing operations*, which include: (1) B actors decreasing the value of rewards offered by A_1, thereby reducing Actor B's dependence on Actor A_1; (2) B actors increasing the number of alternative resources that are only offered presently by A_1—that is, finding $A_{2,3,4...n}$ and thus reducing dependence upon the original A or any Actor A who possesses the valued resource; (3) any actor B can attempt to increase the value of resources that it provides for A_1, thereby making actor A_1 more dependent on this B actor; and (4) B actors can seek to reduce Actor A's alternatives for the resources provided by Actors $B_{1,2,3,4...n}$. This way of expressing the argument is less dramatic than in Marx or Blau, but it communicates pretty much the same information on one of the fundamental process of exchange, whether among individuals, corporate units, whole societies, or any two actors who exchange resources under conditions of inequality. Tension and conflict inhere in inequalities and power-use by advantaged actors over their dependent exchange partners.

Basic Exchange Structures

One of the great innovations in Emerson's theory is that he developed a more precise conception of social structure built around network analysis (see pp. 150–160 in Chapter 9). Actors are seen as points and nodes in a network of relations. Actors possessing and exchanging different resources are denoted by different letters, such as A and B. Actors possessing the same resources for exchange are denoted by the same letter, subscripting the actual number of such actors as is done above in B_1, B_2, B_3, B_4. Lines connecting letters denote an exchange relationship, and by creating different configurations of lines, different structures are revealed. For example, the structure outlined in Figure 5.1 is a very common structure in which a central node exchanges with three subsets of actors possessing different resources that are passed along from the periphery of the network to this central figure. Such networks are, Emerson notes, inherently unstable because actors B_1, B_2, and B_3 resent passing on their bounty of resources from the actors dependent upon them, or Actors C_1, C_2, C_3. . . .$_n$ in the figure.

As this resentment of the B actors increases, they begin to engage in one of the balancing operations listed above. Let me put some substantive content on this network structure. Say that Actor A is the king of a feudal system; the B actors are his lords of the realm; and the C actors are those who work on the manorial estate and give their production to the lords who then pass on a portion of their bounty to the king. Why do they do so? Why not keep it all for themselves? They would like to do so, but kings offer a very valuable resource: coordination of lords and their armies, in conjunction with the king's own army, in the face of invasion by other empires. When times are dangerous, lords perceive that their exchange with the king is useful—material resources from estates for coordination and control resources to protect the feudal kingdom. But, when life is more secure, or perceived to be so, the lords—that is, the Actor Bs in this network—begin to resent

Figure 5.1 Network With Two Sets of Central Nodes

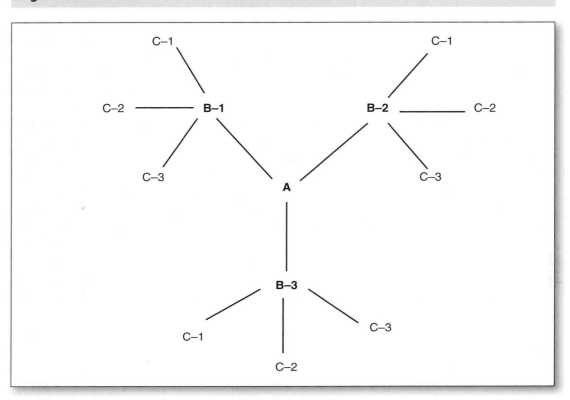

giving up much of their economic surplus for protection that they no longer think is needed. And so, they adopt any of the balancing operations, including banding together to overthrow the king. This is why feudal systems are unstable, but they are also vulnerable because greed often leads lords to get rid of the one person who can control competition and self-destructive infighting among the lords and who can mobilize them to protect the feudal kingdom.

With these kinds of network diagrams, coupled with the simple notions of inequalities in exchanges and the balancing operations, many different kinds of social structures can be described in general theoretical terms, and the exchange ideas in Emerson's and his collaborators' work as well as among the students of his students allow us to see how structures are built up and how they begin to erode and eventually collapse. Moreover, because the network structure is generic, it can apply to small-scale or larger-scale socio-cultural formations and explain them both with the same basic ideas about exchange processes.

The Rationality of Social Structural Formations

All exchange theories seek to explain the emergence, change, and perhaps disintegration of social structures and their cultures. Another distinctive exchange theoretic tradition, rivaling that proposed by Emerson and, in fact, more pervasive throughout the social sciences, is *rational choice theory*.[15] This approach is closest to the utilitarian arguments pioneered by Adam Smith and championed by neo-classical economics, but it adds what most economists never really examine: the effects of social structure on exchange processes, and vice versa, and the building up of social structures from exchanges among rational, often utility-maximizing actors.

One of the early pioneers of rational choice theory in the social sciences was James S. Coleman.[16] To illustrate Coleman's approach, let me summarize from his last theoretical work ideas that he had been developing for over thirty years. Sometimes it is rational, Coleman argued, for profit-maximizing actors to transfer some of their rights to act to external actors, such as the state or legal system, to make decisions for them. Why would actors who try to maximize their utilities and minimize their costs and investments give over some of their rights to do so and give power to external powers that will, to some degree, regulate what they can do? His answer is that actors are experiencing *negative externalities* or high costs and punishments in their regular exchange activities that are beyond their control. For example, if there is widespread fraud, criminality, cheating, and other dissociative processes in markets or in established relations, costs become very high and rewards uncertain, thereby significantly lowering profits. Under these conditions, rational actors see the need to develop and impose new kinds of regulatory norms that are monitored for conformity and that impose sanctions for violation of these norms. Any individual actor cannot do this alone, and so actors must agree to release rights to act to external actors who then impose norms and sanctions, and in so doing, negative externalities are reduced, and actors costs and punishments decline in relation to more certain payoffs.

These dynamics account for the history of how legal and political systems evolve in society. Without them, societies become seedbeds of negative externalities that impose high costs and make receipt of rewards from regularized exchanges difficult to secure on a consistent basis. For example, if there are thieves in the forest of a feudal system (like Robin Hood, but maybe not so "good"), those with wealth will lose much of this wealth to banditry when they move about, and hence, they will incur high costs in trying to protect this wealth. It is easier and cheaper to pay more taxes to cede this power to catch and prosecute thieves to an external authority like regional sheriffs and other political actors who can enact laws and coercively enforce them.

Thus, social structures emerge and are built up when actors in society are experiencing negative externalities in their ongoing exchange activities. In addition, it often becomes rational to give some resources to external actors in order to increase the receipt of rewards in a more secure environment. Actors, whether individuals or corporate units, typically hate to give up control, but they do so when it is rational; and it is rational to create more inclusive structures when negative externalities are rising and profits from exchanges, as a result, are falling.

Exchange Processes, Social Solidarity, and Commitments Behaviors

Another major focus of exchange theories is to explain processes of solidarity among actors in networks or any kind of social structure where exchanges are ongoing. How individuals

---

[15]This approach has different names in other disciplines, but the core ideas come from neo-classical and game theory in economics and political science and, to an extent, in sociology and anthropology.

[16]See, for examples: James S. Coleman, *Individual Interests and Collective Action: Selected Essays* (Cambridge: Cambridge University Press, 1986). His most important work was *Foundations of Social Theory* (Cambridge, MA: Belknap, 1990).

become committed to each other (to continue exchanging) and to the larger social structures of whole societies in which these exchanges occur? How can these processes be explained if actors are indeed selfish and oriented to receiving rewards for the least costs? For solidarity requires work as well as other cost, while and often compromising maximal profits to experience solidarity. Similarly, commitments to larger social structures mean attaching oneself to more remote social structures and, to some degree, giving these structures resources, such as commitments to incur costs during war or emotional feelings that for most of human history were only given over to kindred and small groups of persons.

Groups at the micro level of social organization are more viable through solidarity, as are the organizations that organize these groups; societies are only viable when people give up some resources—extrinsic resources like money in taxes and intrinsic resources like commitments and legitimacy—to remote social structures like the state, society as a whole, or some of its institutions such as religion and law. Why would profit-maximizing actors do so? Both Emerson's exchange-network approach and rational choice theory can explain these critical dynamics, but in somewhat different ways.

Rational Choice Theories of Solidarity

Michael Hechter[17] has developed one of the most influential theories of how selfish, rational actors can gain high levels of reward by participating in high-solidarity groups. Like all rational choice theorists, Hechter assumes that humans are goal oriented, that they have hierarchies of preferences, and that in selecting lines of conduct, they invoke this preference hierarchy and pursue those actions that bring the most reward and the least costs forgone, thereby maximizing utilities. Like Coleman, he also emphasizes that social structures are constructed and sustained as a consequence of utility-maximizing decisions of individuals. Thus, what many consider an extreme assumption—utility maximization—is often retained in rational choice versions of exchange theory.

Hechter begins his analysis of solidarity by emphasizing that individuals must almost always seek resources that give them utility in groups. Utilities are conceptualized as "goods," as would be the case if individuals seek companionship. Companionship thus becomes a *good* in the theory. This is a good that can only be secured by interaction with others, typically in groups. Groups thus exist to provide goods for their members. Some goods are *public* in that the group produces a good through their joint coordinated activities for consumption by non-group members. If, for example, a group builds a highway, this *public good* can be used by non-group members. In contrast, there are *private goods* that are produced to be consumed *only* by group members. For example, groups can produce a sense of solidarity, and this private good is intended only for consumption by the group members who experience rewards from the positive emotions associated with group solidarity.

The basic problem of order from this rational choice perspective on group solidarity is *free-riding*, or the problem of individuals securing goods that they not work at producing. For example, individuals who use public goods but do not pay for them (through highway taxes or tolls) are free-riding on all those who have paid for the production of this public good, or individuals who do not engage or work at the joint production of a sense of solidarity but enjoy the emotional benefits of this solidarity are also free-riding. The reason that free-riding

---

[17]Michael Hechter, *Principles of Group Solidarity* (Berkeley: University of California Press, 1987); "Rational Choice Foundations of Social Order," in *Theory Building in Sociology*, ed. J. H. Turner (Newbury Park, CA: Sage, 1988).

becomes a problem is that, if everyone free rides, then the goods do not get produced, and the viability of social structures declines.

How, then, do groups structure themselves to avoid free-riding? This is a question of social order because, ultimately, all other social structures are made up from groups—e.g., organizations, communities, whole societies. And, hence, if the outputs of goods are consumed by free-riders, who do not pay for the good by fees or participation in group activities, groups will fail and so will the social structures built from these failing groups.

In the above summary, there is a distinction to be made between *extrinsic goods* and *intrinsic goods*. Extrinsic goods are produced to be consumed by others, as is the case for any product produced by joint actions of groups working for a company that sells its products—cars, TVs, clothes, etc.—in markets. Intrinsic goods are those that are made for consumption by the very people producing the good. Thus, most intrinsic goods provide rewards revolving around emotions, friendship, companionship, and social solidarity; and while they are not a "hard good," they can be highly valuable to those producing and receiving them. Yet, even for intrinsic goods, it is rational for actors to avoid the costs of producing this intrinsic good and enjoy the rewards of experiencing an intrinsic good like solidarity. But, if everyone free-rides in the production of solidarity, there will be no intrinsic good to consume. So, as emphasized above, free-riding can be a problem for the production of both hard and soft goods, because too much free-riding destroys the group and the availability of the goods that it produces.

How, therefore, is free-riding mitigated? Hechter outlines the basis of social control that all groups employ to limit free-riding, labeling these social control processes a group's *control capacity*. Control is achieved by (1) *dependence* of members on the group for valued resources that are not easily gotten elsewhere or only at higher costs; (2) *monitoring* of members effort at producing a public or private good; and (3) *sanctioning* those negatively who do not contribute their fair share to the production of goods, while bestowing positive sanctions on those who do. There are two basic types of groups. One is what Hechter terms *obligatory groups* where members produce a joint good, typically intrinsic, for their own consumption; the second basic type is *compensatory groups* where individuals are compensated (e.g., paid) for their contributions to joint goods usually consumed by others. Most groups producing public goods are compensatory, while those producing private goods are obligatory.

The type of group determines the nature of social control. In compensatory groups, people are "bought off" with monetary compensation to engage in the activities necessary to produce a good for consumption by others. Yet, it is still rational for a resource-maximizing individual to take the pay and not work hard, and so, most compensatory groups must have higher levels of supervision to make sure that people work hard enough, and they are ready to impose negative sanctions on those who do not. If dependence is high on the resource offered by a group—i.e., the persons need the pay offered as compensation—workers are often motivated to work hard in order to secure this valued resource. Still, it is rational to do less for this pay than do more, and so some monitoring and sanctioning procedures need to be in place. The most effective monitoring occurs informally, as when employees monitor and sanction each other for free-riding rather than having to put another layer of costly supervisory personnel in place to monitor and sanction.

Obligatory groups almost always engage in informal monitoring and sanctioning, and moreover, individuals are typically dependent upon the group for the valued resource—say, positive emotions and sense of solidarity—jointly produced and consumed by group members. Thus, social control costs in obligatory groups are lower, but if groups get large, then informal monitoring will become less effective, leading to more formal monitoring and sanctioning procedures. Several conditions, then, increase solidarity in obligatory groups. First, individuals find the intrinsic goods produced to be highly rewarding; and since each group will produce its own types of intrinsic good, this valued resource in one group is typically not available in other groups. Moreover, individuals make investments of their time, energy, and emotions that can never be retrieved if this person leaves the group. There are no "roll over" programs for sunk costs and investments in obligatory groups when people leave the group and seek to join another group. This dependence on the group increases its power over individuals, with individuals feeling a greater sense of obligation to contribute the production of its private, intrinsic rewards. Second, if this private good is not easily secured in other groups, dependence increases; and individuals are likely to see exiting the group as very costly. Third, if group members can monitor and sanction each other in the normal course of their joint activities, the solidarity-dampening effects of external supervision are avoided, as is the extra costs of such supervision. Fourth, if the architecture and ecology of the group's locale is open and enables individuals to see each other, then monitoring and positive sanctioning become part of the very process of producing an intrinsic, jointly produced good like social solidarity. Fifth, if groups can develop *extensive normative obligations* for joint production—indeed, if these obligations can be moralized—they operate to ensure not only the production of the joint good but also operate as very effective means of social control because to violate a moral norm is to invite guilt. Increasing group size can undermine these conditions of group solidarity, as can compensation for joint efforts to produce extrinsic groups for consumption by non-group members.

It is for this reason that compensatory groups typically evidence much lower levels of solidarity because all of the solidarity-producing conditions listed above are more difficult to put in play, and especially so if a group gets larger or the organization in which a group is lodged becomes large. Yet, there are compensatory groups that can meet many of the conditions for solidarity. Dot.com companies like Google, Facebook, and others have effectively created group environments where members receive more than just a paycheck and stock options; they also experience the intrinsic rewards that come from the joint activities of the group per se, above and beyond their extrinsic compensation. Such solidarity becomes an intrinsic, jointly produced private good that is highly rewarding and that can only be produced by individuals in daily, emotion-arousing interactions. Group members become dependent upon this extra, private good; they will generally work hard without much supervision to secure this private good, thus reducing monitoring and sanctioning costs. It is also no coincidence that organizations of these work groups tend to be ecologically open and to de-emphasize inequalities in authority. The result is that they can meet the conditions increasing the solidarity in groups. Academia is another place where most professors work because of the intrinsic rewards of their labor, especially in research universities but also in more teaching-oriented universities as well; the result is comparative high solidarity when compared to an organization like an automobile factory where the work is not intrinsically rewarding and where compensation and monitoring as well as sanctioning by supervisory personnel are critical to worker performance.

Thus, a society is built from mixes of compensatory and obligatory groups, as well as from groups that have elements of both. Free-riding is a problem, but less so in obligatory groups where dependence is high for receiving the joint private good and where monitoring and sanctioning are part of the very joint activities producing the private good that is rewarding to all members. Thus, the control capacity of obligatory group keeps rational actors from free-riding on the efforts of fellow group members to incur the costs of joint activity producing the private good. In contrast, the control capacity of a compensatory group is much lower with the result that the production of a private good is less likely or, if produced, less intensely gratifying—thus making free-riding a more pressing problem for the group and the organization in which the group operates. If free-riding is high in either compensatory or obligatory groups, rational actors will need to increase the groups control capacity through more active monitoring and sanctioning; and so, it is always rational to limit free-riding because in Coleman's terms, free-riding becomes a "negative external-ity" that forces a group to build up its control capacity.

Exchange-Network Analyses of Commitments to Exchange Partners

The process of generating commitments can be seen as irrational in this sense: commitments limit rational actors' efforts to explore alternatives sources of rewards because they are committed to an exchange partner who often can provide fewer rewards than potential alternative exchange partners. Why would commitments be so pervasive among actors whose basic behaviors are driven by assessment of rewards, alternatives, costs, and investments? An answer to this question illustrates the power of exchange theories to explain how longer-term relations and commitments to larger social structures are generated.[18]

Early work on commitments in experimental settings emphasized that commitments can be rational because they reduce an important cost in all exchange relations: uncertainty. When exchange partners develop commitments to form relations, the costs imposed by uncertainty (associated with finding alternative partners) are reduced, thereby increasing the net rewards when lower costs are factored into relations with others providing less than maximal rewards. Another line of argument is that commitments are much like solidarity, an intrinsic and valu-able resource, which is generated when individuals sustain an exchange relation. So, even if a person receives less of an extrinsic reward, like money, with commitments to exchange part-ners, there is another reinforcer or reward in play—positive emotions and solidarity with those to whom commitments develop.

Exchange-Network Analysis of Commitments to Social Structures

Edward Lawler and his colleagues demonstrated that when exchanges involve actors who are approximately equal in their control of valued resources and who are equally dependent upon each other for rewards and resources with no actor enjoying a power advantage, these actors are more likely to engage in frequent exchanges that produce mild positive emotions—interest, excitement, pleasure/satisfaction—that lead to commitment behaviors, such as token gift-giving, staying in the

---

[18]Edward J. Lawler and Jeongkoo Yoon, "Commitment in Exchange Relations: A Test of a Theory of Relational Cohesion," *American Sociological Review* 61 (1996): pp. 89–108; Edward Lawler, Jeongkoo Yoon, Mouraine R. Baker, and Michael D. Large, "Mutual Dependence and Gift Giving in Exchange Relations," *Advances in Group Processes* 12 (1995): pp. 271–298; Edward J. Lawler and Jeongkoo Yoon, "Power and the Emergence of Commitment Behavior in Negotiated Exchange," *American Sociological Review* 58 (1993): pp. 465–481. For earlier works on commitment dynamics within power-dependence theorizing see Karen S. Cook and Richard M. Emerson, "Power, Equity, and Commitment in Exchange Networks," *American Sociological Review* 43 (1978): pp. 721–739; Karen S. Cook and Richard M. Emerson, "Exchange Networks and the Analysis of Complex Organizations," *Research on the Sociology of Organizations* 3 (1984): pp. 1–30; Peter Kollock, "The Emergence of Exchange Structures: An Experimental Study of Uncertainty, Commitment and Trust," *American Journal of Sociology* 100 (1994): pp. 315–345.

relationship even though other attractive alternative exists, and contributing resources to joint activities, even risky ones.[19] What is remarkable about these findings is that actors never see each other because, in fact, they are all interacting with a computer algorithm rather than a real person. Still, they develop positive emotions and commitment behaviors because it appears that these positive emotions are a valuable intrinsic good that, in Hechter's terms, is still rewarding. Thus, additional resources come into play during the exchange: positive emotions and commitment behaviors. These intrinsic rewards are as highly rewarding as whatever extrinsic goods are also being exchanged. Figure 5.2 models these empirical findings.

Thus, individuals who are equal in resources and equally dependent upon each other for resources will engage in more frequent exchanges, with this frequency increasing positive emotions that lead them to engage in commitment behaviors. Again, additional resources that are highly valued, even when given to individuals by a computer, generate the fundamental behaviors that hold groups together.

Lawler then began to ask the question of how commitments more generally are made to larger-scale social structures, given what Lawler and colleagues also learned in other experiments:[20] Positive emotions have a *proximal bias* in that individuals will see themselves and local others as responsible for generating these emotions, whereas negative emotions have a *distal bias* with individuals blaming more remote others and social structures for experiencing negative emotions. How, then, do commitments to larger scale structures—state and society—ever develop with these two types of cognitive-emotional biases in play in most social relations? How can the proximal bias trapping positive emotions be broken so that these emotions will drift outward, thereby overcoming the negativity of the distal bias? An answer to these questions explains how societies sustain themselves.

Figure 5.2   Equal Power, Exchange, Frequency, and Commitment Behaviors

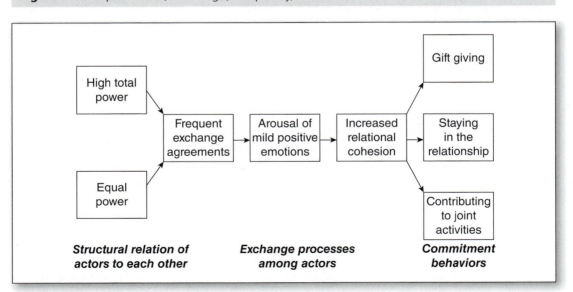

[19]Edward J. Lawler, Shane R. Thye, and Jeongkoo Yoon, *Social Commitment in a Depersonalized World* (New York: Russell Sage Foundation, 2009).

[20]Lawler, "An Affect Theory of Social Exchange" (cited in note 9).

Type of exchange—enumerated earlier—has an effect on whether or not individuals can begin to make these more *distal attributions* for positive emotions, thereby breaking the hold of the *proximal bias*. *Productive exchanges* are the most likely to generate the kinds of emotions that lead to more distal attributions for positive emotions.[21] In productive exchanges, it is difficult to separate the respective contributions of others to achieving group goals because activities are coordinated and conflated to a collective, as opposed to individual goal. This *non-seprability* of contributions causes individuals to experience strong positive and negative emotions, depending on whether or not the coordinated actions have been successful in realizing goals. People in productive exchanges also have a sense of *shared responsibility*, and they will thus experience positive and negative emotions collectively rather than individually. It is the group rather than individuals that has been successful or failed; and when joint actions in the group have been successful, the shared positive emotions become, in Hechter's terms, a *private good* that is highly valuable when consumed by group members. When productive exchanges have been unsuccessful in meeting goals, the group as a whole rather than any one person feels the negative emotions that come with failure, but these emotions tend to motivate the group to try harder, thus creating a highly rewarding sense of collective purpose and solidarity even with failure.

From these dynamics come *attributions* about the causes of success or failure; and the more productive exchanges *do not separate* each person's contribution, the more they generate a sense of *shared responsibility*, and the more they also produce a *sense of efficacy* among individuals in their productive activities, the more likely are attributions to be made toward *the group as a whole*. Attributions for positive emotions will then begin to break the hold of the proximal bias, and once attributions move to the group level, they can begin to travel to ever-larger and more inclusive social structures. Why would this movement of attributions continue to go outward to larger structures?

The answer to this question resides in fact that groups are typically embedded in organizations, which are embedded in communities, which in turn are lodged in institutions (e.g., economy, polity, education, etc.) that are part of a larger society. These layers of structure, with smaller structures lodged in larger structures, create conduits for positive emotions created in the group to move out and target larger structures. This movement thus creates external attributions to potentially very macro-level structures, like the whole society, which is viewed as responsible for the positive emotions that individuals feel in their productive exchanges that have increased their shared sense of joint, collective activity, their sense of shared responsibility for outcomes, and their sense of efficacy as a collective enterprise.

It is difficult in productive exchanges for individuals to make self-attributions or attributions to specific others for positive emotions, as would normally be the case because of the power of the proximal bias. The respective contributions of individuals are too conflated with each other, and so individuals begin to see the group and larger networks and structures in which the group is embedded as responsible for their positive feelings. As these external or distal attributions are made, people develop commitments not only to their productive exchanges conducted to realize goals but also to the more macro structures within which these exchanges are embedded. So, once the power of the proximal bias is broken, positive emotions can be attached to distal objects like social structures, leading people to develop commitments to macrostructures. Thus, the more a set of productive exchanges is embedded in successive layers of increasingly larger social structures,

---

[21]Lawler, Thye, and Yoon, *Social Commitment* (cited in note 19).

the more likely are positive feelings to move outward toward macrostructures, thereby increasing commitments to these macrostructures. In this way, people legitimize macrostructures and, in so doing, make macrostructures and whole societies more viable.

Thus, the greater is the number of productive exchanges operating in a society (as a proportion of all other types of exchange), the greater is the non-separability of joint tasks, the more people feel that they are collectively engaged in a common enterprise, the more they have a shared sense of responsibility (as opposed to individual responsibility). And, the more they feel a sense of efficacy in join activities, the more likely will they make more distal attributions and develop commitments to remote social structures. The positive emotions that come from these forces circulate as a private good for group members, but equally important, these emotions push attributions up layers of embedded structures that are seen as ultimately responsible for success in more micro-level productive exchanges.

Lawler and his colleagues also note that once these dynamics are operative, they increase the general and diffuse *sense of trust* that individuals have in each other but also in the larger social structures in which groups are embedded. And these dynamics are reinforced when people's *sense of identity* is caught up in the success of productive exchanges. In all situations, people see themselves as objects and develop an identity about themselves in situations (see next chapter on symbolic interaction for more details on how self and identity operate). As they do so, identities become tied to, and dependent upon, productive exchanges that will allow for more distal attributions about success in activities, seeing macrostructures as at least partially responsible. As these more distal attributions are made, people also begin to see their sense of self and specific identities as connected to, and dependent upon, the operation of macrostructures. And, once people see this connection between macrostructures and the verification and viability of their sense of self, they become even more committed to macro-level structures.

Thus, what Lawler and his colleagues Shane Thye and Jeongkoo Yoon[22] have accomplished is the use a theory of exchange to explain some of the most important processes that sustain societies. They have, in essence, connected the micro-level universe of exchanges among individuals to not only local solidarities, but to generalized sense of trust in others and structures and, most importantly, to feelings of commitment to macrostructures. When these processes operate smoothly, societies become more viable and stable.

Conclusion

I have not reviewed all exchange theories, but only some of the most important. I have focused on particular theories because they represent the current leading edge of exchange theory, but many other theories are part of this more general movement to use exchange theories to explain both micro- and macro-level social phenomena. Let me conclude by expanding upon the list of assumptions from early exchange theory listed earlier in order to offer a more robust sense for the key idea in all exchange theories today.

1. All human behavior is goal oriented, with individuals making decisions—whether consciously or more implicitly—about the rewards to be gained by pursuing alternative lines of activity.

---

[22]Ibid.

2. As individuals make decisions about actions in situations, they make a set of related calculations, sometimes consciously but probably more often implicitly, with respect to

   A. The rewards to be potentially gained

   B. The probability that these rewards will be forthcoming

   C. The costs in rewards forgone, as well as in time and energy that will be incurred in seeking a given reward

   D. The level of investments required (accumulated costs) to realize a given reward

   E. the level of reward that would be considered minimally fair and just

3. Collective or corporate units engage in these same calculations as they seek to realize goals.

4. The likelihood that corporate units or individuals will pursue a given line of conduct is related to the level of reward relative to assessments of the cost inhering in the considerations listed in 2B-E above.

5. There are at least four basic types of exchange:

   A. Productive

   B. Negotiated

   C. Reciprocal

   D. Generalized

6. There are several basic processes by which exchanges unfold, whether the actors are individuals or corporate units:

   A. *Attraction* of actors to each other because of their resources that are available for exchange

   B. The *exchange of rewards*, along the basic types listed in 5A-D

   C. *Competition* for power and prestige through the mutual displays by actors of the value of their rewards, relative to those of exchange partners

   D. *Differentiation* of actors by *esteem and power*, depending upon the relative dependence of actors on other actors for valued rewards, with differentiation increasing to the extent that one set of actors is dependent upon another actor for a valued resource, especially when there are no other alternative sources for this valued resource, and actors become highly dependent on another actor for this resource

   E. *Strains toward integration* among differentiated actors through

      1. Legitimation of power differences

      2. Social control by subordinates

      3. Coalitions among actors

   F. *Strains toward opposition*, which increases with

      1. Inequalities in the distribution of valued resources

      2. Denial of expected rewards from power holders

      3. Violation of normal of fair exchange and justice

      4. Violations of reciprocity in exchanges

    5. Collective experience of deprivations by dependent/subordinate actors

    6. Mobilization for conflict among, which increases among those actors dependent on, and subordinate to, a powerful actor, with the potential for mobilization increasing with

        a. Ecological concentration of actors

        b. Communication among actors

        c. Collective experience of deprivations in exchanges

        d. Collective experience of injustice in exchanges

        e. Increased collective solidarity of subordinates

  G. *Strains toward balancing* tactics by subordinates, including

    1. Reduce the value to subordinates of subordinate's resources

    2. Search subordinates for alternative sources of resources controlled by subordinates

    3. Increase the value of resources given by subordinates to superordinates

    4. Reduce the number sources of the resources given to superordinates by subordinates

7. The likelihood that an exchange relationship will reveal tension, conflict, and balancing activities increases with the level of inequality in the exchange of resources arising from dependence of subordinates actors on the resources of superordinates actors and the degree of power-use by superordinate to extract ever-more resources from subordinates.

8. The likelihood that exchange relationships will generate solidarity increases with

  A. The production and consumption by group members of private goods that are highly valued by group members and consumed by group members

  B. The development of obligatory norms to contribute to the production of this joint good

  C. The control capacity of the group, which increases with

    1. The dependence of members on the group for private goods, which increases with

        a. The value of the private good

        b. The difficulty of securing the good in other groups

        c. The high exit costs from the group imposed by loss of investments in the group

    2. The ease of informal monitoring of free-riding

    3. The use of informal sanctioning of free-riders as part of the normal interaction among group members

9. The likelihood of solidarity in groups decreases with

  A. The use of extrinsic rewards to produce public goods for consumption by non-group members

  B. The size of the group and/or organization in which a group is embedded

  C. The inability for groups to produce and consume an intrinsic private good for their own consumption

D. Reduced control capacity, which is related to

1. Group size

2. Formal monitoring of free-riding by formal authority

3. Sanctioning by formal authority

4. Low dependence of group for private goods

5. Low exit costs due to alternative sources of extrinsic rewards used to motivate group members

10. The level of commitment to groups by individuals increases with the solidarity of groups, which increases with the conditions listed under 8 above and decreases with the conditions listed under 9 above, and the following additional conditions:

A. Low inequality among group members and equal dependence on each other for rewards

B. Productive exchanges, where

1. Respective tasks and contributions of individuals to group goals are non-separable

2. Generalized positive emotions are aroused because of frequent exchanges as a course of productive activity

3. Perceptions of shared responsibility for outcomes of joint activities are strong

4. Group members experience a strong sense of efficacy

C. Member identities are defined by joint activities and affirmed when these activities are successful in meeting group norms

11. The movement of commitments to more macro-level social structures increases with the conditions listed under 10, above and

A. The degree to which attributions for the positive emotions arising from success in realizing goals targets the group as a whole rather than individual members, which increases with the conditions listed under 10, above, rather than individuals members of the group or self

B. The extent and degree to which the group is embedded in larger and more inclusive network structures and successive layers of increasingly macro-level social structures

C. The clarity of the linkages of groups to larger networks and layers of social structure in a society

D. The proportion of exchange activities in groups within a society that

1. Involve the production and consumption of intrinsic and private goods, even when groups produce goods for public consumption by non-group members

2. Productive exchanges that produce a sense of joint activity, shared responsibility, efficacy, and self-verification

CHAPTER 6

Symbolic Interactionist Theorizing

M ost of early sociology was decidedly macro in its concerns with the big changes in human societies that came with industrialization and modernity. There are hints of a more micro-level focus in Emile Durkheim's analysis of religion and rituals, in Georg Simmel's analysis of the modern self in complex societies revealing multiple and cross-cutting group affiliations, in Max Weber's analysis of four types of action undergirding legitimated orders, in Herbert Spencer's concern with ceremonial institutions, and even in Karl Marx's portrayal of alienation and the emotional arousal accompanying mobilization for conflict. But, most of this work was intended to explain more macro-social forces and societal-level evolutionary trends.

In the United States, in the last two decades of the nineteenth century and into the first three decades of the twentieth century, there was a convergence of thought from diverse disciplines on understanding human behavior and social interaction. The most important figure in this more micro analysis was George Herbert Mead[1] who was a philosopher at the University of Chicago and advocate for a school of philosophy known as *pragmatism*.

Pragmatism argued that humans constantly seek to make adjustments in their actions so as to adapt to ongoing social processes. People do "what works," and this criterion of adaptation can explain a great deal about the development of persons from their first moments in societies. Pragmatism was a broad intellectual movement that still has adherents, but several generations ago, many more key figures in the history of philosophy, psychology, and sociology considered themselves pragmatists. And, it is from the synthesis of their ideas by George Herbert Mead that micro sociology was born, despite the fact, which perhaps is embarrassing for the discipline, that Mead was not a sociologist.

George Herbert Mead's Synthesis

Mead not only followed the general philosophy of pragmatism, but he also saw an affinity of pragmatism with behaviorism, utilitarianism, and Darwinism. To him, these theoretical

---

[1]Mead's most important sociological ideas can be found in the published lecture notes of his students from his course in social psychology. His most important exposition is found in his *Mind, Self, and Society*, ed. C. W. Morris (Chicago: University of Chicago Press, 1934). Other useful sources include George Herbert Mead, *Selected Writings* (Indianapolis: Bobbs-Merrill, 1964) and Anselm Strauss, ed., *George Herbert Mead on Social Psychology* (Chicago: University of Chicago Press, 1964).

approaches in, respectively, psychology, economics, and biology described *human behavior as adaptation*.[2] If behaviorism is freed from its strict methodology of avoiding the black box of human cognition, then behaviors hidden in the human brain—that is, capacities to learn language, think and make decisions, see and evaluate self from the perspective of others and cultural codes, and cooperate with others in organized groupings—can be seen as behaviors that are learned because they bring the rewards associated with cooperating with others in societies. Similarly, the utility-seeking, rational, and decision-making actors of utilitarianism and neo-classical economics are also doing the same thing: trying to adjust and adapt to social circumstances in order to maximize utilities or rewards. And Darwin's notion of natural selection can be applied to social behaviors, whereby those behaviors that facilitate adjustment and adaptation to the social environment are retained in the behavioral repertoire of a person.

And so, for Mead, the basic question was this: What behavioral capacities do humans learn during the course of their lives that enable them to adapt to ongoing coordinated actions in societies? His answer to this question pulls ideas from philosophy and the social sciences; and in bringing related strands of thinking together, Mead accomplished what no one else had ever done: uncover fundamental processes of social interaction among human beings. Human behavior, interaction, and social organization are possible by virtue of several unique human abilities, beginning with the capacity to use and read *conventional* or *significant gestures* that mean the same thing to the sending and receiving organism. Mead incorrectly thought that only humans had this capacity to develop conventional meanings for words and body gestures that mean the same thing to all parties in an interaction, but still, humans can probably engage in interactions using arbitrary symbols and signs more than any other animal. With the ability to use significant gestures, humans learn to *take the role of the other* or *role take*, by which he meant humans' capacity to read the conventional gestures of others, put themselves in each other's place, anticipate the role they are likely to play out, and then make the necessary adjustments to others so as to facilitate cooperation.

With the ability to read, interpret, and use conventional gestures and, then, to role take with others come additional capacities. One is the capacity for *mind* that Mead adopted from his colleague at the University of Chicago, John Dewey.[3] For Dewey, mind is the ability to imaginatively rehearse covertly alternative lines of conduct, to perceive the likely consequences of these alternatives in a situation, and then to select that alternative that would facilitate adjustment to, and cooperation with, others. If an organism can engage in such covert behaviors, Dewy asserted, it had the behavioral capacity for *mind*. Thus, for Dewy and Mead, mind is not a thing, but rather, a behavioral ability that is learned like any other behavior response: if it brings reinforcement and rewards by facilitating adjustment and adaptation to the social environment, it will be retained in the behavioral repertoire of an individual. Thus, while minded behaviors have a biological basis, this basis is only used when it is mobilized to facilitate adjustment and adaptation of individuals to ongoing social contexts. Because humans must cooperate in groups to survive, having the abilities outlined by Dewy for mind would be highly rewarding. With mind, role-taking can be much more subtle and complex, and this too is rewarding because it makes cooperation more viable.

---

[2]Jonathan H. Turner, *Contemporary Sociological Theory* (Thousand Oaks, CA: Sage, 2012), pp. 312–313.

[3]John Dewey, *Human Nature and Human Conduct* (New York: Henry Holt, 1922), p. 190. For an earlier statement of these ideas, see John Dewey, *Psychology* (New York: Harper & Row, 1886).

With the ability to read and use conventional gestures, to role take, and anticipate likely responses of others to various lines of behavior (i.e., to have a facility for mind), another critical behavioral capacity is acquired: The ability to see one's self as an object in a situation. Mead borrowed this idea from Charles Horton Cooley[4] at the University Michigan, where Mead had begun his career, and from the famous pragmatist psychologist, William James.[5] Cooley used the interesting phrase "looking glass self" to outline self-related behaviors. People read the conventional gestures of others as if looking into a mirror (or, the "looking glass," which was a term used for "mirror" in the nineteenth century). By looking into this mirror, one's self is reflected, or at least the reactions of others are reflected; and as a person interprets these gestures of other, this person will experience self-feelings ranging from *pride* at the positive end of emotions to *shame* at the negative end of the continuum. By seeing "oneself as an object" (reflected in the gestures of others operating as a kind of mirror), individuals make adjustments to their behaviors so as to sustain a positive reflection of themselves. William James added to this kind of analysis the notion that people's images of themselves, as reflected in the mirror of others gestures, will crystallize over time into more enduring views of self that persons carry with them. James also emphasized that individuals develop different types of selves—material, social, and spiritual, for example—that become relevant to them in various situations and that they seek to verify in the eyes of others.

Mead took these ideas and developed a view of individuals as deriving a self-image from the responses of others, which they evaluate for what these responses of others say about a person's conduct in ongoing groups; then, he added James' key idea: from these self-images that arise in every interaction, people's sense of self becomes codified into a more stable and enduring *self-conception*. This self-conception is more stable, and it represents the fundamental cognitions, feelings, and evaluations of self that emerge over a person's lifetime. It is this self-conception that, once formed by young adulthood, gives persons' actions a certain predictability and constancy because people's behaviors reflect the kind of persons that they consider themselves to be.

Mead added several refinements to his notion of self. He recognized that individuals do not just role take with specific others in a situation. The can often role take with others who are not co-present but who are important to an individual and whose evaluation is particularly significant. A person can imagine what these others would say, do, or think about their actions, as if they are present in the situation; and often, people are responding to these distant drummers more than the people right in front of them. Mead then added yet another critical idea: people role take with what he termed the *generalized other* or a "community of attitudes" and the broader perspective of a situation. Indeed, Mead felt that people's capacities for role-taking were not complete until they could assume the perspective—the values, beliefs, collective attitudes—of communities of others. These communities of attitudes can be the immediate group, to ever-larger and more encompassing structures, including a whole society. Thus, in Mead's view, culture comes to individuals through role-taking with generalized others.

These are the basic ideas in Mead's theory of interaction, and they capture the core processes of face-to-face interaction that have served sociology for one hundred years. These ideas have been expanded upon, as we will see in this and the next chapter, but without Mead's synthesis, none of

---

[4]Charles Horton Cooley, *Human Nature and the Social Order* (New York: Scribner's, 1902) and *Social Organization: A Study of the Larger Mind* (New York: Scribner's, 1916).

[5]William James, *The Principles of Psychology* (New York: Henry Holt, 1890), vol. 1, pp. 292–299.

this subsequent elaboration of his scheme would have been possible. Mead's ideas have been carried forward through a theoretical perspective known as *symbolic interactionism*. This label was given to Mead's work by Herbert Blumer[6] who took over Mead's famous social psychology course at the University of Chicago upon his death. I am not sure that Mead would have approved of this label, but it has stuck as the name for theorizing in the Meadian tradition. The label, symbolic interactionism, denotes a wide range of phenomena, from the mutual signaling of gestures in interaction to the codification of a self-conception, but it is last element of Mead's scheme—the social self—that has been the focus of symbolic interactionists over the last few decades.

Contemporary Symbolic Interactionism and the Analysis of Identities

For some decades, the terms self-image, self, and self-conception were used by symbolic interactionists, but in recent decades, the label *identity* has become more widespread. The reason for this shift in terminology is that sociologists have increasingly theorized many dimension, types, and forms of self, and clearly, the notion of identities captures this emphasis. As Mead recognized but did not elaborate upon, people have multiple selves that differ along a number of potential dimensions, including: How emotional attached are individuals to diverse identities? How general or situation-specific are various identities? How connected to culture and its moral codes are various identities? How salient or relevant are various identities in particular situations? And, how high or low in a hierarchy of identities is any particular identity? These kinds of question have become increasingly important as theorists pursued Mead's and the sources of Mead's ideas over the last thirty years.

Multiple Identities

For many decades after Mead's great synthesis, theorists followed Mead's lead and distinguished between identities tied to particular situations—family, work, school, church, team, etc.—and the general self-conception that a person has of himself or herself. But, empirical research has revealed that people have potentially many more identities, including a general conception of themselves as a certain kind of person, as well as a host identities tied to various types of situations. There is no consensus about basic types of identities, but a set of distinctions that I work with captures the current state of theorizing on types of identities. Figure 6.1 outlines four basic types and levels of identity in terms of their generality and emotional content.[7] Some identities are very general and, moreover, are always with a person, much like a shell on the back of a snail. We walk around with them, and they are almost always relevant and salient to a certain degree. At the other extreme, some identities are tied to a particular role in a particular social structure. For example, I have an identity of myself as a professor as a role in a particular type of organization. A female may have an identity of herself as mother in a family structure. These identities are clearly narrower than a

---

[6]Herbert Blumer, *Symbolic Interaction* (Englewood Cliffs, NJ: Prentice Hall, 1969).

[7]Jonathan H. Turner, *Face-to-Face: Toward a Sociological Theory of Interpersonal Behavior* (Stanford, CA: Stanford University Press, 2002); See also, Jonathan H. Turner, *Theoretical Principles of Sociology, Volume 2 on Microdynamics* (New York: Springer, 2011).

more general self-conception. Yet, we need to be careful here because some role-identities may also be central to a person's more general self-conception. For example, the longer that I have been a professor, the more of my general identity is tied up with my role as professor, and such is often the case for women's role-identities as a mother.

In Figure 6.1, I placed what I term as *core-identity* at the top of a hierarchy that also emphasizes two dimensions of identities: (1) the emotions tied to them and (2) the degree to which we are cognizant of the nature of an identity. I would argue that people will have some difficulty in articulating their core-identity or what some now call *person-identity*. The reason for this is that some dimensions of this identity are unconscious, or even repressed, but these elements still influence how persons act and even how they evaluate themselves. A great deal of emotion is tied up in identities, especially core-identities, and people react very emotionally to failure to verify this level of identity. As a result, they often push the negative emotions that come with failure below the level of consciousness, but this does not mean the emotions go away or the evaluations of others about core-identities are ignored. They are pushed below the level of consciousness, but eventually, the emotions will come out, often in rather transmuted form, as we will see later in discussing more psychoanalytic theories of symbolic interactionists.

At the bottom of the hierarchy in Figure 6.1 are *role-identities*, which people can usually describe with accuracy. Thus, if you asked someone what kind of father, student, professor, mother, worker, etc. they are, they can usually respond with clarity and specificity. These identities are evaluated by

Figure 6.1   Types and Levels of Identity Formation

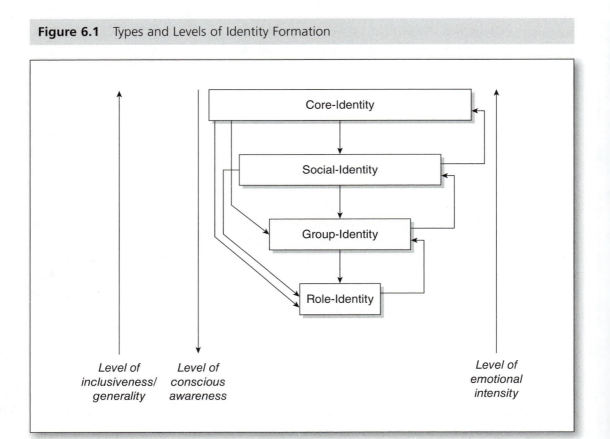

individuals, and so like all identities, there is emotion attached to them, but not to the extent of a core- or person-identity. Yet, as noted above, if a particular role is bound up with a person's fundamental feelings about themselves at the person-identity level, then there will be much more emotion inhering in individuals' description of a particular role-identity.

Between these levels of core- and role-identities are two others that I typically highlight. One is a *group-identity*, which is a step up from a role-identity. These are identities built around membership in, desire to be a member in, or vicarious identification with a group or organization. A fan of a sports team is a good example of group-identity built around often excessive identification. As is all too evident, rabid sports fans are quite emotional about their identification with a team; they can talk about their identity at quite some length, often endlessly. As a student, even after graduation, you may have the identity of once being a member and now an alumnus of a university or college, and people vary enormously in how important this group-identity is. A worker usually has some sense of identity with his or her place of work, even if it is negative, and we rarely have any trouble talking about how we see our workplace. Indeed, like role-identities, group-identities (as well as organizational and community) can carry emotion but remain cognitive in that people can articulate the nature of the identity. Moreover, the identity is generally confined and not highly general, unless group membership in an important part of a person- or core-identity. The final level and type of identity is what is called a *social-identity* in the psychological literature; this identity is about broad social categories that people belong to, such as gender, ethnicity, religion, age, social class, and any social category that is salient in a society. These identities are quite general and must be carried around like person-identities because our gender, age, ethnicity, and other memberships in social categories are often quite visible, but more importantly, there are beliefs, evaluations, expectations, and norms associated with each of these social-identities.[8] People may not like them, or embrace evaluations and expectations, but emotions are almost always tied to social-identities. People have cognitive awareness of the nature of this identity, but if they are ashamed of their social-identity, then emotions and defense mechanisms distort these cognitions, with the result that people's ability to describe their social-identity accurately is less than is normally the case for describing their group- and role-identities.

These are not the only identities found in theory and research on self. Recently, for example, some have argued that there is a separate "moral identity"[9] whereby people have conceptions about how moral they are and how they feel about this morality. This moral identity might be considered a component of a core-identity, but since so much research is being conducted on this question of conscience and morality, it may become a distinctive identity in social science typologies, if only because it has been studied as a distinct level and type of self. But, those who make the argument for a moral identity point out that it affects all of the other levels of identity enumerated in Figure 6.1. Time will tell on how this, and other potential candidates for a new type of identity, shake out in the theoretical literature over the next decade.

---

[8]In the expectation-states literature, these memberships in categoric units are conceptualized as "diffuse status characteristics" about which there are status beliefs about the worth and characteristics of members. These translate into a series of expectations for how these members of social categories should behave.

[9]See, for example, Steven Hitlin, ed., *Handbook of The Sociology of Morality* (New York: Springer, 2010); Steven Hitlin, *Moral Selves, Evil Selves: The Social Psychology of Conscience* (London, UK: Palgrave/Macmillan, 2008)

Hierarchies of Salience and Prominence

Much theorizing on identities sees identity dynamics as revolving around a hierarchy of salience and prominence. The underlying idea in these approaches is that identities constitute a hierarchy of *how important they* are to people in *how many situations*. The more people present a particular identity in situations, the higher in the hierarchy it is, and the more important is this identity to a person. If the identity is verified and accepted by others, it remains in the hierarchy. However, if people do not accept this identity, and consistently so, it will move down the hierarchy and, in extreme cases, disappear. Thus, this literature brings an important force into interaction: people seek to have others verify and confirm those identities that are high in a hierarchical ranking of all identities. Much of what goes on in interaction is an effort to present to others a particular identity with the hope and expectation that others will accept this presentation and, thereby, verify this identity. Identities that get consistently verified, then, will move up and stay high in the hierarchy of salience and prominence. At times, social-structural and cultural constraints restrict the range of identities that can be presented to others, as might be the case in a formal office setting, but even with these restrictions, people can often present multiple identities, and when an identity is high in the salience hierarchy, it is sure to be one of those identities that is added to a person's presentation of self to others. There are some variations in theories using this basic idea of hierarchy, and so, let me outline two of the most important theories.

Stryker's Theory of Identity Salience

Sheldon Stryker[10] argues that people become committed to identities, for a variety of reasons: an identity is positively valued by others and by broader cultural definitions; it is congruent with the perceived expectations of others on whom one will be dependent for identify verification; it is an identity that is part of a more extensive network of persons who have expectations for this identity; and it may be an identity that larger numbers of people, regardless of their network location, expect a person to play.

Identities to which persons have commitments move up the *salience hierarchy*, with the result that individuals will emit role performances to others that are consistent with this highly salient identity. Moreover, identities high in the salience hierarchy are likely to push individuals to perceive that a given situation is an opportunity to present this identity; and more generally, persons are likely to seek out situations where they can present this salient

---

[10]Sheldon Stryker, *Symbolic Interactionism: A Structural Version* (Menlo Park, CA: Benjamin/Cummings, 1980); "Identity Salience and Role Performance: The Relevance of Symbolic Interaction Theory for Family Research," *Journal of Marriage and the Family* (1968): pp. 558–564; "Fundamental Principles of Social Interaction," in *Sociology,* 2nd ed., Neil J. Smelser, ed. (New York: Wiley, 1973), pp. 495–547. For a more recent version of the theory, see Sheldon Stryker and Richard T. Serpe, "Commitment, Identity Salience, and Role Behavior," in *Personality, Roles, and Social Behavior,* eds. William Ickes and Eric Knowles (New York: Springer-Verlag, 1982), pp. 199–218; Richard T. Serpe and Sheldon Stryker, "The Construction of Self and the Reconstruction of Social Relationships," *Advances in Group Processes,* 4 (1987): pp. 41–66; and Sheldon Stryker, "Exploring the Relevance of Social Cognition for the Relationship of Self and Society," in *The Self-Society Dynamic: Cognition, Emotion, and Action,* eds. Judith Howard and Peter L. Callero (Cambridge: Cambridge University Press, 1991), pp. 19–41.

identity. However, if the identity is not verified by others, for whatever reason, it will move down the hierarchy.

Identities link people to structures because people are more likely to play identities that are consistent with cultural beliefs and values, with norms in situations where they have opportunities to present an identity, with networks of persons who have expectations for certain kinds of role performances, and situations where a person is allowed to present an identity. These pressures mean that there will generally be *correspondence* between identities that are highly salient to a person and the expectations inhering in social structures and the cultures of these structures. The self-esteem of a person is dependent upon playing a highly salient identity, and thus self-esteem is also dependent upon meeting the expectations of networks, social structures, and culture. In this way, person, salient identity, roles displaying this identity, social structure, and culture are lined up and generally compatible.

If the structure and culture of a situation change, however, then identity salience and commitment will change, and any identity can change if it is consistent with the person's value commitments. When people experience strong negative emotions in situation, this almost always means that there is discordance with the identity presented and situational expectations generated by networks, social structures, and culture. Individuals will, therefore, frequently have to alter their commitments to an identity and seek out a new identity that is compatible with a situation that has changed. Thus, the emotions attached to an identity are both an early warning system that something is amiss as well as the motivational force that pushes individuals to find either a whole new network of relations or alter an identity. The latter is more likely because people are generally not free to change social structures on which they depend, and thus, an unverified identity will move down the hierarchy, and an identity more consistent with situational expectations will move up the hierarchy.

McCall and Simmons' Hierarchy of Prominence

George McCall and J. L. Simmons focus on role-identities.[11] Role-identities are tied to roles, and these roles are, in turn, tied to social structures and culture. While social structure and culture constrain the roles that a person can play, and how they play these roles, there is always a certain amount of latitude in how a person presents himself or herself to others in a situation. McCall and Simmons posit a *hierarchy of prominence* among various role-identities, which consists of several elements: (a) the idealized view that individuals have of themselves (e.g., smart, funny, intelligent, etc.) that will determine not only which role they will play but also how they will play this role; (b) memories about the extent to which these ideal views of self have been supported by audiences; (c) emotional commitments to those roles that, in the past, have been supported; and (d) the amount of previous investment in time and energy for a particular identity that has been played out in a role.

Because most interactions are somewhat underspecified about how one should behave, this ambiguity gives individuals some flexibility in presenting roles to others. This ambiguity can be reduced by role-taking with other individuals, and through what McCall and Simmons call *an*

---

[11]George P. McCall and J. L. Simmons, *Identities and Interactions* (New York: Basic Books, 1960). A second edition of this book was published in 1978, although the theory remained virtually unchanged.

inner forum (or minded deliberations in G. H. Mead's scheme), persons adjust their roles and the identities embedded in them to accommodate others' dispositions and likely actions, if they can. There are always expressive strategies for orchestrating gestures in order to present a certain kind of self to others during their role-taking, and these expressive and strategically presented gestures will typically present a role-identity high in a person's hierarchy of prominence.

Undergirding this strategic presentation of self is an exchange dynamic (see previous chapter). There can be *extrinsic rewards* in a situation, such as money, and there are almost always *intrinsic rewards*, such as satisfaction, pride, happiness, sense of efficacy, and role support by others. Indeed, one of the most important intrinsic rewards is others' support for a role-identity that a person presents, and individuals are highly motivated to secure this support because it offers the most reward for presenting a role-identity. There is, McCall and Simmons argue, a kind of marketplace for exchanges of rewards, and like any exchange in a quasi markets, individuals try to exchange similar rewards that allow both parties to an interaction to realize a profit—rewards less costs and investments in securing roles. There is also always a calculation of fairness and justice that determines if rewards given to each person are proportional to their respective costs and investments in a particular role-identity.

McCall and Simmons distinguish between *situated self* and *ideal self*. A situated self is the role-identity to which a person is committed in a situation and is most likely to present to others. The elements of a situated self will vary, depending upon the situation where individuals can have somewhat different hierarchies of prominence. The ideal self, like G. H. Mead's self-conception or core-self (see Figure 6.1 above) is more permanent and is almost always present in self-presentations; and thus, this ideal self is generally the self that is highest in the prominence hierarchy. This self, then, is the most salient identity, and individuals fill in elements of other role-identities around this ideal self.

Finally, McCall and Simmons anticipate more psychoanalytically oriented symbolic interactionist approaches by noting that when a self-presentation is not fully accepted by others, individuals will engage in *defensive strategies* to protect themselves. They list a number of potential strategies: (1) *selective perception* of others' gestures so as to ensure identity verification and support; (2) *selective interpretation* of others' gestures; (3) *disavowal of a performance* as not truly indicative to self and *disavowal of the audience* as not important or relevant to self-evaluation; and (4) *riding out* the temporary incongruity between sense of self and others' evaluations of self by drawing upon past memories in which the self presented has indeed been verified. These defensive strategies will not always work, but they can allow individuals to get through situations where self is not perceived to have been verified by others. Since support and verification of a role-identity are the most valuable intrinsic rewards for individuals, emotions run high in the process of mutual role-taking and presentation of role-identities; and so it is not surprising that individuals seek to protect self from painful negative emotions like *shame*.

Emotions, Defensive Strategies, and Defense Mechanisms

A basic principle in all symbolic interactionist theorizing about identity is this: When an identity goes unverified by others, persons will experience powerful negative emotions and be motivated to bring the identity presented and the responses of others back in line, or congruity. McCall and Simmons emphasize adjustments to role behaviors as well as defensive strategies. Another theory that has addressed this issue is Peter J. Burkes' and, at times, Jan E. Stets' Identity Control Theory.[12]

Burke' and Stets' Identity Control Theory

Peter Burke first developed this approach to identity dynamics, and he and Jan E. Stets have recently expanded the theory.[13] The basic argument is that individuals have multiple identities that are only loosely arranged in a hierarchy. Using the identity levels in Figure 6.1, they posit that people evidence a person-level identity or what is also called core-identity in the figure, a number of social-identities, and many potential role-identities. For each of these identities there is what they term a *comparator*, which is an identity standard against which the behaviors of a person and the responses of others are compared to see if indeed behavioral *outputs* by a person and role-taking *inputs* subject to *reflective appraisal* meet identity standards. If they do, then a person experiences positive emotions and continues to play out an identity. If, however, there is a lack of congruence between the comparator, on the one hand, and behavioral outputs of the individual, inputs of people' reaction to behavioral outputs, and reflective appraisal, on the other, then a person will experience negative emotions such as *distress*, *anxiety*, *sadness*, *shame*, and other negative emotions about self.

Humans are cybernetic organisms in that they seek to sustain an equilibrium for each identity. Thus, when an identity goes unverified, and a person experiences negative emotions, this individual will work to restore the balance by (a) adjusting behavioral outputs that allows others to verify the identity and (b) presenting a new identity with a different identity standards and comparator. There is of course an alternative, not part of Burke and Stet's theory: invoke one of the defensive strategies suggested by McCall and Simmons—selective perception and interpretation of others' responses, disavowal of the audience's right to evaluate a set of behavioral outputs, or disavowal the behavioral outputs as indicative a person's self. This is about as far as most identity theories will go, but another, much smaller group of symbolic interactionists emphasizes repression and use of more powerful defense mechanisms to sustain, at the least, a sense of equilibrium. But, once emotions are repressed, the dynamics of self change significantly. Repressed emotions will often transmute to other negative emotions, and individual will no longer have full cognitive access to the original repressed feelings, with the result that this person's actual behaviors may not correspond to self-perceptions of these behaviors. Moreover, others' evaluation of these behaviors will be difficult to interpret because these others may be reacting to emotional cues about which the person has little awareness.

---

[12]Peter J. Burke, "The Self: Measurement Implications from a Symbolic Interactionist Perspective," *Social Psychology Quarterly* 43 (1980): pp. 18–20; "An Identity Model for Network Exchange," *American Sociological Review* 62 (1997): pp. 134–150; "Attitudes, Behavior, and the Self," in *The Self-Society Dynamic,* eds. Judith Howard and Peter L. Callero (cited in note 10), pp. 189–208, "Identity Processes and Social Stress," *American Sociological Review* 56 (1991): pp. 836–849; P. J. Burke and D. C. Reitzes, "An Identity Theory Approach to Commitment," *Social Psychology Quarterly* 54 (1991): pp. 239–251; P. J. Burke and Jan E. Stets, "Trust and Commitment through Self Verification," *Social Psychology Quarterly* 62 (1999): pp. 347–366; and Peter J. Burke and Jan E. Stets, *Identity Theory* (New York: Oxford University Press).

[13]Peter J. Burke and Jan E. Stets, *Identity Theory* (New York: Oxford University Press, 2009).

Thus, in Burke's (and Stet's) theory, the more salient an identity in a role, the more motivated are individuals to achieve a sense of congruence between the expectations established by the identity standard and the responses of others in a situation. When the responses of others match the expectations dictated by an identity standard, the more positive are the emotions experienced by individuals and the greater is their level of self-esteem. People experience enhanced positive emotions when self is verified by others; and as a result, they develop positive emotions, trust, and commitments to these others. In contrast, the less responses of others match an identity standard, the more likely are the emotions experienced by individuals to be negative, with such incongruence between expectations set by an identity standard and the responses of others increasing when individuals have (a) multiple and incompatible identity standards from two or more role-identities, (b) an over-controlled self in which the elements of the identity are tightly woven into inflexible identity standards, (c) little practice in displaying an identity in a role, and (d) consistent failure in their efforts to change and/or leave the situation.

The intensity of negative emotions from these failures to verify an identity increases with (a) the salience of an identity in the situation, (b) the significance of the others who have not verified an identity, and (c) the degree of incongruity whether above or below expectations associated with an identity standard. In contrast, the intensity of negative emotions from the failure to verify an identity will decrease over time as the identity standard is readjusted downward so as to lower expectations, thereby making congruence between identity standards and reflected appraisals of people's response to behavior output. Yet, like so many symbolic interactionist approaches, the Burke-Stets model does not consider another way to create congruence: repression of the negative emotions aroused when an identity is not verified or supported by others. This oversight has called for more psychoanalytical theories.

Psychoanalytic Symbolic Interactionist Theories

Thomas Scheff and Jonathan Turner are the most prominent theorists who have blended identity theories from symbolic interactionism with the basic argument of psychoanalytical theory. The general line of argument is that when interpersonal behaviors lead individuals to experience *shame*, persons often repress in some way this very painful emotion. When they do so, the person no longer has direct access to this shame but will experience other emotions such as *anger* and will act in ways that further disrupt interpersonal processes. The important point is that people often protect self by repressing negative emotions—*shame* but also other emotions like *anger*, *guilt*, *humiliation*, *frustration*, etc.—that signal incongruity between people's presentations of self and others' negative responses to efforts to get this self verified. Let me first review Scheff's theory.

Scheff on Pride, Shame, and Interpersonal Attunement

One of the great shortcomings of George Herbert Mead's synthesis is that emotions are not examined. The potential to address emotions surrounding self and identity was there in the sources of Mead's synthesis; indeed, Charles Horton Cooley[14] emphasized that people have feelings about themselves as they read the gestures of others in role-taking.

---

[14]Cooley, *Human Nature and the Social Order* (full citation in note 4).

For Cooley, people are in a constant state of low-level *pride* and *shame*, depending upon what they "see" in the looking glass. When the gestures of others signal that a person has behaved properly, this person will experience mild levels of *pride*. But, when the gestures of others signal that a person has acted inappropriately, the negative feelings about self will revolve around various levels of *shame*.

Symbolic interactionists who have followed Cooley as much as Mead have generally been sympathetic to psychoanalytic theorizing because, as Sigmund Freud[15] emphasized, negative emotions like *shame* and *guilt* are painful, and individuals will often invoke defense mechanisms to protect self. Thomas Scheff has for many decades been the most persistent advocate of incorporating at least elements of psychoanalytical theory into symbolic interactionism, although he has been reluctant to characterize his theory as I have (that is, as "psychoanalytic").

Scheff[16] adopts Cooley's view that humans are in a constant state of self-feeling, particularly with respect to *pride* and *shame*. This state of self-feeling is an outcome of the fact that people are also in a constant state of self-evaluation, even when they are alone and think back on situations; in addition, as they evaluate themselves in situations, they will experience either *pride* or *shame*. Pride is a positive emotion that verifies self and thus generates a sense of well-being; moreover, pride generally makes individuals more attuned to others and more willing to offer supportive responses to these others. Thus, pride is a key mechanism by which strong social bonds and social solidarity are generated in face-to-face encounters and, ultimately, in societies. In contrast, *shame* is a negative emotion and, if unrecognized by a person, leads to a loss of attunement with others and, if widespread among many others, in a society as a whole.

Thus, *pride* and *shame* not only have consequences for individuals' self-feelings; they also affect attunement in social relations and, potentially, the viability of larger-scale social structures, including the society as a whole. Pride and shame, Scheff argues, are emotions that are essential to the social order; and yet, they are virtually invisible, for several reasons. One is that they are generally experienced at relatively low levels of intensity. Another is that they can be repressed to a certain degree—*pride* because a person does not want to reveal "too much" pride to others (less they see it as *vanity*) or too much shame to others and to oneself. Another reason for the apparent invisibility of *shame* is that it is often repressed. Scheff borrows from the psychoanalyst, Helen Lewis,[17] to emphasize that shame is often unacknowledged, denied, or repressed. When such is the case, a shame-anger cycle can be initiated in which *shame* is transmuted to *anger*, with each outburst of anger causing more *shame* that is denied in ways escalating the intensity of the next outburst of *anger*.

Following Lewis, Scheff emphasizes that one path to denying shame is through the experience of *overt, undifferentiated shame*, in which the person has painful feelings that come with *shame* but hides from the real source of these feelings: shame. The shame is disguised

---

[15]Sigmund Freud, *The Interpretation of Dreams* (London: Hogarth Press, 1900).

[16]For examples of Scheff's work, see "Shame and Conformity: The Deference-Emotion System," *American Sociological Review* 53 (1988): pp. 395–406; "Socialization of Emotion: Pride and Shame as Causal Agents," in *Research Agendas in The Sociology of Emotions*, ed. T. Kemper (Albany, NY: SUNY Press), pp. 281–304; "Shame and the Social Bond: A Sociological Theory," *Sociological Theory* 18 (2000): pp. 84–99; "Shame and Community: Social Components in Depression," *Psychiatry* 64 (2001): pp. 212–224; "Shame and Self in Society," *Symbolic Interaction* 26 (2002): pp. 239–262.

[17]Helen Lewis, *Shame and Guilt in Neurosis* (New York: International Universities Press, 1971).

by words and gestures signaling feelings other than shame. People can blush, slow their speech, lower the auditory levels of their voices, and utter such words as "foolish," "silly," "stupid," and other such labels that denote negative feelings but hide that fact that these feelings have arisen because of shame.

Another path to denying the shame is to *bypass the shame*. When this defense mechanism is employed, individuals engage in hyperactive behavior such as rapid speech and demonstrative gesturing before the shame can be fully experienced for what it is. The result is for individuals to avoid the pain of shame but at a high cost of having to live with unacknowledged shame that, in turn, will often disrupt social relations.

Later, Scheff began to term these two paths to denial of shame *underdistancing* (overt, undifferentiated) and *overdistancing* (bypassed) shame. In both cases, the shame is repressed from conscious awareness and, ultimately, leads to anger and hostility that, in turn, disrupt interpersonal attunement. Without attunement, it is difficult for individuals to develop mutual respect and solidarity. In Figure 6.2, I have drawn out Scheff's underlying model.

Across the top of the figure, the receipt of deference from others leads to positive self-evaluations and a sense of pride, which encourages interpersonal attunement, mutual respect, and social solidarity. It is the dynamics below this top row of processes that is the cause of problems for persons and, potentially, larger-scale social structures. When individuals perceive that others exhibit a lack of deference, they experience negative self-evaluations that cause shame. If, however, the shame can be "acknowledged" and seen for what it is, it can lead to efforts at *interpersonal attunement* between a person and others, ultimately causing mutual respect, and social solidarity. When the same is denied by overdistancing or underdistancing, it can initiate the anger-shame cycle that ensures that individuals will lack proper deference to others and perceive a lack of deference from others. In turn, the negative evaluations will cause shame that, if acknowledged at this point, can perhaps lead to attunement and mutual respect, but if the anger-shame cycle becomes habitual, then the denial of shame only stokes the emotional hostility that sustains the cycle at the bottom of Figure 6.2.

Figure 6.3 outlines some of the more macrostructural implications of the anger-shame cycle outlined in Figure 6.2.[18] If social structures and the culture in the broader society systematically generate shame, as is often the case when relations are hierarchical, but at the same time, impose prohibitions against acknowledging shame, societies can reveal the potential for collective violence. If enough persons in enough encounters over long periods of time are forced to endure shame but cannot acknowledge it but, instead, must repress their shame, the lack of interpersonal attunement and the *shame–anger–more shame–more hostility* cycle is sustained, individuals in this state can be mobilized for collective action, often of a highly violent nature. Thus, if the experience of shame is widespread and if cultural prohibitions inhibit individuals from acknowledging their shame, denial of this negative emotion can become an emotional powder keg in a society. Events at the micro-interpersonal level can, therefore, have far reaching consequences for the stability of macrostructural formations and their cultures.

---

[18]See for examples of work on conflict and violence from repressed shame the following: Thomas J. Scheff and Suzanne M. Retzinger, *Emotions and Violence: Shame and Rage in Destructive Conflicts* (Lexington, MA: Lexington Books, 1991). For an example of work arguing much the same as Scheff from a psychiatrist, see Vamik Volkan, *Killing in the Name of Identity: A Study in Bloody Conflicts* (Charlottesville, VA: Pitchstone Press, 2006), *Bloodlines: From Ethnic Pride to Ethnic Terrorism* (Charlottesville, VA: Pitchstone Press, 1999).

Figure 6.2 Scheff's Model of Emotions, Attunement, and Solidarity

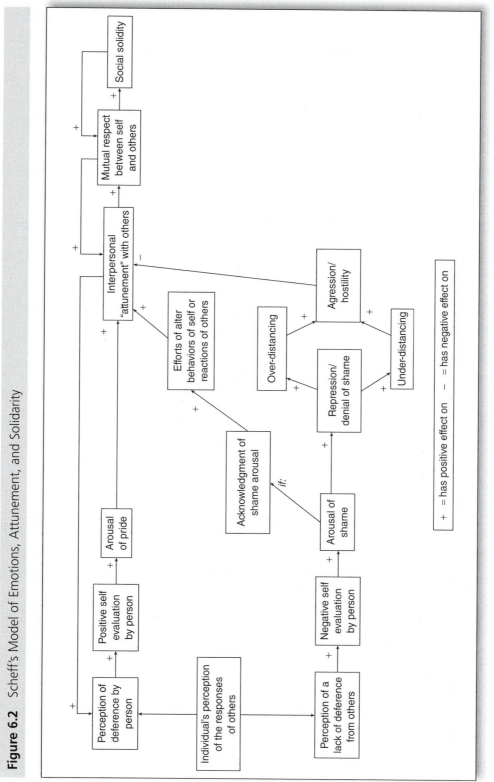

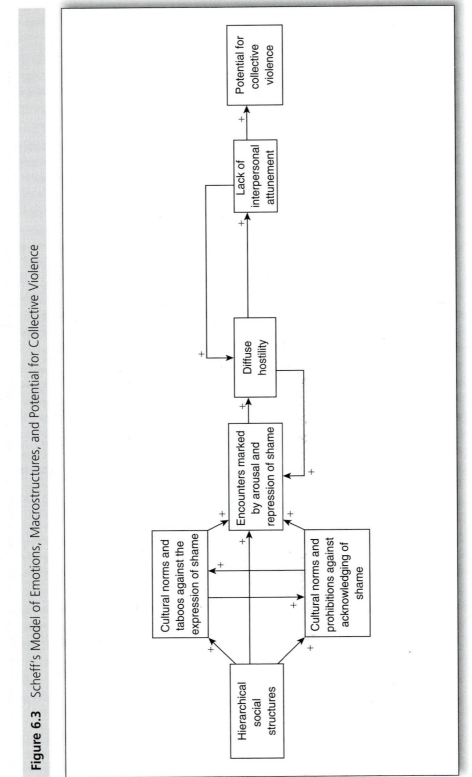

Figure 6.3 Scheff's Model of Emotions, Macrostructures, and Potential for Collective Violence

Jonathan Turner's Theory of Transactional Needs

As part of my general theory of microdynamic processes,[19] I see *transactional needs* as a critical force in human interaction. Humans have certain fundamental need-states that, to varying degrees, are always activated when individuals interact. These are transactional needs in two senses: First, some of these needs and typically all of them are activated during interaction; and second, success or failure in meeting these needs dramatically affects the flow of interaction. Here, I will only focus on the most important need in this hierarchy of need-states: the need to verify the identities making up self. As Figure 6.1 on page 100 summarizes, I have come to visualize self as composed of four fundamental *identities*, although people can probably have an identity about almost anything. For example, as noted earlier, recently there has been great interest in people's moral identities or the extent to which, and the arenas into which, people see themselves as "moral." Still, the most central identities are (1) *core-identity*, or the fundamental cognitions and feelings that people have about themselves that are generally salient in almost all situations (some have termed this *person-identity*); (2) *social-identities*, or the cognitions and feelings that people have of themselves as members of social categories (for example, gender, sexual preference, ethnicity, class, or any social category) that define people as distinctive and that generally lead to differential evaluation of memberships in social categories; (3) *group-identities*, or cognitions and feelings about self that stem from membership in, or identification with, corporate units revealing divisions of labor (groups, communities, and organizations being the most likely sources of a group identity); and (4) *role-identities* or the roles that people play in any social context, but particularly the roles associated with membership in the divisions of labor in corporate units and, at times, memberships in social categories or what I term *categoric units*.[20] I am skeptical that there is a neat linear hierarchy of prominence or salience among identities, as is posited by most identity theories, but I do believe that some are more general than others, as was summarized in Figure 6.1.

The dynamics of identities reveal many of the cybernetic processes outlined in Burke's theory. People orchestrate their behaviors in an effort to verify any or all of the four identities in a situation; if others signal their acceptance of an identity or identities, a person will experience positive emotions from *satisfaction* at the lower-intensity end to *joy* and *pride* at the higher-intensity end of positive emotions. In contrast, if an identity is not verified, individuals will experience negative emotions such as *anger*, *fear*, *embarrassment*, *shame*, *guilt*, and many other negative emotions. When people become aware of their negative emotions, these emotions signal to them that, *a la* Stryker's argument, something has gone wrong in the presentation of self and that,

---

[19]See, for examples, my *A Theory of Social Interaction* (Stanford, CA: Stanford University Press, 1988); *Face-to-Face* and *Theoretical Principles of Sociology, Volume 2 on Microdynamics* (cited in note 7); *Human Emotions: A Sociological Theory* (London: Routledge, 2008); "Toward a Theory of Embedded Encounters," *Advances in Group Processes* 17 (2000): pp. 285–322; Jonathan H. Turner and Jan E. Stets, "The Moral Emotions," in *Handbook of The Sociology of Emotions*, Jan E. Stets and Jonathan H. Turner, eds. (New York: Springer, 2006), pp. 544–568; Jonathan H. Turner, "Emotions and Social Structure: Toward a General Theory," in *Emotions and Social Structure*, D. Robinson and J. Clay-Warner, eds. (New York: Elsevier, 2008), pp. 319–342; Jonathan Turner, "Self, Emotions, and Extreme Violence: Extending Symbolic Interactionist Theorizing," *Symbolic Interaction* 30 (2008): pp. 275–30l; "Toward A Theory of Interpersonal Processes," in *Sociological Social Psychology*, J. Chin and J. Cardell, eds. (Boston, MA: Allyn and Bacon, 2008), pp. 65–95; Jonathan Turner, "Identities, Emotions, and Interaction Processes," *Symbolic Interaction* 34 (2011): 330–339.

[20]See Turner, *Face-to-Face* and *Theoretical Principles of Sociology*, volume 2 (both cited in note 7).

following Burke's theory, motivates individuals to re-appraise their behavior and modify their actions so as to secure verification of an identity. But, these dynamics only unfold *if* a person becomes fully aware that an identity has not been verified.

As McCall and Simons suggest, people often invoke a variety of "defensive strategies" to protect self from this fate. People can engage in selective perception and/or interpretation of the responses of others; they often disavow the audience that has rejected their claims to verification; and they often leave situations where they cannot have identities confirmed by others. Yet, I do not think that McCall and Simons go far enough; people often repress the negative emotions that have come from failure to verify an identity. They simply push these feelings below the level of consciousness and do not feel them consciously, although the emotions may still be evident to others or become transmuted to a new, often more volatile negative emotion that others must endure. Thus, true defense mechanisms break the cybernetic cycle outlined by Burke and implied in other identity theories. The break prevents individuals from accurate "reflected appraisals" among their identity standard, behaviors, and others responses to behaviors.

In Table 6.1, I enumerate various types of *defense mechanisms*, seeing *repression* as the master mechanism that removes emotions from consciousness; then, additional types of defense mechanism may be subsequently activated: *displacement* (venting emotions directed at self on others), *projection* [imputing the repressed emotion(s) to other(s)], *sublimation* (converting negative emotions into positive emotional energy), *reaction formation* (converting intense negative emotions into positive emotions directed at others who caused the negative emotion), and *attribution* (imputing the source cause of emotional reactions). The first five defense mechanisms are those often posited by those working in the psychoanalytic tradition, while the last— *attribution*—comes from cognitive psychology (and earlier, from Gestalt psychology).

Attribution is generally not considered a defense mechanism, but I think that it may be the most sociologically important mechanism. People make attributions for their experiences, and they generally make self-attributions (that is, see themselves as responsible) when experiencing positive

Table 6.1   Repression, Defense, Transmutation, and Targeting Emotions

Repressed Emotions	Defense Mechanism	Transmutation to	Target
anger, sadness, fear shame, guilt, and alienation	displacement	anger	others, corporate units and categoric units
anger, sadness, fear, shame, guilt, and alienation	projection	little, but some anger	imputation of anger, sadness, fear, shame or guilt to dispositional state of others
anger, sadness, fear, shame, guilt, and alienation	reaction formation	positive emotions	others, corporate units, categoric units
anger, sadness, fear, shame, guilt, and alienation	sublimation	positive emotions	tasks in corporate units
anger, sadness, fear shame, guilt, and alienation	attribution	anger	others, corporate units, categoric units

emotions, whereas with negative emotions, they may blame others, categories of others, and social structures in an effort to protect self from having negative self-feelings.

This *proximal bias* for positive emotions to be attributed to self or others in the immediate situation and the *distal bias* for negative emotions to target more remote objects as responsible for these negative feelings have important implications for people's commitment to others and social structures. People feel positive emotions about themselves and perhaps immediate others when experiencing the positive emotions that come with identity verification. They feel that they have been positively sanctioned and have met situational expectations, and in so doing, they feel good about themselves because their identity or identities have been verified. In contrast, when people have not met expectations, have been negatively sanctioned, and hence have failed to confirm an identity in a situation, the negative emotions aroused, such as *shame*, are too painful and are repressed; then more remote social units, such as members of a social category or the social structures of a corporate unit, are blamed for their feelings. In this way, despite feeling negative emotions, a person can protect self by seeing objects outside of self as causally responsible for his or her negative feelings. These negative emotions generate prejudices against members of social categories (by gender, ethnicity, religious affiliation, for example) and alienation and/or loss of commitment to social structures. In contrast, positive emotions increase commitments to others and situations.

Yet, if emotions have these proximal and distal biases, how are more remote objects, such as social structures, to be the targets of commitments by individuals when self-verification, meeting expectations, and receiving positive sanctions from others activate the proximal bias—thereby, remaining local, tied to encounters at the micro level of social organizations? What would allow for positive emotions to break the centripetal force of the proximal bias built into attribution processes? My answer is that when people *consistently experience* positive emotions in particular types of situations, they begin to make attributions to the larger social structures in which these situations are embedded. As they do so, they develop positive feelings about, and commitments to, these structures because they see these structures as causally responsible for the verification of self and the positive feelings that arise from identity verification.

In this manner, consistent self-verification will ultimately lead to commitments to those social structures in which encounters have aroused the positive emotions that come with self-verification. And, the more identities that are verified, the greater will these commitments ultimately be. Indeed, if a group-identity with particular types of corporate units or even a whole society did not already exist, it is likely to form when individuals validate other identities within a particular type of social structure. And to the extent that other identities are tied to roles in divisions of labor and are verified in encounters within this division of labor, identity dynamics become the underlying force behind commitments to this social structure and perhaps the larger institutional domain in which this structure is lodged. For example, a good student who has consistently been rewarded and had the role-identity of student verified will, over time, develop commitments to successive schools and eventually the entire institutional domain of education (compare my argument with Lawler et al., pp. 86–91, whose exchange theory is very much like my theory from entirely different sources and traditions).

In this way, forces like transactional needs for verification of self can have large effects on more macro-level social structures, and vice versa. Macrostructures that set people up for success in verifying role-identities and any other identities tied to these roles in groups and organizations will reap what they sow: commitments from individuals. And these commitments may eventually move to the institutional domains or whole society in which these groups and organizations are embedded.

Conclusion

Symbolic interactionism has carried the synthesis of George Herbert Mead into the twenty-first century, and in so doing, it has come to emphasize the importance of identities in interaction and the dynamics revolving around individuals' efforts to have their identities verified. But, as is evident with Stryker's, McCall and Simons', Burke and Stets', Scheff's, and my theories, there has also been a serious effort to connect these identity dynamics to social structures and cultures. Identities can only be played out within the confines of culture and structure, which set limits on which identities can be presented in what manner; and once the verification of identities becomes tied to social structure and culture, they can operate to sustain and reinforce social structures. Identities that are not viable in a situation will move down the hierarchy of salience or prominence, and new identities more compatible with structure and culture will move up, thus increasing congruence among self, social structure, and culture in a society.

In more psychoanalytic oriented theories, the arousal of negative emotions around self-presentations to others, the negative emotions experienced when others do not verify self or accept particular lines of behavior more generally, lead a person to experience negative emotions like *shame*, which if not fully acknowledged and/or if repressed will transmute into other emotions and associated behaviors that break the social bond. Once the social bond is broken, interactions become disruptive and destroy group solidarity. When emotions are repressed, they often transmute into anger and other negative emotions that disrupt interaction and ensure that persons will have trouble verifying their identities, which only leads to more negative emotions.

Emotions aroused at the level of interpersonal behavior are subject to attributions by individuals as to who or what causes these emotions. Positive emotions lead to positive sanctions toward others and, typically, stay local in the situations where they were first aroused. Negative emotions tend to be more distal because of the effects of repression to protect self. When negative emotions are repressed, they often transmute into anger and anger-driven cognitive states like prejudice that target social structures, culture, and categories of others—thereby protecting self and the local situation. Thus, many macro-level processes, such as conflict, ethnic violence, and mass mobilizations of angry persons can be often tied to what people have experienced at the level of interaction and in their efforts to get identities verified.

Verification of identities consistently across situations begins to break the proximal bias of positive emotions, causing people to make external attributions to local groups, and then the larger social structures in which groups are almost always embedded. This embedding generates conduits for positive emotions to move outward to macrostructures and potentially the whole society, creating commitments and legitimacy for macrostructures built ultimately from individuals at the micro level to verify key identities across many diverse micro-level interactions.

Thus, theoretical sociology has taken Mead's ideas considerably beyond his original formulation, and so we can conclude by outlining the basic elements of symbolic interactionism as it has developed over the last one-hundred years.

1. Individuals are born into ongoing social activity constrained by social structures and regulated by culture. Individuals will learn and retain in their behavioral repertoire those behaviors that facilitate adaptation to ongoing patterns of cooperative behavior.

2. The first critical behavioral capacity that individuals learn is *conventional gestures* that carry the same meaning for the person sending and receiving communication. Such capacities are adaptive because they allow individuals to effectively communicate their needs and intentions.

3. With the adaptive capacity for using conventional gestures, individuals acquire the capacity to *role take* with other and to place themselves in the role of these others and to determine their perspective on, and likely course of action in, a situation, and thereby, to cooperate with these others in ongoing coordinated activity. Over time, the ability to role take expands so that individuals can role take with

   A. Multiple others at the same time engaged in coordinated activities

   B. Others who are not present in the situation

   C. Generalized others that personify values, beliefs, attitudes, and perspectives of situations, groups, organizations, communities, institutional domains, and even the entire society

4. With role-taking comes the capacity for *mind*, or the ability to imagine alternative courses of action, to visualize their likely consequences in a situation, and to select that course of action that will best facilitate cooperation with others.

5. With the capacity for (2), (3), and (4) above, individuals acquire the ability to see themselves as an object in a situation, to read and interpret the gestures of others for what they say about a person's presentation of self, to evaluate self from the perspective of others and generalized others, and to derive images and conceptions of themselves in a situation.

6. These images of self will, over time, crystallize into *conceptions of self* that make up a series of identities that, in turn, individuals seek to verify in their interactions with others. These identities can develop along several basic dimensions:

   A. *Core- or person-identity*, which is the more permanent and stable cognitions and emotions that persons feel about themselves in all situations

   B. *Social-identities*, which are those conceptions, evaluations, and emotions of self tied to memberships in social categories that are salient in a situation and, more broadly, in a society

   C. *Group-identities*, which are conceptions of self and states of emotional arousal tied to identification with, or membership in, groups, organizations, and communities

   D. *Role-identities*, which are conceptions of self and emotions of self arising from incumbency in social structures and playing roles in this structure

7. Identities can be arranged into hierarchies of prominence and salience, which determine how often, when, and where a particular identity will be presented to others.

8. Identities are one of the most powerful motivating forces in human action because all identities in all situations are presented with an eye to having others verify the identity

   A. When identities are verified by others, individuals will experience positive emotions, positively sanction others, and develop commitments to others and the situation

   B. When identities are not verified by others, individuals will experience negative emotions and seek to bring their identity presentations and reactions of others into congruence through a number of ways:

      1. Adjusting behaviors so that others will verify an identity

      2. Changing the identity presented to others

      3. Avoiding situations where identities are not verified

      4. Engaging in defensive strategies, including the following:

         a. Selective perception of the responses of others

         b. Selective interpretation of the responses of others

         c. Disavowing behaviors that led to a failure to verify self

         d. Disavowing the audience as having the right to evaluate self

         e. Using credits from past experiences where identity was verified to ride out a particular situations where it was not

         f. Repressing negative emotions associated with failure to verify self

9. Verification or failure to verify self at any identity level can have repercussions for person's commitments to others, situation, and broader social structure, depending upon the attributions that individuals make for their emotional experiences

   A. When self and identities are verified, individuals develop positive emotions for self and others and commitments to others and the local situation

   B. When self and identities are verified consistently across a larger number of situations within a variety of institutional domains in a society, individuals will experience positive emotions that will begin to target macrostructures and, thereby, lead them to develop commitments to more macro social structures and their cultures

   C. When self and identities are not verified, individuals will generally make more external attributions to categories of others and external social structures rather than to self or others in the local situation and, in so doing, lower their commitments to these external social structures

10. Patterns of social organization and culture constrain individuals are created, sustained, and changed by individuals revealing the above behavioral capacities, with verification of self leading to commitments that sustain social structure and culture and with failure to verify self leading to negative emotions targeting external social structures and their cultures. Thus, the positive emotions arising for verification of self sustain and legitimate social structures, whereas the negative emotions arising from failure to verify self can lead to change in social structure and cultures when sufficient numbers of individuals have such negative emotional experiences.

CHAPTER 7

Dramaturgical Theorizing

The Durkheimian Roots of Dramaturical Theory

In the late 1890s, Emile Durkheim began to search for the mechanisms generating solidarity in human societies.[1] Durkheim had long taught a course on the sociology of religion, but his thinking began to change once he started searching more explicitly for the mechanisms producing solidarity. In his last great work—*The Elementary Forms of the Religious Life*[2]—Durkheim reviewed the data on what he thought to be the most primitive society—the Arunta aboriginals of central Australia. By removing the complexity of more industrial societies, Durkheim felt that he could see the essential mechanisms for social solidarity. From the descriptions of the Arunta in and around Alice Springs, Australia, the Arunta from outlying areas would periodically gather, which in turn set off animated talk and emotions, or what Durkheim termed "effervescence," among those gathered. Over time, apparently, the Arunta began to see an external force pushing on them as they gathered in what can best be described as a kind of carnival; furthermore, feeling this force, they needed to symbolize it with totems celebrating the power of supernatural forces. Once in place, these totems would be the objects of rituals reaffirming the sense of solidarity in these preliterate societies. Durkheim thought that these carnivals were the origins of religion, but for his purposes, they were also the basis of group solidarity. It is through (a) interaction, (b) contagious emotional effervescence, (c) symbolic representations of the power of this effervescence in totems, and (d) rituals directed to these totems that solidarity ultimately arises. Among preliterate populations, these forces led to the creation of religion as the Arunta and other preliterate populations symbolized the power of their own relations, believing it to be the power of the supernatural, when in fact, it was the power of people themselves.

Durkheim also began to realize that in his earlier work in 1892—*The Division of Labor in Society*[3]—he had not quite captured a key element of integration in complex societies. When societies are differentiated, it is still possible to develop society-wide solidarities—emotionally charged commitments to the social whole—by rituals directed as highly generalized symbols

---

[1]Emile Durkheim, *The Elementary Forms of the Religious Life* (New York: Free Press, 1947, originally published in 1912), but long before publishing this book, Durkheim had wondered about whether he had missed a key force of societal integration in his earlier work.

[2]Ibid.

[3]Emile Durkheim, *The Division of Labor in Society* (New York: Free Press, 1947, originally published in 1892).

representing the entire society. People may lead somewhat different daily lives because of their diverse locations in the divisions of labor in differentiated societies, but they can still "worship" like the Arunta the larger social whole—for Durkheim, all of French society—by enacting emotion-arousing rituals to totems symbolizing the society. The totems did not have to be physical objects like an actual totem pole; they could be other forms of symbolism, such as the French's long standing insistence on not "polluting" their language with words and phrases from other languages. Indeed, Durkheim as a dominant figure in education worked to have the school systems secularized in France, with the teacher substituting for the priest in religion and leading students in daily rituals directed at totems, such as the flag and other symbols of France.

This line of argument had enormous influence on a number of modern-day theorists, such as Randall Collins's analysis of interaction rituals in his conflict theory (see Chapter 3), but Collins was influenced not just by Durkheim but also by the founder of dramaturgical theorizing in the United States, Erving Goffman. I have emphasized Durkheim above because dramaturgy is often seen as a variant of symbolic interactionism, but Goffman did not see himself as an intellectual descendant of George Herbert Mead (see last chapter), the intellectual founder of symbolic interactionism. Goffman always claimed that he was a Durkheimian, focusing on the processes by which ritualized actions of individuals in face-to-face encounters make societies possible. He saw self as important in this process because individuals do make self-presentations to others, but these are not so much reflective of a deeply sedimented sense of identity as strategic practices in a given situation to carry out a line of action vis-à-vis others. He was doubtful that people have stable identities that they are always seeking to verify; instead, self is part of a strategic game to bring off an interaction and realize whatever purposes are being pursued by individuals. Thus, there is a very large shift in emphasis with dramaturgy compared to symbolic interactionism.

Erving Goffman's Dramaturgical Theory of Encounters

The Dramaturgical Metaphor

Goffman's approach is termed *dramaturgy* because of the analogy made to the theater—an analogy that is as least as old as Shakespeare. For Goffman, interaction typically has a normative script or a relatively clear set of expectations about how individuals are supposed to behave. Yet, within the script, a considerable amount of dramatic license is possible; individuals can play the role demanded by the script in many ways, with a personal style reflecting the kind of "line" that a person is taking in his or her self-presentations. There is also a stage that has an ecology (configuration of space) and props that can be used to carry off a dramatic performance. There is always an audience, whether actually present or imagined by actor. Self is presented to establish a particular kind of connection with the audience. Finally, Goffman emphasized that actors are always behaving strategically; they often have agendas, and their behaviors to an audience reflect their agenda, even if the agenda is hidden from the audience. For example, a "con man" strategically presents self to the audience (e.g., sincere, trustworthy, honest) but, in fact, hides the real strategic purposes (e.g., to cheat the "mark" of money). So, the analogy to the theater is tempered by the people that deliberately manipulate their self-presentation so as "to put on an act" for strategic and often nefarious purposes.

Encounters

Goffman generally employed the terms *unfocused* and *focused* to denote two basic types of interaction. *Unfocused interaction* "consists of interpersonal communications that result solely by virtue of persons being in one another's presence, as when two strangers across the room from each other check up on each other's clothing, posture, and general manner, while each modifies his (her) own demeanor because he himself is under observation."[4] Such unfocused interaction is, Goffman argued, an important part of the interaction order, for much of what people do is exchange glances and monitor each other in public places. *Focused interaction*, in contrast, "occurs when people effectively agree to sustain for a time a single focus of cognitive and visual attention, as in a conversation, a board game, or a joint task sustained by a close face-to-face circle of contributors."[5]

Focused Encounters

An encounter is defined as *focused* interaction revealing the following characteristics:[6]

1. A single visual and cognitive focus of attention

2. A mutual and preferential openness to verbal communication

3. A heightened mutual relevance of acts

4. An eye-to-eye ecological huddle, maximizing mutual perception and monitoring

5. An emergent "we" feeling of solidarity and flow of feeling

6. A ritual and ceremonial punctuation of openings, closings, entrances, and exits

7. A set of procedures for corrective compensation for deviant acts

To sustain itself, an encounter develops a *membrane*, or penetrable barrier to the larger social world in which the interaction is located. The membrane of an encounter is sustained by a set of rules. In *Encounters*, Goffman lists several; later, in what is probably his most significant work, *Interaction Ritual*, he lists several more.[7] Let me combine both discussions by listing the rules that guide focused interaction in encounters:

1. *Rules of irrelevance*, which "frame" a situation as excluding certain materials (attributes of participants, psychological states, cultural values and norms, etc.)

2. *Rules of transformation*, which specify how materials moving through the membrane created by rules of irrelevance are to be altered to fit into the interaction

---

[4]Erving Goffman, *Encounters: Two Studies in the Sociology of Interaction* (Indianapolis, IN: Bobbs-Merrill, 1961), p. 30.

[5]Ibid., p 31.

[6]Ibid., p. 33; see the key earlier work where these ideas were first developed: Erving Goffman, *The Presentation of Self in Everyday Life* (Garden City, NY: Anchor, 1959).

[7]Erving Goffman, *Interaction Ritual: Essays on Face-to-Face Behavior* (Garden City, NY: Anchor, 1967).

3. *Rules of realized resources*, which provide a general schemata and framework for expression and interpretation for activities among participants

4. *Rules of talk*, which are the procedures, conventions, and practices guiding the flow of verbalizations with respect to

   a. Maintaining a single focus of attention

   b. Establishing "clearance cues" for determining when one speaker is done and another can begin

   c. Determining how long and how frequently any one person can hold the floor

   d. Regulating interruptions and lulls in the conversation

   e. Sanctioning participants whose attention wanders to matters outside the conversation

   f. Ensuring that nearby people do not interfere with the conversation

   g. Guiding the use of politeness and tact, even in the face of disagreements

5. *Rules of self-respect*, which encourage participants to honor with tact and etiquette their respective efforts to present themselves in a certain light

Interaction is thus guided by complex configurations of rules that individuals learn how to use and apply in different types of encounters, logged in varying types of gatherings and social occasions. The "reality" of the world is, to a very great extent, sustained by people's ability to invoke and use these rules. When these rules are operating effectively, individuals develop a "state of euphoria," or what Randall Collins has termed enhanced "emotional energy" (see Chapter 3). However, encounters are vulnerable to "dysphoria" or tension when these rules do not exclude troublesome external materials or fail to regulate the flow of interaction. Such failures are seen by Goffman as incidents or *breaches*. When these breaches can be effectively handled by tact and corrective procedures, they are then viewed as integrations because they are blended into the ongoing encounter. The key mechanism for avoiding dysphoria and maintaining the integration of the encounter is the use of ritual.

Ritual

In *Interaction Ritual*, Goffman's great contribution is the recognition that minor, seemingly trivial, and everyday rituals—such as "Hello, how are you?" "Good morning," "Please, after you," and other standardized forms of talk—are crucial to the maintenance of social order—just as much as the larger rituals emphasized by Durkheim among the Arunta aborigines were seen to sustain the social order. In Goffman's own words, his goal is to reformulate "Émile Durkheim's social psychology in a modern dress"[8] by recognizing that, when individuals gather and begin to interact, their behaviors are highly ritualized. That is, actors punctuate each phase of interpersonal contact with stereotypical sequences of behavior that invoke the rules of the encounter and, at the same time, become the medium or vehicle by which the rules are followed. Rituals are thus essential for (a) mobilizing individuals to participate in interaction; (b) making them cognizant of the relevant rules of irrelevance,

---

[8]Ibid. p. 39, especially Durkheim's later work in *The Elementary Forms of the Religious Life* (see note 1 for full citation).

transformation, resource use, and talk; (c) guiding them during the course of the interaction; and (d) helping them correct for breaches and incidents.

Among the most significant are those rituals revolving around deference and demeanor. *Deference* pertains to interpersonal rituals that express individuals' respect for others, their willingness to interact, their affection and other emotions, and their engagement in the encounter. In Goffman's words, deference establishes "marks of devotion" by which an actor "celebrates and confirms his (her) relationship to a recipient."[9] Thus, seemingly innocuous gestures—"It's nice to see you again," "How are things?" "What are you doing?" "Good-bye," "See you later," and many other stereotypical phrases as well as bodily movements—are rituals that present a demeanor invoking relevant rules and guiding the opening, sequencing, and closing of the interaction.

Deference rituals, Goffman argued, can be of two types: (1) *avoidance rituals* and (2) *presentational rituals*. Avoidance rituals are those that an individual uses to keep distance from another and to avoid violating the "ideal sphere" that lies around the other. Such rituals are most typical among unequals. Presentational rituals communicate how a person regards others—as equals, inferiors, or superiors—and how he expects others to treat this person. Goffman saw interaction as constantly involving a dialectic between avoidance and presentational rituals as individuals respect each other and maintain distance while trying to make contact and get things done.

In contrast, *demeanor* is ceremonial behavior revolving around deportment, dress, and general bearing that informs others about an individual as a person of certain desirable or undesirable qualities. Through demeanor rituals, individuals present images of themselves to others and, at the same time, communicate that they are reliable, trustworthy, and tactful—even if this is just a ruse.

Thus, through deference and demeanor rituals, individuals plug themselves into an encounter by invoking relevant rules and demonstrating their capacity to follow them, while indicating their respect for others and presenting themselves as certain kinds of individuals. The enactment of such deference and demeanor rituals in concrete gatherings, especially encounters but also including unfocused situations, provides a basis for the integration of society.

Roles

As people present a front, invoke relevant rules, emit rituals, and offer demeanor and deference behaviors, they also try to orchestrate a role for themselves vis-à-vis others. Roles are bundles of activity that others recognize as marking a particular line of behavior or role. Indeed, persons are expected to try and make a role for themselves, and this role should be consistent with the personal qualities that a person has tried to communicate to others through their demeanor, self-presentations, and fronts (stage props, expressive equipment, appearance). If there is inconsistency between the attempted role and these additional aspects of a performance, then others in the situation are likely to sanction the individual through subtle cues and gestures. These others are driven to do so because discrepancy between another's role and other performance cues disrupts the definition of the situation and the underlying sense of reality that this definition promotes. Thus, role-playing is a highly contingent on the responses and reactions of others. Once approved by others, it is difficult to change a role in a situation because this would require too much work on part of others and would disrupt the established routines in a situation.

---

[9]Goffman, *Interaction Ritual*, pp. 56–67 (see note 7).

Yet, people often get stuck in roles that they perceive to be incompatible with their image of themselves. Under these conditions, persons will display what Goffman termed *role distance*, whereby a "separation" of the person from a role is communicated. Such distancing, Goffman argued,[10] allows the individual to (a) release the tension associated with a role considered to be "beneath his (her) dignity," (b) present additional aspects of self that extend beyond the role, and (c) remove the burden of "complete compliance to the role," thereby making minor transgressions less dramatic and troublesome for others.

Role distance is one aspect of the more general process of *role embracement*. Persons will reveal varying degrees of attachment and involvement in the role, with one extreme being *role distance* and with the other extreme being *engrossment*, or complete involvement in a role. Roles over which individuals have control are likely to involve high degrees of embracement, whereas those roles in which the individual is subordinate will be played with considerable role distance.

Self

Goffman's views self as highly situational and contingent on the responses of others. Although one of the main activities of actors in a situation is to present themselves to others, Goffman was highly skeptical about a "core," "person-level," or "transituational" self-conception that is part of an individual's "personality." For Goffman, individuals do *not* have an underlying "personality" or "identity" that is carried from situation to situation—as most symbolic interactionists would argue (see last chapter). Still, people present images of themselves in a particular situation, and others' reactions to this presentation are central dynamics in all encounters. Individuals constantly emit demeanor cues that project images of themselves as certain kinds of persons; people are thus always engaged in a performance, as they *act out a line*. Individuals seek to *stay in face* or to maintain face by presenting an image of themselves through their line that is supported by the responses of others and, if possible, sustained by impersonal agencies in a situation. Conversely, a person is in wrong *face* or *out of face* when the line emitted is inappropriate and unacceptable to others. Thus, a person's face is only on loan because others must approve of an individual's line of conduct.

Yet, people will generally try to allow another to present and stay in a given face, if they can. They communicate with subtle body gestures and verbal utterances their verification of a given face; in so doing, they confirm the definition of the situation and promote a sense of a common reality. Because people's sense of what is real depends upon an agreed definition of the situation, a given line and face in an encounter will be difficult to change, once established. For, to alter face (and the line by which it is presented) would require redefining the situation and recreating a sense of reality—which can be stressful and which can often breach the interaction.

Face engagements are usually initiated with eye contact, and once initiated, they involve ritual openings appropriate to the situation (as determined by length of last engagement, amount of time since previous engagement, level of inequality, and so forth). During the course of the face engagement, each individual uses tact to maintain, if possible, each others presentations of "face" and the line of conduct that this presentations of self requires. Participants seek to avoid "a scene" or breach in the situation, and so they use tact and etiquette to save their own face and that of others. Moreover, as deemed appropriate for the type of encounter (as well as for the larger gathering and more

---

[10]Goffman, *Encounters*, p. 113 (see note 4).

inclusive social occasion), individuals will attempt to maintain what Goffman sometimes termed the *territories of self*, revolving around such matters as physical props, ecological space, personal preserve (territory around one's body), and conversational rights (to talk and be heard), which are necessary for people to execute their line and maintain face. In general, the higher the rank of individuals, the greater their *territories of self* in an encounter. To violate such territories disrupts or breaches the situation, forcing remedial action by participants to restore their respective lines, face, definitions of the situation, and sense of reality.

Talk

Throughout his work, Goffman emphasized the significance of verbalizations for focusing people's attention.[11] Talk is used to open and close interactions, to seek intersubjectivity among individuals, to frame what should be talked about, to rhythmically structure the interaction through turn-taking in a conversation, and to shift topics. Talk is thus a crucial mechanism for drawing individuals together, focusing their attention, and adjudicating an overall definition of the situation. Because talk is so central to focusing interaction, it is normatively regulated and ritualized. Other forms of quasi talk are also regulated and ritualized. For example, response cues or "exclamatory interjections which are not full-fledged words"—"Oops," "Wow," "Oh," and "Yikes"—are regulated as to when they can be used and the way they are uttered. Verbal fillers—"ah," "uh," "um," and the like—are also ritualized and are used to facilitate "conversational tracking." In essence, they indicate that "the speaker does not have, as of yet, the proper word but is working on the matter" and that he or she is still engaged in the conversation. Even seemingly emotional cues and tabooed expressions, such as all the "four-letter words," are not so much an expression of emotion as "self-other alignment" and assert that "our inner concerns should be theirs." Such outbursts are normative and ritualized because this "invitation into our interiors tends to be made only when it will be easy to other persons present to see where the voyage takes them."[12]

In creating a definition of the situation, Goffman argued, talk operates in extremely complex ways. When individuals talk, they create *a footing*, or assumed foundation for the conversation and the interaction. Because verbal symbols are easily manipulated, people can readily change the footing or basic premises underlying the conversation. Such shifts in footing are, however, highly ritualized and usually reveal clear markers. For example, when a person says something like "Let's not talk about that," the footing of the conversation is shifted, but in a ritualized way; similarly, when someone utters a phrase like "That's great, but what about . . . ?" this person is also changing the footing through ritual.

Shifts in footing raise a question that increasingly dominated Goffman's later works: the issue of embedding. Goffman came to recognize that conversations are layered and, hence, embedded in different footings. There are often multiple footings for talk, as when someone "says one thing but means another" or when a person "hints" or "implies" something else. These "layerings" of conversations, which embed them in different contexts, are possible because speech is capable of generating subtle and complex meanings. For example, irony, sarcasm, puns, wit, double-entendres, inflections, shadings, and other manipulations of speech

[11]Erving Goffman, *Forms of Talk* (Philadelphia: University of Pennsylvania Press, 1981).

[12]Ibid., p. 85.

demonstrate the capacity of individuals to shift footings and contextual embeddings of a conversation (for example, think of a conversation in a work setting involving romantic flirtations; it will involve constant movement in footing and context). Yet, for encounters to proceed smoothly, these alterations in footing are, to some extent, normatively regulated.

Disruption and Repair

Goffman stressed that disruption in encounters is never a trivial matter.[13] When a person emits gestures that contradict normative roles, present a contradictory front, fail to enact appropriate rituals, seek an inappropriate role, attempt a normatively or ritually incorrect line, or present a wrong face, there is potential for *a scene*. From the person's point of view, there is a possibility of embarrassment, to use Goffman's favorite phrase; once embarrassed, an individual's responses can further degenerate in an escalating cycle of ever greater levels of embarrassment. From the perspective of others, a scene disrupts the definition of the situation and threatens the sense of reality necessary for them to feel comfortable. Individuals implicitly assume that people are reliable and trustworthy, that they are what they appear to be, that they are competent, and that they can be relied on. Thus, when a scene occurs, these implicit assumptions are challenged and threaten the organization of the encounter (and, potentially, the larger gathering and social occasion in which the encounter is embedded).

For this reason, an individual will seek to repair a scene caused by the use of inappropriate gestures, and others will use tact to assist the individual in such repair efforts. The sense of order of a situation is thus sustained by a variety of corrective responses by individuals and by the willingness of others to use tact in ignoring minor mistakes and, if this is not possible, to employ tact to facilitate an offending individual's corrective efforts. People "disattend" much potentially discrepant behavior, and when this is no longer an option, they are prepared to accept apologies, accounts, new information, excuses, and other ritually and normatively appropriate efforts at repair. Of course, this willingness to accept people as they are, to assume their competence, and to overlook minor interpersonal mistakes makes them vulnerable to manipulation and deceit.

Unfocused Encounters

Goffman was one of the few sociologists to recognize that behavior and interaction in public places, or in *unfocused* settings, are important features of the interaction order and, by extension, of social organization in general.[14] Such simple acts as walking down the street, standing in line, sitting in a waiting room or on a park bench, standing in an elevator, going to and from a public restroom, and many other activities represent a significant realm of social organization. These unfocused situations in which people are co-present but not involved in prolonged talk and "face encounters" represent a crucial topic of sociological inquiry—a topic that is often seen as trivial but that embraces much of people's time and attention.

---

[13]Goffman, *Interaction Ritual* (see note 7).

[14]Erving Goffman, *Behavior in Public Places: Notes on the Social Organization of Gatherings* (New York: Free Press, 1963); Erving Goffman, *Relations in Public: Micro Studies of the Public Order* (New York: Harper Colophon, 1972), originally published in 1971 by Basic Books.

Unfocused gatherings are like focused interactions in their general contours: They are normatively regulated; they call for performances by individuals; they include the presentation of a self; they involve the use of rituals; they have normatively and ritually appropriate procedures for repair; and they depend on a considerable amount of etiquette, tact, and inattention. Let me explore each of these features in somewhat greater detail.

Much like a focused interaction, unfocused gatherings involve normative rules concerning spacing, movement, positioning, listening, talking, and self-presentation. But, unlike focused interaction, norms do not have to sustain a well-defined membrane. There is no closure, intense focus of attention, or face-to-face obligations in unfocused encounters. Rather, rules pertain to how individuals are to comport themselves *without* becoming the focus of attention and involved in a face encounter. Rules are thus about how to move, talk, sit, stand, present self, apologize, and perform other actions necessary to sustain public order without creating a situation requiring the additional interpersonal "work" of focused interaction.

When in public, individuals still engage in performances, but because the audience is not involved in a face engagement or prolonged tracks of talk, the presentation can be more muted and less animated. Goffman used a variety of terms to describe these presentations, two of the most frequent being *body idiom*[15] and *body gloss*.[16] Both terms denote the overall configuration of gestures, or demeanor, that an individual makes available and gleanable to others. (Conversely, others are constantly scanning to determine the content of others' body idiom and body gloss.) Such demeanor denotes a person's direction, speed, resoluteness, purpose, and other aspects of a course of action. In *Relations in Public*, Goffman enumerated three types of body gloss:[17] (1) *orientation gloss*, or gestures giving evidence to others confirming that a person is engaged in a recognizable and appropriate activity in the present time and place; (2) *circumspection gloss*, or gestures indicating to others that a person is not going to encroach on or threaten the activity of others; and (3) *overplay gloss*, or gestures signaling that a person is not constrained or under duress and is, therefore, fully in charge and control of his or her other movements and actions. Thus the public performance of an individual in unfocused interaction revolves around providing information that one is of "sound character and reasonable competency."[18]

In public and during unfocused interactions, the territories of self become an important consideration. Goffman listed various kinds of territorial considerations that can become salient during unfocused interaction, including[19] (a) *fixed geographical spaces* attached to a particular person, (b) *egocentric preserves* of non-encroachment that surround individuals as they move in space, (c) *personal spaces* that others are not to violate under any circumstances, (d) *stalls* or bounded places that an individual can temporarily claim, (c) *use-spaces* that can be claimed as an individual engages in some instrumental activity, (f) *turns* or the claimed order of doing or receiving something relative to others in a situation, (g) *possessional territory* or objects identified with self and arrayed around an individual's body, (h) *informational preserve* or the

---

[15]Goffman, *Behavior in Public* (see note 14), p. 8.

[16]Ibid.

[17]Ibid., p. 129–138.

[18]Ibid., p. 162.

[19]Ibid., Chapter 2.

body of facts about a person that is controlled and regulated, and (i) *conversational preserve* or the right to control who can summon and talk to an individual. Depending on the type of unfocused interaction, as well as on the number, age, sex, rank, position, and other characteristics of the participants, the territories of self will vary, but in all societies, there are clearly understood norms about which configuration of these territories is relevant, and to what degree it can be invoked.

These territories of self are made visible through what Goffman termed *markers*. Markers are signals and objects that denote the type of territorial claim, its extent and boundary, and its duration. Violation of these markers involves an encroachment on a person's self and invites sanctioning, perhaps creating a breach or scene in the public order. Indeed, seemingly innocent acts—such as inadvertently taking someone's place, butting in line, cutting someone off, and the like—can become a violation or "befoulment" of another's self and, as a result, invite an extreme reaction. Thus, social organization in general depends on the capacity of individuals to read those markers that establish their territories of self in public situations.

Violations of norms and territories create breaches and potential scenes, even when individuals are not engaged in focused interaction. These are usually repaired through ritual activity, such as (a) *accounts* explaining why a transgression has occurred (ignorance, unusual circumstances, temporary incompetence, "unmindfulness," and so on), (b) *apologies* (some combination of expressed embarrassment or chagrin, clarification that the proper conduct is known and understood, disavowal and rejection of one's behavior, penance, volunteering of restitution, and so forth), and (c) *requests*, or a preemptive asking for license to do something that might otherwise be considered a violation of a norm or a person's self.[20] The use of these ritualized forms of repair sustains the positioning, movement, and smooth flow of activity among people in unfocused situations; without these repair rituals, tempers would flair and other disruptive acts would overwhelm the public order.

The significance of ritualized responses for repair only highlights the importance of ritual in general for unfocused interaction. As individuals move about, stand, sit, and engage in other acts in public, these activities are punctuated with rituals, especially as people come close to contact with each other. Nods, smiles, hand gestures, bodily movements, and if necessary, brief episodes of talk (especially during repairs) are all highly ritualized, involving stereotyped sequences of behavior that reinforce norms and signal individuals' willingness to get along with and accommodate each other.

In addition to ritual, much unfocused interaction involves tact and inattention. By simply ignoring or quietly tolerating small breaches of norms, self, and ritual practices, people can gather and move about without undue tension and acrimony. In this way, unfocused interactions are made to seem uneventful, enabling individuals to cultivate a sense of obdurate reality in the subtle glances, nods, momentary eye contact, shifting of direction, and other acts of public life. Since so much action in complex differentiated societies occurs among strangers moving about in public spaces, the dynamics of unfocused interactions are critical to sustaining the social order of the society as a whole.

Extensions of Goffmanian Dramaturgy

Goffman was, rather surprisingly, one of the first contemporary sociologists to conceptualize emotions. Indeed, sociology in general tended to ignore the topic of emotions between Charles Horton

---

[20]Ibid., 102–120.

Cooley's analysis of pride and shame in the first decade of the twentieth century to the late 1960s and 1970s—a significant gap in theorizing given the significance of emotions in human affairs.[21] Yet, Goffman never developed a robust theory of emotions but, instead, frequently mentioned the importance of *embarrassment*, or what we might see as a mild form of *shame*. When an individual cannot successfully present a self, and when he or she fails to abide by the script by talking inappropriately, incorrectly using rituals, failing to stay within the frame, inappropriately categorizing a situation, misusing stage props, or expressing inappropriate emotions, the negative emotions aroused in the audience will lead to negative sanctioning of the person who will, in turn, experience embarrassment. Often, the audience will not actually need to sanction those who have breached an encounter because individuals will typically recognize the breach and feel embarrassed. Under these conditions, a sequence of *repair rituals* ensues, revolving around sanctions, apologies, and re-presentation of a more appropriate face and line. People are motivated to do so because they implicitly recognize that the social fabric and moral order are at stake. Encounters depend upon the smooth flow of interaction that sustains the moral order. People in encounters are thus highly attuned to the cultural script and the mutual presentations of self in accordance with the script.

Even though Goffman himself did not develop a very robust conception of emotions, many of those who followed him did. The sociology of emotions did not exist in sociology during most of Goffman's career, but by the time he died in the 1980s, the study of emotions and, hence, theorizing about emotional dynamics had become more prevalent and, today, is one of the leading edges of micro theorizing in sociology. Let me follow up on this observation by reviewing a sample of the sociologists who used the dramaturgical perspective pioneered by Goffman to develop new theories of emotional processes.

Arlie Hochschild on Emotional Labor

Emotion Culture

Arlie Russell Hochschild[22] was one of the first sociologists to develop a view of emotions as managed performances by individuals within the constraints of situational norms and broader cultural ideas about what emotions can be felt and presented in front of others. For Hochschild, the *emotion culture*[23] consists of a series of ideas about how and what people are supposed to experience in various types of situations, and this culture is filled with emotional ideologies about the appropriate attitudes and feelings for specific spheres and activities. Emotional markers are events in the biographies of individuals that personify and symbolize more general emotional ideologies.

In any context, Hochschild emphasizes, there are norms of two basic types: (1) *feeling rules* that indicate (a) the amount of appropriate emotion that can be felt in a situation, (b) the direction, whether positive or negative, of the emotion, and (c) the duration of the emotion; and (2) *display rules* that indicate the nature, intensity, and style of expressive behavior to be emitted. Thus, for any

---

[21]See for reviews, Jonathan H. Turner and Jan E. Stets, *The Sociology of Emotions* (Cambridge, UK: Cambridge University Press, 2005); Jan E. Stets and Jonathan H. Turner, eds., *Handbook of the Sociology of Emotions* (New York: Springer, 2006).

[22]Arlie R. Hochschild, "Emotion Work, Feeling Rules, and Social Structure," *American Journal of Sociology* 85 (1979): pp. 551–575; *The Managed Heart: The Commercialization of Human Feeling* (Berkeley: University of California Press, 1983).

[23]Hochschild, *The Managed Heart* (cited in note 22).

interaction, feeling and display rules circumscribe what can be done. These rules reflect ideologies of the broader emotion culture, the goals and purposes of groups in which interactions are lodged, and the distribution of power and other organizational features of the situation.

Emotion Work

The existence of cultural ideologies and normative constraints on the selection and emission of emotions forces individuals to manage the feelings that they experience and present to others. At this point, Hochschild's analysis becomes dramaturgic, for much like Goffman before her, she sees actors as having to manage a presentation of self in situations guided by a cultural script of norms and broader ideologies. There are various types of what Hochschild terms *emotion work* or mechanisms for managing emotions and making the appropriate self-presentation: (1) *body work* whereby individuals actually seek to change their bodily sensations in an effort to evoke the appropriate emotion (for example, deep breathing to create calm); (2) *surface acting* where individuals alter their external expressive gestures in ways that they hope will make them actually feel the appropriate emotion (for instance, emitting gestures expressing joy and sociality at a party in the attempt to feel happy); (3) *deep acting* where individuals attempt to change their internal feelings, or at least some of these feelings in the hope that the rest of the appropriate emotions will be activated and fall into place (for example, evoking feelings of *sadness* in an effort to feel sad at a funeral); and (4) *cognitive work* where the thoughts and ideas associated with particular emotions are evoked in an attempt to activate the corresponding feelings.

As Hochschild stresses, individuals are often put in situations where a considerable amount of emotion work must be performed. For example, in her pioneering study of airline attendants,[24] the requirement that attendants always be friendly, pleasant, and helpful even as passengers were rude and unpleasant placed an enormous emotional burden on the attendants. They had to manage their emotions through emotion work and present themselves in ways consistent with highly restrictive feeling and display rules. Virtually all encounters require emotion work, although some, such as the one faced by airline attendants, are particularly taxing and require a considerable amount of emotion management in self-presentations.

The Marxian Slant

In emphasizing emotion work, Hochschild not only incorporates elements of Erving Goffman's analysis of emotions but also adds a critical edge that is more reminiscent of Karl Marx's views on alienation. For Hochschild, individuals often engage in strategic performances that are not gratifying. Cultural scripts thus impose requirements on how they feel. As a general rule, then, emotion work will be most evident when people confront emotion ideologies, emotion rules, and display rules that go against their actual feelings, and especially when they are required by these rules to express and display emotions that they do not feel. Complex social systems with hierarchies of authority, or market systems forcing sellers of goods and providers of services to act in certain ways to customers who have more latitude in expression of emotions, are likely to generate situations where individuals must engage in emotion work. Since these types of systems are more typical of industrial and post-industrial societies, Hochschild sees modernity as dramatically increasing the amount of emotion work that people must perform. Such work is always costly because people

---

[24]Ibid.

must, to some degree, repress their "true emotions" as they try to present themselves in ways demanded by the cultural script.

The Strategic Slant

Another extension of this line of reasoning is more in tune with Erving Goffman's repeated fascination with how individuals "con" one another. If the feeling and display rules are known by all participants in an encounter, an individual is in a position to manipulate gestures in order to convince others that she also feels the same emotions and has the same goals when, in fact, she may have a devious purpose. A good "con man (or woman)," for instance, can appear to be helpful to people experiencing difficulty by displaying gestures indicating that he or she feels their pain and that he or she is doing his or her best to help them out of a difficult situation when, in reality, this individual is trying to cheat them. Yet, most of the time in most situations, individuals make a good faith effort to feel and express the appropriate emotions because the rules of culture have a moral quality that invites negative feelings and sanctions for their violation, even in seemingly trivial interactions. Thus, people implicitly understand that to violate feeling and display rules is to disrupt the encounter and, potentially, the larger social occasion.

Candace Clark's Theory on the Dramaturgy

Candace Clark has extended the dramaturgical perspective with the detailed analysis of sympathy as both a dramatic and strategic process[25]—two points of emphasis in Goffmans' theory. Like all dramaturgical theories, Clark visualizes a *feeling culture* consisting of beliefs, values, rules, logics, vocabularies, and other symbolic elements that frame and direct the process of sympathizing. Individuals are implicitly aware of these cultural elements, drawing upon them to make dramaturgical presentations and displays on a stage in front of an audience of others. Although there are cultural rules guiding behavior, many dimensions of culture do not constitute a clear script but, instead, operate more like the rules of grammar that allow actors to organize feeling elements, such as feeling ideologies, feeling rules, feeling logics, and feeling vocabularies, into a framework for emitting and responding to sympathy.

Each individual feels the weight of expectations from culture about how sympathizing is to occur, and each must engage in a performance using whatever techniques are appropriate to feeling and displaying the appropriate emotions. In particular, surface acting, deep acting, and use of rituals to arouse and track emotions are often employed by actors who are seeking to present a self in accordance with a script assembled from relevant cultural elements.

Strategic Dimensions of Sympathy Giving

There are also a strategic dimension to sympathizing, a point of emphasis that follows Goffman's view of encounters as highly strategic. Individuals do not passively play roles imposed by a cultural

---

[25]Candace Clark, *Misery and Company: Sympathy in Everyday Life* (Chicago, IL: University of Chicago Press, 1997); "Sympathy Biography and Sympathy Margin," *American Journal of Sociology* 93 (1987): pp. 290–321; and "Emotions and Micropolitics in Everyday Life: Some patterns and Paradoxes," in *Research Agendas in The Sociology of Emotions*, T. D. Kemper, ed. (Albany, NY: State University of New York Press, 1990).

script; rather, they also engage in games of *microeconomics* and *micropolitics*. With respect to *micro-economics*, Clark argues that emotions are often exchanged in the sympathy giving and taking, and even sympathy as an act of kindness and altruism is subject to these exchange dynamics. Feeling rules often require that recipients of sympathy must to give back to their sympathizers emotions like *gratitude*, *pleasure*, and *relief*. In regard to *micropolitics*, individuals always seek to enhance their place or standing vis-à-vis others, even when they remain unaware of their efforts to gain standing at the expense of others. Such contests over *place* vis-à-vis others introduce inequalities into encounters and, hence, the tensions that always arise from inequality. Sympathy, like any set of emotions, can be an important tool for individuals to enhance their place or standing in an encounter. By giving sympathy to someone, a person establishes that they are in a higher place since the person receiving sympathy needs help. There is a kind of strategic dramaturgy involved, and Clark outlines several strategies for gaining a favorable place: display mock sympathy that draws attention to another's negative qualities; bestow an emotional gift in a way that underscores another's weakness, vulnerability, problems; bestow sympathy on superordinates to reduce distance between places marked by inequalities; remind others of an emotional debt by pointing out problems for which sympathy is given, thereby not only lowering the other's place but also establishing an obligation for the recipient of sympathy to reciprocate; use sympathy in ways that makes the others feel negative emotions such as *worry*, *humiliation*, *shame*, or *anger*, thereby lowering their place.

Integrative Effects of Sympathy

Even though there is a darker side to sympathy processes in games of microeconomics and micropolitics, sympathy at the level of the encounter has integrative effects on the larger social order. First, positive emotions are exchanged—that is, sympathy for other positive emotions like *gratitude*, thereby making both parties to the exchange feel better. Second, the plight of those in need of sympathy is acknowledged by those giving sympathy, thus reinforcing social bonds per se, above and beyond whatever exchange will eventually occur. Third, sympathy operates as a "safety valve" in allowing those in difficulty a temporary release from normal cultural proscriptions and prescriptions while remobilizing their energies to meeting cultural expectations in the future. Fourth, sympathizing is also the enactment of a moral drama because it always involves invoking cultural guidelines about justice, fairness, and worthiness for those who receive the emotions marking sympathy. Fifth, even though games of micropolitics can make one party superior and another inferior (the receiver of sympathy), they do establish hierarchies that order social relations, although they also create the potential for negative emotional arousal and conflict.

Societal Changes and the Extension of Sympathy

Clark argues that the range of plights for which sympathy can be claimed is expanding. Part of the reason for this change is that high levels of structural differentiation, especially in market-driven systems emphasizing individualism, have isolated the person from traditional patterns of embeddedness in social structures. As a result, culture highlights the importance of the individual and the problems that individuals confront. Sympathy is now to be extended to "emotional problems" that individuals have, such as stress, identity crises, divorce, loneliness, criminal victimization, difficult relationships, dissatisfaction at work, home, school, and many other plights of individuals in complex societies. This same differentiation has created new professions that operate as "sympathy entrepreneurs" who highlight certain plights and advocate their inclusion in the list of conditions invoking sympathetic responses. The expansion of medicine and psychotherapy has added a host of new ills, both physical and mental, that are to be objects of sympathy. The social sciences have added even more, including the plight of people subject to racism, sexism, patriarchy, discrimination, urban blight, lower class position, poor job skills, difficult family life, and the like. Thus, modern societies, at least those in the West, have greatly expanded the list of conditions calling for sympathetic responses.

Given the wide array of plights that can be defined as deserving of sympathetic responses, there are implicit sorting mechanisms or cultural logics that enable actors to assemble from cultural elements definitions of who is worthy of sympathy. One cultural logic revolves around establishing responsibility for a person's plight. Americans, for example, implicitly array a person's plight, Clark argues, on a continuum ranging from blameless at one pole to blameworthy at the other. Those who are blameless are deserving of sympathy, whereas those who are blameworthy deserve less sympathy. "Bad luck" is one way in which blame is established; those who have had bad luck deserve sympathy, while those who have brought problems on themselves are not deserving of sympathy.

Clark adds a list of competing rules for "determining what plights were unlucky for members of a category" and, hence, deserving of sympathy. One rule is "the special deprivation principle" that highlights deprivations experienced by individuals that are out of the ordinary. Another is "the special burden principle" emphasizing that those who have particularly difficult tasks to perform are entitled to sympathy. Still another is "the balance of fortune principle" that those who lead fortunate and pampered lives (celebrities, rich people, and the powerful) deserve less sympathy than the ordinary person or the unfortunate individual. Still another rule is "the vulnerability principle" stressing that some categories of persons (e.g., children, the aged, women) are more vulnerable to misfortune than others and are thereby deserving of sympathy. Another rule is "the potential principle" arguing that those whose futures have been cut short or delayed (e.g., children) are more deserving of sympathy than those who have already had a chance to realize their potential (e.g., elderly). Yet another rule is "the special responsibility principle" arguing that those who have special abilities and knowledge, but who do not use them well or wisely, are less deserving of sympathy. And a final rule that is particularly important in establishing whether or not people are deserving of sympathy is "the social worth principle" emphasizing that people who are worthy by virtue of possessing status, power, wealth, cultural capital, and other resources are entitled to sympathy. There is, then, a cultural script for deciding who is deserving of how much sympathy in a society.

Clark notes that there are "off-the-shelf" ways in contemporary societies for expressing sympathy that involve a considerable reduction of the emotion work that a person giving sympathy must endure. These include: greeting cards, offerings (like flowers), prayers, tolerance of behaviors, time off from obligations, easing the pressure, listening, visitations, stereotyped rituals of touching and talk, composure work giving people time to put on a face, offers of help, and the like. But the use of standardized ways to offer sympathy still require some emotion work as the sympathizer tries to decide upon the right combination of these off-the-shelf actions.

One of the most interesting concepts in Clark's conceptualization is the notion of *lines of sympathy credit* given to individuals. Each individual has, in essence, a *sympathy margin*, which is a line of emotional credit indicating how much sympathy is available to a person. These sympathy margins are, like all credit, subject to negotiation; just how much of a margin an individual can claim depends upon the individual's moral worth, their past history of being a good individual who has been sympathetic to others, and the nature of their plight. Cultural rules dictate that family members get the largest sympathy margins, that people who have social value (in terms of wealth, education, authority, beauty, fame, and other forms of social capital) receive large margins, that those who have demonstrated kindness and goodness in their other roles be given large margins, and that the deserving poor (and others in plight) who are trying to help themselves receive large sympathy margins.

There is, however, a limit to sympathy margins. If a person has used all of his or her sympathy credits, no more credit will be offered. And in fact, others will often feel and express negative emotions to those who have sought to overextend their line of credit. Moreover, if individuals who have been given sympathy credits do not attempt to pay others back with the appropriate emotions, those who extended the sympathy credits will withdraw further credit and experience negative emotional arousal.

Sympathy Etiquette

The processes of claiming, accepting, and repaying credit are guided, Clark argues, by "sympathy etiquette"—an idea that pervades Goffman's analysis of encounters. Indeed, if the rules of sympathy etiquette have been breached in the past actions of a person, this individual will have his or her line of credit reduced. Thus, individuals calculate whether a person has a flawed biography or problem credit rating when deciding how much sympathy to offer. There are several basic cultural rules, Clark's data indicate, that guide efforts by individuals to claim sympathy. These are phrased as prohibitions about claiming sympathy: Do not make false claims; do not claim too much sympathy; do not take sympathy too readily; do not take it for granted; be sure to secure some sympathy to keep your emotional accounts open and emotional credit rating high; and reciprocate with gratitude and appreciation to those who have given sympathy.

To these rules are corresponding rules for sympathizers: do not give sympathy that is not due; do not give too much sympathy out of proportion to the plight; and do not give sympathy that goes unacknowledged or underappreciated. People can under-invest or over-invest in sympathy. Over-investors do not follow the rules above, whereas under-investors do not keep their sympathy accounts open so that they can, if needed, make claims to sympathy in future.

Randall Collins on Interaction Rituals

Randall Collins' conflict theory was examined in Chapter 3. At the core of this theory is the notion of interaction rituals, the elements of which roughly correspond to Goffman's analysis of the encounter.[26] For Collins, interaction rituals contain the following elements: (1) a physical assembly of co-present individuals; (2) mutual awareness of each other; (3) a common focus of attention; (4) a common emotional mood among co-present individuals; (5) a rhythmic coordination and synchronization of conversation and nonverbal gestures; (6) emotional entrainment of participants; (7) a symbolic representation of this group focus and mood with objects, persons, gestures, words, and ideas among interacting individuals; (8) circulation of particularized cultural capital; and (8) a sense of moral righteousness about these symbols marking group membership. Figure 3.3 on page 49 portrays the dynamics of such rituals.

---

[26]Randall Collins, *Conflict Sociology: Toward an Explanatory Social Science* (New York: Academic Press, 1975).

In Collins' view, there is a kind of market for interaction rituals, which increases people's strategic actions in interaction rituals. Individuals weigh the costs in time, energy, cultural capital, and other resources that they must spend to participate in the various rituals available to them; then, they select those rituals that maximize emotional profits. In this sense, Collins proclaimed emotional energy to be the common denominator of rational choice.[27] Thus, rather than representing an irrational force in human interaction, Collins sees the pursuit of emotions as highly rational: People seek out those interaction rituals in a marketplace of rituals that maximize profits (costs less the positive emotional energy produced by the ritual). The search for emotional energy is, therefore, the criterion by which various alternative encounters are assessed for how much emotional profit they can generate.

Humans are, in a sense, "emotional junkies," but they are implicitly rational about it. They must constantly balance those encounters where interaction rituals produce high levels of positive emotional energy (such as love-making, family activities, religious participation, and gatherings of friends) with those more practical and work activities that give them the material resources to participate in more emotionally arousing encounters. Indeed, those who opt out of these work-practical activities and seek only high-emotion encounters (such as drop-outs in a drug culture) soon lose the material resources to enjoy emotion-arousing encounters. Moreover, within the context of work-practical activity, individuals typically seek out or create encounters that provide increases in emotional energy. For example, workers might create an informal subculture in which social encounters produce emotional energy that makes work more bearable, or as is often the case with professionals, they seek the rituals involved in acquiring power, authority, and status on the job as highly rewarding and as giving them an emotional charge (such is almost always the case, for instance, with "workaholics" who use the work setting as a place to charge up their levels of emotional energy).

Not only are there material costs as well as expenditures of cultural capital in interaction rituals, but emotional energy is, itself, a cost. People spend their emotional energy in interaction rituals, and they are willing to do so as long as they realize an emotional profit—that is, the emotional energy spent is repaid with even more positive emotions flowing from the common focus of attention, mood, arousal, rhythmic synchronization, and symbolization. When interaction rituals require too much emotional energy without sufficient emotional payoff, then individuals gravitate to other interaction rituals where their profits are higher.

What kinds of rituals provide the most positive emotional energy for the costs involved? For Collins, those encounters where individuals can have power (the capacity to tell others what to do) and status (the capacity to receive deference and honor) are the most likely to generate high emotional payoffs. Hence, those who possess the cultural capital to command respect and obedience are likely to receive the most positive emotional energy from interaction rituals.

Meso- and macro-level social orders are built up, sustained, and changed by interaction rituals, depending upon the degree to which they generate positive and negative emotional energy. When the elements in Collins' model (Figure 3.3) portrayed on page 49 are working successfully, people develop positive emotions, experience increases in their cultural capital, and develop commitments to groups. When these processes do not flow smoothly, or are breached, then the converse ensues—a line of argument consistent with Goffman's analysis of when encounters are breached.

---

[27]Randall Collins, "Emotional Energy as the Common Denominator of Rational Action," *Rationality and Society* 5 (1993): pp. 203–230.

Finally, interaction rituals impose barriers to violent conflict at the micro level[28] because individuals in a conflict situation have a legacy of the gravitational pull of interaction rituals, which are the opposite of violent conflict, and because potential conflict activates fear. This combination keeps individuals from participating in conflict and generally limits the duration and intensity of interpersonal violence. Yet, if interaction rituals can be chained together toward the pursuit of conflict, then violence is more likely to occur, but even then, fear and the pull of successful interaction rituals reduces the involvements of many who are organized for conflict.

If Goffman were developing the theory, he would make much the same argument, indicating that people derive positive emotions from encounters and are highly motivated to repair them when they are breached. Encounters thus sustain the social and moral orders of more meso and macro social organization, and they pull people away from interpersonal violence. Only when encounters are organized for violence that is perceived to sustain a moral order can they effectively be used for longer-term violence.

Conclusion

While symbolic interactionism and dramaturgy are often conflated, there is a significant difference in emphasis. Symbolic interactionists emphasize self and its verification as central to understanding behavior and the dynamics of interpersonal processes, whereas dramaturgy stresses that the script, stage, audience, roles, and rituals are more important. True, people present a self, a line, seek a footing, and other activities marking self, but much of this activity involves an effort to strategically position self in a situation and in the eyes of others. Self is not so much a motive force, as in symbolic interactionism, but a strategic force as persons play out roles on a stage in front of an audience. By comparing the assumptions and basic thrust of theorizing of dramaturgy listed below with similar lists in the last chapter, these differences become even more dramatic.

1. Interaction is a theatrical process of individuals making self-presentations to each other in light of several key properties of any dramatic performance:
    A. A script or normatively prescribed activities that should occur
    B. A stage or locale in which a variety of props can be used by individuals in their dramatic performances
    C. An audience of others who witness performances on a stage and offer their judgments of the quality of these performances
    D. Roles which are delineated in the script but which can offer individuals to add their own dramatic expressive interpretation of the role

2. Interactions are of two basic forms:
    A. *Focused encounters* where individuals are face-to-face with a common focus of attention, which is sustained by
        1. *Rituals* marking openings, closings, and shifts in the flow of interaction

---

[28]Randall Collins, *Violence: A Micro-sociological Theory* (Princeton, NJ: Princeton University Press, 2008).

2. *Forms of talk* appropriate for the situation that sustain the sense of intersubjectivity among persons and that allow interaction to be multilayered and complex

3. Tact and respect for others

4. Ritualized repairs to breaches in the interaction

5. Definitions of the situation, which are reached through 1 to 4 above and several additional processes

    a. Self-presentations that establish a line and footing of an interaction that is consistent with the collective definition of the situation

    b. Role enactments that are consistent with the script and emerging definition of the situation

B. *Unfocused encounters* in which individuals monitor each other's actions but avoid face engagement, which would focus the encounter. Unfocused encounters are sustained by

1. Body idiom in which individuals signal that they are engaged in a legitimate and recognizable behaviors, which are non-threatening

2. Respect for the normatively prescribed territories of self surrounding an individual and that can be used in unfocused interactions

3. Mutual understanding of the markers that define territories of self

4. Ritualized accounts, apologies, or requests for actual or potential transgressions of the rules governing non-face engagement in public places

3. While all interaction involves a dramatic presentation on a stage to audiences, much human behavior is strategic in which individuals manipulate their self-presentations for specific goals, sometimes falsely and ingenuously.

4. Interaction always raises the potential for the arousal of emotions through breaches to an interaction caused by

A. Failure to meet conditions listed under 2A and 2B above

B. Failure to avoid face engagement in unfocused encounters and failure to sustain face engagement in focused encounters

5. Because encounters can be breached and arouse emotions, the expression of emotions is regulated by several layers of culture:

A. *Feeling ideologies* that specify what emotions should and ought to be displayed in general classes and types of situations

B. *Feeling rules* that specify the emotions that should be felt and *display rules* that specify what emotions should be visible to others in a particular situation

6. The cultural regulation of emotions often creates problems for individuals to abide by feeling ideologies and feeling rules, forcing them to engage in *emotion work* to present the appropriate emotions, even if these emotions are not felt.

7. The display of emotions can often be used strategically to present a disingenuous self and goals and in games of micropolitics to gain place vis-à-vis others and of microeconomics to gain resources vis-à-vis others.

CHAPTER 8

Structural Theorizing

Social Structure: An Embarrassing Confession

It is perhaps a bit embarrassing, but sociology does not have a clear conception of one of its most fundamental concepts: social structure. Societies are social structures, and so are all of the other units—encounters, groups, organizations, communities, stratification systems, institutional domains, social categories, etc.—from which societies are ultimately built. And yet, despite the importance of social structure to sociological analysis, definitions are either vague (e.g., "patterns of social relationships that persist over time and that regulate actions") or more idiosyncratic to a particular theoretical approach, which ensures that there will be no consensus over a conception of social structure.

For some, of course, this lack of clarity is not a theoretical problem because the notion of social structure is simply a generalized way of talking about constraints that circumscribe human actions. Moreover, for many sociologists, the goal is to emphasize human agency or the capacity of persons to reconstruct the very structures that constrain them. Indeed, some go so far as to proclaim that there can never be a consensual definition of social structure, nor universally accepted laws of social structure, because humans have the capacity to change the fundamental nature of social structure—thus, obviating the ability to formulate timeless laws about the dynamics of structures.

Still, since just about every sociologist who has ever lived has used the notion of social structure to explain human action and the dynamics of societies more generally, it would seem that there should be at least some commonality in views about this central topic. If we look over the many conceptualizations of social structure, certain basic ideas consistently appear in theories, including the following:

1. Human social relations, including relations among corporate or collective actors, evidence patterns of relationships that persist over time and place.

2. This persistency is created and sustained by social structure and the cultural symbol systems that are attached to social structures.

3. Social structures are composed of relations among social units, with these relations constrained by

   A. The network location of individuals and collective units in physical and relational space

B. The flow of extrinsic and intrinsic resources among actors—individual and collective—across this physical and relational space

C. The emergence of relations of reciprocity as well as power and authority to regulate the flow of resources

D. The development of systems of cultural symbols—norms specifying obligations and prohibitions for actors, ideologies attaching general values to domains of activities in social structures, which moralize relations among actors

F. Configurations of *integration* among actors in social structures, including

1. *Segmentation* of social units, or the production of the same basic type of units that are structurally and culturally equivalent

2. *Differentiation* of social units, or the creation of units that are different in their structures and cultures as well as being engaged in different activities

3. Configurations of *structural interdependencies* among social units, whether segmented or differentiated, including

   a. Structural and cultural equivalence among segmented units in which individuals and collective actors operating in the same basic types of units hold similar orientations because they must respond to the same structural and cultural constraints

   b. *Exchanges* of resources among units in which social units give up resources in order to receive other resources from other units, thereby creating an integrative tie among units

   c. *Embedding* of smaller inside larger social units, leading to integration of the structure and culture of diverse size and types of units

   d. *Overlaps* of boundaries and sectors of diverse social unit

   e. *Domination* of one (set of) social units over other social units by the mobilization and use of power, with relations among units structured by the control capacity of dominant units

   f. *Stratification* of social units in hierarchies of differential and unequal distributions of resources so that units with similar types of levels of resources being structurally equivalent and with those holding larger shares of resources able to mobilize power over those with fewer resources

   g. *Segregation* in time and space among social units engaged in incompatible activities so that these units do not come into conflict, thereby promoting integration

4. Social structures are also composed of persons integrated into the structure by status positions and normatively regulated roles circumscribed by beliefs and ideologies and by successive patterns of micro to macro embedding of

   A. Encounters inside groups and social categories (e.g., gender, ethnicity, religious affiliation, class)

   B. Groups inside organizations

    C. Organizations inside communities

    D. Organizations and communities inside institutional domains (e.g., economy, education, religion, kinship, etc.)

    E. Social categories or categoric units inside stratification systems

    F. Institutional domains and stratification systems inside societies

    G. Societies inside systems of societies

5. Social structures and their cultures constrain the actions of individuals at the micro level of social organization, while also being reproduced by the interaction of individuals in micro encounters. Micro encounters generate commitments to social structures and their cultures through the arousal of positive emotions, while decreasing commitments and increasing the potential for change in structures when negative emotions are aroused.

Different theories emphasize varying aspects of the properties of social structure listed above. For example, let me illustrate some theories from classical figures in sociological theory. Herbert Spencer emphasized differentiation as the key property of social structure, with integration of differences achieved through structural interdependences via market exchanges and domination by centers of power and law. Emile Durkheim also emphasized differentiation, with integration achieved by normatively regulated structural interdependencies and by commitments to generalized beliefs and values through ritual activities in encounters and groups directed at the totems symbolizing the culture of a society. Karl Marx emphasized differentiation as essentially a stratifying process held together by domination of centers of power controlled by those owning the means of production and by cultural ideologies legitimating inequalities and stratification. Max Weber stressed the development of legitimated orders composed of networks among complex organizations and patterns of domination creating systems of stratification legitimated by cultural ideologies. Georg Simmel stressed differentiation of social units, integrated primarily by patterns of group affiliation and market relations among individuals pursuing their preferences.

These are obviously rather superficial portrayals, but they are intended to highlight that each theorist conceptualized *somewhat different properties* of social structure as I have laid them out above, although there is also commonality in Spencer's, Weber's, and Simmel's focus on differentiation and integration. Furthermore, I should note that these are macro theories of social structure, which further biases the selection of properties. A more micro theory would emphasize status and role dynamics, as well as ritual, as these build up solidarities in groups, from which organizations and other types of social structure are built up and integrated.

Anthony Giddens' "Structuration" Theory

Over the last forty years, Anthony Giddens has been one of the most prominent critics of the scientific pretensions of sociology. Yet, at the same time, he has developed a relatively formal abstract conceptual scheme for analyzing the social world. In his *The Constitution of Society*,[1] Giddens brought elements of his advocacy together into an important theoretical synthesis of diverse theoretical traditions—structuralism, Marxism, dramaturgy, psychoanalysis, and even elements of functionalism—into what he had earlier titled "structuration theory." This theory represents one of more creative theoretical efforts of the second half of the twentieth century. Although Giddens has developed theoretical interests in modernity and, indeed, has become an important contributor to the debate about modernity and post-modernity,[2] his theoretical contribution still resides primarily in the more formal statement of structuration theory.

Giddens' Critique of Science in Sociology

Anthony Giddens reasoned that there can never be any universal and timeless sociological laws,[3] like those in physics or the biological sciences. Humans have the capacity for agency, and hence, they can change the very nature of social organization—thereby obviating any laws that are proposed to be universal. At best, "the concepts of theory should for many research purposes be regarded as sensitizing devices, nothing more."[4]

Structuration

Because Giddens does not believe that abstract laws of social action, interaction, and organization exist, his "theory of structuration" is not a series of propositions. Instead, as Giddens' critique of science would suggest, his "theory" is a cluster of sensitizing concepts, linked together discursively. The key concept is *structuration*, which is intended to communicate the duality of structure.[5] That is, social structure is used by active agents; in so using the properties of structure, they transform or reproduce this structure. Thus the process of structuration requires a conceptualization of the nature of structure, of the agents who use structure, and of the ways that these are mutually implicated in each other to produce varying patterns of human organization.

---

[1]Anthony Giddens, *The Constitution of Society: Outline of the Theory of Structuration* (Oxford: Polity, 1984) and *Central Problems in Social Theory* (London: Macmillan, 1979). The University of California Press also has editions of these two books. For an excellent overview, both sociological and philosophical, of Giddens' theoretical project, see Ira Cohen, *Structuration Theory: Anthony Giddens and the Constitution of Social Life* (London: Macmillan, 1989). For a commentary and debate on Giddens' work, see J. Clark, C. Modgil, and S. Modgil, eds., *Anthony Giddens: Consensus and Controversy* (London: Falmer, 1990). For a selection of readings, see *The Giddens Reader*, ed. Philip Cassell (Stanford, CA: Stanford University Press, 1993).

[2]See, for examples, Anthony Giddens, *The Consequences of Modernity* (Stanford, CA: Stanford University Press, 1990); Ulrich Beck, Anthony Giddens, and Scott Lash, *Reflexive Modernization* (Stanford, CA: Stanford University Press, 1994); Anthony Giddens, *Modernity and Self-Identity* (Stanford, CA: Stanford University Press, 1991).

[3]See, in particular, Anthony Giddens, *Profiles and Critiques in Social Theory* (London: Macmillan, 1982) and *New Rules of Sociological Method: A Positive Critique of Interpretive Sociologies*, 2nd ed. (Stanford, CA: Stanford University Press, 1993).

[4]Giddens, *The Constitution of Society* (cited in note 1), p. 326.

[5]Ibid., pp. 207–213.

Reconceptualizing Structure and Social System

Giddens believes structure can be conceptualized as *rules and resources* that actors use in "interaction contexts" that extend across "space" and over "time." In so using these rules and resources, actors sustain or reproduce structures in space and time.

Rules. Giddens sees rules as "generalizable procedures" that actors understand and use in various circumstances. Giddens posits that a rule is a methodology or technique that actors know about, often only implicitly, and that provides a relevant formula for action.[6] From a sociological perspective, the most important rules are those that agents use in the reproduction of social relations over significant lengths of time and across space. These rules reveal certain characteristics: (1) they are frequently used in (a) conversations, (b) interaction rituals, and (c) the daily routines of individuals; (2) they are tacitly grasped and understood and are part of the "stock knowledge" of competent actors; (3) they are informal, remaining unwritten and unarticulated; and (4) they are weakly sanctioned through interpersonal techniques.[7]

The thrust of Giddens' argument is that rules are part of actors' "knowledgeability." Some can be normative in that actors can articulate and explicitly make reference to them, but many other rules are more implicitly understood and used to guide the flow of interaction in ways that are not easily expressed or verbalized. Moreover, actors can transform rules into new combinations as they confront and deal with one another and the contextual particulars of their interaction.

Resources. As the other critical property of structure, *resources* are facilities that actors use to get things done. For, even if there are well-understood methodologies and formulas—that is, rules—to guide action, there must also be the capacity to perform tasks. Such capacity requires resources, or the material equipment and the organizational ability to act in situations. Giddens visualizes resources as what generates power.[8] Power is not a resource, as much social theory argues. Rather, the mobilization of other resources is what gives actors power to get things done. Thus, power is integral to the very existence of structure: As actors interact, they use resources, and as they use resources, they mobilize power to shape the actions of others.

Giddens visualizes rules and resources as "transformational" and as "mediating."[9] What he means by these terms is that rules and resources can be transformed into many different patterns and profiles. Resources can be mobilized in various ways to perform activities and achieve ends through the exercise of different forms and degrees of power; rules can generate many diverse combinations of methodologies and formulas to guide how people communicate, interact, and adjust to one another. Rules and resources are mediating in that they are what tie social relations together. They are what actors use to create, sustain, or transform relations across time and in space. And, because rules and resources are inherently transformational—that is, generative of diverse combinations—they can lace together many different patterns of social relations in time and space.

---

[6]Ibid., pp. 20–21.

[7]Ibid., p. 22.

[8]Ibid., pp. 14–16.

[9]Here Giddens seems to be taking what is useful from "structuralism" and reworking these ideas into a more sociological approach. Giddens remains, however, extremely critical of structuralism; see his "Structuralism, Post-structuralism and the Production of Culture," in *Social Theory Today*, eds. A. Giddens and J. Turner (Cambridge, England: Polity, 2000).

Giddens developed a typology of rules and resources that is rather vague and imprecise.[10] He sees the three concepts in this typology—*domination, legitimization,* and *signification*—as "theoretical primitives," which is, perhaps, an excuse for defining them imprecisely. The basic idea is that resources are the stuff of domination because they involve the mobilization of material and organizational facilities to do things. Some rules are transformed into instruments of legitimization because they make things seem correct and appropriate. Other rules are used to create signification, or meaningful symbolic systems, because they provide people with ways to see and interpret events. Actually, the scheme makes more sense if the concepts of domination, legitimation, and signification are given less emphasis, and the elements of his discussion are selectively extracted to create the typology presented in Figure 8.1.

Figure 8.1   Social Structure, Social System, and the Modalities of Connection

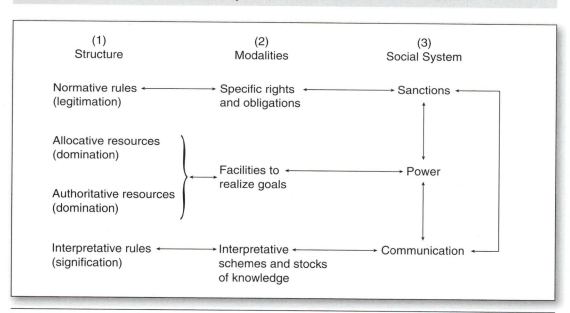

Source: Figure 28.1 on p. 615 of Turner, J. *Contemporary Sociology Theory,* © SAGE Publications Inc., 2013

In the left column of Figure 8.1, structure is viewed by Giddens as composed of rules and resources. Rules are transformed into two basic types of mediating processes: (1) *normative,* or the creation of rights and obligations in a context; and (2) *interpretative,* or the generation of schemes and stocks of taken-for-granted knowledge in a context. Resources are transformed into two major types of facilities that can mediate social relations: (1) *authoritative resources,* or the organizational capacity to control and direct the patterns of interactions in a context; and (2) *allocative resources,* or the use of material features, artifacts, and goods to control and direct patterns of interaction in a context.

Giddens sees these types of rules and resources as mediating interaction via three modalities, as is portrayed in Column 2 of Figure 8.1: rights and obligations, facilities, and interpretative schemes. The figure deviates somewhat from Giddens' discussion, but the idea is the same: rules and

---

[10]*The Constitution of Society,* p. 29 and *Central Problems in Social Theory,* pp. 97–107 (both cited in note 1).

resources are attached to interaction (or "social system" in Giddens' terms) via these three modalities. These modalities are then used to (a) generate the power that enables some actors to control others, (b) affirm the norms that, in turn, allow actors to be sanctioned for their conformity or nonconformity, and (c) create and use the interpretative schemes that make it possible for actors to communicate with one another.

Giddens also stresses that rules and resources are interrelated, emphasizing that the modalities and their use in interaction are separated only analytically. In the actual flow of interaction in the real empirical world, they exist simultaneously, thereby making their separation merely an exercise of analytical decomposition. Thus, power, sanctions, and media of communication are interconnected, as are the rules and resources of social structure. In social systems, where people are co-present and interact, power is used to secure a particular set of rights and obligations as well as a system of communication; conversely, power can be exercised only through communication and sanctioning.

Giddens, then, sees social structure as something used by actors, not as some external reality that pushes and shoves actors around. Social structure is defined as the rules and resources that can be transformed as actors use them in concrete settings. But, the question arises: How is structure to be connected to what people actually do in interaction settings, or what Giddens terms "social systems"? The answer is the notion of modalities, whereby rules and resources are transformed into power, sanctions, and communication. In Giddens' conceptualization, social structure is transformative and flexible, it is "part of" actors in concrete situations, and it is used by them to create patterns of social relations across space and through time.

Moreover, this typology allows Giddens to emphasize that, as agents interact in social systems, they can reproduce rules and resources (via the modalities) or they can transform them. Thus, social interaction and social structure are reciprocally implicated. Structuration is, therefore, the dual processes in which rules and resources are used to organize interaction across time and in space and, by virtue of this use, to reproduce or transform these rules and resources.

Reconceptualizing Institutions

Giddens believes that institutions are systems of interaction in societies that endure over time and that distribute people in space. Giddens uses phrases like "deeply sedimented across time and in space in societies" to express the idea that, when rules and resources are reproduced over long periods of time and in explicit regions of space, then institutions can be said to exist in a society. Giddens offers a typology of institutions showing the weights and combinations of rules and resources that are implicated in interaction.[11] If signification (interpretative rules) is primary, followed, respectively by domination (allocative and authoritative resources) and then legitimization (normative rules), a "symbolic order" exists. If authoritative domination, signification, and legitimization are successively combined, political institutionalization occurs. If allocative dominance, signification, and legitimization are ordered, economic institutionalization prevails. And if legitimization, dominance, and signification are rank ordered, institutionalization of law occurs. Table 8.1 summarizes Giddens' argument.

In this conceptualization of institutions, Giddens seeks to avoid a mechanical view of institutionalization, in several senses. First, systems of interaction in empirical contexts are a mixture of

---

[11]*Central Problems in Social Theory*, p. 107 and *The Constitution of Society*, p. 31 (both cited in note 1).

institutional processes. Economic, political, legal, and symbolic orders are not easily separated; there is usually an element of each in any social system context. Second, institutions are tied to the rules and resources that agents employ and thereby reproduce; they are not external to individuals because they are formed by the use of varying rules and resources in actual social relations. Third, the most basic dimensions of all rules and resources—signification, domination, and legitimization—are all involved in institutionalization; it is only their relative salience for actors that gives the stabilization of relations across time and in space to its distinctive institutional character.

Structural Principles, Sets, and Properties

The extent and form of institutionalization in societies are related to what Giddens terms *structural principles*.[12] These are the most general principles that guide the organization of societal totalities. These are what "stretch systems across time and space," and they allow for "system integration," or the maintenance of reciprocal relations among units in a society. For Giddens, "structural principles can thus be understood as the principles of organization which allow recognizably consistent forms of time-space distanciation on the basis of definite mechanisms of societal integration."[13] The basic idea seems to be that rules and resources are used by active agents in accordance with fundamental principles of organization. Such principles guide just how rules and resources are transformed and employed to mediate social relations.

On the basis of their underlying structural principles, three basic types of societies have existed: (1) "tribal societies," which are organized by structural principles that emphasize kinship and tradition as the mediating force behind social relations across time and in space; (2) "class-divided

Table 8.1 The Typology of Institutions

Type of Institution		Rank Order of Emphasis on Rules and Resources
1. Symbolic orders, or modes of discourse, and patterns of communication	are produced and reproduced by	the use of interpretative rules (signification) in conjuction with normative rules (legitimation) and allocative as well as authoritative resources (domination).
2. Political institutions	are produced and reproduced by	the use of authoritative resources (domination) in conjuction with interpretative rules (signification) and normative rules (legitimation).
3. Economic institutions	are produced and reproduced by	the use of allocative resources (domination) in conjuction with interpretative rules (signification) and normative rules (legitimation).
4. Legal institutions	are produced and reproduced by	the use of normative rules (legitimation) in conjuction with authoritative and allocative resources (domination) and interpretative rules (signification).

Source: Turner, Jonathan. (2013). *Contemporary Sociology Theory,* Table 28.1, p. 617. SAGE Publications, Inc.

---

[12]*The Constitution of Society* (cited in note 1), pp. 179–193.

[13]Ibid., p. 181.

societies," which are organized by an urban/rural differentiation, with urban areas revealing distinctive political institutions that can be separated from economic institutions, formal codes of law or legal institutions, and modes of symbolic coordination or ordering through written texts and testaments; and (3) "class societies," which involve structural principles that separate and yet interconnect all four institutional spheres, especially the economic and political.[14]

Structural principles are implicated in the production and reproduction of "structures" or "structural sets." These structural sets are rule and resource bundles, or combinations and configurations of rules and resources, which are used to produce and reproduce certain types and forms of social relations across time and space. Giddens offers the example of how the structural principles of class societies (differentiation and clear separation of economy and polity) guide the use of the following structural set: private property-money-capital-labor-contract-profit. The details of his analysis are less important than the general idea that the general structural principles of class societies are transformed into more specific sets of rules and resources that agents use to mediate social relations. This structural set is used in capitalist societies and, as a consequence, is reproduced. In turn, such reproduction of the structural set reaffirms the more abstract structural principles of class societies.

As these and other structural sets are used by agents and as they are thereby reproduced, societies develop "structural properties," which are "institutionalized features of social systems, stretching across time and space."[15] That is, social relations become patterned in certain typical ways. Thus the structural set of private property-money-capital-labor-contract-profit can mediate only certain patterns of relations; that is, if this is the rule and resource bundle with which agents must work, then only certain forms of relations can be produced and reproduced in the economic sphere. Hence the institutionalization of relations in time and space reveals a particular form, or in Giddens' terms, structural property.

Structural Contradiction

Giddens always emphasizes the inherent "transformative" potential of rules and resources. Structural principles, he argues, "operate in terms of one another but yet also contravene each other."[16] In other words, they reveal contradictions that can be either primary or secondary. A "primary contradiction" is one between structural principles that are formative and constitute a society, whereas a "secondary contradiction" is one that is "brought into being by primary contradictions."[17] For example, there is a contradiction between structural principles that mediate the institutionalization of private profits, on the one hand, and those that mediate socialized production, on the other. If workers pool their labor to produce goods and services, it is contradictory to allow only some to enjoy profits of such socialized labor.

Contradictions are not, Giddens emphasizes, the same as conflicts. Contradiction is a "disjunction of structural principles of system organization," whereas conflict is the actual struggle between

---

[14]For an extensive discussion of this typology, see Giddens' *A Contemporary Critique of Historical Materialism: Power, Property and the State* (London: Macmillan, 1981).

[15]*The Constitution of Society* (cited in note 1), p. 185.

[16]Ibid., p. 193.

[17]Ibid.

actors in "definite social practices."[18] Thus, the contradiction between private profits and socialized labor is not, itself, a conflict. It can create situations of conflict, such as struggles between management and labor in a specific time and place, but such conflicts are not the same as contradiction.

For Giddens, then, the institutional patterns of a society represent the creation and use by agents of very generalized and abstract principles. These principles represent the development of particular rules and the mobilization of certain resources; such principles generate more concrete "bundles" or "sets" of rules and resources that agents actively use to produce and reproduce social relations in concrete settings; and many of these principles and sets contain contradictory elements that can encourage actual conflicts among actors. In this way, structure "constrains" but is not disembodied from agents. Rather, the "properties" of total societies are not external to individuals and collectivities but are persistently reproduced through the use of structural principles and sets by agents who act. Let us now turn to Giddens' discussion of these active agents.

Agents, Agency, and Action

As is evident, Giddens visualizes structure as a duality, as something that is part of the actions of agents. And so, in Giddens' approach, it is essential to understand the dynamics of human agency. He proposes a "stratification model," which is an effort to synthesize psychoanalytic theory, phenomenology, ethnomethodology, and elements of action theory. This model is depicted in the lower portions of Figure 8.2. For Giddens, "agency" denotes the events that an actor perpetrates rather than "intentions," "purposes," "ends," or other states. Agency is what an actor actually does in a situation that has visible consequences (not necessarily intended consequences). To understand the dynamics of agency, it is required to analyze each element in the model.

As drawn, the model in Figure 8.2 actually combines two overlapping models in Giddens' discussion, but its intent is reasonably clear: humans "reflexively monitor" their own conduct and that of others; in other words, they pay attention to, note, calculate, and assess the consequences of actions.[19] Monitoring is influenced by two levels of consciousness.[20] One is "discursive consciousness," which involves the capacity to give reasons for or rationalize what one does (and presumably to do the same for others' behavior). "Practical consciousness" is the stock of knowledge that one implicitly uses to act in situations and to interpret the actions of others. This knowledgeability is constantly used, but rarely articulated, to interpret events—one's own and those of others. Almost all acts are indexical in that they must be interpreted by their context, and this implicit stock of knowledge provides these contextual interpretations and frameworks.

There are also unconscious dimensions to human agency. There are many pressures to act in certain ways, which an actor does not perceive. Indeed, Giddens argues that much motivation is unconscious. Moreover, motivation is often much more diffuse than action theories portray. That is, there is no one-to-one relation between an act and a motive. Actors might be able to rationalize through their capacity for discursive consciousness in ways that make this one-to-one relationship seem to be what directs action. But much of what propels action lies below consciousness and, at best, provides very general and diffuse pressures to act. Moreover,

---

[18]Ibid., p. 198.

[19]Ibid., pp. 5–7; see also *Central Problems in Social Theory* (cited in note 1), pp. 56–59.

[20]His debt to Alfred Schutz and phenomenology is evident here, but he has liberated it from its subjectivism. See Chapter 6 on the rise of interactionist theorizing.

Figure 8.2 The Dynamics of Agency

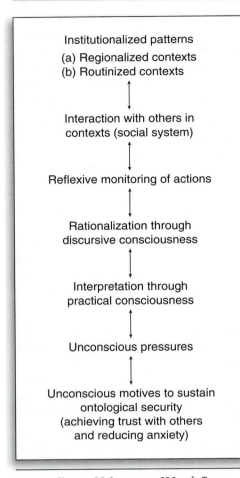

Institutionalized patterns
(a) Regionalized contexts
(b) Routinized contexts

↑
↓

Interaction with others in
contexts (social system)

↑
↓

Reflexive monitoring of actions

↑
↓

Rationalization through
discursive consciousness

↑
↓

Interpretation through
practical consciousness

↑
↓

Unconscious pressures

↑
↓

Unconscious motives to sustain
ontological security
(achieving trust with others
and reducing anxiety)

Source: Figure 28.2 on p. 620 of Turner, J. *Contemporary Sociology Theory*, © SAGE Publications Inc., 2013

much action might not be motivated at all; an actor simply monitors and responds to the environment.

In trying to reintroduce the unconscious into social theory, Giddens adopts Erik Erikson's psychoanalytic ideas.[21] The basic "force" behind much action is an unconscious set of processes to gain a "sense of trust" in interaction with others. Giddens terms this set of processes the ontological security system of an agent. That is, one of the driving but highly diffuse forces behind action is the desire to sustain ontological security or the sense of trust that comes from being able to reduce anxiety in social relations. Actors need to have this sense of trust. How they go about reducing anxiety to secure this sense is often unconscious because the mechanisms involved are developed before linguistic skills emerge in the young and because psychodynamics, such as repression, might also keep these fundamental feelings and their resolution from becoming conscious. In general, Giddens argues that ontological security is maintained through the routinization of encounters with others, through the successful interpretation of acts as practical or stock knowledge, and through the capacity for rationalization that comes with discursive consciousness.

As the top portions of Figure 8.2 emphasize, institutionalized patterns have an effect on, while being a consequence of, the dynamics of agency. As we will see shortly, unconscious motives for ontological security require routinized interactions (predictable, stable over time) that are regionalized (ordered in space). Such regionalization and routinization are the products of past interactions of agents and are sustained or reproduced through the present (and future) actions of agents. To sustain routines and regions, actors must monitor their actions while drawing on their stock knowledge and discursive capacities. In this way, Giddens visualizes institutionalized patterns implicated in the very nature of agency. Institutions and agents cannot exist without each other, for institutions are reproduced practices by agents, whereas the conscious and unconscious dynamics of agency depend on the routines and regions provided by institutionalized patterns.

Routinization and Regionalization of Interaction

Both the ontological security of agents and the institutionalization of structures in time and space depend on routinized and regionalized interaction among actors. Routinization of interaction

---

[21] *The Constitution of Society* (cited in note 1), pp. 45–59.

patterns is what gives them continuity across time, thereby reproducing structure (rules and resources) and institutions. At the same time, routinization gives predictability to actions and, in so doing, provides a sense of ontological security. Thus, routines become critical for the most basic aspects of structure and human agency. Similarly, regionalization orders action in space by positioning actors in places relative to one another and by circumscribing how they are to present themselves and act. As with routines, the regionalization of interaction is essential to the sustenance of broader structural patterns and ontological security of actors, because it orders people's interactions in space and time, which in turn reproduces structures and meets an agent's need for ontological security.

Routines

Giddens sees *routines* as the key link between the episodic character of interactions (they start, proceed, and end), on the one hand, and basic trust and security, on the other hand. Moreover, "the routinization of encounters is of major significance in binding the fleeting encounter to social reproduction and thus to the seeming 'fixity' of institutions." In a very interesting discussion in which he borrows heavily from Erving Goffman (but with a phenomenological twist), Giddens proposed several procedures, or mechanisms, that humans use to sustain routines: (1) opening and closing rituals, (2) turn taking, (3) tact, (4) positioning, and (5) framing. Each of these is discussed below.[22]

1. Because interaction is serial—that is, it occurs sequentially—there must be symbolic markers of opening and closing. Such markers are essential to the maintenance of routines because they indicate when in the flow of time the elements of routine interaction are to begin and end. There are many such interpersonal markers—words, facial gestures, positions of bodies—and there are physical markers, such as rooms, buildings, roads, and equipment, that also signal when certain routinized interactions are to begin and end (note, for example, the interpersonal and physical markers for a lecture, which is a highly routinized interaction that sustains the ontological security of agents and perpetuates institutional patterns).

2. Turn-taking in a conversation is another process that sustains a routine. All competent actors contain in their practical consciousness, or implicit stock of knowledge, a sense of how conversations are to proceed sequentially. People rely on "folk methods" to construct sequences of talk; in so doing, they sustain a routine and, hence, their psychological sense of security and the larger institutional context (think, for example, about a conversation that did not proceed smoothly in conversational turn-taking; recall how disruptive this was for your sense of order and routine).

3. Tact is, in Giddens' view, "the main mechanism that sustains 'trust' or 'ontological security' over long time-space spans." By tact, Giddens means "a latent conceptual agreement among participants in interaction" about just how each party is to gesture and respond and about what is appropriate and inappropriate. People carry with implicit stocks of knowledge that define for them what would be "tactful" and what would be "rude" and "intrusive." And they use this sense of tact to regulate their emission of gestures, their talking, and their relative

---

[22]This list has been created from what is a much more discursive text.

positioning in situations "to remain tactful," thereby sustaining their sense of trust and the larger social order. (Imagine interactions in which tact is not exercised—how they disrupt our routines, our sense of comfort, and our perceptions of an orderly situation.)

4. Giddens rejects the idea of "role" as very useful and substitutes the notion of "position." People bring to situations a position or "social identity that carries with it a certain range of prerogatives and obligations," and they emit gestures in a process of mutual positioning, such as locating their bodies in certain points, asserting their prerogatives, and signaling their obligations. In this way interactions can be routinized, and people can sustain their sense of mutual trust as well as the larger social structures in which their interaction occurs. (For example, examine a student/student or professor/student interaction for positioning and determine how it sustains a sense of trust and the institutional structure.)

5. Much of the coherence of positioning activities is made possible by "frames," which provide formulas for interpreting a context. Interactions tend to be framed in the sense that there are rules that apply to them, but these are not purely normative in the sense of precise instructions for participants. Equally important, frames are more implicitly held, and they operate as markers that assert when certain behaviors and demeanors should be activated. (For example, compare your sense of how to comport yourself at a funeral, at a cocktail party, in class, and in other contexts that are "framed.")

In sum, social structure is extended across time by these techniques that produce and reproduce routines. In so stretching interaction across time in an orderly and predictable manner, people realize their need for a sense of trust in others. In this way, then, Giddens connects the most basic properties of structure (rules and resources) to the most fundamental features of human agents (unconscious motives).

Regionalization

Structuration theory is concerned with the reproduction of relations not only across time but also in space. With the concept of *regionalization* of interaction, Giddens addresses the intersection of space and time.[23] For interaction is not just serial, moving in time; it is also located in space. Again borrowing from Goffman and also from time and space geography, Giddens introduces the concept of *locale* to account for the physical space in which interaction occurs as well as the contextual knowledge about what is to occur in this space. In a locale, actors are not only establishing their presence in relation to one another but they are also using their stocks of practical knowledge to interpret the context of the locale. Such interpretations provide them with the relevant frames, the appropriate procedures for tact, and the salient forms for sequencing gestures and talk.

Giddens classifies locales by their "modes." Locales vary in (1) their physical and symbolic boundaries, (2) their duration across time, (3) their span or extension in physical space, and (4) their character, or the ways they connect to other locales and to broader institutional patterns. Locales also vary in the degree to which they force people to sustain high public presence (what Goffman termed frontstage) or allow retreats to back regions where public presence is reduced

---

[23]Ibid., pp. 110–144.

(Goffman's backstage).[24] They also vary in how much disclosure of self (feelings, attitudes, and emotions) they require, some allowing "enclosure" or the withholding of self and other locales requiring "disclosure" of at least some aspects of self.

Regionalization of interaction through the creation of locales facilitates the maintenance of routines. In turn, the maintenance of routines across time and space sustains institutional structures. Thus, it is through routinized and regionalized systems of interaction that the reflexive capacities of agents reproduce institutional patterns.

Figure 8.3 represents one way to summarize Giddens' conceptual scheme and the theoretical traditions from which he has drawn. In a rough sense, as one moves from left to right, the scheme gets increasingly micro, although Giddens would probably not visualize his theory in these macro versus micro terms. But the general message is clear: Rules and resources are used to construct structures; these rules and resources are also a part of structural principles that include structural sets; these structural properties are involved in institutionalization of systems of interaction; such interaction systems are organized by the processes of regionalization and routinization; and all these processes are influenced by practical and discursive consciousness that, in turn, are driven by unconscious motives, especially needs for ontological security.

Giddens would not consider his "theory" anything more than a conceptual scheme for describing, analyzing, and interpreting empirical events. Moreover, he would not see this scheme as representing timeless social processes, although the reason his works are read and respected is because these do seem like basic and fundamental processes that transcend time, context, and place.

Figure 8.3   Key Elements of "Structuration Theory"

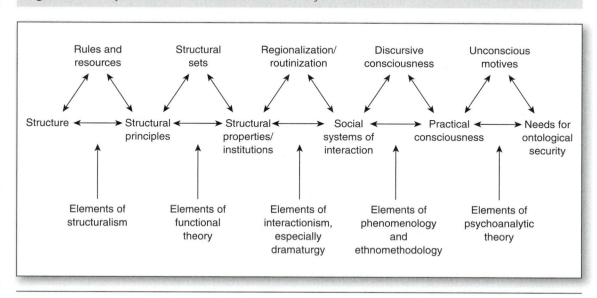

Source: Figure 28.3 on p. 625 of Turner, J. *Contemporary Sociology Theory,* © SAGE Publications Inc., 2013

---

[24]See Erving Goffman, *The Presentation of Self in Everyday Life* (Garden City, NY: Doubleday, 1959); see also Chapter 7 on dramaturgical theorizing.

Network Theorizing On Structure

The Development of Network Analysis

During the last forty years,[25] work within anthropology, social psychology, sociology, communications, psychology, geography, and political science has converged on the conceptualization of "structure" as "social networks." During this period, rather metaphorical and intuitive ideas about networks have been reconceptualized in various types of algebra, graph theory, and probability theory. This convergence has, in some ways, been a mixed blessing. On the one hand, grounding concepts in mathematics can give them greater precision and provide a common language for pulling together a common conceptual core from the overlapping metaphors of different disciplines. On the other hand, the extensive use of mathematics and computer algorithms far exceeds the technical skills of most social scientists. More importantly, the use and application of quantitative techniques per se have become a preoccupation among many who seem less and less interested in explaining how the actual social world operates.[26]

Nonetheless, despite these drawbacks, the potential for network analysis as a theoretical approach is great because it captures an important property of social structure—patterns of relations among social units, whether people, collectivities, locations, or status positions. As Georg Simmel emphasized, at the core of any conceptualization of social structure is the notion that structure consists of *relations and links among entities*. Network analysis forces us to conceptualize carefully the nature of the entities and relations as well as the properties and dynamics that inhere in these relations.

---

[25]For some references on early pioneers in network analysis in anthropology, sociology, and psychology, see S. F. Nadel, *The Study of Social Structure* (London: Cohen and West, 1957); J. Clyde Mitchell, "The Concept and Use of Social Networks," in Jeremy F. Boissevain and J. Clyde Mitchell, eds., *Network Analysis: Studies in Human Interaction* (The Hague: Mouton, 1973); John A. Barnes, "Social Networks" (Addison-Wesley Module, no. 26, 1972). See also his "Network and Political Processes," in J. F. Boissevain and J. C. Mitchell, eds., *Network Analysis: Studies in Human Interaction* (The Hague: Mouton, 1973); Elizabeth Bott, *Family and Social Network: Roles, Norms, and External Relationships in Ordinary Urban Families* (London: Tavistock, 1957, 1971); Jacob L. Moreno, *Who Shall Survive?* (Washington, DC: Nervous and Mental Diseases Publishing, 1934; republished in revised form by Beacon House, New York, 1953); Alex Bavelas, "A Mathematical Model for Group Structures," *Applied Anthropology* 7 (3) (1948): pp. 16–30; Harold J. Leavitt, "Some Effects of Certain Communication Patterns on Group Performance," *Journal of Abnormal and Social Psychology* 56 (1951): pp. 38–50; Harold J. Leavitt and Kenneth E. Knight, "Most 'Efficient' Solution to Communication Networks: Empirical versus Analytical Search," *Sociometry* 26 (1963): pp. 260–267;Theodore M. Newcomb, "An Approach to the Study of Communicative Acts," *Psychological Review* 60 (1953): pp. 393–404. See his earlier work where these ideas took form: *Personality and Social Change* (New York: Dryden, 1943).

[26]For example, D. König, *Theorie der Endlichen und Undlichen Graphen* (Leipzig, Teubner, 1936 but reissued, New York: Chelsea, 1950) is, as best I can tell, the first work on graph theory. It appears that the first important application of this theory to the social sciences came with R. Duncan Luce and A. D. Perry, "A Method of Matrix Analysis of Group Structure," *Psychometrika* 14 (1949): pp. 94–116, followed by R. Duncan Luce, "Connectivity and Generalized Cliques in Sociometric Group Structure," *Psychometrika* 15 (1950): pp. 169–190. Frank Harary's Graph Theory (Reading, MA: Addison-Wesley, 1969) later became a standard reference, which had been preceded by Frank Harary and R. Z. Norman, *Graph Theory as a Mathematical Model in Social Science* (Ann Arbor: University of Michigan Institute for Social Research, 1953), and Frank Harary, R. Z. Norman, and Dorin Cartwright, *Structural Models: An Introduction to the Theory of Directed Graphs* (New York: Wiley, 1965); Dorin Cartwright and Frank Harary, "Structural Balance: A Generalization of Heider's Theory," *Psychological Review* 63 (1956): pp. 277–293. For more recent work, see their "Balance and Clusterability: An Overview," in Holland and Leinhardt, eds., *Perspectives on Social Network Research* (New York: Academic, 1979).

Basic Theoretical Concepts in Network Analysis

Points and Nodes

The units of a network can be persons, positions, corporate or collective actors, or virtually any entity that can be connected to another entity. In general, these units are conceptualized as *points or nodes*, and they are typically symbolized by letters or numbers. In Figure 8.4, a very simple network is drawn with each letter representing a point or node in the network. One goal of network analysis, then, is to array in visual space a pattern of connections among the units that are related to each other. In a mathematical sense, it makes little difference what the points and nodes are, and this has great virtue because it provides a common set of analytical tools for analyzing very diverse phenomena. Another goal of network analysis is to explain the dynamics of various patterns of ties among nodes, although this goal is often subordinated to developing computer algorithms for representing the connections among points and nodes in more complex networks than the one portrayed in Figure 8.4.

Links, Ties, and Connections

The letters in Figure 8.4 represent the nodes or points of a structure. The lines connecting the letters indicate that these points are attached to each other in a particular pattern. The concept of *tie* is the most frequent way to denote this property of a network, and so in Figure 8.4, there are ties between A and B, A and C, A and D, B and E, C and D, and D and E. We not only need to know that points in a network are connected, but we also must have some idea of what it is that connects these points. That is, what is the nature of the tie? What resources flow from node to node? From the point of view of graph theory, it does not make much difference, but when the substantive concerns of sociologists are considered, it is important to know the nature of the ties. In the early sociograms constructed by Jacob Moreno, the ties involved emotional states such as liking and friendship, and the nodes themselves were individual people. But the nature of the tie can be diverse: the flow of information, money, goods, services, influence, emotions, deference, prestige, and virtually any force or resource that binds actors to each other.

Often, as we saw in Chapter 5 on exchange network theory, the ties are conceptualized as resources. When points or nodes are represented by different letters, this denotes that actors are exchanging different resources, such as prestige for advice, money for services, deference for information, and so on. Conversely, if they were exchanging similar resources, the nodes would be represented by the same letter and subscripted numbers, such as A_1, A_2, and A_3. But this is only one convention; the nature of the tie can also be represented by different kinds of lines, such as dotted, dashed, or colored lines. In graph theory, the lines can also reveal direction, as indicated by arrows. Moreover, if multiple resources

Figure 8.4   A Simple Network

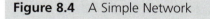

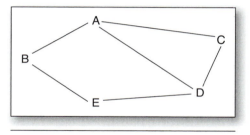

Source: Figure 29.1 on p. 628 of Turner, J. *Contemporary Sociology Theory,* © SAGE Publications Inc., 2013

are connecting positions in the graph, multiple lines (and, if necessary, arrows specifying direction) would be used. Thus, the graph represented in Figure 8.4 is obviously very simple, but it communicates the basic goal of network analysis: to represent in visual space the structure of connections among units.

One way to rise above the diversity of resources examined in network analysis is to visualize resource flows in networks for three generic types: materials, symbols, and emotions. That is, what connects persons, positions, and corporate actors in the social world is the flow of (1) symbols (information, ideas, values, norms, messages, etc.); (2) materials (physical things and perhaps symbols, such as money, that give access to physical things); and (3) emotions (approval, respect, liking, pleasure, and so forth). In non-sociological uses of networks, the ties or links can be other types of phenomena, but when the ties are social, they exist along material, symbolic, and emotional dimensions.

The configuration of ties can also be represented as a matrix, and in most network studies, the matrix is created before the actual network diagram. Moreover, when large numbers of nodes are involved, the matrix is often a better way to grasp the complexity of connections than a diagram, which would become too cumbersome to be useful. Figure 8.5 presents the logic of a matrix, using the very simple network. The mathematics of such matrices can become very complicated, but the general point is clear: to cross-tabulate which nodes are connected to each other (as is done inside the triangular area of the matrix in Figure 8.5). If possible, once the matrix is constructed, it can be used to generate a graph, something like the one in Figure 8.4. With the use of sophisticated computer algorithms in network analysis, the matrix is the essential step for subsequent analysis; an actual diagram might not be drawn because the mathematical manipulations are too complex. Yet, most matrices will eventually be converted in network analysis into some form of visual representation in space—perhaps

Figure 8.5 A Simple Matrix

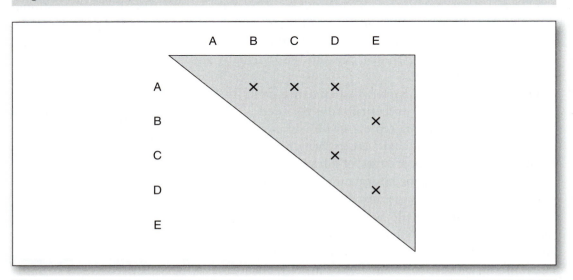

Source: Figure 29.2 on p. 630 of Turner, J. *Contemporary Sociology Theory,* © SAGE Publications Inc., 2013

not a network digraph but some other technique, such as three dimensional bar graphs or clusters of points, will be used to express in visual space the relations among units.

Patterns and Configurations of Ties[27]

From a network perspective, social structure is conceptualized as the form of ties among positions or nodes. That is, what is the pattern or configuration among what resources flowing among what sets of nodes or points in a graph? To answer questions like this, network sociology addresses several properties of networks. The most important of these are number of ties, directedness, reciprocity of ties, transitivity of ties, density of ties, strength of ties, bridges, brokerage, centrality, and equivalence. Each of these is briefly described below.

Number of Ties

An important piece of information in performing network analysis is the total number of ties among all points and nodes. Naturally, the number of potential ties depends on the number of points in a graph and the number of resources involved in connecting the points. Yet, for any given number of points and resources, it is important to calculate both the actual and potential number of ties that are (and can be) generated. This information can then be used to calculate other dimensions of a network structure.

Directedness

It is important to know the direction in which resources flow through a network; so, as indicated earlier, arrows are often placed on the lines of a graph, making it a digraph. As a consequence, a better sense of the structure of the network emerges. For example, if the lines denote information, we would have a better understanding of how the ties in the network are constructed and maintained, because we could see the direction and sequence of the information flow.

Reciprocity of Ties

Another significant feature of networks is the reciprocity of ties among positions. That is, is the flow of resources one way, or is it reciprocated for any two positions? If the flow of resources is reciprocated, then it is conventional to have double lines with arrows pointing in

---

[27]For some readable overviews on network analysis, see Barry Wellman, "Network Analysis: Some Basic Principles," *Sociological Theory* (1983), pp. 155–200; Jeremy F. Boissevain and J. Clyde Mitchell, eds., *Network Analysis* (The Hague: Mouton, 1973) and *Social Networks in Urban Situations* (Manchester: Manchester University Press, 1969); J. A. Barnes, "Social Networks" (Addison-Wesley Module, no. 26, 1972); Barry S. Wellman and S. D. Berkowitz, *Social Structures: A Network Approach* (Cambridge: Cambridge University Press, 1988). Somewhat more technical summaries of recent network research can be found in Samuel Leinhardt, ed., *Social Networks: A Developing Paradigm* (New York: Academic, 1977); Paul Holland and Samuel Leinhardt, eds., *Perspectives in Social Network Research* (New York: Academic, 1979); Ronald S. Burt, "Models of Network Structure," *Annual Review of Sociology* 6 (1980): pp. 79–141; Peter Marsden and Nan Lin, eds., *Social Structure and Network Analysis* (Newbury Park, CA: Sage, 1982). For advanced research on networks, consult recent issues of the journal *Social Networks*.

the direction of the resource flow. Moreover, if different resources flow back and forth, this too can be represented. Surprisingly, conventions about how to represent this multiplicity of resource flows are not fully developed. One way to denote the flow of different resources is to use varying-colored lines or numbered lines; another is to label the points with the same letter subscripted (that is, A_1, A_2, A_3, and so forth) if similar resources flow and with varying letters (that is, A, B, C, D) if the resources connecting actors are different. But, whatever the notation, the extent and nature of reciprocity in ties become an important property of a social network.

Transitivity of Ties

A critical dimension of networks is the level of transitivity among sets of positions. *Transitivity* refers to the degree to which there is a "transfer" of a relation among subsets of positions. For example, if nodes A_1 and A_2 are connected with positive affect, and positions A_2 and A_3 are similarly connected, we can ask, will positions A_1 and A_3 also be tied together with positive affect? If the answer to this question is yes, then the relations among A_1, A_2, and A_3 are transitive. Discovering patterns of transitivity in a network can be important because it helps explain other critical properties of a network, such as density and the formation of cliques.

Density of Ties

A significant property of a network is its degree of connectedness, or the extent to which nodes reveal the maximum possible number of ties. The more the actual number of ties among nodes approaches the total possible number among a set of nodes, the greater is the overall *density* of a network.[28] Figure 8.6 compares the same five-node network under conditions of high and low density of ties.

Figure 8.6   High- and Low-Density Network

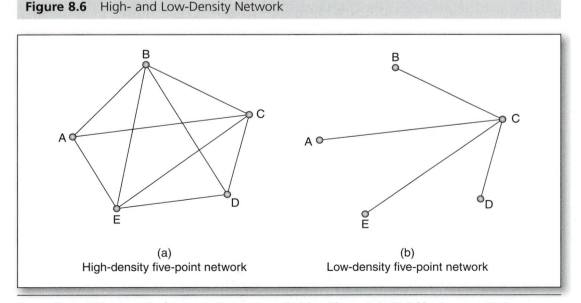

(a)
High-density five-point network

(b)
Low-density five-point network

Source: Figure 29.3 on p. 632 of Turner, J. *Contemporary Sociology Theory,* © SAGE Publications Inc., 2013

[28]There are other ways to measure density; this definition is meant to be illustrative of the general idea.

Of even greater interest are subdensities of ties within a larger network structure. Such subdensities, which are sometimes referred to as *cliques*, reveal strong, reciprocated, and transitive ties among a particular subset of positions within the overall network.[29] For example, in Figure 8.7, there are two clusters of relatively dense ties in the network, thus revealing two distinct subcliques within the larger network.

Figure 8.7   A Network With Brokerage Potential

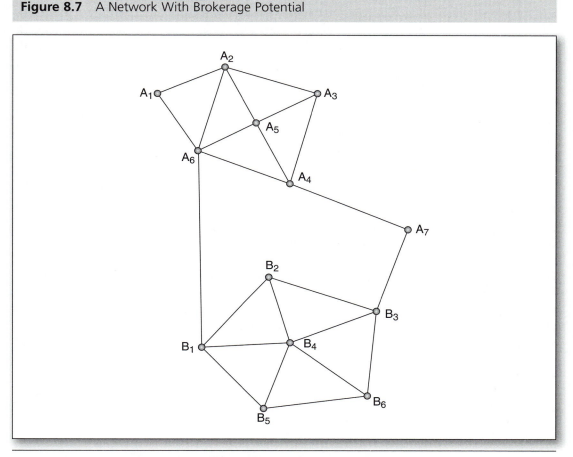

Source: Figure 29.5 of Turner, J. *Contemporary Sociology Theory,* © SAGE Publications Inc., 2013

Strength of Ties

Yet another crucial aspect of a network is the volume and level of resources that flow among positions. A weak tie is one where few or sporadic amounts of resources flow among positions, whereas a strong tie evidences a high level of resource flow. The overall structure of a network is significantly influenced by clusters and configurations of strong and weak ties. For example, if the ties in the cliques in Figure 8.7 are all strong, the network is composed of cohesive subgroupings that have relatively sparse ties to one another. On the other hand, if the ties in these subdensities

---

[29]The terminology on subdensities varies. "Clique" is still the most prominent term, but "alliances" has been offered as an alternative. Moreover, the old sociological standbys "group" and "subgroup" seem to have made a comeback in network analysis.

are weak, then the subgroupings will involve less intense linkages,[30] with the result that the structure of the whole network will be very different than would be the case if these ties were strong.

Bridges

When networks reveal subdensities, it is always interesting to know which positions connect the subdensities, or cliques, to one another. For example, in Figure 8.7, A_6 and B_1 are directly connected and thus constitute a bridge between the two subdensities in the overall network. Such bridging ties connecting subdensities are crucial in maintaining the overall connectedness of the network. Indeed, if one removed one of these positions or severed the tie, the structure of the network would be very different—it would become three separate networks, except for A_7. These bridging ties are typically weak,[31] because each position in the bridge is more embedded in the flow of resources of a particular subdensity or clique. But, nonetheless, such ties are often crucial to the maintenance of a larger social structure; it is not surprising that the number and nature of bridges within a network structure are highlighted in network analysis.

Brokerage

At times, a particular position is outside subsets of positions but is crucial to the flow of resources to and from these subsets. This position is often in a brokerage situation because its activities determine the nature and level of resources that flow to and from subsets of positions.[32] In Figure 8.7, position A_7 is potentially a broker for the flow of resources from subsets consisting of positions A_1, A_2, A_3, A_4, and A_5 to B_1, B_2, B_3, B_4, B_5, and B_6. Position A_7 can become a broker if (1) the distinctive resources that pass to, and from, these two subsets are needed or valued by at least one of these subsets, and (2) direct ties, or bridges, between the two subsets do not exist. Indeed, a person or actor in a brokerage position often seeks to prevent the development of bridges like the one between A_6 and B_1 and to manipulate the flow of resources such that at least one, and if possible both, subsets are highly dependent on its activities.

Centrality

An extremely important property of a network is *centrality*. There are several ways to calculate centrality:[33] (1) the number of other positions with which a particular position

---

[30]At one time, "intensity" appears to have been used in preference to "strength." See Mitchell, "The Concept and Use of Social Networks." It appears that Granovetter's classic article shifted usage in favor of "strength" and "weakness." See note 31.

[31]See Mark Granovetter, "The Strength of Weak Ties," *American Journal of Sociology* 78 (1973): pp. 1360–1380; and "The Strength of Weak Ties: A Network Theory Revisited," *Sociological Theory* (1983): pp. 201–233. The basic network "law" from Granovetter's original study can be expressed as follows: *The degree of integration of a network composed of highly dense subcliques is a positive function of the extensiveness of bridges, involving weak ties, among these subcliques.*

[32]Ronald S. Burt has, perhaps, done the most interesting work here. See, for example, his *Toward a Structural Theory of Action* (New York: Academic, 1982) and "A Structural Theory of Interlocking Corporate Directorships," *Social Networks* 1 (1978–1979): pp. 415–435.

[33]The definitive works here are Linton C. Freeman, "Centrality in Social Networks: Conceptual Clarification," *Social Networks* 1 (1979): pp. 215–239; and Linton C. Freeman, Douglas Boeder, and Robert R. Mulholland, "Centrality in Social Networks: Experimental Results," *Social Networks* 2 (1979): pp. 119–141. See also Linton C. Freeman, "Centered Graphs and the Structure of Ego Networks," *Mathematical Social Sciences* 3 (1982): pp. 291–304, and Philip Bonacich, "Power and Centrality: A Family of Measures," *American Journal of Sociology* 92 (1987): pp. 1170–1182.

is connected, (2) the number of points between which a position falls, and (3) the closeness of a position to others in a network. Although these three measures might denote somewhat different points as central, the theoretical idea is fairly straightforward: Some positions in a network mediate the flow of resources by virtue of their patterns of ties to other points. For example, in Figure 8.7 (b), points A_5 and B_4 are more central than other positions because they are directly connected to the most actors in the two cliques and, hence, a higher proportion of resources will tend to pass through these two positions in the two cliques evident in Figure 8.7. A network can also reveal several nodes of centrality, as is evident in Figure 8.8. Moreover, patterns of centrality can shift over time. Thus many of the dynamics of network structure revolve around the nature and pattern of centrality.

Equivalence

When positions stand in the same relation to another position, they are considered *equivalent*. When this idea was first introduced into network analysis, it was termed *structural equivalence*, and it is restricted to situations in which a set of positions is connected to another position or set of positions in exactly the same way.[34] For example, positions A_2, A_3, A_4 and A_6 in Figure 8.7 are structurally equivalent because they reveal the same relation to position A_5. Figure 8.8 provides another illustration of structural equivalence, as well. A_2, A_3, and A_4 are structurally equivalent to A_1; similarly, D_2, D_3, and D_4 are equivalent to D_1; and A_1, C_1, and D_1 are structurally equivalent to B.

This original formulation of equivalence was limited, however, in that positions could be equivalent only when *actually connected to the same position*. We might also want to consider all positions as equivalent when they are connected to different positions but in the same form, pattern, or manner. For instance, in Figure 8.8, A_2, A_3, A_4, D_2, D_3, D_4, C_2, C_3, and C_4 can all be seen as equivalent because they bear the *same type* of relation to another position—that is to A_1, D_1, and C_1, respectively. This way of conceptualizing equivalence is termed *regular equivalence*[35] and, in a sense, subsumes the original notion of *structural equivalence*. That is, structural equivalence, wherein the equivalent *positions must actually be connected to the same position in the same way*, is a particular type of a more general equivalence phenomenon. These terms, "structural" and "regular," are awkward, but they have become conventional in network analysis, so we are stuck with them. The critical idea is that the number and nature of equivalent positions in a network have

---

[34]François Lorrain and Harrison C. White, "Structural Equivalence of Individuals in Social Networks," *Journal of Mathematical Sociology* 1 (1971): pp. 49–80; Harrison C. White, Scott A. Boorman, and Ronald L. Breiger, "Social Structure from Multiple Networks: I. Block Models of Roles and Positions," *American Journal of Sociology* 8 (1976): pp. 730–780.

[35]Lee Douglas Sailer, "Structural Equivalence," *Social Networks* 1 (1978): pp. 73–90; John Paul Boyd, "Finding and Testing Regular Equivalence," *Social Networks* 24 (2002): pp. 315–331; John Paul Boyd and Kai J. Jonas, "Are Social Equivalences Ever Regular? Permutation and Exact Tests," *Social Networks* 32 (2001): pp. 87–123; Katherine Faust, "Comparison of Methods for Positional Analysis: Structural Equivalence and General Equivalence," *Social Networks* 10 (1988): pp. 313–341.

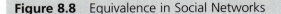

Figure 8.8 Equivalence in Social Networks

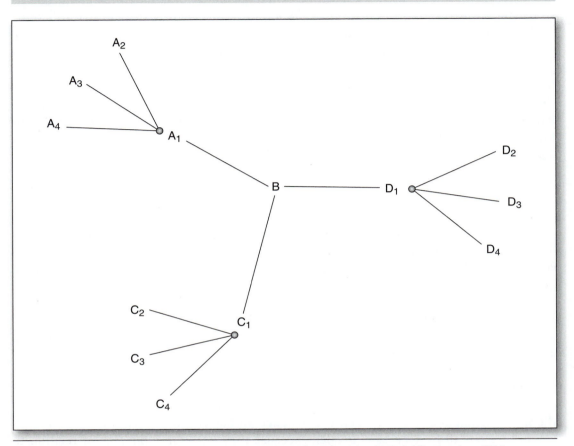

Source: Figure 29.6 on p. 636 of Turner, J. *Contemporary Sociology Theory,* © SAGE Publications Inc., 2013

important influences on the dynamics of the network.[36] The general hypothesis is that actors in structurally equivalent or regularly equivalent positions will behave or act in similar ways.[37]

---

[36]In many ways, for example, Karl Marx's idea that those who stand in a common relationship to the means of production have common interests is an equivalence agreement. Thus, the idea of equivalence is not new to sociology—just the formalism used to express it is new.

[37]There are, of course, some notable exceptions to this statement. For an example, John Levi Martin, *Social Structures* (Princeton, NJ: Princeton University Press, 2009), "Structures of Power in Naturally Occurring Communities," *Social Networks* 20 (1998): pp. 197–225, and "Formation and Stabilization of Veridical Hierarchies among Adolescents," *Social Psychology Quarterly* (2010); Ronald S. Burt, *Toward a Structural Theory of Action* (cited in note 27), *Structural Holes: The Social Structure of Competition* (Cambridge, MA: Harvard University Press, 1992); Noah E. Friedkin, *A Structural Theory of Social Influence* (Cambridge, UK: Cambridge University Press, 1998).

Can Network Analysis Make Conceptions of Structure More Precise?

The mathematics of network analysis can become quite complicated, as can the computer algorithms used to analyze data sets of the processes outlined above. This listing of concepts is somewhat metaphorical because it eliminates the formal and quantitative thrust of much network analysis. Indeed, much network analysis bypasses the conversion of matrices into graphs like those in the various figures presented and, instead, performs mathematical and statistical operations on just the matrices themselves. Yet, if network analysis is to realize its full theoretical (as opposed to methodological) potential, it might be wise to use concepts, at least initially, in a more verbal and intuitive sense.

Few would disagree with the notion that social structure is composed of relations among positions. But is this all that social structure is? Can the concepts denoting nodes, ties, and patterns of ties (number, strength, reciprocity, transitivity, bridges, brokerage, centrality, and equivalence) capture all the critical properties of social structure?

The answer to these questions is probably "no." Social structure probably involves other crucial processes that are not captured by these concepts. Yet a major property of social structure *is* its network characteristics, as Georg Simmel was perhaps the first to really appreciate. For, whatever other dimensions social structure might reveal—cultural, behavioral, ecological, temporal, psychological, and so forth—its backbone is a system of interconnections among actors who occupy positions relative to one another and who exchange resources. And, so, network analysis has great potential for theories of social structure. Has this potential been realized? Probably not, for several reasons.

First, as just noted, network analysis is overly methodological and concerned with generating quantitative techniques for arraying data in matrices and then converting the matrices into descriptions of particular networks (whether as graphs or as equations). As long as this is the case, network sociology will remain primarily a tool for empirical description.

Second, there has been little effort to develop principles of network dynamics per se. Few[38] seem to ask theoretical questions within the network tradition itself. For example, how does the degree of density, centrality, equivalence, bridging, and brokerage influence the nature of the network and the flow of relations among positions in the network? There are many empirical descriptions of events that touch on this question but few actual theoretical laws or principles.[39]

Third, network sociology has yet to translate traditional theoretical concerns and concepts into network terminology in a way that highlights the superiority, or at least the viability, of using network theoretical constructs for mainstream theory in sociology. For example, power, hierarchy, differentiation, integration, stratification, conflict, and many other concerns of sociological theory have not been adequately reconceptualized in network terms, and hence it is unlikely that sociological theory will adopt or incorporate a network approach until this translation of traditional questions occurs.

All these points, however, need to be qualified because numerous sociologists have actually sought to develop laws of network processes and to address traditional theoretical concerns

---

[38]Mark Granovetter, "The Theory-Gap in Social Network Analysis," in *Perspectives on Social Network Research*, eds. P. Holland and S. Leinhardt (New York: Academic, 1979).

[39]For example, see my three volume: *Theoretical Principles of Sociology*, volumes 1, 2, and 3 (New York: Springer, 2011–2012). Volume 1 addresses macrodynamics, volume 2 microdynamics, and volume 3 mesodynamics.

with network concepts. Although these efforts are far from constituting a coherent theory of network dynamics, they do illustrate the potential utility of network sociology, as we saw, for example, in the review of network exchange theory in Chapter 5.

Toward a More Simplified Conception of Social Structure

For some years now, I have been advocating a simplified orientation to social structure. In my view, humans have created only a few basic types of social structures at the three basic levels of social reality: micro, meso, macro. To be sure, the distinctions among micro, meso, and macro summarized in Table 8.2 are analytical distinctions, but they are also denote the actual way that social reality has unfolded during the growth and increasing complexity of societies (see Chapter 11 on stage models of evolution). At each of these three levels have emerged just a few basic types of social structure. At the micro level of social organization where interpersonal behaviors are carried out, there is only the encounter, which as Table 8.2 emphasizes can be of two types: focused and

Table 8.2 Structures of the Social Universe

Macro-Level Structures
Institutional domains: Society-wide structures built from corporate units that arise in response to adaptive problems facing a population (e.g., economy, polity, kinship, religion, law, education, etc.)
Stratification systems: Society-wide structures that arise from the unequal distribution of resources in corporate units and that create categories of individuals defined and evaluated by their shares of valued resources (e.g., social classes, ethnic subpopulations, gender categories, etc.)
Inter-societal systems: Structures generated by interrelations between societies, typically key institutional domains of societies, that establish patterns of longer-terms relations among societies.
Meso-Level Structures
Corporate units: Structures that organize individuals into a division of labor in pursuit of goals, however vaguely defined these goals may be. There have been three basic types of corporate units created by humans: groups of face-to-face interaction that persist over time and are often embedded in organizations, which link groups together in the pursuit of goals and communities that provide the geo-political organization of space where organizations and groups reside.
Categoric units: Structures created by differences that members of a society notice and evaluate. When individuals are placed into a social category, they become members of a categoric unit that contains expectations for, and evaluations of, members of this categoric unit.
Micro-Level Structures
Focused encounters: Episodes of face-to-face interaction among individuals that generate momentary solidarities, which can be iterated over time.
Unfocused encounters: Episodes of mutual monitoring of others as individuals move and occupy public space but, at the same time, seek to avoid face-engagement, which would force the encounter to become more focused.

unfocused. Encounters are, however, fleeting structures; they assemble and then disassemble, although they can often be chained together over time as successive gatherings in an encounter. But for this to occur, encounters need to be embedded in meso-level structures, which provide a certain solidity and continuity to encounters. On the one hand, encounters are the building blocks of meso-level structures, while on the other hand, meso-level structures provide the mortar that holds these encounters together and gives them continuity over time.

At the meso level, there are *corporate units* revealing a division of labor, and in the history of human societies, there have been only three different types of corporate units: groups, organizations, and communities. What gives corporate units their solidity as structures is that they are embedded in each other. First, encounters are almost always embedded in a more permanent group, which in turn is embedded in an organization that is located and hence embedded in a community. For example, each meeting of a class is an encounter, but this class is embedded in an organization (the college or university, for example), which is located in a community. The organization provides the culture and material resources for organizing groups (departments, classes, etc.), while groups provide the parameters for organizing chains of face-to-face encounters. The community provides the location in geographical space and the key resources for an organization, such as roads to and from the college, electricity, governance of the community, and other environmental resources necessary for any organization to function.

The other type of meso structure is, at first, hard to visualize as a structure: social categories. People are classified on the basis of various markers of difference, such as age, gender, ethnicity, social class position, religious affiliation, or anything that makes a subpopulaton distinctive and different from others. I have come to term these categoric distinctions *categoric units* because associated with membership in categoric units are cultural expectations and evaluations of members, and these have very large effects on what transpires in encounters. Just as the structure of a corporate unit, such as the authority system in its division of labor, constrains what transpires at the micro level of social organization in encounters, so beliefs about the characteristics of members in categoric units affect how individuals behave. For example, an encounter composed of all males will be different than one composed of all females, or a mixed-gender encounter. An encounter of old and young will be very different than one composed of only people or younger persons. And, to the extent that people's behaviors reinforce the expectations of categoric unit memberships, they reproduce the categoric unit, much as they reproduce the authority system in the division of labor of a corporate unit when individuals behave appropriately.

Macro-level structures at the societal level—institutional domains and stratification systems—are built, respectively, from corporate and categoric units. And once built up, these macro structures constrain what transpires in meso-level and micro-level social structures. *Institutional domains* are composed of embedded corporate units created to deal with society-wide adaptive problems in a society; and as they evolve, they develop a distinctive culture (norms and ideologies) that constrains the culture of all corporate units within a domain, and all encounters within these corporate unit building blocks of an institutional domain.

Stratification systems are composed of categoric units, where the distribution of valued resources is correlated with categoric-units memberships. For example, a social class is a categoric unit typified by a particular level of income and wealth. Other categoric units are often typified by the resources that they are able to secure in the stratification system. For example, if males make more money than females, then there will be a gender dimension to the stratification system. For if members of particular ethic subpopulations, for instance, earn less that other ethnic subpopulations, then there is an ethnic dimension to the stratification system. The ideologies built up in institutional domains are often combined to generate an ideology that legitimates the unequal distribution of resources, thus giving the stratification system some solidity, even as it generates tensions over inequalities. For example, the ideologies of the economy (work hard for your living) and education (acquire skills and knowledge by working hard in schools) are combined to become a major part of the ideology justifying and legitimating inequality. Those who work hard and get educational credentials *should* earn more than those who do not; at least, this is the way American think about inequalities.

Societies are often linked, typically through various institutional domains like the economy or polity, to other societies, thereby forming an inter-societal system, which is the largest social structure created thus far by humans. Indeed, the growth of the world global system through market relations has increased dramatically over the last fifty years and promises to grow further, perhaps punctuated by periodic collapses.

In Figure 8.9, I lay about this vision of social structure as composed of the structural formations and their cultures at the three levels of social organization. The lines connecting social structures are intended to emphasize that they are connected to each other, and many of the

Figure 8.9   A Simple Conceptual Scheme for Analyzing Social Structure

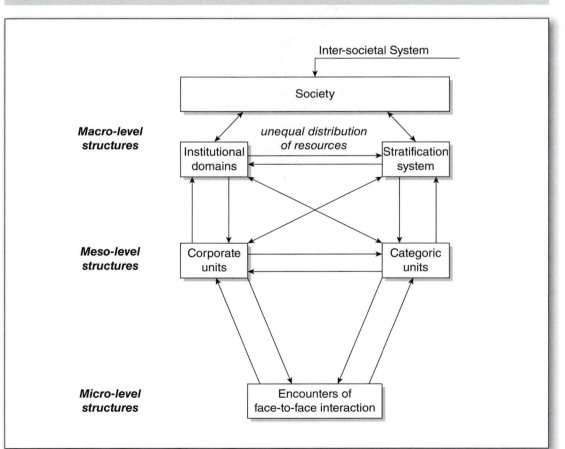

dynamics of social structure revolve around and influence each other. For example, it is corporate units that distribute resources unequally, thus creating the inequalities of the stratification system. Or, it is the successive embedded in corporate units that give particular institutional domain their structure as, for example, workers in encounters are lodged in groups that are the building blocks of organizations embedded in communities, which are ultimately the building blocks of the institutional domain of the economy.

One of the critical questions in this view of social structure is to explain how all of these structural elements at each level of social organization are integrated into larger social structures; and so, many of the ideas in the theories presented thus far become relevant for understanding how this integration occurs. I have outlined in detail these dynamics,[39] but my point here is just to lay out the general terrain of a structuralist approach that, in the end, is a bit more straightforward than many that now exist in sociology.

Conclusion

Theorizing on social structure is highly diverse, perhaps not so surprisingly, given the lack of a clear definition of what the concept of "structure" denotes. As the theories reviewed here demonstrate, there is a cultural dimension of structure, consisting of rules, beliefs, ideologies, and value premises. There are also sets of principles or underlying logics that, in still unknown ways, generate structures; some of these may be cultural, while others are potentially lodged in human neurology. There is also a relational property of social structure consisting of positions and nodes that are connected by the movement of resources among actors at particular nodes. What sociology has, then, is the contours of a more rigorous conceptualization of the properties of structure, although the dynamic aspects of structure can be found in the many theories that are outlined in the chapters of this book. These dynamics inhere in the forms of networks in the levels of power, inequality, and conflict, in the nature of interaction and exchange, in the dramaturgical presentations, in the dynamics of roles and status locations, and in many other topics of theoretical sociology. What has not been done, however, is integrate these into a more general theory on the properties and dynamics of structures. Giddens' structuration theory is one example of an effort to achieve this necessary integration, and while it is provocative, it is also incomplete. Network analysis is another provocative approach—also incomplete. Thus, the agenda for structural sociology is clear: define the properties and dimensions of structures, and then use existing theories in various combinations to explain the operative dynamics that produce, reproduce, and change these properties and dimensions of structure.

---

[39]Jonathan H. Turner, *Theoretical Principles of Sociology*, 3 Volumes (New York: Springer, 2010–2012).

CHAPTER 9

Cultural Theorizing

Another Embarassing Confession

Like the concept of social structure, the conceptualization of culture in sociology is rather vague, despite a great deal of attention by sociologists to the properties and dynamics of culture. There has always been the recognition that culture is attached to social structures, and vice versa, with the result that sociologists often speak in terms of sociocultural formations or sociocultural systems and structures. This merging of structure and culture rarely clarifies but, instead, further conflates a precise definition of culture. And so, sociology's big idea—culture—is much like the notion of social structure. Its conceptualization is somewhat metaphorical, often rather imprecise, and yet highly evocative. There is no consensus in definitions of culture beyond the general idea that humans create symbol systems, built from our linguistic capacities, which are used to regulate conduct. And even this definition would be challenged by some.

Since the 1980s and accelerating with each decade, the amount of cultural theorizing has dramatically increased. Mid-twentieth-century functional theory had emphasized the importance of culture but not in a context-specific or robust manner; rather, functionalism viewed culture as a *mechanism* by which actions are controlled and regulated,[1] whereas much of the modern revival of culture has viewed culture in a much more robust and inclusive manner. When conflict theory finally pushed functionalism from center stage, it also tended to bring forth a more Marxian view of culture as a "superstructure" generated by economic substructures. Culture became the sidekick, much like Tonto for the Lone Ranger, to social structure, with the result that its autonomy and force independent of social structures were not emphasized and, in some cases, not even recognized. Yet, such had not always been the case.

---

[1]For example, Talcott Parsons saw it as an action system that provided the necessary information of regulating social systems and the status-role and normative structure of social systems that, in turn, regulated the psychological action system and even the organismic system (see Chapter 2). Or, in Niklas Luhmann's work, ideology is seen as mechanisms, which is critical to the integration of institutional domains; see his *The Differentiation of Society*, trans. S. Holmes and C. Larmore (New York: Columbia University Presss, 1982).

Early Sociological Conceptions of Culture

Auguste Comte and Emile Durkheim

From its beginnings in France, sociological theorizing has always emphasized the power of culture. For Auguste Comte[2] and Emile Durkheim,[3] as well as the French philosophers of the eighteen century, society was seen as held together by commitments of individuals to a common cultural core. The exact nature of this core was always a bit vague in French philosophy and sociology, but in today's vocabulary, it denotes systems of cultural symbols that carry meanings shared by members of a population and that have the power to regulate the actions of individuals and corporate units. Culture was built from language and carried a populations' history, traditions, and lore, while also codifying these into values, beliefs and ideologies, norms, and laws that direct actions and interactions among social units. The late Durkheim increasingly emphasized that differentiated societies require a common cultural core and that this core is invoked by individuals when they engage in rituals directed at totems symbolizing key elements of this core. Through emotion-arousing rituals, culture was not only recognized but also *moralized* as emotions were attached to key elements of culture, giving culture an imperative character and causing guilt and shame for all those who would violate this imperative power of moral codes. Emotions thus gave "teeth" to culture because emotions can be negative and, hence, painful when persons fail to abide by cultural directives in situations.

Karl Marx and Max Weber

German sociologists like Karl Marx and Max Weber also emphasized culture, but in somewhat different ways. For Marx,[4] as noted above, culture is part of the *superstructure* of a society. This superstructure is controlled by those owning the means of production and is codified into ideologies supported by the state—another part of the social superstructure. Once codified, the ideologies of cultural superstructures legitimate the interests of powerful owners of capital and the means of production. Culture was thus an obfuscating force because it blinds workers and the oppressed from recognizing their true interests in changing the system of production and power in a society. Yet, Marx also recognized that counter-ideologies by subordinates in the system of inequality were critical to arousing emotions and motivating subordinates to incur the risk of conflict with superordinates. As part of a revolutionary force,

---

[2]Auguste Comte, *The Course of Positive Philosophy*, translated and condensed by Harriet Martineau as *The Positive Philosophy of Auguste Comte* (London: Bell and Sons, 1898). See also Comte's *System of Positive Polity* (Burt Franklin, 1875, originally published in 1851).

[3]Emile Durkheim's notion of the collective conscience gave priority to culture as an integrative force in the *Division of Labor in Society* (New York: Macmillan, 1933, originally published in 1892), and later, he gave even more emphasis to culture in his analysis of rituals as the link between culture and the individuals' commitment to culture in *The Elementary Forms of the Religious Life* (New York: Free Press, 1947, originally published in 1912). Comte and Spencer were only continuing the tradition set a century earlier by the French philosophes, who all emphasized the importance of culture as an integrative force, as well as a force for change.

[4]Karl Marx and Friedrich Engels, *The German Ideology* (New York: International, 1946, originally published in 1846).

then, culture can gain some autonomy in Marx's eyes because it pushes actors to seek alternative forms of social structure. As they do so, subordinates codify a counter-ideology that gives direction to their pursuit of conflict with superordinates.

Marx Weber[5] did not go so far as to see culture as "merely" a superstructure; indeed, he felt that culture could be seen as an autonomous force driving social structural arrangements. His famous typology on the Protestant ethic and worldly asceticism[6] emphasizes that structural change can occur when particular structural conditions are in place—e.g., markets, labor markets, money, urban centers, stable polity, etc. Once in place, new beliefs and ideologies can emerge to push a society over to an entirely new pattern of social organization. Thus, in his eye, the industrial revolution and capitalism were chance events that only emerged with alternations in religious beliefs and with the development of a more secular ideology of worldly asceticism (see footnote 6) that codified the moral imperatives of Protestantism into an ideology that could drive actors to form new kinds of economic relations. He also, like Marx, recognized that *legitimated social orders* (what today we might call institutional domains) and stratification systems were legitimated by ideologies and that if these were ever to change, mobilization of actors with new counter-ideologies and charismatic leaders would be necessary.

George Herbert Mead

At the more micro level of social organization, George Herbert Mead's[7] notion of the *generalized other* is very similar to Durkheim's ideas about the *collective conscience* (a term central to early Durkheim but later abandoned). Individuals not only role take with real persons; they also assume the perspective of generalized others attached to all social structures. The generalized other is, for Mead, a "community of attitudes" or set of beliefs that is shared by persons and that drives their conduct and self-evaluations as they role take in a situation. Too much is probably packed into the notion of generalized other (collective values, beliefs, norms, perspectives, attitudes, sentiments, etc.), but Mead provided a mechanism—role-taking with the generalized other—by which individuals invoke culture to regulate their conduct and to evaluative themselves. Mead did not, however, develop Durkheim's ideas about ritual as another key mechanisms by which culture exerts it power. For, as individuals make ritual appeals to totems symbolizing the power of the supernatural that is, in reality, the collective order of a society and its culture, individuals come under the power of culture and, moreover, legitimate its sanctity. Still, both the late Durkheim and Mead were seeking the more micro basis of social organization, and this search led them to try and understand how culture becomes internalized and part of persons' worldviews and perceptions of proper forms of conduct.

---

[5]Max Weber, *The Protestant Ethic and the Spirit of Capitalism*, trans. T. Parsons (New York: Scribners, 1948, original published in two parts between 1904 and 1905. See also Stephen Kallberg's translation for Roxbury Press, 2002).

[6]Worldly asceticism emphasizes hard work, diligence, frugality, savings and accumulation of capital, and rationality—all in the name of God.

[7]George Herbert Mead, *Mind, Self, and Society* (Chicago: University of Chicago Press, 1934).

Alfred Schutz

In Germany and later, after his immigration to the United States, the more phenomenological sociologist Alfred Schutz[8] also began to explore how individuals store knowledge, including knowledge and emotional tags for cultural directives, and how they make this knowledge available in concrete situations. Schutz's famous phrase, partially borrowed from the philosopher Edmund Husserl, "stocks of knowledge at hand," indicates that culture is highly robust, and it postulates vast stores of knowledgeability that can be drawn upon to facilitate interaction among individuals. These stores are accumulated during a lifetime, and they are often implicit and not easy to articulate, but they are available when needed; thus, culture is more than just norms, beliefs, ideologies, and values, but stores and stocks of information relevant to persons in concrete situations. Other phenomenological thinkers in Europe, in varying ways, also emphasized this more robust and seemingly amorphous body of culture sitting in the human brain, which can be drawn upon rapidly and be assembled to give guidance in varying types of situations. This more robust view of culture also became part of the modern revival of cultural sociology.

The Mid-Century Legacy of Claude Levi-Strauss

Another legacy from early sociology is what is sometimes termed *structuralism*, which is a mix of Durkheim's ideas and those of early twentieth-century structural linguistics. The details of this mixing are less critical than what was left on the table long after structuralism faded from its mid-twentieth-century prominence. Claude Levi-Straus was perhaps the critical figure here because he initially followed Durkheim's and Marcel Mauss'[9] lead of seeing cultural logics as reflecting the structural, including ecological, arrangements of societies. That is, basic categories of thought about such matters as time, space, and causation are a reflection of how societies are organized. Later, Levi-Strauss was to "turn Durkheim on his head" to argue that the structure of culture arises from programming lodged in the neuro-anatomy of the human brain.[10] There are *deep structures* of generative rules, logics, assumptions, conceptions of time/space/others, and other properties of culture that undergird all cultural phenomena, but for the later Levi-Strauss, they are hardwired in the brain.

Even if one does not want to go as far as Levi-Strauss in seeing elements of culture as manifestations of bioprogrammers in the neurology of the brain, the notion that culture as used by people in their daily lives is but a *surface structure* driven by deeper structures of culture—that is, underlying rules and logics—that are more fundamental to understanding culture than simple empirical examination of surface structures. For example, a cultural myth, value premises, ideologies, norms, stories of traditions, and virtually all surface culture are to be understood much better when the *deeper structures* systematically generating these cultural phenomena are isolated and examined as the root source of culture.

---

[8]Alfred Schutz, *The Phenomenology of the Social World* (Evanston, IL: Northwestern University Press, 1967, originally published in 1932).

[9]Emile Durkheim and Marcel Mauss, *Primitive Classification* (Chicago, IL: University of Chicago Press, 1963, originally published in 1903).

[10]Claude Levi-Strauss, *Myth and Meaning* (New York: Schocken, 1979); *A World Without Wane* (London: Hutchinson, 1961); *Structural Anthropology* (Paris: Plon, 1964).

Along with this line of argument from structuralism came rather metaphorical uses of ideas from the emerging field on computer sciences, although these ideas had also appeared in Durkheim's later work. Culture, for example, was seen as structured by binary oppositions, such as good/bad, tall/short, present/past, and in fact, the diversity of culture and its capacity for restructuring itself inheres in this binary structure because one cultural or moral code about what is right also implies what is "not right," or codes pushing people to think in the present or future also imply what it means to think about the past. These metaphors still exist in structuralism and many other approaches in sociology[11]—for example, Giddens'[12] structuration theory summarized in the previous chapter or in functional theories like that developed by Niklas Luhmann,[13] who argued that each cultural code makes "negative copies of itself," which is another way of expressing the notion of binary oppositions.

To capture variations in the application of these ideas in contemporary cultural sociology,[14] I have selected several theorists for review: Robert Wuthnow, Pierre Bourdieu, Jeffrey Alexander, Gary Alan Fine, and my own theoretical excursions into cultural theorizing. Wuthnow extends the Durkheimian tradition in interesting ways; Bourdieu dramatically improves Marx's analysis of class structures from a cultural perspective; Alexander and colleagues are the most prominent advocates for "the strong program" in cultural sociology where the autonomy of culture as a force is emphasized; Fine develops a theory of idioculture that emphasizes the importance of group processes; and I seek to rehabilitate older ideas from functionalism on culture in more acceptable guise.

Cultural Analysis Today

Robert Wuthnow's Theory of Cultural Meanings

Robert Wuthnow's theory of culture[15] is one of the more creative approaches to structuralism, primarily because it blends structuralist concerns about relations among symbolic codes

---

[11]For some general works reviewing structuralism, see Anthony Giddens, "Structuralism, Post-structuralism and the Production of Culture," in *Social Theory Today*, eds. A. Giddens and J. H. Turner (Cambridge, UK: Polity Press, 2000); S. Clarke, *The Foundations of Structuralism* (Sussex, UK: Harvester, 1981); J. Sturrock, ed., *Structuralism and Science* (Oxford: Oxford University Press, 1979); W. G. Runciman, *"What Is Structuralism?" in Sociology in Its Place* (Cambridge: Cambridge University Press, 1970); Ino Rossi, *From the Sociology of Symbols to the Sociology of Signs* (New York: Columbia University Press, 1983) and Ino Rossi, ed., *Structural Sociology* (New York: Columbia University Press, 1982); Jacques Ehrmann, *Structuralism* (New York: Doubleday, 1970); Philip Pettit, *The Concept of Structuralism: A Critical Analysis* (Berkeley, CA: University of California Press, 1977); Charles C. Lemert, "The Uses of French Structuralism in Sociology," and Michelle Lamont and Robert Wuthnow, "Recent Cultural Sociology in Europe and the United States," in *Frontiers of Social Theory*, G. Ritzer, ed. (New York: Columbia University Press, 1990).

[12]Anthony Giddens, *The Constitution of Society* (Berkeley, CA: University of California Press, 1984).

[13]Niklas Luhmann, *The Differentiation of Society* (see note 1).

[14]For some reviews, see Robert Wuthnow and Marsha Witten, "New Directions in the Study of Culture," *Annual Review of Sociology* 14 (1988): pp. 149–167. See also Robert Wuthnow, James Davidson Hunter, Albert Bergesen, and Edith Kurzweil, *Cultural Analysis: The World of Peter L. Berger, Mary Douglas, Michel Foucault, and Jurgen Habermas* (London: Routledge & Kegan Paul, 1984).

[15]For examples of Robert Wuthnow's work on religion, see his *The Consciousness Reformation* (Berkeley: University of California Press, 1976) and *Experimentation in American Religion* (Berkeley: University of California Press, 1978).

with other theoretical traditions.[16] Among these other traditions are elements of dramaturgy, institutional analysis, and subjective approaches drawn from phenomenology.

Cultural Structure, Ritual, and Institutional Context

In Wuthnow's view, it is best to move away from an overemphasis on attitudes, beliefs, and meanings held by individuals in the analysis of culture. These are difficult to measure, and so instead, it is best to focus on observable communications of interacting individuals to understanding culture. Once emphasis shifts away from cultural meaning per se to the structure of culture in social contexts and in socially produced texts, other theoretical approaches become useful.

Dramaturgy (Chapter 7) is one essential supplement because of its emphasis on ritual as a mechanism for expressing and dramatizing symbols—an emphasis that clearly owes its root to Durkheimian theory. In a sense, individual interpersonal rituals as well as collective rituals express deeply held meanings, but at the same time, they affirm particular cultural structures. In so doing, ritual performs such diverse functions as reinforcing collective values, dramatizing certain relations, denoting key positions, embellishing certain messages, and highlighting particular activities.

Another important theoretical supplement is institutional analysis. Culture does not exist as an abstract structure in its own right. Nor is it simply dramatic and ritualized performances; it is also embedded in organized social structures. Culture is produced by actors and organizations that require resources—material, organizational, and political—if they are to develop systems of cultural codes, ritualize them, and transmit them to others. Once the institutional basis of cultural activity is recognized, then the significance of inequalities in resources, the use of power, and the outbreak of conflict become essential parts of cultural analysis.

The Moral Order

Wuthnow labels this view of culture as the study of *the moral order*. The moral order revolves around (1) the construction of systems of cultural codes, (2) the emission of rituals, and (3) the mobilization of resources to produce and sustain these cultural codes and rituals. Let me examine each of these in turn.

The Structure of Cultural Codes

A cultural code is a set of symbolic elements that define "the nature of commitment to a particular course of behavior." Contrary to views of cultural codes as having a tight logic, as Levi-Strauss had argued, Wuthnow only sees sets of cultural elements that have an "identifiable structure," which can be used "to make sense of" situations and areas that can generate problems in establishing the nature of moral obligations. Wuthnow sees three such distinctions as crucial to structuring a moral order from cultural codes: (1) moral objects versus real programs, (2) core self versus enacted social roles, and (3) inevitable constraints versus intentional options. Below, I review each of these.

---

[16]Robert Wuthnow, *Meaning and Moral Order: Explorations in Cultural Analysis* (Berkeley, CA: University of California Press, 1987). For a review of this work, see Jonathan H. Turner, "Cultural Analysis and Social Theory," *American Journal of Sociology* 94 (July 1988): pp. 637–644.

1. *Moral Objects and Programs.* The structure of a moral order distinguishes between (a) the *objects of commitment* and (b) the activities or *real programs* in which the committed are engaged. The objects of commitment can vary—a person, a set of beliefs and values, a text, and so on. Real program can be almost any kind of activity. The critical points that the objects of moral commitment and the behavior emitted to demonstrate this commitment are "connected" and, yet, "different." For example, one's object of commitment might be "making a better life for one's children," which is to be realized through "hard work" and other activities or real programs. For the structure of a moral order to be effective, it must implicitly distinguish and, at the same time, connect such objects and real programs.

2. *Real Self and Roles.* The structure of moral codes must also, in Wuthnow's view, distinguish between (a) the person's "real self" or "true self" and (b) the various "roles" that this person plays. Moral structures always link self-worth and behavior but, at the same time, allow them to be distinguished so that there is a "real me" who is morally worthy and who can be separated from the roles that can potentially compromise this sense of self-worth. For example, when someone reveals "role distance," an assertion is being made that a role is beneath one's dignity or self-worth.

3. *The Inevitable and Intentional.* Moral codes must also distinguish between (a) those forces that are out of people's control and (b) those that are within the realm of their will. That is, the inevitable must be distinguished from the intentional. In this way, cultural codes posit a moral evaluation of those behaviors that can be controlled through intent and will power, while forgiving or suspending evaluation for what is out of a person's control. Without this distinction, it would be impossible to know what kinds of behaviors of individuals are to be subject to moral evaluations.

Thus, the structure of a moral order revolves around three basic types of codes that denote and distinguish commitments with respect to (1) moral objects/real programs, (2) self/roles, and (3) inevitable constraint/intentional options. These three basic types of codes indicate what is desirable by separating and, yet at the same time, also linking objects, behavior, self, roles, constraints, and intentions. Without this denotation of, and a distinction along, these three axes, a moral order and the institutional system in which it is lodged will reveal crises and will begin to break down. If objects and programs are not denoted, distinguished, and yet linked, then cynicism becomes rampant; if self and roles are confused, then loss of self-worth spreads; and if constraints and control are blurred, then apathy or frustration increases.

The Nature of Ritual

A moral ritual dramatizes collective values and demonstrates individuals' moral responsibility for such values through the enactment of emotion-arousing rituals. In so doing, rituals operate to maintain the moral order—that is, the system of symbolic codes ordering moral objects/real programs, self/roles, and constraints/options. Such rituals can be embedded in normal interaction as well as in more elaborate collective ceremonies, and they can be privately or publicly performed. But the key point is that ritual is a basic mechanism for sustaining the moral order—as idea clearly borrowed from Durkheim and extended in Goffman's dramaturgy (see Chapter 7).

Ritual is also used to cope with uncertainty in the social relations regulated by the codes of the moral order. Whether through increased options, uses of authority, ambiguity in expectations, lack of clarity in values, "equivocality" in key symbols, or unpredictability in key social relations, uncertainty will often be invoked to deal with these varying bases of uncertainty. Uncertainty is thus one of the sources of escalated ritual activity. However, such uses of ritual are usually tied to efforts at mobilizing resources in institutional contexts to create a new moral order.

Institutional Context and Resources

For a moral order to exist, it must be produced and reproduced, and for new moral codes to emerge—seen by Wuthnow as *ideologies*—these new ideologies also must be actively produced by actors using resources. Thus systems of symbolic codes depend on material and organizational resources. If a moral order is to persist, and if a new ideology is to become a part of the moral order, it must have a stable supply of resources for actors to use in sustaining the moral order, or in propagating a new ideology. That is, actors must have the material goods necessary to sustain themselves and the organizations in which they participate; they must have organizational bases that depend not only on material goods, such as money, but also on organizational "know-how," communication networks, and leadership; and at times, they must also have power. Thus, the moral order is anchored in institutional structures revolving around material goods, money, leadership, communication networks, and organizational capacities.

Ideology

Wuthnow defines ideologies as symbols that express and/or dramatize some aspect of the moral order. The basic idea appears to be that an ideology is a subset of symbolic codes emphasizing a *particular aspect* of the more inclusive moral order. The moral order is altered through the development and subsequent institutionalization of new ideologies, and ideologies are the driving force of change—much as Marx emphasized.

The production, use in mobilizing individuals, and eventual institutionalization of ideologies are all dependent upon (1) the mobilization of other types of resources (leaders, communication networks, organizations, and material goods) and (2) the development and use of rituals highlighting the morality of an ideology. New ideologies must often compete with one another for attention, with the consequence that ideologies with superior resource bases are more likely to survive this competition and become a part of the moral order. There is, then, an ecological dimension to ideologies as competing in resource niches composed of potential adherents to the ideology.

The Dynamics of the Moral Order

Wuthnow employs an ecological framework for the analysis of dynamics (see Chapter 4). If a moral order (1) does not specify the ordering of moral objects/real programs, self/roles, and inevitable constraints/intentional controls, (2) cannot specify the appropriate communicative and ritual practices for its affirmation and dramatization, and as a result of these conditions, (3) cannot reduce the risks associated with various activities, then there will be some ambiguity in most situations. The consequence of this ambiguity is that individuals will not have sufficient guidance, and their actions will be somewhat unpredictable. Under conditions of uncertainty and ambiguity, new ideologies become likely to emerge as a way of reducing these conditions. New ideological production will increase with (1) high degrees of heterogeneity in the types of social units—classes, groups, organizations, and so forth—in a society; (2) high levels of diversity in resources and their distribution; (3) high rates of change (realignment of power, redistribution of resources, establishment of new structures, creation of new types of social relations); (4) inflexibility in cultural codes (created by tight connections among a few codes); and (5) reduced capacity of political authority to repress new cultural codes, rituals, and mobilization of resources.

In an ecological perspective, these processes increase "ideological variation" that, in turn, increases the level of "competition" among ideologies. Some ideologies are "more fit" to survive this competition and, as a consequence, are "selected." Such "fitness" and "selection" depends on an ideology's capacity to accomplish several goals: (1) define social relations in ways reducing uncertainty (over moral objects, programs, self, roles, constraints, options, risks, ambiguities, and unpredictability); (2) reveal a flexible structure consisting of many elements weakly connected; (3) secure a resource base (particularly money, adherents, organizations, leadership, and communication channels); (4) specify ritual and communicative practices; (5) establish autonomous goals; and (6) achieve legitimacy in the eyes of political authority and in terms of existing values and procedural rules.

The more that these six conditions can be met, the more likely is an ideology to survive in competition with other ideologies and the more likely it is to become institutionalized as part of the moral order. In particular, the institutionalization of an ideology depends on the establishment of rituals and modes of communication affirming the new moral codes within organizational arrangements that allows for *ritual dramatization* of new codes reducing uncertainty, that secures a stable resource base, and that eventually receives acceptance by political authority.

Different types of ideological movements will emerge, Wuthnow appears to argue, under varying configurations of conditions that produce variation, competition, selection, and institutionalization.

Pierre Bourdieu's Constructivist Structuralism[17]

Pierre Bourdieu has characterized his work as "constructivist structuralism" or "structuralist constructivism."[18] Structures constrain action, but this constraint is not absolute. People use their capacities for thought, reflection, and action to *construct* social and cultural phenomena. They do so within the parameters of existing structures, but these structures are repositories of materials and resources that can be used for a wide variety of social and cultural constructions. Acknowledging his structuralist roots, Bourdieu analogizes to the relation of grammar and language in order to make this point: The grammar of a language only loosely constrains the production of actual speech; it can be seen as defining the possibilities for new kinds of speech acts.[19] So it is with social and cultural structures: They exist independently of agents and guide

---

[17]This section is coauthored with Stephan Fuchs.

[18]Indeed, Bourdieu has been enormously prolific, having authored some twenty-five books and hundreds of articles in a variety of fields, including anthropology, education, cultural history, linguistics, philosophy, and sociology. His empirical work covers a wide spectrum of topics—art, academics, unemployment, peasants, classes, religion, sports, kinship, politics, law, and intellectuals. See Loic J. D. Wacquant, "Towards a Reflexive Sociology: A Workshop with Pierre Bourdieu," *Sociological Theory* 7 (1, Spring 1989): pp. 26–63. This article also contains a selected bibliography on Bourdieu's own works as well as secondary analyses and comments on Bourdieu.

[19]Pierre Bourdieu, "Social Space and Symbolic Power," *Sociological Theory* 7 (1, Spring, 1989): p. 14.

their conduct, and at the same time, they also create options, possibilities, and paths for creative actions and for the construction of new and unique cultural and social phenomena.

Bourdieu's Cultural Conflict Theory

Bourdieu has explored many topics, but the conceptual core of his sociology is a vision of social classes and the cultural forms associated with these classes.[20] In essence, Bourdieu combines a Marxian theory of objective class position in relation to the means of production with a Weberian analysis of status groups (lifestyles, tastes, prestige) and politics (organized efforts to have one's class culture dominate). The key to this reconciliation of Karl Marx's and Max Weber's views of stratification is the expanded conceptualization of *capital* as more than economic and material resources, coupled with elements of French structuralism.[21]

Classes and Capital

To understand Bourdieu's view of classes, it is first necessary to recognize a distinction among four types of capital:[22] (1) *economic capital*, or productive property (money and material objects that can be used to produce goods and services); (2) *social capital*, or positions and relations in groupings and social networks; (3) *cultural capital*, or informal interpersonal skills, habits, manners, linguistic styles, educational credentials, tastes, and lifestyles, and (4) *symbolic capital*, or the use of symbols to legitimate the possession of varying levels and configurations of the other three types of capital.

These forms of capital can be converted into one another, but only to a certain extent. The degree of convertibility of capital on various "markets" is itself at stake in social struggles. The overproduction of academic qualifications, for example, can decrease the convertibility of educational into economic capital ("credential inflation"). As a result, owners of credentials must struggle to get their cultural capital converted into economic gains, such as high-paying jobs. Likewise, the extent to which economic capital can be converted into social capital is at stake in struggles over control of the political apparatus, and the efforts of those with economic capital to "buy" cultural capital can often be limited by their perceived lack of "taste" (a type of cultural capital).

The distribution of these four types of capital determines the objective class structure of a social system. The overall class structure reflects the total amount of capital possessed by various groupings. Hence the dominant class will possess the most economic, social, cultural, and symbolic capital; the middle class will possess less of these forms of capital; and the lower classes will have the least amount of these capital resources.

The class structure is not, however, a simple lineal hierarchy. Within each class are *factions* that can be distinguished by (1) the composition or configuration of their capital and (2) the

---

[20]Pierre Bourdieu, *Language and Symbolic Power* (Cambridge, MA: Harvard University Press, 1989).

[21]Pierre Bourdieu, *Distinction: A Social Critique of the Judgement of Taste* (Cambridge, MA: Harvard University Press, 1984). Pierre Bourdieu, *Homo Academicus* (Stanford, CA: Stanford University Press, 1988).

[22]Pierre Bourdieu, "The Forms of Capital," in *Handbook of Theory and Research in the Sociology of Education*, ed. J. G. Richardson (New York: Greenwood, 1986). Bourdieu, *Outline of a Theory of Practice* (Cambridge: Cambridge University Press, 1977). See also Michele Lamont and Annette P. Larreau, "Cultural Capital: Allusions, Gaps, and Glissandos in Recent Theoretical Developments," *Sociological Theory* 6 (2, Fall 1988): pp. 153–168.

social origin and amount of time that individuals in families have possessed a particular profile or configuration of capital resources.

Table 9.1 represents schematically Bourdieu's portrayal of the factions in three classes. The top faction within a given class controls the greatest proportion of economic or productive capital typical of a class; the bottom faction possesses the greatest amount of cultural and symbolic capital for a class; and the middle faction possesses an intermediate amount of economic, cultural, and symbolic capital. The top faction is the dominant faction within a given class, and the bottom faction is the dominated faction for that class, with the middle faction being both superordinate over the dominated faction and subordinate to the top faction. As factions engage in struggles to control resources and legitimate themselves, they mobilize social capital to form groupings and networks of relations, but their capacity to form such networks is limited by their other forms of capital. Thus, the overall distribution of social capital (groups and organizational memberships, network ties, social relations, and so forth) for classes and their factions will correspond to the overall distribution of other forms of capital. However, the particular forms of groupings, networks, and social ties will reflect the particular configuration of economic, cultural, and symbolic capital typically possessed by a particular faction within a given class.

Bourdieu borrows Marx's distinction between a class "for itself" (organized to pursue its interests) and one "in itself" (unorganized but having common interests and objective location in a class and class faction), and then he argues that classes are not real groups but only "potentialities." As noted earlier, the objective distribution of resources for Bourdieu relates to actual groups as grammar relates to speech: It defines the possibilities for actors but requires actual people and concrete settings to become real. And, it is the transformation of class and class-faction interests into actual groupings that marks the dynamics of a society.

Such transformation involves the use of productive material, cultural, and symbolic capital to mobilize social capital (groups and networks); even more important, class conflict tends to revolve around the mobilization of symbols into ideologies that legitimate a particular composition of resources. Much conflict in human societies, therefore, revolves around efforts to manipulate symbols to make a particular pattern of social, cultural, and productive resources seem the most appropriate. For example, when intellectuals and artists decry the "crass commercialism," "acquisitiveness," and "greed" of big business, this activity involves the mobilization of symbols into an ideology that seeks to demean forms of capital held by elites and, thereby, to mitigate their domination by the owners of the means of production.

But class relations involve more than a simple pecking order. There are also homologies among similarly located factions within different classes. For example, the rich capitalists of the dominant class and the small business owners of the middle class are equivalent in their control of productive resources and their dominant position relative to other factions in their respective classes. Similarly, intellectuals, artists, and other cultural elites in the dominant class are equivalent to schoolteachers in the middle class because of their reliance on cultural capital and because of their subordinate position in relation to those who control the material resources of their respective classes.

These homologies in class factions across different classes make class conflict complex, because those in similar objective positions in different classes—say, intellectuals and schoolteachers—will mobilize symbolic resources into somewhat similar ideologies—in this example, emphasizing learning, knowledge for its own sake, and life of the mind and, at the same time, decrying crass materialism. Such ideologies legitimate their own class position and attack those

Table 9.1   Representation of Classes and Class Factions in Industrial Societies*

Dominant Class: Richest in all forms of capital
Dominant faction: Richest in economic capital, which can be used to buy other types of capital. This faction is composed primarily of those who own the means of production—that is, the classical bourgeoisie.
Intermediate faction: Some economic capital, coupled with moderate levels of social, cultural, and symbolic capital. This faction is composed of high-professionals.
Dominated faction: Little economic capital but high levels of cultural and symbolic capital. This faction is composed of intellectuals, artists, writers, and others who possess cultural resources valued in a society.
Middle Class: Moderate levels of all forms of capital
Dominant faction: Highest in this class in economic capital but having considerably less economic capital than the dominant faction of the dominant class. This faction is composed of petite bourgeoisie (small business owners).
Intermediate faction: Some economic, social, cultural, and symbolic capital but considerably less than the intermediate faction of the dominant class. This faction is composed of skilled clerical workers.
Dominated faction: Little or no economic capital and comparatively high social, cultural, and symbolic capital. This class is composed of educational workers, such as schoolteachers, and other low-income and routinized professions that are involved in cultural production.
Lower Class: Low levels of all forms of capital
Dominant faction: Comparatively high economic capital for this general class. It is composed of skilled manual workers.
Intermediate faction: Lower amounts of economic and other types of capital. It is composed of semi-skilled workers without credentials.
Dominated faction: Very low amounts of economic capital. There is some symbolic capital in uneducated ideologues and intellectuals for the poor and working person.

*I have had to make inferences from Bourdieu's somewhat rambling text, but the table captures the imagery of Bourdieu's analysis. He probably would not like this layered (like a cake) imagery in the table, but the critical point is that individuals and families in factions of different classes often have more in common that individuals and families at different factions within a class. This makes stratification a much more complex phenomenon that is typically portrayed by sociologists.

who dominate them (by emphasizing the importance of those cultural resources that they have more of). At the same time, their homologous positions are separated by the different amounts of cultural capital owned: The intellectuals despise the strained efforts of schoolteachers to appear more sophisticated than they are, whereas the schoolteachers resent the decadent and irresponsible relativism of snobbish intellectuals. Thus, ideological conflict is complicated by the simultaneous convergence of factions within different classes and by the divergence of these factions by virtue of their position in different social classes.

Moreover, an additional complication stems from people sharing similar types and amounts of resources but having very different origins and social trajectories. Those who have recently moved to a class faction—say, the dominant productive elite or intermediate faction of the middle class—will have somewhat different styles and tastes than those who have been born into these classes, and these differences in social origin and mobility can create yet another source of ideological conflict. For example, the "old rich" will often comment on the "lack of class" and on the "ostentatiousness" of the "new rich," or the "solid middle class" will be somewhat snobbish toward the "the poor boy who made good" but who "still has a lot to learn" or who "still is a bit crude."

All those points of convergence and divergence within and between classes and class factions make the dynamics of stratification very complex. Although there is always an "objective class location," as determined by the amount and composition of capital and by the social origins of the holders of this capital, the development of organizations and ideologies is not a simple process. Bourdieu often ventures into a more structuralist mode when trying to sort out how various classes, class factions, and splits of individuals with different social origins within class factions generate categories of thought, systems of speech, signs of distinction, forms of mythology, modes of appreciation, tastes, and lifestyle.

The general argument is that objective location—(1) class, (2) faction within class, and (3) social origin—creates interests and structural constraints that, in turn, allow different social constructions.[23] Such constructions might involve the use of "formal rules" (implicitly known by individuals with varying interests) to construct cultural codes that classify and organize "things," "signs," and "people" in the world. This kind of analysis by Bourdieu has not produced a fine-grained structuralist model of how individuals construct particular cultural codes, but it has provided an interesting analysis of "class cultures." Such "class cultures" are always the dependent variable for Bourdieu, with objective class location being the independent variable and with rather poorly conceptualized structuralist processes of generative rules and cultural codes being the "intervening variables." Yet, the detailed description of these class cultures is perhaps Bourdieu's most unique contribution to sociology and is captured by his concept of *habitus*.

Class Cultures and Habitus

Those within a given class share certain modes of classification, appreciation, judgment, perception, and behavior. Bourdieu conceptualizes this mediating process between class and individual perceptions, choices, and behavior as *habitus*. In a sense, *habitus* is the "collective unconscious" of those in similar positions because it provides cognitive and emotional guidelines that enable individuals to represent the world in common ways and to classify, choose, evaluate, and act in a particular manner.

Habitus creates syndromes of taste, speech, dress, manner, and other responses. For example, a preference for particular foods will tend to correspond to tastes in art, ways of dressing, styles of speech, manners of eating, and other cultural actions among those sharing a common class location. There is, then, a correlation between the class hierarchy and the cultural objects, preferences, and behaviors of those located at particular ranks in the hierarchy. For instance, Bourdieu devotes considerable attention to "taste," which is seen as one of the most visible manifestations of the habitus.

---

[23]Bourdieu, *Distinction* and *Outline of a Theory of Practice* (cited in note 22).

Bourdieu views "taste" in a holistic and anthropological sense to include appreciation of art, ways of dressing, and preferences for foods.[24] Although taste appears as an innocent, natural, and personal phenomenon, it co-varies with objective class location: The upper class is to the working class what an art museum is to television; the old upper class is to the new upper class what polite and distant elegance is to noisy and conspicuous consumption; and the dominant is to the dominated faction of the upper class what opera is to avant-garde theater. Because tastes are organized in a cultural hierarchy that mirrors the social hierarchy of objective class location, conflicts between tastes are class conflicts.

Bourdieu roughly distinguishes between two types of tastes, which correspond to high versus low overall capital, or high versus low objective class position. The "taste of liberty and luxury" is the taste of the upper class; as such, it is removed from direct economic necessity and material need. The taste of liberty is the philosophy of art for its own sake. Following Immanuel Kant, Bourdieu calls this aesthetic the "pure gaze." The pure gaze looks at the sheer form of art and places this form above function and content. The upper-class taste of luxury is not concerned with art illustrating or representing some external reality; art is removed from life, just as upper-class life is removed from harsh material necessity. Consequently, the taste of luxury purifies and sublimates the ordinary and profane into the aesthetic and beautiful. The pure gaze confers aesthetic meaning to ordinary and profane objects because the taste of liberty is at leisure to relieve objects from their pragmatic functions. Thus, as the distance form basic material necessities increases, the pure gaze or the taste of luxury transforms the ordinary into the aesthetic, the material into the symbolic, the functional into the formal. And, because the taste of liberty is that of the dominant class, it is also the dominant and most legitimate taste in society.

In contrast, the working class cultivates a "popular" aesthetic. Their taste is the taste of necessity, for working-class life is constrained by harsh economic imperatives. The popular taste wants art to represent reality and despises formal and self-sufficient art as decadent and degenerate. The popular taste favors the simple and honest rather than the complex and sophisticated. It is downgraded by the "legitimate" taste of luxury as naive and complacent, and these conflicts over tastes are class conflicts over cultural and symbolic capital.

Preferences for certain works and styles of art, however, are only part of "tastes" as ordered by habitus. Aesthetic choices are correlated with choices made in other cultural fields. The taste of liberty and luxury, for example, corresponds to the polite, distant, and disciplined style of upper-class conversation. Just as art is expected to be removed from life, so are the bodies of interlocutors expected to be removed from one another and so is the spirit expected to be removed from matter. Distance from economic necessity in the upper-class lifestyle not only corresponds to an aesthetic of pure form, but it also entails that all natural and physical desires are to be sublimated and dematerialized. Hence, upper-class eating is highly regulated and disciplined, and foods that are less filling are preferred over fatty dishes. Similarly, items of clothing are chosen for fashion and aesthetic harmony, rather than for functional appropriateness. "Distance from necessity" is the motif underlying the upper-class lifestyle as a whole, not just aesthetic tastes as one area of practice.

---

[24]Bourdieu, "The Forms of Capital" (cited in note 22). For another cultural approach to analyzing classes, see Michelle Lamont, *Money, Morals and Manners: The Culture of the French and American Upper-Middle Class* (Chicago, IL: University of Chicago Press, 1992); "Symbolic Boundaries and Status," in *Cultural Sociology*, ed. Lyn Spillman (Malden, MA and Oxford: Blackwell, 2002), pp. 98–119; *The Dignity of Working Men: Morality and the Boundaries of Race, Class, and Immigration* (Cambridge: Harvard University Press and New York: Russell Sage Foundation. Paperback 2002).

Conversely, because they are immersed in physical reality and economic necessity, working-class people interact in more physical ways, touching one another's bodies, laughing heartily, and valuing straightforward outspokenness more than distant and "false" politeness. Similarly, the working-class taste favors foods that are more filling and less "refined" but more physically gratifying. The popular taste chooses clothes and furniture that are functional, and this is so not only because of sheer economic constraints but also because of a true and profound dislike of that which is "formal" and "fancy."

In sum, then, Bourdieu has provided a conceptual model of class conflict that combines elements of Marxian, Weberian, and Durkheimian sociology. The structuralist aspects of Bourdieu's conceptualization of habitus as the mediating process between class position and individual behavior have been underemphasized in this review, but clearly Bourdieu places Durkheim "back on his feet" by emphasizing that class position determines habitus. However, the useful elements of structuralism—systems of symbols as generative structures of codes—are retained and incorporated into a theory of class conflict as revolving around the mobilization of symbols into ideologies legitimating a class position and the associated lifestyle and habitus.

Jeffrey C. Alexander's Approach to Cultural Pragmatics

To many cultural sociologists,[25] much analysis of culture is part of a "weak program" where culture is seen as something that emerges out of structural arrangements and that can only be theorized in reference to social structures. A *strong program*, in contrast, makes culture the main topic rather than, in Marx's works, a "superstructure" to material social-structural conditions. This strong program is to involve "thick descriptions" of symbolic meanings and the mechanisms by which such meanings are constructed. Culture is seen as texts with themes, plotlines, moral evaluations, traditions, frameworks, and other properties that make culture an autonomous realm, separated from social structure.

Much of the work in such a strong program would be empirical, examining specific types of cultural formations and analyzing them in detail. And, only after such a strong program has existed for a time should the relationship between culture and social structure be examined through such processes as rituals and interactions.

Jeffrey Alexander and his colleagues at Yale and other key centers of cultural theorizing have been part of the movement pushing for a strong program. Even though not all cultural sociologists go this far, most cultural sociologists have been influenced by the call for the analysis of culture per se and by the need to engage in rich and thick empirical descriptions of cultural processes. Of course, description does not always lead to theorizing about why the culture described exists and operates the way it does. Thus, even a strong program must eventually begin to explain cultural dynamics more than simply describe empirical manifestations of these

---

[25]See, for example, Jeffrey C. Alexander, Ron Eyerman, Bernard Giessen, and Neil J. Smelser, *Cultural Trauma and Collective Identity* (University of California Press, 2004); Jeffrey Alexander, Bernard Giessen, and Jason Mast, *Social Performance: Symbolic Action, Cultural Pragmatics, and Ritual* (Cambridge, UK: Cambridge University Press, 2006); Philip Smith and A. T. Riley, *Cultural Theory*, 2nd ed. (Oxford, UK: Blackwell); Jeffrey C. Alexander, *The Civil Sphere* (Oxford University Press, 2006); Jeffrey Alexander, *The Meaning of Social Life: A Cultural Sociology* (New York: Oxford University Press, 2005; Jeffrey Alexander, Ronald Jacobs, and Philip Smith, *The Oxford Handbook of Cultural Sociology* (New York: Oxford University Press, 2012).

dynamics. Alexander's work on "cultural pragmatics" is a good illustration of moving beyond description to explain at least a limited range of cultural processes.[26]

In pursuing the goal to develop theories about culture, Alexander blends a heavy dose of Emile Durkheim's analysis of ritual and emotion in *The Elementary Forms of the Religious Life* with Erving Goffman's dramaturgy (see Chapter 7). This mix makes sense because one of the most conspicuous strands of cultural theorizing revolves around rituals and performances that arouse emotions, which bring background "collective representations," "implicit scripts," and "themes" to the foreground of interaction with audiences of others.

History of Ritualized Performances

Alexander draws from Durkheim's distinction between *mechanical* and *organic* solidarity (employed in *The Division of Labor in Society*, but subsequently abandoned) to present a condensed history of ritualized performances. In simple, homogenous societies (mechanical), all of the elements of performances are seamless so that culture is always in the foreground, making individuals experience rituals as personal, immediate, and iconographic. The cultural script, texts, collective representations, stage, props, actors, audience, means for symbolic production, and social powers of individuals are, as he puts it, *fused* together, allowing interaction to seem not only seamless but *authentic* as individuals engage in ritual performances to immediate audiences.

With the differentiation of societies, however, there comes (1) a separation of foreground texts and background symbolic representations, (2) an estrangement of the symbolic means of production from the mass of social actors, and (3) a disconnect between elites who carry out symbolic actions and their mass audiences. The result is that successful performances are no longer automatic but something that takes skill and effort to *re-fuse* the elements of background representations with *texts* that are used in the foreground, on a stage, in ritual performances in front of audiences. Rituals become the means by which the disparate elements of culture are *re*-assembled through effort and performances.

At times in primary groups, re-fusion is not so necessary even in complex societies; interaction rituals proceed smoothly and seamlessly as background comes to foreground in an emotionally gratifying way. Still, the dramatic increase in the number and scale of social spaces and the vast public sphere in modern, complex societies inevitably cause separation among the elements of performances. As a consequence, it is always problematic as to how to re-fuse them through ritual performances among people. The cultural world is fragmented and detached from many performances, giving the modern world problems of cultural integration and meaning in social situations—very old themes that go back to the founding of sociology.

Alexander has, with a different vocabulary, rephrased the basic problem that Durkheim emphasized in his earlier work in *The Division of Labor in Society*. How can performances be made in ways that re-fuse what inevitably gets decomposed with structural and cultural differentiation in a society? For Alexander, a successful performance that re-fuses background to foreground "stands or falls" upon individuals and collective actions to achieve what he terms (1) *cultural extension* of the background representations and its interpretation in a text to the

---

[26]Jeffrey C. Alexander, "Cultural Pragmatics: Social Performances Between Ritual and Strategy," *Sociological Theory* 22 (2004): pp. 512–574.

audience and (2) *psychological* (and emotional) *identification* of the audience with performances and its interpretation of the background representations as text. Only in this way can the fragmentation of complex societies be overcome in performances. Alexander's theory is thus about the steps and strategies of actors in successfully re-fusing culture during their performances. I will come back to these shortly, but let me now backtrack to outline some of the basic assumptions that Alexander makes in developing his theory of cultural pragmatics.

Assumptions About Actors and Performances

Alexander assumes that actors are motivated by moral concerns and that they seek to bring both background representations and scripts of culture to the forefront of action and interaction with audiences. In realizing this fundamental goal, Alexander lists emphasizes several key properties of re-fusing:

1. Actors convert background representation of culture and scripts into *texts* that decode and interpret these background elements of culture.

2. To bring off a successful performance, actors must also achieve *cathexis*, or some kind of emotional attachment to the text as it has been decoded.

3. With interpretations of background representations and scripts that are emotionally valenced, individuals and potentially collective actors are in a better position to engage in cultural extension of the text to the audience; if successful, the audience will psychologically identify with the performance and the underlying text, script, and background representations.

4. In making a performance to an audience, actors always assess the means of symbolic reproduction, or the stage and props that are available for a performance.

5. The dramatic presentation of text thus involves physical and verbal gestures on a stage where props are used to enhance the performance.

6. Performances like all actions are constrained by power, which can delimit, limit, or facilitate access to text as well as the availability of stages, staging props, actors who can engage in performances, and audiences that these actors can reach in interpreting and decoding background cultural elements into a text.

As is evident, the dramatic metaphor is central to cultural pragmatics, which perhaps makes it a part of dramaturgy. Moreover, much like dramaturgy summarized in Chapter 7, there is an emphasis on *strategic* elements in just how to go about (a) reaching or achieving *cultural extension* to an audience and (b) getting the members of the audience to *identify* with the performance and the cultural text.

Challenges and Strategies Employed in Performances

Re-fusing always poses challenges that, in turn, lead actors to adopt various strategies for achieving cultural extension and audience identification with a performance and its underlying text. First, in order to give a successful performance, an effective *script* must be created that compresses background cultural meanings and intensifies these meanings in ways that facilitate an effective performance. Alexander lists several techniques for doing so: (a) *cognitive simplification* of background representations so that audiences do not need to deal with too much complexity, (b) *time-space compression* that collapses elements in time and space so that the elements are highlighted and less dependent upon contextual interpretations, (c) *moral agonism* whereby representations are stated as dichotomies such as good vs. evil, conflicts against enemies, and challenges that must overcome obstacles, and (d) *twistings and turnings* in the plot line that keeps audiences engaged.

Second, re-fusing involves a script, action, and performances as actors "walk and talk" in space. This process is more engaging when writers of scripts leave room for dramatic inventions and interpretations and when directors of staged actions allow for some dramatic license on the part of performers. When scripts, direction, and staging are too tightly orchestrated, performances come off as stiff, artificial and less engaging than when actors are seen as authentically brining to an audience emotionally charged background elements of culture.

Third, re-fusing always involves the use of social power. This power must be mobilized on at least three fronts: (a) the appropriation of relevant symbolic means of production, such as the right venues and stages where a performance can be most effective and reach the right audience; (b) the appropriation of the means of symbolic distribution in which the background representations can be secured and then through performances distributed to audiences; and (c) the appropriation of some control over the subsequent debate, discourse, and criticism of a performance.

Fourth, actors are always in a double re-fusing situation. They have to connect with the (a) text and, then, (b) the audience. The best way to bring off this "double re-fusion" is through giving a performance that seems natural and as part of the ongoing flow of the situation, whereas disjointed performances will only exacerbate the process of re-fusing. This problem is aggravated in complex societies as individuals play different roles in highly diverse social context; under these conditions, it is often difficult to give a performance in all stages that is natural rather than somewhat disjointed. The result is that re-fusing will fail, or partially fail, thereby reducing the extension of culture and audience identification.

And fifth, there is the challenge of re-fusing audience with the performance text because, in complex societies, audiences are frequently diverse, larger, and separated in time and space from actors, as is especially the case with performances that are given through various media. This reality of the stages and audiences in complex societies places enormous demands on actors, directors, and scriptwriters to pull off an effective performance. Some of the strategies listed above—cognitive simplification, time-space compression, moral agonism, and twists and turns are one set of means for overcoming the problems of appealing the larger, more diverse, and separated audiences. These strategies simplify, de-contextualize to a degree, moralize, and make engaging the text and performance in ways that extend the culture to the audience and emotionally pull them in to the point of identifying with the performance and text.

Why Pragmatics?

I have stated Alexander's argument abstractly, as he does, but without examples. The point of the theory, I believe, is to emphasize that fusing of background cultural elements with performances is a generic and universal process that has been made more difficult and challenging in complex, highly differentiated societies. Yet, if the background culture of a society cannot be fused with actors' performances, the problems of integration in complex societies become that much greater. In simple, homogeneous societies of the past, performances were naturally fused, but with complexity, active re-fusing through dramatic performances must occur. This re-fusing, I believe Alexander intends to argue, can occur at many different levels and among different types of actors. The process is perhaps easiest at the level of encounters of face-to-face interaction, but if those interacting are strangers to each other and from different backgrounds, then the interaction will often be awkward and stilted because the script, direction, staging, use of props, and acting in front of the audience are disjointed or unclear. At the other extreme are dramatic performances by (political, economic, religious) actors to large audiences given through mass media, and here the same problems exist. The actors confront a large, diverse, and spatially disconnected audience where the script, performance, text, and staging must somehow pull in diverse audiences who are asked to emotionally identify with the performance and text being brought forward. Relatively few actors can pull this off in natural settings, although good actors in movies and on theatrical stage are often able to pull audiences into their performances, but these successful performances only highlight the difficulty of doing so in real life situations. In between encounters of individuals and media presentations are performances at all the intervening levels of society—groups, organizations, civic meeting, lectures, rallies, protest events, revolutions, and other stages[27]—where actors confront audiences of varying sizes and backgrounds and where they must give a performance that extends culture and pulls the audience into the performance and text so that they identify emotionally with both. Again, only relatively few actors can bring these kinds of performances off and achieve full re-fusion. And yet, the viability of complex societies depends upon some degree of success in such performances.

Thus, ritual performances that connect audience with texts that decode background cultural representations are s key dynamic, in Alexander's view, in all social situations. Yet, many situations in complex societies are fragmented because they have been subject to de-fusion as a simple consequence of the scale and differentiation of society. In these de-fused situations, the importance of performance rituals becomes ever-more evident because performances are not automatic, nor do they seamlessly unfold. Whether it be one person in an encounter writing the script, decoding background representations in a text, appropriating stages and props, and giving the performance or a large team of actors coordinating the writing, directing, staging, marketing, and securing actors and audiences, the dynamics are the same; moreover, they are critical to the integration of societies.

Only with a strong program in cultural sociology, Alexander seems to argue, would this need to bring cultural representations from background to the front stage be seen as critical. Without a prior understanding of the dynamics of culture per se, the ritual performances needed to make cultural assumptions salient, relevant, and engrossing to audiences would not be appreciated and, hence, theorized.

---

[27]For example, the titles of the following books by Alexander reveal that more macro-level effects of performance dynamics: *Performative Revolution in Egypt: An Essay on Cultural Power* (New York: Oxford University Press, 2011); *The Performance of Politics: Obama's Victory and The Democratic Struggle for Power* (New York: Oxford University Press, 2010); and *Peformance of Power* (Cambridge, UK: Polity Press, 2011).

Gary Alan Fine's Theory of Idioculture

For many years, Gary Alan Fine has been the strongest advocate for conceptualizing groups as the critical meso-level structure that mediates between interactions among persons, on the one side, and more macro-level structures such as institutional domains, on the other. Groups give "tensile strength" to interaction by providing spaces for interactions to build up a shared culture that incorporates cultural elements from more macro structures but, even more importantly, generates culture that not only orders relations among micro-level interactions in groups but, potentially, can spread across networks to other groups and up lines of structural embeddedness to macrostructure formations. In his *Tiny Publics: A Theory of Group Action and Culture*,[28] Fine brings together ideas developed in many essays, and while the theory is not tightly integrated, it is highly evocative and adds considerably to the revival of cultural theorizing in sociology.

What Is Idioculture?

For Fine, the defining characteristic of groups is the development of a shared culture, or *idioculture* that consists of "a system of knowledge, beliefs, behaviors, and customs shared by members of an interacting group to which members can refer and that serves as a basis for further interaction."[29] A group and its culture make strips of interaction more coherent and, in so doing, groups reveal a number of important characteristics:

1. *Social Control.* Groups socialize individuals into communal standards, and in so doing, they provide an important mechanism of social control, while also engaging in monitoring and sanctioning of conformity to communal standards, thereby adding an additional form of social control. And, if groups develop differences in power and authority among status locations, they add a third set of social control mechanisms.

2. *Contestation.* Groups provide an arena in which these cultural standards are developed and, if necessary, changed. Groups build up commitments to ideologies and frames for change; in fact, they are the locus of micro mobilizations for change that, if extended across groups and up to organizations, can turn into more meso- and macro-level mobilizations for change. Change, then, comes from the power of a group's idioculture to develop commitments to cultural ideologies that can become a starting point for mass mobilizations for change.

3. *Representations.* Groups provide spaces for the development, appropriation, and interpretation of meaning and objects that carry meanings. It is within groups that culture is created, and people use their cultural resources to create symbolic meanings and ideologies that represent the collective. These systems of symbols can trickle down from more macrostructures and their cultures, or be generated from interactions, but in both cases, these cultural elements become representations of both individuals and the group. And, they can often become symbols operating like totems to represent the culture of the group toward which ritualized performances affirm commitments to the group and its representations are made.

---

[28]Gary Alan Fine, *Tiny Publics: A Theory of Group Action and Culture* (New York: Russell Sage, 2012).

[29]Ibid., p. 8.

4. *Allocation.* Groups are spaces where people negotiate positions in a status order, often a hierarchical order, and in so doing, the culture of the group will include evaluations of, and expectations for, status within the group and, more generally, in the society as a whole.

Thus, as these processes of social control, contestation, representation, and allocation play themselves out in groups, the culture that is created gives groups the solidity to order interactions and, moreover, to provide a vessel to which the culture from other groups or from more macro-level formations can filter into and change the culture of the group. It is thus at the group level that culture takes hold of people, building commitments that have consequences not only for group members but also other types and levels of social structure and culture in a society.

The Dynamics of Idioculture

As soon as people interact, they begin to build up an idioculture by asking about background knowledge, by making collective references, by talking and reciprocally questioning each other during sociable interactions, and by suggesting rules, opinions, and information. As they do so, they begin to create an important property of a group: a history, or what Randall Collins has termed *particularistic cultural capital.* Culture is thus acted out, talked about, and made on the ground as individuals interact, and the more the group provides a structural locus and arena for interaction, the more clear will the idioculture become.

It is these dynamics that are at the core of culture, and for this reason, groups are important to theorizing about culture because this is where people "do" culture and assemble meanings. Groups are also the nexus for the mediation between cultural elements from more macro-structures and the interaction of individuals in a specific context. Idioculture is thus built up through a series of key dynamics, including the following:

1. *Known Knowledge.* In groups, people present and assess their known knowledge. Culture cannot emerge and evolve without this critical space where the respective knowledge of interactants can be presented.

2. *Use of Cultural Elements.* Once presented, individuals must assess and often negotiate over the use of this cultural knowledge. What elements of culture can be used by group members?

3. *Functionality.* People must assess the degree to which cultural elements help a group meet its goals and facilitate the survival and viability of the group. Functionality is a kind of selection process where members assess and negotiate which elements of a culture will facilitate its viability in the environment.

4. *Appropriateness.* Individuals also assess the extent to which culture is appropriate for the structure and existing patterns in the group. Do cultural elements challenge the existing set of arrangements, or are these elements compatible with existing status order and culture?

5. *Triggering Events.* While there are inertial tendencies in groups with an idioculture, events can trigger assessment of new elements of culture; and so, events can set into motion processes 2, 3, and 4 above as individuals in the group reassess what is usable, what is functional, and what is appropriate for the group.

Embedding and Constraints

Groups exist in an environment of other social structures and their cultures, and unlike many theorists, Fine recognizes that there is a *macro-level* foundation to mesostructures and microstructures and their cultures, while also recognizing that macrostructural and macro-cultural formations are built on the solidity of group structures that cement together interactions so that they have the strength to serve as the building blocks of larger-scale sociocultural systems. Thus, the embedding of groups in larger structures operates as a constraint as well as a conduit from larger structures and their cultures to groups and their idiocultures. This "exteriority" is both an obdurate feature of the environment of groups, but it is also a constructed set of perceptions by members of groups who assess the most salient constraints.

These constraints operate as (1) *physical* limitations that constrain movement and actions of group members, (2) *temporal* constraints of when various types of actions can occur, (3) *spatial* constraints on where actions can occur, (4) *institutional* constraints imposed by networks of groups lodged in organizations that make up most institutional domains, and (5) *traditional* burdens where the past "weighs heavily on the present" as a set of cultural traditions as well as structural constraints from institutional embeddedness listed under (4) above, and (6) limitations imposed by organizational primacy, where organizations become reified as objects that impose themselves on group processes because of their embeddedness in institutional domains that invoke the power of all other constraints, but especially (4) and (5) above.

Culture in Action and Performance

Norms are expectations for behaviors, but because they almost always carry an element of evaluation, they are also how individuals evaluate each other. Fine borrows from Erving Goffman the ideas of frame and framing that impose shared values, recognizable motivations, and normative expectations for behaviors. This framing moralizes norms and makes them object of special meanings. Fine emphasizes that individuals do not so much "obey" norms as *perform* them; norms are seen in the ways in which individuals orchestrate their behaviors in a dramatic performance in a situation. Not only do individuals perform norms, they also talk about them in "tellings" as they indicate what norms are and what happens when they are violated. Indeed, norms are often talked about and transformed into stories, which contain the moral message of why norms are important and cannot be violated. Thus, norms are a part of cultural narrations.

Norms are negotiated as individuals seek to determine what expectations are to be relevant in a group. These negotiations are constrained by the structural situation or scene in which interaction occurs and in which the group is embedded. Negotiations also have temporal limits, which must actively be extended in time or, if necessary, revised and reconstituted if conditions on the ground change or changes in the larger social structure require a change in norms.

Ideologies are a linked set of beliefs about the social and political order that are shared by members of a community; these beliefs have a high level of moral and evaluative content, indicating how individuals *should* think about and act in situations. Like norms, people act out ideologies in performances, thereby affirming or, if desired, changing the moral order defined by values, ideologies, and norms. Ideologies are thus behavioral, but they are also "images" of a moral order. Ideologies gain power and effectiveness when (1) the particular scene or situational context can be dramatically linked to widely held moral concerns of individuals, (2) the images connected to beliefs specify what is good, proper, and just, while providing guidelines for making decisions and taking actions, and (3) the situation in which an ideology is invoked is highly relevant to participants in a group.

Like norms, ideologies are not just "held"; they are both personal to individuals and shared with others in a group. As such, they become a characteristic of actors, their enacted relationships with other actors, and resources for presentations of individual actors or the group as a whole. Groups provide the space these enactment processes revolve around:

1. *Identification.* Ideologies served to promote an identification for self, as well as the group or community in which the ideology is enacted. As part of the conception that persons and groups have of themselves, ideology becomes capable of exerting great power.

2. *Rituals.* Ideologies represent one way that groups overcome "free-rider problems" where persons enjoy the benefits produced by group interaction without incurring the necessary costs. This power to limit free-riding relies on ritual performances of actors, reaffirming the moral tenets of an ideology publically and, thereby, making the necessary contribution to sustaining the culture and structure of the group.

3. *Resource Mobilization.* Ideologies are almost always linked to resource and efforts to secure resources necessary to sustain or change the group and, potentially, other groups and even institutional domains. By mobilizing rituals to affirm a moral order, groups can recruit new members and even material resources needed to achieve group goals.

Ideologies exert much of their power by arousing emotions. Ideologies are felt by individuals, and these emotions arouse individuals to engage in the rituals and other enactment processes necessary to sustain or even change ideologies. Decisions by individuals are also constrained by the emotional commitments that persons feel toward an ideology, and these decisions, in turn, determine behavioral enactments in the group. And as individuals engage in ritual performances reaffirming the moral tenets of the ideology, these performances arouse the emotions that attach people to the moral order of a group and to more remote social structures linked to the group.

The Diffusion of Culture

Groups are typically connected to each other via networks among individuals in different groups, or networks among the groups themselves. Institutional domains also knit groups together, often via organizations that ultimately are built from groups. As culture moves out along networks to include more groups, subcultures in a society are generated. And since culture can serve as a mechanism for securing resources, the culture of a group as it moves out from its origins and spreads to other groups can also generate not only subcultures but sub-societies composed of linked groups. Fine outlines a number of mechanisms by which idiocultures diffuse out from local groups to other groups and potentially to more macro-level structures and their culture.

One mechanism extending a group's culture is *multiple group memberships*. Individuals in complex societies are always members of different groups. As they occupy status locations and play roles in diverse groups, they also potentially bring the culture of one group to another.

Moreover, as individuals develop identities around their position in groups, the connection between identity and culture means that this identity will often be carried to other groups and played out, thus bringing the culture of one group through the back door to another group. A second mechanism resides in systems of *weak ties among diverse individuals* and groups. Weak ties also weaken boundaries among those linked by weak ties, with the result that culture can travel along these weak-tie relations and not have much resistance from the boundaries of groups (Conversely, if solidarity is sustained by strong ties among group members, these ties will resist diffusion of new cultural elements.) Third, even when the connection among groups is through marginal actors or stronger *actors in a brokerage situation* (standing between two groups and managing flow of resources), these actors fill in large holes in the network among groups and thus provide conduits by which culture travels across the space between groups. Media in a weak-tie society also allow for the diffusion of culture from one group to another. A fourth mechanism inheres in some *roles that, by their very nature, transcend group boundaries*. Roles such as lecturer, sales person, and all broker roles bring one group culture into another just by the process of playing the role out in diverse settings. A fifth mechanism is the *modes of connection* among groups. Some are hierarchical, as when one group has power over another, whereas another would be more horizontal where groups exchange resources. In both cases, the culture of one group moves into that of another. A sixth mechanism is *embedding* whereby groups are lodged inside communities or organizations and thus exposed to the culture of the more inclusive structure, while the larger structure will also have to reconcile its culture with the culture of its constituent groups. These and other mechanisms, Fine argues, allow groups and their cultures to begin as "a tiny spore from a mighty mushroom grows."[30]

Groups and Civil Society

Fine argues that groups or "tiny publics" carrying a culture are the seedbed of civil society. Groups provide the communal spaces that mitigate individualism and free-riding, while being the locale where "civil society is enacted."[31] As Fine argues, "groups define the terms of civic engagement, provide the essential resources, and link the movements to larger political and cultural domains."[32] Moreover, successful groups that influence civil society often become templates for the formation of similar groups, which also extend the reach and influence of groups. Small groups, then, are the key structures in understanding the dynamics of civic engagement by virtue of

1. *The Framing Function.* Groups provide "interpretative tools" to unpack and frame problems and issues of the larger social context in terms of local meanings in the group. These framing activities in groups can facilitate alignment of group members, as well as members of diverse groups; they can amplify the emerging ideologies about the goals of mobilizations to change some aspect of civil society; and these mobilizations further frame local context within the institutional domains that may require change.

---

[30]Ibid., p. 156.

[31]Ibid., p. 127.

[32]Ibid, p. 128.

2. *The Mobilization Function.* As noted earlier, groups and their ideologies operate to pull resources—new members, material and organizational resources, and cultural resources—into the group. These tiny publics, then, are the "gravitational centers of civic life" by drawing individuals into civic engagement and participation not just by the ideologies that they develop but also by the resources that they can pull into the group to support its goals. Politics is, in many ways, always "local," and local networks among families, friends, and associates are the stage for engagement, the ties that pull people into groups, and the magnate for resource mobilization.

3. *The Creating Citizens Function.* The emotions, cognitive sets, and cultural meanings that are generated in groups will radiate outwards to larger social venues and increase group members' civic identity. In so doing, groups not only increase these members' sense of group identity, but they nurture an identity tied to larger groups and civic structures in the society. In so doing, groups increase commitments at micro-interpersonal level, the meso level of the group and the organizations and communities in which the group is embedded, and the macro level of the society as a whole and/or its key institutional domains.

Groups thus provide the tensile strength for not only society but also for social movements that change the culture and structure of society. Groups provide the face-to-face interaction and ritual activities that charge up emotions and increase solidarity, and these become a *private good* that is highly rewarding to group members. These private goods, such as positive emotions and solidarity, increase commitments to groups and thus give groups power over individuals, while at the same time monitoring their members activities and, if necessary, sanctioning them. Groups also provide reputation resources, membership, and status locations, which also are rewarding to individuals. As a consequence, groups limit free-riding while increasing commitments to groups and their ideology. In so doing, groups become the building block of a social movement as its culture is extended out by the mechanisms of diffusion listed earlier.

The Centrality of Groups to Cultural Analysis

In sum, Fine makes a strong case for what Alexander might see as a "weak culture program" because idiocultures are still very much attached to social structure. Fine would argue, I think, that culture exerts influence because it is groups that are the necessary structure to develop idiocultures and commitments to these cultures; it is through the mechanisms linking groups that culture can diffuse outward, thereby opening up opportunities for ideological mobilizations for change that, again, ultimately start with groups.

Jonathan Turner's Explicitly "Weak" Cultural Program

Analytical Theorizing and Weak Programs of Cultural Analysis

Much cultural analysis before the revival of the "strong" program in cultural sociology was decidedly weak in two senses: First, there was less effort to separate structure and culture; instead, there was a clear emphasis on their connectedness, without a preference for declaring structure or culture as more primary. And second, the goal was not so much to tease out the empirically unique and robust nature of symbol systems but, rather, to emphasize the *generic* elements that always exist when culture emerges in *any* structural contexts emerge. Talcott Parsons' analysis of culture within his functional action theory (see Chapter 2) represented one type of weak program, while the emphasis on ideology and belief systems in analytical conflict theory was another example of a weak program (see Chapter 3). Just whether the strong program proposed by Alexander and his colleagues is needed as a corrective to previous under-emphasis on culture as a force in its own right can be debated, but even Gary Alan Fine's theoretical approach, which draws from very detailed and insightful qualitative research projects on a variety of groups is closer to the weak than strong program. In fact, as Alexander's theory demonstrates, once emphasis is on the explanatory theory rather than the empirical and historical details of culture, the theories all converge and seem to become part of a weaker program, as I will note when summing up cultural theory in the conclusions.

For the present, I will introduce my views of cultural dynamics as they can be theorized. I will draw from the outline of basic structural formations as different levels of social organization in Figure 8.9 on page 162 to illustrate an alternative form of cultural analysis. Social structure unfolds at three levels: the micro level of face-to-face interaction; the meso level of corporate units (groups, organizations, communities) and categoric units (social categories carrying evaluations and expectations); and the macro level of institutional domains, stratification systems, societies, and inter-societal systems (see Figure 8.9 on page 162 for an outline and page 160 for definitions of each of these universal structures). I have tended to call this distribution of basic structural forms at three levels of reality *sociocultural formations* because this is just what they are: They are social structures of a basic type with a culture that, I believe, can be conceptualized in more generic terms than a strong program would allow. That is, whatever the exact content of culture in these generic and universal types of social structures at the three fundamental levels (micro, meso, and macro), there are also generic types of cultural systems necessary for their operation.

A Weak Model of Culture and Levels of Social Organization

By comparing Figure 9.1 with Figure 8.9 on page 162, it is evident that I have attached cultural systems to the generic social structures of macro, meso, and micro levels of social reality. The arrows are intended to emphasize certain causal connections within and between levels, and it is in these connections that many of the dynamics of culture from an analytical standpoint occur. By emphasizing these aspects of culture, I am asserting that they are *the most important dimensions* of culture in understanding how sociocultural formations operate and interact with each other. I am, in many ways, going back to earlier analytical theories and suggesting what is needed for an explanation of cultural processes is simplification rather than an endless search for robust and situational meanings of culture in their unique historical context. The outline in Figure 9.1 is not the explanation but, rather, the guide to developing models and proposition describing cultural dynamics. In this short review, I cannot outline these dynamics in detail, but they can be found in other works.[33]

---

[33]Jonathan H. Turner, *Theoretical Principles of Sociology*, volumes 1, 2, and 3 (New York: Springer 2010–2012).

Figure 9.1 Levels of Culture

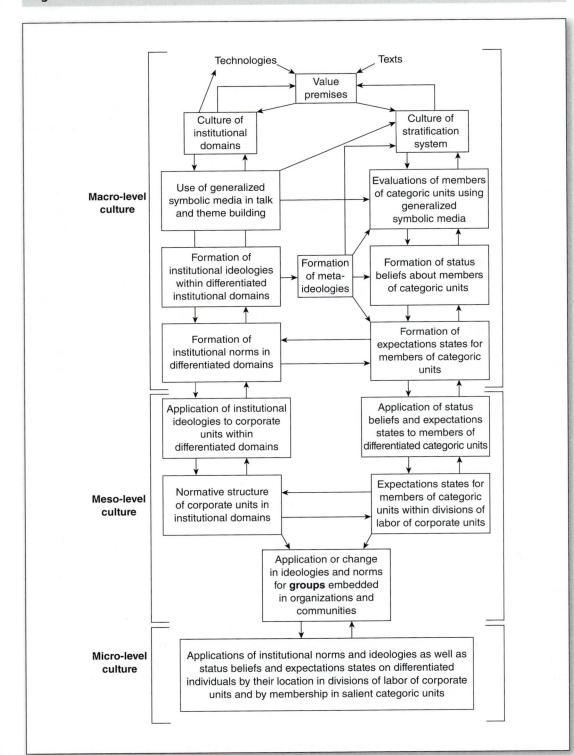

The Figure 9.1 is set up to emphasize the embedding of micro in meso-sociocultural, and the meso in macro-sociocultural formations. For culture, this means that value premises of a society, as influenced by the level of technology and the accumulated texts (history, traditions, philosophy, lore, etc.) of a society are the most general systems of symbols relevant for understanding many basic social processes. *Value premises* are emphasized because these are highly abstract cultural codes denoting of right/wrong and appropriate/inappropriate that constrain all other elements of culture that affect behavior and social organization. Values can vary considerably by their number, their consistency with each other, the level of consensus over key tenets among members of diverse subpopulations, and of course, their actual content, but as a general rule, the greater the consensus over values, the greater will be their influence on ideologies and norms as these develop at the meso and micro levels of social organization.

Ideologies are a prominent force in all cultural sociologies, but my take on them is more in tune with a reconstructed functionalism than is typically the case. *Ideologies* are evaluative beliefs that draw from the basic tenets of value premises to state what is right and correct within an institutional domain, such as economy, kinship, religion, education, law, polity, science, medicine, etc. Ideologies are built up from *generalized symbolic media* that begin as a means for ordering communication among actors as institutional domains are first being built up. These generalized media are used in discourse among actors and eventually evolve into general moral themes and, over time, become codified into a distinctive ideology for an institutional domain. Thus, values are made relevant to actors by virtue of their influence on the formation of ideologies as these are built up from generalized symbolic media. Table 9.3 lists in a very rough way the generalized media for a number of basic institutions. Generalized media have some very special characteristics: First, they are the terms and media of discourse, but they always carry elements of evaluation because they are drawn from more general value premises. Second, as emphasized above, they are the building blocks of ideologies that form within institutional domains. And third, they are also the valued resource unequally distributed by the corporate units that make up each institutional domain. For example, *money* is a generalized medium, but it is also the valued resource unequally distributed by corporate units in the economy and in modern societies in many other institutional domains. *Power* is the medium or terms of discourse for constructing political ideologies, and at the same time, it is the valued resource unequally distributed. Thus, stratification systems unequally distribute *money, power, learning, health, love/loyalty, piety/sacredness*, and other media, and these become the resources unequally distributed in the stratification system. Because generalized symbolic media carry moral connotations, at the very least, and moral imperatives at the most, they always have effects on how individuals, and especially members of what I term *categoric units*, are evaluated. Thus, members of different social classes as well as other social categories, such as ethnicity, gender, age, religious affiliation, etc. are all evaluated by the moral tenets that are implicit in generalized symbolic media, as is denoted by the arrow from generalized symbolic media to evaluations of members of categoric units.

As these media are used in forging *corporate units* of an institutional domain, they are codified into an ideology that adds an additional layer of moral coding. These ideologies constrain the formation of institutional norms at the macro level, as well as the culture of corporate units at the meso level, as is indicated by the downward arrows on the left side of Figure 9.1. The arrow going from institutional ideologies to formation of *status beliefs* about members of categoric units emphasizes that, once codified, ideologies provide the evaluative

Table 9.2 Generalized Symbolic Media of Institutional Domains

Kinship	**Love/loyalty,** or the use of intense positive affective states to forge and mark commitments to others and groups of others
Economy	**Money,** or the denotation of exchange value for objects, actions, and services by the metrics inhering in money
Polity	**Power,** or the capacity to control the actions of other actors
Law	**Influence,** or the capacity to adjudicate social relations and render judgments about justice, fairness, and appropriateness of actions
Religion	**Sacredness/Piety,** or the commitment to beliefs about forces and entities inhabiting a non-observable supernatural realm and the propensity to explain events and conditions by references to these sacred forces and beings
Education	**Learning,** or the commitment to acquiring and passing on knowledge
Science	**Knowledge,** or the invocation of standards for gaining verified knowledge about all dimensions of the social, biotic, and physico-chemical universes
Medicine	**Health,** or the concern about and commitment to sustaining the normal functioning of the human body
Sport	**Competitiveness,** or the definition of games that produce winners and losers by virtue of the respective efforts of players
Arts	**Aesthetics,** or the commitment to make and evaluate objects and performances by standards of beauty and pleasure that they give observers

Note: These and other generalized symbolic media are employed in discourse among actors, in articulating themes, and in developing ideologies about what should and ought to transpire in an institutional domain. They tend to circulate within a domain, but all of the symbolic media can circulate in other domains, although some media are more likely to do so than others.

yardstick for forming beliefs about the worth and merit of members of diverse categoric units. Much of this influence of ideologies on status beliefs is, however, mediated by what I term *meta-ideologies*, which are combinations of the ideologies from the dominant institutions in a society. Thus, for example, if the ideologies of economy, education, science, and democratic polity dominate, their basic tenets will be combined and reconciled to create a meta-ideology that then becomes the moral standard by which individuals are evaluated and judged, especially members of categoric units (see arrow from ideology to meta-ideology to formation of status beliefs). In contrast, if the dominant institutions are religion, kinship, and non-democratic polity, then a very different meta-ideology will be formed and become the moral standard by which people are judged in terms of their relative worth.

Moving down Figure 9.1 to the meso level of social reality, ideologies of a domain will influence the normative structure of corporate units (groups, organizations, and communities). If a corporate unit such as a community is embedded in multiple domains, a meta-ideology will be formed to give community norms a moral character. Status beliefs as part of the culture of the stratification system will incorporate tenets of ideologies and meta-ideologies, and these become specified as expectation states for how members of different categoric units are likely to behave and, indeed, *should* behave. There is considerable empirical and theoretical literature supporting the power of these expectation states, and they all draw from status beliefs that, in turn, are pulled from ideologies and meta-ideologies.[34] These expectation states represent implicit norms about how people in valued and devalued categories are to behave, and these expectations tend to be enforced at the level of the encounter. Similarly, the norms in the division of labor of corporate units also are applied to encounters. Following Fine, I argue that group corporate units are particularly important in this process because they provide the space and structure for housing ideologies, norms, and expectation states that can then be applied to interacting individuals. Moreover, it is at the level of groups that variously categorized individuals meet other cultural elements; if there is resentment about expectation states for categoric unit members or about norms in organizations or communities, the resentment is expressed here as a challenge to expectations states and norms. And, as much of the social movement literature documents, it is at the level of the group that counter-ideologies ferment and then begin to spread up the ladder of embedding among the cultural elements portrayed in Figure 9.1 and/or out to other groups via the "mechanisms" outlined in Fine's theory. Thus, the arrows all indicate connection among cultural elements, which gives them great power, but at the same time, if resentments over inequalities and inequities of stratification associated with ideologies, status beliefs, and expectations states increase, these very same networks and patterns of embedding become a highway for the rapid movement of change-oriented ideologies.

There is not sufficient space to trace out all of these dynamics, but what a more analytical approach communicates is this: There are relatively few levels of culture in play for most actions, interactions, and social structures; these elements of culture are always moralized, to a degree, and they lead to differential evaluation of persons by their membership in various social categories. And as these legitimating ideologies for stratification and for corporate-unit organization generate resentment of people at the level of the encounter and group, they can set into motion powerful cultural forces for social change of the structure and culture of corporate units and the culture and structure of status beliefs and categoric units, and change at this meso level will, eventually, affect institutional domains and the society-wide stratification system, and hence the whole society and perhaps even inter-societal relations of societies with each other. All of the processes and dynamics denoted by the boxes and arrows connecting them can, therefore, be specified in greater detail with models and theoretical principles.[35]

---

[34]For a summary of this literature, see Jonathan H. Turner and David Wagner, "Status Theorizing," in Jonathan H. Turner, *Contemporary Sociological Theory* (Thousand Oaks, CA: Sage, 2012).

[35]See, for example, Turner, *Theoretical Principles of Sociology* (see note 33); Jonathan H. Turner, *Face-to-Face: Toward a Sociological Theory of Interpersonal Processes* (Stanford, CA: Stanford University Press, 2002).

Conclusion

With the conflict critique on functional theories in the 1960s and 1970s, especially the approach of Talcott Parsons who *did* emphasize cultural processes, sociological attention shifted to the material bases of society as they generated conflicts of interests that, under various conditions, led to varying types of conflict. Culture was not irrelevant in this conceptual shift, but it was relegated to the analysis of beliefs and ideologies as they arouse parties to conflict or legitimated oppressive social structures. Just as conflict theory reacted to functionalism, I suspect that the new cultural sociology emerged as a reaction to the simplification of cultural analysis when it was seen as the sidekick of conflict dynamics, ultimately generated by the material conditions of societies.

There were intellectual traditions, such as phenomenology and hermeneutics, that remained viable during this period, but they did not explore culture in all of its manifestations; these were specialized theories that were often more cognitive than cultural. It is obvious, but surprisingly underappreciated, that everything humans do when they act and organize is cultural. Ideas are expressed with language, not just words but the language of emotions; ideas take hold when they are used by interacting persons and collective actors to build up social structures, reproduce such structures, or tear them down, only to rebuild them in another form. But, culture is more—new cultural theories appear to argue—because it is a domain of reality where symbols are organized and stored, and then brought into use in dramatic performances. They are not simple superstructures to material social structures, but an autonomous set of dynamics that need to be theorized and, eventually, connected to the structural properties of social reality. The notion of *performances* seems to be one wedge for recognizing the autonomous dynamics of culture per se and the necessity of bringing culture to stages and props in social settings that are part of social structures. It is the capacity to extend cultural representations to audiences and to get audiences to emotionally identify with these representations through scripts, direction, texts, staging, and acting that culture that exerts their power over actions of persons and corporate units as they build up, reproduce, dismantle, and build up anew social structures.

In somewhat different ways, Wuthnow, Bourdieu, Alexander, Fine, and Turner have sought to highlight the properties of culture and how culture is used in social settings. Each explicitly, or more implicitly in the case of Bourdieu, sees ritual and performances as critical in generating the emotions necessary to give culture its power to influence how people behave and how social structures are created, reproduced, or changed. Yet, when theorized by these scholars and others, the conceptualization of culture becomes a bit vague—*moral order, habitus, cultural and symbolic capital, background representations, texts, scripts, idioculture,* and the like. These are not precise conceptualizations. They are evocative, to be sure, but they are not denotative in any precise sense. From empirical descriptions of these in real empirical contexts, perhaps it will be possible to isolate the properties and dynamics of each of these evocative terms, which I think would represent a much stronger program in cultural sociology. For the present, let me summarize by listing some of the key assumptions and topics that are a part of the new cultural theorizing:

1. Culture is all the systems of symbols carrying meanings that have been produced by individual and collective actors in a population.

2. Culture is composed of texts, lore, traditions, technologies, and stocks of knowledge that can be stored in the minds of persons, in social structures of corporate units, in the definitions of categoric units, and in cultural warehouses (libraries, computer files, etc.) available in a society, but the most important dimensions of culture are those that are consistently used by actors in micro-, meso-, and macro-level social structures.

3. Virtually any aspect of culture has an effect on the substance of symbol systems used by actors at the micro, meso, and macro levels of social reality, but for virtually all situations, certain elements of culture are most critical to understanding the dynamics of the moral order generated by culture.

   A. At the macro level, the moral order consists of society-wide and highly abstract *value premises* that moralize all situations and provide the premises for action at all levels of social reality.

   B. At the meso level of social reality, value premises are drawn into evaluative beliefs within institutional domains and within the stratification systems.

      1. Evaluative beliefs within institutional domains can be viewed as *ideologies*, which specify in moral terms proper conduct and action for all actors in a given domain. Such ideologies are built from *generalized symbolic media* that are used in discourse and exchanges of resources among actors within and between institutional domains.

         a. These ideologies, and the symbolic media from which they are built, are used to legitimate institutional domains.

         b. The generalized symbolic media from which ideologies are built also denote the valued resources that are unequally distributed by corporate units operating within institutional domains and, hence, also become mechanism by which stratification systems are legitimated.

         c. The culture of corporate units—their normative systems and general culture—are constrained by the ideologies of the institutional domain in which they are embedded as well as by the ideologies that circulate into a given domain from other domains. Norms governing actions and interactions within corporate units carry the moral overtones of institutional ideologies.

         d. The beliefs evaluating the moral worth of members of diverse social classes in the stratification and other categoric units associated with the system of inequality are constrained by the combination of ideologies from institutional domains used to legitimate inequalities. *Status beliefs* about the worth of members of categoric units carry the moral overtones of the ideologies legitimating inequality, while generating the expectation states for members of categoric units during their action and interactions.

   C. At the micro level, individuals are guided by the norms of the corporate units in which episodes of interaction are embedded and by the expectations states of categoric units that are derived from status beliefs and ideologies legitimating inequality.

4. Culture is created, sustained, and changed by ritualized acts and performances that arouse emotions and generate commitments to, or alienation from, symbol systems.

5. The more positive are the emotions aroused in ritual acts, the greater will be commitments to the moral tenets of a system of symbols, and the more likely will interactions lead to

   A. A fusing of person, action, interaction, social structure, and background elements of culture so as to produce high levels of solidarity among individuals involved in ritual acts and performances

   B. Self-identification with the moral order and, thus, enhanced commitments to this order since self-definitions depend upon the viability of this order

   C. Marking of group boundaries with symbols having a totemic quality and, thereby, reinforcing the common culture of those acting within these boundaries marked by totemic symbols

   D. Development of idiocultures at the group level that frame for group members social issues and problems from the broader society

6. Systems of symbols can be viewed as valued resources or a form of capital that are distributed unequally and, hence, become part of the stratification system. As such, classes and factions within classes in the stratification system will differ by the nature of the cultural capital that they possess and by the symbols available to legitimate or to challenge the existing system of inequality.

7. Culture is always used to legitimate existing systems but also to challenge existing ideologies and the social structural formations that these ideologies legitimate.

8. Those social formations and the actors in them that can use culture, especially ideologies but other cultural systems as well, to secure resources are more likely to be able to sustain themselves and, indeed, spread their culture to other social formations, whereas those formations that cannot successfully use culture to secure resources, will not have their culture diffuse outward and may, in fact, see their culture disappear or be absorbed by a more resource-rich social formation and its culture.

9. The outcome of the dynamics described in (7), (8), and (9) above will revolve around the relative success of actors in groups possessing a given culture in

   A. Recruiting new members committed to a particular culture and its ideology

   B. Acquiring material resources to sustain the formation

   C. Developing forms of organizational structure that can absorb new members and engage in recruiting and extending their culture outward

   D. Using networks among groups to extend one group's idioculture outward within and between organizations, communities, and categoric units, which becomes more likely in multiple group affiliations of group members, the existence of brokerage roles, roles that transcend group boundaries, weak ties within and between groups, and prominence of mass media

   E. Using a group's culture to legitimate its viability vis-à-vis the culture and ideology of other structural formations

   F. Focusing their idioculture on civic issues of public importance that are salient to all members of a population

CHAPTER 10

Critical Theorizing on Modernity and Postmodernity

ociology, as a discipline, was a product of Enlightenment thinking. One legacy of the Enlightenment, which grew out of the Renaissance and the Age of Science in the seventeenth century, was the notion of progress. Science could be used to make a better world and lead to progress in the organization of societies. This legacy endures today, and it was a central idea in the classical era of sociology between 1830 and 1930.[1] Sociology was born during early modernization because scholars and lay persons alike wanted to understand the large-scale changes occurring in societies—changes revolving around industrialization, urbanization, bureaucratization, democratization, and other seismic shifts in the structure and culture of societies. Early sociologists, just like sociologists today, debated the degree to which these changes were harmful and, if harmful, what could be done about them. The same is true today, over 180 years since Comte gave the discipline of sociology its name.

Those who saw aspects of modernity as harmful developed a more critical attitude in their sociological theorizing—with Karl Marx being perhaps the paragon of a critical approach. Others were more tempered but, nonetheless, worried about the changes that it would bring. For example, Max Weber was clearly concerned about the passionless world of rational-legal domination and the spread of the "steel enclosure" or "iron cage" of bureaucracy; Emile Durkheim's sociology was built around the problems—lack of coordination and integration, anomie, egoism, forced divisions of labor—accompanying the transition to from simple to highly differentiated and complex societies. Others such as George Simmel[2] and Herbert Spencer saw the changes as more emancipatory than oppressive as group affiliations became more voluntary than ascriptive, as markets allowed for more choice in meeting individual preferences, and as polities became more democratic. The implicit debates over the consequences of modernity of early theoretical sociology have continued to the present, and some of the debate has shifted to concerns about the new *postmodern* stage of societal evolution that has emerged in post-industrialization and the new information age, although the criticisms of postmodernists look surprisingly similar to criticisms of modernity by classical theorists and critical theorists in the initial periods of more contemporary theorizing in the early to mid-twentieth century.

---

[1]Jonathan H. Turner, "Founders and Classics: A Canon in Motion," in *The Student Sociologist's Handbook*, ed. C. Middleton, J. Gubbay, and C. Ballard (Oxford: Blackwell, 1997).

[2]Georg Simmel, *The Philosophy of Money*, trans. T. Bottomore and D. Frisbie (Boston: Routledge & Kegan Paul, 1978, originally published in 1907).

The Delimma of Early Critical Theory

Marx's Emancipatory Optimism vs. Weber's Pessimism

Karl Marx argued that humans' unique capacity for thought leads them to conceive of, and then act to create, a better social world.[3] Action in the real world and theoretical understandings of this world work together in *praxis* to create better social universe, ultimately Marx's communist utopia. As I outlined in Chapter 3, Marx argued that societies were evolving through successive epochs of revolutionary conflict toward communism in which inequalities and oppression would be eliminated. By understanding the dialectical nature of societies—that is, successive eras of control of the means of production, oppression of those who do not have resources, growing discontent, and revolutionary change—societies had been marching toward communism since they left the Garden of Eden of primitive communism. Capitalism would be the last stage of this dialectical process, and as the contradictions of capitalism were exposed by critical theorists like Marx and by the innate reflective capacities of oppressed segments of the population, the last great revolutionary movement would topple capitalism and usher in communism.[4] Such was Marx's utopian dream supported, he felt, by his analysis of history and the dynamics of capitalism.

Marx Weber, however, had a much less optimistic scenario of what capitalism had brought.[5] Rather than creating the conditions for the last great emancipatory revolution, modernity revolved around the process of *rationalization*, or the increasing expansion into all areas of social life of rational-legal domination through law and the expansion of bureaucratic modes of social organization of virtually all social life. Older traditions, group affiliations, and even emotions were being ground down by the penetration of means-end rationality into ever-more spheres of social life. Markets and rational-legal authority do bring new freedom from domination by religious dogmatism, community, class, and other traditional forces, but in their place comes a new kind of domination by impersonal economic forces, such as markets and corporate bureaucracies, and by the vast administrative apparatus of the ever-expanding state.

By the mid-1930s, Weber's pessimistic view of modernity seemed to be a more accurate assessment than Marx's optimistic scenario about what capitalism would bring. The Russian Revolution had degenerated into Stalinism and bureaucratic totalitarianism of the Communist Party; in the West, workers were willing to sell their alienated labor in markets for increased pay; political fascism in Germany and Italy were creating new authoritarian states; and in general, the social world looked rather gloomy and oppressive. How, then, could this pessimistic picture of modernity be reconciled with Marx's emancipatory vision? This was the question that became central to early critical theories.

---

[3]Karl Marx, *Capital: A Critical Analysis of Capitalist Production*, volume 1 (New York: International, 1967, originally published in 1867); Karl Marx and Friedrich Engels, *The Communist Manifesto* (New York: International, 1971, originally published in 1848).

[4]Karl Marx and Friedrich Engels, *The German Ideology* (New York: International, 1947, written in 1846).

[5]Max Weber, *Economy and Society*, trans. G. Roth (Berkeley: University of California Press, 1978).

The Rise of the Frankfurt School

The first generation of critical theorists,[6] who are frequently referred to as the Frankfurt School because of their location in Germany and their explicit interdisciplinary effort to interpret the oppressive events of the twentieth century,[7] confronted the dilemma of how to reconcile Marx's emancipatory dream with the stark reality of modern society as conceptualized by Max Weber. Thus, modern critical theory in sociology was born in a time when there was little reason to be optimistic about realizing emancipatory goals. Three members of the Frankfurt School are most central: György Lukács, Max Horkheimer, and Theodor Adorno. Lukács' major work appeared in the 1920s, whereas Horkheimer and Adorno were active well into the 1960s. In many ways, Lukács was the key link in the transition from Marx and Weber to modern critical theory, because Horkheimer and Adorno were reacting to much of Lukács analysis and approach. All these scholars are important because they directly influenced the intellectual development and subsequent work of Jürgen Habermas, the most prolific contemporary critical theorist whose work is examined shortly.

György Lukács[8]

Borrowing from Marx's analysis of the "fetishism of commodities," Lukács employed the concept of *reification* to denote the process by which social relationships become "objects" that can be manipulated, bought, and sold in markets. Then, reinterpreting Weber's notion of "rationalization" to mean a growing emphasis on the process of "calculation" of exchange values, Lukács combined Weber's and Marx's ideas. As traditional societies change, he argued, there is less reliance on moral standards and processes of communication to achieve societal integration; instead, there is more use of money, markets, and rational calculations. As a result, relations are coordinated by exchange values and by people's perceptions of one another as "things."

Lukács painted himself into a conceptual corner, however. If indeed such is the historical process, how is it to be stopped? Lukács' answer was to resurrect a contrite Hegel; that is, rather than look to contradictions in material conditions or economic and political forces, one must examine the dialectical forces inherent in human consciousness. There are limits, Lukács argued, to how much reification and rationalization people will endure. Human subjects have an inner quality that keeps rationalization from completely taking over.

This emphasis on the process of consciousness is very much a part of critical theory that borrows much from the early Marx and that, at the Frankfurt School, had a heavy dose of Freud and

---

[6]For descriptions of this activity, see Martin Jay, *The Dialectical Imagination* (Boston: Little, Brown, 1973) and "The Frankfurt School's Critique of Marxist Humanism," *Social Research* 39 (1972): pp. 285–305; David Held, *Introduction to Critical Theory* (Berkeley: University of California Press, 1980), pp. 29–110; Robert J. Antonio, "The Origin, Development, and Contemporary Status of Critical Theory," *Sociological Quarterly* 24 (Summer 1983): pp. 325–351; Phil Slater, *Origin and Significance of The Frankfurt School* (London: Routledge & Kegan Paul, 1977); "Justification of Norms," *California Sociologist* 4 (Winter 1981): pp. 33–53.

[7]Other prominent members included Friedrich Pollock (economist), Erich Fromm (psychoanalyst, social psychologist), Franz Neumann (political scientist), Herbert Marcuse (philosopher), and Leo Loenthal (sociologist). During the Nazi years, the school relocated to the United States, and many of its members never returned to Germany.

[8]György Lukács, *History and Class Consciousness* (Cambridge, MA: MIT Press, 1968, originally published in 1922).

psychoanalytic theory. As a result, unlike its sources of inspiration, Marx and Weber, early critical theory was subjectivist and failed to analyze *intersubjectivity*, or the ways people interact through mutually shared conscious activity. Emphasizing the inherent resistance of subjects to their total reification, Lukács could only propose that the critical theorist's role is to expose reification at work by analyzing the historical processes that have dehumanized people. As a consequence, Lukács made critical theory highly contemplative, emphasizing that the solution to the problem of domination resides in making people more aware and conscious of their situation through a detailed, historical analysis of reification.

Max Horkheimer and Theodor Adorno

Both Horkheimer[9] and Adorno were highly suspicious of Lukács' Hegelian solution to the dilemma of reification and rationalization. These processes do not imply their own critique, as Hegel would have suggested. Subjective consciousness and material reality cannot be separated. Consciousness does not automatically offer resistance to those material forces that commodify, reify, and rationalize. Critical theory must, therefore, actively (1) describe historical forces that dominate human freedom and (2) expose ideological justifications of these forces. Such is to be achieved through interdisciplinary research among variously trained researchers and theorists who confront one another's ideas and use this dialogue to analyze concrete social conditions and to propose courses of ameliorative action. This emphasis on *praxis*—the confrontation between theory and action in the world—involves developing ideas about what oppresses and what to do about it in the course of human struggles. Such critical theory is, Horkheimer claimed, guided by a "particular practical interest" in the emancipation of people from class domination. Thus, critical theory is tied, in a sense that Marx might have appreciated, to people's practical interests.

Theodor Adorno[10] was more philosophical and, yet, research oriented than Horkheimer. Adorno was very pessimistic about the chances of critical theory making great changes, although his essays were designed to expose patterns of recognized and unrecognized domination of individuals by social and psychological forces. At best, his "negative dialectics" could allow humans to "tread water" until historical circumstances were more favorable to emancipatory movements. The goal of negative dialectics was to sustain a constant critique of ideas, conceptions, and conditions. This critique could not by itself change anything, for it operates only on the plane of ideas and concepts. But it can keep ideological dogmatisms from obscuring conditions that might eventually allow emancipatory action.

---

[9]Max Horkheimer, *Critical Theory: Selected Essays* (New York: Herder and Herder, 1972) is a translation of essays written in German in the 1930s and 1940s; *Eclipse of Reason* (New York: Oxford University Press, 1947, reprinted by Seabury in 1974) was the only book by Horkheimer originally published in English. It takes a slightly different turn than earlier works, but it does present ideas that emerged from his association with Theodor Adorno. See also Horkheimer, *Critique of Instrumental Reason* (New York: Seabury, 1974). See David Held, *Introduction to Critical Theory* (cited in note 6), pp. 489–491, for a more complete listing of Horkheimer's works in German.

[10]Theodor W. Adorno, *Negative Dialectics* (New York: Seabury, 1973, originally published in 1966) and with Max Horkheimer, *Dialectic of Enlightenment* (New York: Herder and Herder, 1972, originally published in 1947). See Held, *Introduction to Critical Theory* (cited in note 6), pp. 485–487, for a more complete listing of his works. See also "From Lukács to Adorno: Rationalization as Reification," pp. 339–399 in Jürgen Habermas, *The Theory of Communicative Action*, vol. 1 (Boston: Beacon, 1984); contains Habermas' critique of Lukács, Horkheimer, and Adorno.

Both Horkheimer and Adorno emphasized that humans' "subjective side" is restricted by the spread of rationalization. In conceptualizing this process, they created a kind of dualism between the subjective world and the realm of material objects, seeing the latter as oppressing the former. From their viewpoint, critical theory must expose this dualism, and it must analyze how this "instrumental reason" (means/ends rationality) has invaded the human spirit. In this way, some resistance can be offered to these oppressive forces.

Gramsci's Theory of Ideological Hegemony

Antonio Gramsci[11] was an Italian Marxist who, obviously, cannot be considered part of the Frankfurt School. Yet, he is a key figure in continuing what the Frankfurt School emphasized: Criticism acknowledging that the capitalist systems of the twentieth century's midpoint were generating prosperity and that the working classes in these systems did not seem particularly disposed to revolution. Gramsci completed the turning of Marx's ideas back into a more Hegelian mode. Marx believed that ideology and the "false consciousness" of workers were ideological obfuscations created and maintained by those who controlled the material (economic) "substructure." Marx had argued that those who control the means and modes of production also control the state which, in turn, generates ideologies justifying this control and power. In this way, the proletariat is kept, for a time until the full contradictions of capitalism become clear, from becoming a class "for themselves" ready to pursue revolutionary conflict with their oppressors. Gramsci simply turned this argument around: The "superstructure" of state and ideology drives the organization of society and the consciousness of the population.

Gramsci believed the ruling social class is *hegemonic*, controlling not only property and power, but ideology as well. Indeed, the ruling class holds onto its power and wealth by virtue of its ability to use ideologies to manipulate workers and all others. The state is no longer a crude tool of coercion, nor an intrusive and insensitive bureaucratic authority; it has become the propagator of culture and the civic education of the population, creating and controlling key institutional systems in more indirect, unobtrusive and, seemingly, inoffensive ways. Thus, the views of capitalists become the dominant views of all, with workers believing in the appropriateness of the market-driven systems of competition; the commodification of objects, signs, and symbols; the buying and selling of their labor; the use of law to enforce contracts favoring the interests of the wealthy; the encouragement of private charities, the sponsorship of clubs and voluntary organizations; the state's conceptions of a "good citizen"; the civics curriculum of the schools; and virtually all spheres of institutional activity that are penetrated by the ideology of the state. Culture and ideology are, in Albert Bergesen's words,[12] "no longer the thing to be explained but . . . now a thing that does the explaining." A dominant material class rules, to be sure, but it does so by cultural symbols, and the real battle in capitalist societies is over whose symbols will prevail. Or, more accurately, can subordinates generate alternative ideologies to those controlled by the state?

---

[11]Antonio Gramsci, *Selections from the Prison Notebooks* (New York: International, 1971, originally published in 1928).

[12]Albert Bergesen, "The Rise of Semiotic Marxism," *Sociological Perspectives* 36 (1993): p. 5.

This view of critical theory takes much of the mechanical menace out of Weber's "iron cage" metaphor, because the state's control is now "soft" and "internal." It has bars that bend flexibly around those whose perceptions of the world it seeks to control. The Marxian view of emancipation is still alive in Gramsci's theories, because the goal of theory is to expose the full extent to which ideology has been effectively used to manipulate subordinates. Moreover, the recognition that systems of symbols become the base of society is a theme that resonated well with postmodernists (see later discussion).

Althusser's Structuralism

Initially, Louis Althusser seems more strictly orthodox in his Marxism than Gramsci;[13] yet, he was also a French scholar in a long line of structuralists whose emphasis is on the logic of the deeper, underlying structure of surface empirical reality. Althusser remains close to Marx in this sense: The underlying structure and logic of the economy are ultimately determinative. But, having said this, he then developed a theory of "The Ideological State Apparatus," which gave prominence to the state's use of ideology to sustain control within a society.

For Althusser, economic, political, and ideological systems reveal their own structures, hidden beneath the surface and operating by their own logics. The economic might be the dominant system, circumscribing the operation of political and ideological structures, but these latter have a certain autonomy. History is, in essence, a reshuffling of these deep structures, and the individual actor becomes merely a vessel through which the inherent properties of structures operate. Individual actions, perceptions, beliefs, emotions, convictions, and other states of consciousness are somehow "less real" than the underlying structure that cannot be directly observed. To analogize the structuralist theories from which Althusser drew inspiration, social control comes from individuals perceiving that they are but words in a grammatical system generated by an even more fundamental structure. Each actor is at a surface place in the economic and political structures of a society, and their perceptions of these places also put them within an ideological or cultural sphere. But these places and spheres are only one level of reality; people also see themselves as part of a deeper set of structures that, in essence, defines who and what they are. Under these conditions, ideology has even more power because it is doing much more than blinding the subjects to some other reality, such as their objective class interests. Ideology is also defining actors' places in a reality beyond their direct control and a reality operating by its own logic of structure.

Thus, unlike Marx or Gramsci who believe ideology is a tool—an invidious and insidious one—used by those in power, Althusser sees the *Ideological State Apparatus* as more controlling because it is perceived not just as conventions, rules, mores, traditions, and beliefs, but instead as the essence of order and persons' place in this order. The subject is thus trapped in the deeper logics of economic, political, and ideological systems that erode human capacities for praxis and agency.

The Transformation of Marx's Project

In sum, by the middle of the twentieth century when the contemporary period of sociological theory began, Marx's emancipatory project had been turned into something very

---

[13]Louis Althusser, *For Marx* (New York: Pantheon, 1965); *Lenin and Philosophy* (New York: Monthly Review Press, 1971); Louis Althusser and Etienne Balabar, *Reading Capital* (London: New Left, 1968).

different than he had visualized. His and Engel's *The Communist Manifesto* was a call to arms, based on a view of the inherent contradictions in the nature of capitalist systems. Within one hundred years of this call, critical theory had become decidedly more philosophical. Indeed, Marx's dismissal of the Young Hegelians in *The German Ideology* had apparently not worked; they were back in different forms and guises, but they increasingly dominated critical theorizing in the twentieth century. The Young Hegelians, so viciously criticized by Marx and Engels, had considered themselves revolutionaries, but Marx saw them as more concerned with ideas about reality than with reality itself. They were accused of "blowing theoretical bubbles" about ideals and essences, and it could be imagined that he and Engels might make the very same criticisms of the critical theories that developed in the second half of the twentieth century, especially as these theories began to merge with postmodernism, as we will see shortly.

Contemporary Frankfurt School

The German philosopher-sociologist, Jürgen Habermas, undoubtedly has been the most prolific descendant of the original Frankfurt School. As with the earlier generation of Frankfurt School social theorists, Habermas' work revolves around several important questions: (1) How can social theory develop ideas that keep Karl Marx's emancipatory project alive, and yet, at the same time, recognize the empirical inadequacy of his prognosis for advanced capitalist societies? (2) How can social theory confront Max Weber's historical analysis of rationalization in a way that avoids his pessimism and thereby keeps Marx's emancipatory goals at the center of theory? (3) How can social theory avoid the retreat into subjectivism of earlier critical theorists, such as György Lukács, Max Horkheimer, and Theodor Adorno, who increasingly focused on states of subjective consciousness within individuals and, as a consequence, lost Marx's insight that society is constructed from, and must therefore be emancipated by, the processes that sustain social relations among individuals? (4) How can social theory conceptualize and develop a theory that reconciles the forces of material production and political organization with the forces of intersubjectivity among reflective and conscious individuals in such a way that it avoids (a) Weber's pessimism about the domination of consciousness by rational economic and political forces, (b) Marx's naive optimism about inevitability of class consciousness and revolt, and (c) early critical theorists' retreat into the subjectivism of Hegel's dialectic, where oppression mysteriously mobilizes its negation through increases in subjective consciousnesses and resistance?

Jurgen Habermas' Conception of "The Public Sphere"

In his first major publication, *Structural Transformation of the Public Sphere*, Habermas traced the evolution and dissolution of what he termed the *public sphere*.[14] This sphere is a realm of social life where people can discuss matters of general interest; where they can discuss and debate these issues without recourse to custom, dogma, and force; and where they can resolve differences of opinion by rational argument.

---

[14]Jürgen Habermas, *Struckturwandel der Offentlichkeit* (Neuwied, Germany: Luchterhand, 1962); Jürgen Habermas, *Zur Logik der Sozialwissenchaften* (Frankfurt: Suhrkamp, 1970).

These forums of the public helped erode the basic structure of feudalism, which had been legitimated by religion and custom rather than by agreements that have been reached through public debate and discourse. The public sphere was greatly expanded, Habermas argued, by the extension of market economies and the resulting liberation of the individual from the constraints of feudalism. Free citizens, property holders, traders, merchants, and members of other new sectors in society could now be actively concerned about the governance of society and could openly discuss and debate issues. But, in a vein similar to Weber's analysis of rationalization, Habermas concluded that the public sphere was eroded by some of the very forces that stimulated its expansion. As market economies experience instability, the powers of the state are extended in an effort to stabilize the economy; with the expansion of bureaucracy to ever-more contexts of social life, the public sphere is constricted. And, increasingly, the state seeks to redefine problems as technical and soluble by technologies and administrative procedures rather than by public debate and argumentation.

All of the key elements of critical theory are contained in Habermas' first major work—the decline of freedom with the expansion of capitalism and the bureaucratized state as well as the seeming power of the state to construct and control social life. The solution to these problems is to resurrect the public sphere, but how is this to be done given the growing power of the state? Thus, in this early work, Habermas had painted himself into the same conceptual corner as his teachers in the Frankfurt School. The next phase of his work extended this critique of capitalist society, but he also tried to redirect critical theory so that it does not have to retreat into the contemplative subjectivism of Lukács, Horkheimer, and Adorno. Habermas began this project in the late 1960s with an analysis of knowledge systems and a critique of science.

The Critique of Science

Like much critical theory, science is viewed as part of the problem with modernity.[15] Habermas' long statement on this point is this: Science becomes an ideology that legitimates those seeking technical control of members of a society, and this ideology contributes to what he terms a "legitimation crisis." Like all ideologies, science as an ideology masks the interests of a sector of society, making its actions seem right and proper. And in the case the ideology of science and the political and economic actors that it legitimates, problems in the society are viewed as "technical problems" that "social engineers" can solve for society, whereas in fact, this ideology justifies the power and influence of those controlling economy and polity in a society. But the ideology of science does more, it pushes out other forms of knowledge, such as the critical, which examines contradictions in societies and the hermeneutic/historical forms of knowledge that give meaning to life. And so, the critique of science is meant to highlight the goal of critical knowledge and the interests of those in developing critical knowledge: to understand the processes by which people come to understand one another in ways that give meaning and a sense of continuity to social life.

---

[15]Jürgen Habermas, *Knowledge and Human Interest*, trans. J. Shapiro (London: Heinemann, 1970, originally published in German in 1968). The basic ideas in *Zur Logik der Sozialwissenschaften* and *Knowledge and Human Interest* were stated in Habermas' inaugural lecture at the University of Frankfurt in 1965 and were first published in "Knowledge and Interest," *Inquiry* 9 (1966): pp. 285–300.

Legitimation Crisis in Societies

As Habermas had argued in his earlier work, there are several historical trends in modern societies: (1) the decline of the public sphere, (2) the increasing intervention of the state into the economy, and (3) the growing dominance of science in the service of the state's interests in technical control. These ideas are woven together in *Legitimation Crisis*,[16] which argues that government or the state translate political issues into "technical problems" that are not topics for public debate. Rather, they require the use of technologies by experts in bureaucratic organizations. As a result, there is a "depoliticization" of practical issues by redefining them as technical problems. To do this, the state propagates a "technocratic consciousness" that Habermas believed represents a new kind of ideology. Unlike previous ideologies, however, it does not promise a future utopia; but, like other ideologies, it is seductive in its ability to veil problems, to simplify perceived options, and to justify a particular way of organizing social life. At the core of this technocratic consciousness is an emphasis on "instrumental reason," or what Weber termed means/ends rationality. That is, criteria of the efficiency of means in realizing explicit goals increasingly guide evaluations of social action and people's approach to problems. This emphasis on instrumental reason displaces other types of action, such as behaviors oriented to mutual understanding.

This reliance on the ideology of technocratic consciousnesses creates, however, new dilemmas of political legitimation. Capitalist societies can be divided into three basic subsystems: (1) the economic, (2) the politico-administrative, and (3) the cultural (what he later calls *lifeworld*). From this division of societies into these subsystems, Habermas then posits four points of crises: (1) an "economic crisis" occurs if the economic subsystem cannot generate sufficient productivity to meet people's needs; (2) a "rationality crisis" exists when the politico-administrative subsystem cannot generate a sufficient number of instrumental decisions; (3) a "motivation crisis" exists when actors cannot use cultural symbols to generate sufficient meaning to feel committed to participate fully in the society; and (4) a "legitimation crisis" arises when actors do not possess the "requisite number of generalized motivations" or diffuse commitments to the political subsystem's right to make decisions. Much of this analysis of crises is described in Marxian terms but emphasizes that economic and rationality crises are perhaps less important than either motivational or legitimation crises. For, as technocratic consciousness penetrates all spheres of social life and creates productive economies and an intrusive state, the crisis tendencies of late capitalism shift from the inability to produce sufficient economic goods or political decisions to the failure to generate (a) diffuse commitments to political processes and (b) adequate levels of meaning among individual actors.

In *Legitimation Crisis*, there is an early form of what becomes an important distinction: *Systemic processes* revolving around the economy and the politico-administrative apparatus of the state must be distinguished from *cultural processes*. This distinction will later be conceptualized as *system* and *lifeworld,* respectively, but the central point is this: In tune with his Frankfurt School roots, Habermas is shifting emphasis from Marx's analysis of the economic crisis of production to crises of meaning and commitment; if the problems or crises of capitalist societies are in these areas, then critical theory must focus on the communicative and interactive processes by which humans generate understandings and meanings among themselves. If

---

[16]Jürgen Habermas, *Legitimation Crisis*, trans. T. McCarthy (London: Heinemann, 1976, originally published in German in 1973).

instrumental reason, or means/ends rationality, is driving out action based on mutual understanding and commitment, then the goal of critical theory is to expose this trend and to suggest ways of overcoming it, especially because legitimation and motivational crises make people aware that something is missing from their lives and, therefore, makes them more receptive to emancipatory alternatives. So, the task of critical theory is to develop a theoretical perspective that allows the restructuring of meaning and commitment in social life. This goal will be realized, Habermas increasingly argues, by further understanding of how people communicate, interact, and develop symbolic meanings.

Early Analysis of Speech and Interaction

By the early 1970s, Habermas begins to view the mission of critical theory as emphasizing *the process of interaction as mediated by speech*.[17] But such speech acts draw on stores of knowledge—rules, norms, values, tacit understandings, memory traces, and the like—for their interpretation. These ideals of the speech process represent a restatement of the romanticized public sphere, where issues were openly debated, discussed, and rationally resolved. What Habermas has done, of course, is to restate this view of "what is good and desirable" in more theoretical and conceptual terms, although it could be argued that there is not much difference between the romanticized portrayal of the public sphere and the ideal-typical conceptualization of speech. But with this conceptualization, the goal of critical theory must be to expose those conditions that distort communication and that inhibit realization of the ideal speech situation. Habermas' utopia is thus a society where actors can communicate without distortion, achieve a sense of one another's subjective states, and openly reconcile their differences through argumentation that is free of external constraint and coercion. In other words, he wants to restore the public sphere but in a more encompassing way—that is, in people's day-to-day interactions.

Habermas moved in several different directions in trying to construct a rational approach for realizing this utopia. He borrows metaphorically from psychoanalytic theory as a way to uncover the distortions that inhibit open discourse, but this psychoanalytic journey is far less important than his growing concentration on the process of communicative action and interaction as the basis for creating a society that reduces domination and constraint. Thus, by the mid-1970s, he labels his analysis *universal pragmatics*, whose centerpiece is the "theory of communicative action."[18] Communication involves more than words, grammar, and syntax; it also involves what Habermas terms *validity claims*. There are three basic types of claims essential to communicate actions: (1) those asserting that a course of action as indicated through speech is the most effective and efficient means for attaining ends; (2) those claiming that an action is correct and proper in accordance with relevant norms; and

---

[17]Jürgen Habermas, "On Systematically Distorted Communication," *Inquiry* 13 (1970): pp. 205–218; Jürgen Habermas, "Toward a Theory of Communicative Competence," *Inquiry* 13 (1970): pp. 360–375. For an early statement, see "Some Distinctions in Universal Pragmatics: A Working Paper," *Theory and Society* 3 (1976): pp. 155–167.

[18]Jürgen Habermas, *The Theory of Communicative Action*, 2 vols. (cited in note 19). The subtitle of volume 1, *Reason and the Rationalization of Society*, gives some indication of its thrust. The translator Thomas McCarthy has done an excellent service in translating very difficult prose. Also, his "Translator's Introduction" to volume 1, pp. v–xxxvii, is the best summary of Habermas' recent theory that I have come across.

(3) those maintaining that the subjective experiences as expressed in a speech act are sincere and authentic. All speech acts implicitly make these three claims, although a speech act can emphasize one more than the other two. Those responding to communication can accept or challenge these validity claims; if challenged, then the actors contest, debate, criticize, and revise their communication. They use, of course, shared "stocks of knowledge" about norms, means/ends effectiveness, and sincerity to make their claims as well as to contest and revise them. This process (which restates the public sphere in yet one more guise) is often usurped when claims are settled by recourse to power and authority. But if claims are settled by the "giving of reasons for" and "reasons against" the claim in a mutual give-and-take among individuals, then Habermas sees it as "rational discourse."

Thus, built into the very process of interaction is the potential for rational discourse that can be used to create a more just, open, and free society. Such discourse is not merely means/ends rationality, for it involves adjudication of two other validity claims: those concerned with normative appropriateness and those concerned with subjective sincerity. Actors thus implicitly assess and critique one another for effectiveness, normative appropriateness, and sincerity of their respective speech acts; so the goal of critical theory is to expose those societal conditions that keep such processes from occurring for all three types of validity claims.

Habermas' Reconceptualization of Social Evolution

Like Marx, Habermas develops his views about communicative action within an evolutionary framework of stages of societal development (see next chapter), but in Habermas' case, his views of evolution are more reminiscent of functional stage models and Marxist models.[19] Habermas views evolution as the process of structural differentiation and the emergence of integrative problems—arguments at the core of Auguste Comte's, Herbert Spencer's, Emile Durkheim's, and Talcott Parsons' views on societal development. He also borrows from Herbert Spencer, Talcott Parsons, and Niklas Luhmann when he argues that the integration of complex systems leads to an adaptive upgrading, increasing the capacity of the society to cope with the environment. For example, a society with only religious mythology will be less complex and less able to respond to environmental challenges than a more complex society with large stores of technology and stocks of normative procedures determining its organization principles.

The basis for societal integration in societies resides in the processes of communication that allow individuals to develop mutual understandings and stores of knowledge. To the extent that these interactive processes are arrested by the patterns of economic and political organization, the society's learning capacity is correspondingly diminished. One of the main integrative problems of capitalist societies is the integration of the material forces of production (economy as administered by the state), on the one side, and the cultural stores of knowledge that are produced by communicative interaction, on the other side. Societies that differentiate materially in the economic and political realms without achieving integration on a normative and cultural level (that is, shared understandings) will remain unintegrated and experience crises.

---

[19]Jürgen Habermas, *Communication and the Evolution of Society*, trans. T. McCarthy (London: Heinemann, 1979).

Built into these dynamics of communication is, therefore, the solution to the problems of advanced, capitalist societies. The processes of "communicative interaction" that produce and reproduce unifying cultural symbols have the potential to produce a more open, free, and just society.

The human species maintains itself through the socially coordinated activities of its members, and this coordination is established through communication—and in certain spheres of life, through communication aimed at reaching agreement. And so, the reproduction of the species also requires satisfying the conditions of a rationality inherent in communicative action.

The Changing Balance Between *System* and *Lifeworld* (Cultural) Processes

The evolution of societies has altered the balance between "system" and "lifeworld" processes. System processes revolving around political and economic development, or system processes, increasingly invade cultural or lifeworld processes; with this invasion, or what Habermas often terms "colonization," comes means-end rationality that displaces those processes that generate meaning among actors or lifeworld processes. The result is legitimation crises revolving around a lack of individual motivations leading to a loss of diffuse commitments to the society, which in turn, spawn a crisis of legitimation.

The crisis is inherent in structural differentiation of societies because each emerging institutional system—economy, polity, law, education, medicine, for instance—increasingly defines its problems in technical terms and, thereby, separates culture from the system-level processes. However, if the lifeworld that gives meaning to actions becomes separated from system processes, it is the task of critical theory to highly this disjunction between system and lifeworld processes. In doing so, critical theory points the way to solving legitimation crises and re-integrating societies.

The goal of critical theory, then, becomes one of specifying where and how *communicative rationality* (as opposed to means-end rationality) built around the validity claims evident in the ideal speech act, needs to be restored. As long as the media of power and money dominate institutional domains, rather than culture, complex differentiated societies cannot be integrated.

Habermas has now circled back to this initial concern and those of early critical theorists. He has recast the Weberian thesis by asserting that "true rationality" inheres in communicative action, not the means-end or strategic and instrumental action of Weber. And Habermas has redefined the critical theorist's view on modern crises; they are not crises of rationalization, but crises of *colonization* of those truly rational processes that inhere in the speech acts of communicative action, which reproduce the lifeworld so essential to societal integration. Thus, built into the integrating processes of differentiated societies is the potential for a critical theory that seeks to restore communicative rationality despite the power of impersonal steering mechanisms like money and power of system processes. If system differentiation occurs through the expansion of "de-linguistified media" like money and power, and if these reduce the reliance on communicative action, then crises are inevitable. The resulting collective frustration over the lack of meaning in social life can be used by critical theorists to mobilize people to restore the proper balance between system and lifeworld processes. Thus, crises of material production will not be the impetus for change, as Marx contended. Rather, the *crises of lifeworld reproduction* will serve as the stimulus to societal reorganization. And returning to his first work, Habermas sees such reorganization as involving (1) the restoration of the public sphere in politics, where re-linguistified debate and argumentation, rather than de-linguistified power and authority, are used to make political decisions (thus reducing "legitimation crises"), and (2) the extension of communicative action back into those spheres—family, work, and social relations—that have become increasingly dominated by de-linguistified steering media (thereby eliminating the "motivational crises").

The potential for this reorganization inheres in the nature of societal integration through the rationality inherent in the communicative actions that reproduce the lifeworld. The purpose of critical theory is to show the path as to how to release this rational potential.

The Postmodern Turn in Critical Theorizing[20]

Postmodern critical theory begins with a prolonged attack on the scientific pretensions of social science. This attack is multi-pronged, and I will take just a moment to outline the basic prongs. One is a critique of scientific theory as providing "true" or "objective" explanations. Scientific explanations are, some postmodernists argue, "grand narratives" about society that are no more objective than those of anyone else, and yet, scientist seek to "privilege" their narrative over all others.[21] Another critique is that science tends to see itself as above politics, interests, and other distorting influences, when in fact, such is not the case. The search for laws of the social universe inevitably serves some interests over others, and scientific research serves the interests of those who fund it. Science assumes that knowledge accumulates over time, which was the hallmark of modernity, but in fact, there are discontinuities in knowledge and no knowledge is, once again, free from shifts in the interests of dominant factions in society. Science assumes that there is an objective world "out there" that reveals fundamental properties that can be explained by theory, but the world out there is constantly changing its fundamental nature as actors pursue their diverse interests. These and similar lines of attack are not particularly new, but postmodernists have often taken them to extremes.

Curiously, their own work in positing the nature of new, postmodern societal formations is equally vulnerable to these lines of attack. Postmodernists, despite their qualifying of their explanations, produce grand narratives, assume that something is out there to talk about (i.e., postmodernity), clearly pursue interests (academic advancement in academia), and so on for all the criticisms hurled at science. What makes postmodernism critical theory is that most of its practitioners view the postmodern condition as somehow harmful; and thus, the description of postmodern conditions, and efforts to explain their emergence and functioning all assume, like many modernist critical theorists, that the word as it is now structured is somehow pathological.

More interesting than these somewhat tired assertions is the substance of postmodern critical theorizing. This substantive view is divided into (1) economic postmodernists who are

---

[20]The rest of this chapter is coauthored with Kenneth Allan.

[21]Richard Rorty, "Philosophy as a Kind of Writing: An Essay on Derrida," *New Literary History* 10 (1978): pp. 141–160; *Philosophy and the Mirror of Nature* (Princeton: Princeton University Press, 1979); "Method, Social Science, and Social Hope," in *The Postmodern Turn; New Perspectives on Social Theory*, ed. Steven Seidman (Cambridge: Cambridge University Press, 1994).

closer to the classical theorists, particularly Marx, and (2) cultural postmodernists who emphasize the growing dominance of culture over economic conditions.

Economic Postmodernism

Economic postmodernists are concerned with *capital*, especially its *overaccumulation* (that is, overabundance), as well as its level of dispersion and rapid movement in the new world system of markets driven and connected by information technologies. Moreover, culture or systems of symbols are seen to emerge from economic processes, but they exert independent effects on not only the economy but also every other facet of human endeavor. Indeed, for some economic postmodernists, advanced capitalism has evolved into a new stage of human history[22] that, like earlier modernity, is typified by a series of problems, including the loss of a core or essential sense of self, the use of symbolic as much as material means to control individuals, the increased salience of cultural resources as both tools of repression and potential resistance, the emotional disengagement of individuals from culture, and the loss of national identities and a corresponding shift to local and personal identities. This list, and other "pathologies" of the postmodern era, sound much like those that concerned early sociologists when they worried about such matters as anomie and egoism (Emile Durkheim), alienation (Karl Marx), marginal and fractured self (Georg Simmel), ideological control and manipulation by the powerful (Marx and, later, Antonio Gramsci and Louis Althusser), political-ideological mobilization as resistance (Marx), over-differentiation and fragmentation of social structure (Adam Smith, Herbert Spencer, and Durkheim), rationalization and domination by over-concern with efficiency (Max Weber), and so on. Thus, economically oriented postmodernists evidence many of the same analytical tendencies of those who first sought to theorize about modernity.

The scholars examined in this section emphasize the dynamics of capitalism as they generate a new, postmodern condition.

Fredric Jameson

Among the central figures in economic postmodernism, Fredric Jameson is the most explicitly Marxist.[23] Although his theory is about the complex interplay among multinational capitalism, technological advance, and the mass media, the real dynamics in postmodernism revolve around the nature of capital. Jameson argues that capitalism has gone through three distinct phases, with each phase linked to a particular kind of technology. Early-market capitalism was linked to steam-driven machinery; mid-monopoly capitalism was characterized by steam and combustion engines; and late-multinational capitalism is associated with nuclear power and electronic machines.

Late-multinational capitalism is the subject of postmodern theory in which the machines of symbolic reproduction—cameras, computers, videos, movies, tape recorders, fax machines— remove the direct connection between human production and its symbolic representation. These machines generate sequences of signs on top of signs that alter the nature of the

---

[22]See, for example, Stephen Crook, Jan Pakulski, and Malcolm Waters, *Postmodernization* (London: Sage, 1992).

[23]Fredric Jameson, *The Postmodern Condition* (Minneapolis: University of Minnesota Press, 1984).

relationship between thought and action, or *praxis* in Marx's terms. The relationship between the symbolic and material world has changed, with layers of symbols mediating relations that people have with material conditions. As a result, it becomes difficult to think about the material world when persons have only a tenuous sense for it because thinking is now dominated by symbols on symbols often far removed from the real process of production. The instruments of symbolic reproduction now distort thought and thus inhibit meaningful action.

Drawing from Marx's philosophy of knowledge, Jameson still attempts to use the method of praxis to critique the social construction of reality in postmodernity. Marx argued that reality did not exist in concepts, ideas, or reflexive thought but in the material world of production. Indeed, he broke with the Young Hegelians over this issue, seeing them as, noted earlier, "blowing theoretical bubbles" about the reality of ideas—very much like the earlier generation of critical theorists in the first decades of the twentieth century (although those of the late twentieth and early twenty-first centuries sound even more Hegelian). According to Jameson, the creation of consciousness through production was unproblematically represented by the aesthetic of the machine in earlier phases of capitalism, but in multinational capitalism, electronic machines like movie cameras, videos, digital recorders, and computers do not have the same capacity for signification because they are machines of reproduction rather than of production.

Thus, the foundation of thought and knowledge in postmodernity is not simply false, as Marx's view of "false consciousness" emphasized; it is nonexistent. Because the machines of late capitalism reproduce knowledge rather than produce it and because the reproduction itself is focused more on the medium than on the message, the signification chain from object to sign has broken down. Jameson characterizes this breakdown as the "schizophrenia of culture." The relationship between signifiers and the signified is broken; the signification chain indicates that each sign stands alone, or in a relatively loose association with fragmented groups of other signs, and that meaning is free-floating and untied to any clear material reality.

Moreover, in a postmodern world dominated by machines of reproduction, language loses the capacity to ground concepts to place, to moments of time, or to objects in addition to losing its ability to organize symbols into coherent systems of concepts about place, time, and objects. As language loses these capacities, time and space become disassociated. If a sign system becomes detached and free-floating and if it is fragmented and without order, the meaning of concepts in relation to time and space cannot be guaranteed. Indeed, meaning in any sense becomes problematic. The conceptual connection between the "here-and-now" and its relation to the previous "there-and-then" has broken down, and the individual experiences "a series of pure and unrelated presents in time."[24]

Jameson goes on to argue that culture in the postmodern condition has created a *fragmented* rather than Marx's alienated subject. Self is not so much alienated from the failure to control his or her own productive activities; rather, self is now a series of images in a material world dominated by the instruments of reproduction rather than production. In addition, the decentering of the postmodern self produces a kind of emotional flatness or depthlessness "since there is no longer any self to do the feeling . . . [emotions] are now free-floating and impersonal."[25]

---

[24]Ibid., p. 92.

[25]Ibid., p. 64.

Subjects are thus fragmented and dissolved, having no material basis for consciousness or narratives about their situation; under these conditions, individuals' capacity for praxis—using thought to act and using action to generate thought—is diminished. Of course, this capacity for praxis is not so diminished that Jameson cannot develop a critical theory of the postmodern condition, although the action side of Marx's notion of praxis is as notably absent, if not impotent, as it was for the first generation of Frankfurt critical theorists.

David Harvey

Like Jameson, David Harvey[26] posits that capitalism has brought about significant problems associated with humans' capacity to conceptualize time and space. Yet, for Harvey, the cultural and perceptual problems associated with postmodernism are not new. Some of the same tendencies toward fragmentation and confusion in political, cultural, and philosophical movements occurred around the turn into the twentieth century.

Unlike Jameson, however, Harvey does not see the critical condition of postmodernity as the problem of praxis—of anchoring signs and symbols in a material reality that can be changed through thought and action—but, rather, as a condition of *overaccumulation*, or the modes by which too much capital is assembled and disseminated. All capitalist systems—as Marx recognized—have evidenced this problem of overaccumulation, because capitalism is a system designed to grow through exploitation of labor, technological innovation, and organizational retrenchment. At some point, there is overabundance: too many products to sell to nonexistent buyers, too much productive capacity that goes unused, or too much money to invest with insufficient prospects for profits.

This overaccumulation is met in a variety of ways, the most common being the business cycle where workers are laid off, plants close, bankruptcies increase, and money is devalued. Such cycles generally restore macro-level economic controls (usually by government) over money supply, interest rates, unemployment compensation, bankruptcy laws, tax policies, and the like. But Harvey emphasizes another response to overaccumulation: absorption of surplus capital through temporal and spatial *displacement*.

Temporal displacement occurs when investors buy "futures" on commodities yet to be produced, when they purchase stock option in hopes of stock prices rising, when they invested in other financial instruments (mortgages, long-term bonds, government securities), or when they pursue any strategy for using time and the swings of all markets to displace capital and reduce overaccumulation.

Spatial displacement involves moving capital away from areas of overaccumulation to new locations in need of investment capital. Harvey argues that displacement is most effective when both its temporal and spatial aspects are combined, as when money raised in London is sent to Latin America to buy bonds (which will probably be resold again in the future) to finance infrastructural development.

The use of both spatial and temporal displacement to meet the issue of overaccumulation can contribute to the more general problem of time and space displacement. Time and space displacement occurs because of four factors: (1) advanced communication and transportation

---

[26]David Harvey, *The Conditions of Postmodernity: An Inquiry into the Origins of Cultural Change* (Oxford: Blackwell, 1989).

technologies, (2) increased rationalization of distribution processes, (3) meta- and world-level money markets that accelerate the circulation of money, and (4) decreased spatial concentration of capital in geographical locations (cities, nations, regions). These changes create a perceived sense of time and space compression that must be matched by changes in beliefs, ideologies, perceptions, and other systems of symbols. As technologies combine to allow us to move people and objects more quickly through space—as with the advent of travel by rail, automobile, jet, rocket—space becomes compressed; that is, distance is reduced and space is not as forbidding or meaningful as it was at one time. Ironically, as the speed of transportation, communication, market exchanges, commodity distribution, and capital circulation increases, the amount of available time *decreases*, because there are more things to do and more ways to do them. Thus, our sense of time and space compresses in response to increases in specific technologies and structural capacities. If these technological and structural changes occur gradually, then the culture that renders the resulting alterations in time and space understandable and meaningful will evolve along with the changes. But, if the changes in structure and technology occur rapidly, as in postmodernity, then the modifications in symbolic categories will not keep pace, and people will be left with a sense of disorientation concerning two primary categories of human existence, time and space. The present response to overaccumulation, "flexible capitalism," helps create a sense of time and space compression as capital is rapidly moved and manipulated on a global scale in response to portfolio management techniques.

In addition, because the new mode of accumulation is designed to move capital spatially and temporally in a flexible and thus ever-changing manner, disorientation ensues as the mode of regulation struggles to keep up with the mode of accumulation. For example, if capital sustaining jobs in one country can be immediately exported to another with lower-priced labor, beliefs among workers about loyalty to the company, conceptions about how to develop a career, commitments of companies to local communities, ideologies of government, import policies, beliefs about training and retraining, conceptions of labor markets, ideologies of corporate responsibility, laws about foreign investment, and many other cultural modes for regulating the flow of capital will all begin to change. Thus, in postmodernity, physical place has been replaced by a new social space driven by the new technologies of highly differentiated and dynamic markets, but cultural orientations have yet to catch up with this pattern of time and space compression.

As with most economic postmodernists, Harvey emphasizes that markets now distribute services as much as they deliver commodities or "hard goods", and many of the commodities and services that are distributed concern the formation of an image of self and identity. Cultural images are now market driven, emphasizing fashion and corporate logos as well as other markers of culture, lifestyle, group membership, taste, status, and virtually anything that individuals can see as relevant to their identity. As boredom, saturation, and imitation create demands for new images with which to define self, cultural images constantly shift—being limited only by the imagination of people, advertisers, and profit-seeking producers. As a result, the pace and volatility of products to be consumed accelerates, and producers for markets as well as agents in markets (such as advertisers, bankers, investors) search for new images to market as commodities or services.

Given a culture that values instant gratification and easy disposability of commodities, people generally react with sensory block, denial, a blasé attitude, myopic specialization, increased nostalgia (for stable old ways), and an increased search for eternal but simplified truths and collective or personal identity. To the extent that these reactions are the mark of postmodernity,

Harvey argues that they represent the lag between cultural responses to new patterns of capital displacement over time and place. Eventually, culture and people's perceptions will catch up to these new mechanisms for overcoming the latest incarnation of capital overaccumulation.

Scott Lash and John Urry

Like David Harvey, Scott Lash and John Urry argue that a postmodern disposition occurs with changes in advanced capitalism that shift time and space boundaries.[27] In their view, shifting conceptualizations of time and space are associated with changes in the distribution of capital. Moreover, like most postmodern theorists, they stress that postmodern culture is heavily influenced by the mass media and advertising. Yet, revealing their Marxian roots, they add that the postmodern disposition is particularly dependent on the fragmentation of class experience and the rise of the service class.

Also like Harvey, Lash and Urry do not see postmodern culture as entirely new, but unlike Harvey, they are less sure that it is a temporary phase waiting for culture to catch up to changed material conditions. Lash and Urry believe that postmodern culture will always appeal to certain audiences with "postmodern dispositions." These dispositions emerge in response to three forces: First, the boundary between reality and image must become blurred as the media, and especially advertising, present ready-made rather than socially constructed cultural images. Second, the traditional working class must be fractured and fragmented; at the same time, a new service class oriented to the consumption of commodities for their symbolic power to produce, mark, and proclaim distinctions in group memberships, taste, lifestyle, preferences, gender orientation, ethnicity, and many other distinctions must become prominent. And third, the construction of personal and subjective identities must increasingly be built from cultural symbols detached from physical space and location, such as neighborhood, town, or region; as this detachment occurs, images of self become ever-more transitory. As these three forces intensify, a postmodern disposition becomes more likely, and these dispositions can come to support a broader postmodern culture where symbols marking difference, identity, and location are purchased by the expanding service class.

Although Lash and Urry are reluctant to speak of causation, it appears that at least four deciding factors bring about these postmodern conditions. The first factor involves the shift from Taylorist or regimented forms of production, such as the old factory assembly line, to more flexible forms of organizing and controlling labor, such as production teams, "flex-time" working hours, reduced hierarchies of authority, and deconcentration of work extending to computer terminals at home. Like Harvey, Lash and Urry believe that these shifts cause and reflect decreased spatial concentration of capital and expanded communication and transportation technologies, spatial dispersion, deconcentration of capital, and rapid movement of information, people, and resources are the principle dynamics of change. The second factor concerns large-scale economic changes—the globalization of a market economy, the expansion of industry and banking across national boundaries, and the spread of capitalism into less developed countries. A third factor is increased distributive capacities that accelerate and

---

[27]Scott Lash and John Urry, *The End of Organized Capitalism* (Madison: University of Wisconsin Press, 1987); *Economies of Signs and Space* (Newbury Park, CA: Sage, 1994).

extend the flow of commodities from the local and national to international markets. This increased scope and speed of circulation can empty many commodities of their ethnic, local, national, and other traditional anchors of symbolic and affective meaning. This rapid circulation of commodities increases the likelihood that many other commodities will be made and purchased for what they communicate aesthetically and cognitively about ever-shifting tastes, preferences, lifestyles, personal statements, and new boundaries of prestige and status group membership. And, a fourth factor is a set of forces that follows from the other factors: (a) the commodification of leisure as yet one more purchased symbolic statement; (b) the breakdown of, and merger among, previously distinct and coherent cultural forms (revolving around music, art, literature, class, ethnic, or gender identity, and other cultural distinctions in modernism); (c) the general collapse of social space, designated physical locations, and temporal frames within which activities are conducted and personal identifications are sustained; and (d) the undermining of politics as tied to traditional constituencies (a time dimension) located in physical places like neighborhoods and social spaces such as classes and ethnic groups.

Together, these factors create a spatially fragmented division of labor, a less clear-cut working class, a larger service class, a shift to symbolic rather than material or coercive domination, a use of cultural more than material resources for resistance, and a level of cultural fragmentation and pluralism that erodes nationalism. But Lash and Urry argue, in contrast with Jameson, this emptying out process is not as deregulated as it might appear. They posit that new forms of distribution, communication, and transportation all create networks in time, social spaces, and physical places. Economic governance occurs where the networks are dense, with communications having an increasingly important impact on the difference between core and peripheral sites. Core sites are heavily networked communication sites that function as a "wired village of noncontiguous communities."

All these economic postmodernists clearly have roots in Marxian analysis, both the critical forms that emerged in the early decades of the last century and the world-system forms of analysis that arose in the 1970s and continue to the present day. Early critical theorists had to come to terms with the Weberian specter of coercive and rational-legal authority as crushing emancipatory class activity, but this generation of postmodern critics has had to reconcile their rather muted emancipatory goals to the spread of world capitalism as the preferred economic system; the prosperity generated by capitalism; the breakdown of the proletariat as a coherent class (much less a vanguard of emancipation); the commodification of everything in fluid and dynamic markets; the production and consumption of symbols more than hard goods (as commodities are bought for their symbolic value); the destruction of social, physical, and temporal boundaries as restrictions of space and time are changed by technologies; the purchase of personal and subjective identities by consumer-driven actors; and the importance of symbolic and cultural superstructures as driving forces in world markets glutted with mass media and advertising images. Given these forced adaptations of the Marxian perspective, it is not surprising that many postmodernists have shifted their focus from the economic base to the cultural superstructure of society and, in many ways, turning Marx on his head just as Marx had turned Hegel on his head.

Cultural Postmodernism

All postmodern theories emphasize the fragmenting character of culture and the blurring of differences marked by symbols. Individuals are seen as caught in these transformations, participating in, and defining self from, an increasing array of social categories, such as race, class, gender, ethnicity, or status, while being exposed to ever-increasing varieties of cultural images as potential markers of self. At the same time, individuals lose their sense of being located in stable places and time frames. Many of the forces examined by economic postmodernists can account for this fragmentation of culture, decline in the salience of markers of differences, and loss of identity in time, place, and social space, but cultural postmodernists place particular emphasis on mass media and advertising because these are driven by markets and information technologies.

Jean Baudrillard

The strongest postmodern statement concerning the effects of the media on culture comes from Jean Baudrillard,[28] who sees the task before the social sciences today as challenging the "meaning that comes from the media and its fascination."[29] In contrast with philosophical postmodernism, Baudrillard's theory is based on the assumption that there is a potential equivalence or correspondence between the sign and its object, and based on this proposition, Baudrillard posits four historical phases of the sign.

In the first phase, the sign represented a profound reality, with the correlation and correspondence between the sign and the obdurate reality it signified being very high. In the next two phases, signs dissimulated or hid reality in some way: In the second phase, signs masked or counterfeited reality, as when art elaborated or commented on life, whereas in the third phase, signs masked the absence of *any* profound reality, as when mass commodification produced a plethora of signs that have no real basis in group identity but have the appearance of originating in group interaction.

The second phase roughly corresponds to the period of time from the Renaissance to the Industrial Revolution, whereas the third phase came with the Industrial Age, as production and new market forces created commodities whose sign values marking tastes, style, status, and other symbolic representations of individuals began to rival the use value (for some practical purpose) or exchange value (for some other commodity or resource like money) of commodities. In Baudrillard's view, then, the evolution of signs has involved decreasing, if not obfuscating, of their connection to real objects in the actual world.

The fourth stage in the evolution of the sign is the present postmodern era. In this age, the sign "has no relation to any reality whatsoever: It is its own pure simulacrum."[30] Signs are about themselves and, hence, are simulations or simulacrums of other signs with little connection to the basic nature of the social or material world. Baudrillard's prime example of simulacrum is Disneyland. Disneyland presents itself as a representation of American, embodying the values and joys of American life. Disneyland is offered as imagery—a place to symbolically celebrate and enjoy all that is good in the real world. But Baudrillard argues that Disneyland is presented as imagery to hide the fact that it is American reality itself. Life in the surrounding "real" communities, for example, Los Angeles and Anaheim, consists simply of emulations of past realities:

---

[28]Jean Baudrillard, *For a Critique of the Political Economy of the Sign* (St. Louis: Telos, 1972, 1981); *The Mirror of Production* (St. Louis: Telos, 1973, 1975); *Simulacra and Simulation* (Ann Arbor: University of Michigan Press, 1981, 1994); *Symbolic Exchange and Death* (Newbury Park, CA: Sage, 1993).

[29]Baudrillard, *Simulacra and Simulation* (cited in note 28), p. 84.

[30]Ibid., p. 6.

People no longer walk as a mode of transportation; rather, they jog or power walk. People no longer touch one another in daily interaction; rather, they go to contact-therapy groups. The essence of life in postmodernity is imagery; behavior is determined by image potential and is thus simply image. Baudrillard depicts Los Angeles as "no longer anything but an immense scenario and a perpetual pan shot."[31] Thus, when Disneyland is presented as a symbolic representation of life in America, when life in America is itself an image or simulation of a past reality, then Disneyland becomes a simulation of a simulation with no relationship to any reality whatsoever, and it hides the nonreality of daily life.

Baudrillard argues that the presentation of information by the media destroys information. This destruction occurs because there is a natural entropy within the information process; any information about a social event is a degraded form of that event and, hence, represents a dissolving of the social. The media is nothing more than a constant barrage of bits of image and sign that have been removed an infinite number of times from actual social events. Thus, the media does not present a surplus of information, but on the contrary, what is communicated represents total entropy of information and, hence, of the social world that is supposedly denoted by signs organized into information. The media also destroys information because it stages the presentation of information, presenting it in a prepackaged meaning form. As information is staged, the subjects are told what constitutes their particular relationship to that information, thereby simulating for individuals their place and location in a universe of signs about signs.

Baudrillard argues that the break between reality and the sign was facilitated by advertising. Advertising eventually reduces objects from their use-value to their sign-value; the symbols of advertisements become commodities in and of themselves, and image more than information about the commodity is communicated. Thus, advertisements typically juxtapose a commodity with a desirable image—for example, a watch showing one young male and two young females with their naked bodies overlapping one another—rather than providing information about the quality and durability of the commodity. So, that what is being sold and purchased is the image rather than the commodity itself. But, further, advertising itself can become the commodity sought after by the consuming public rather than the image of the advertisement. In the postmodern era, the form of the advertisement rather than the advertisement itself becomes paramount. For example, a currently popular form of television commercials is what could be called the "MTV style." Certain groups of people respond to these commercials not because of the product and not simply because of the images contained within the advertisements, but because they respond to the overall form of the message and not to its content at all. Thus, in postmodernity, the medium is the message, and what people are faced with, according to Baudrillard, are simulations of simulations and an utter absence of any reality.

Kenneth Gergen

The self is best understood, in Kenneth Gergen's view,[32] as the process through which individuals categorize their own behaviors. This process depends on the linguistic system used in

---

[31]Ibid., p. 13.

[32]Kenneth J. Gergen, *The Saturated Self* (New York: Basic Books, 1991); *The Concept of Self* (New York: Holt, Rinehart and Winston, 1971).

the physical and social spaces that locate the individual at a given time. Because conceptualizations of self are situational, the self generally tends to be experienced by individuals as fragmented and sometimes contradictory. Yet, people are generally motivated to eliminate inconsistencies in conceptualizations, and though Gergen grants that other possible factors influence efforts to resolve inconsistencies, people in Western societies try to create a consistent self-identity because they are socialized to dislike cognitive dissonance in much the same way they are taught to reason rationally. Gergen thus sees an intrinsic relationship between the individual's experience of a self and the culture within which that experience takes place, a cultural stand that he exploits in his understanding of the postmodern self.

Gergen argues that the culture of the self has gone through at least three distinct stages—the romantic, modern, and current postmodern phase. During the romantic period, the self as an autonomous individual and agent was stressed as individuals came out from the domination of various institutions including the church and manorial estate; during the modern period, the self was perceived as possessing essential or basic qualities, such as psychologically defined inherent personality traits. But the postmodern self consists only of images, revealing no inherent qualities, and most significantly, has lost the ability as well as desire to create self-consistency. Further, because knowledge and culture are fragmented in the postmodern era, the very concept of the individual self must be questioned and the distinction between the subject and the object dropped. According to Gergen, the very category of the self has been erased as a result of postmodern culture.

Thus, like Baudrillard, Gergen sees the self in postmodern culture as becoming saturated with images that are incoherent, communicating unrelated elements in different languages. And corresponding to Baudrillard's death of the subject, Gergen posits that the category of the self has been eradicated because efforts to formulate consistent and coherent definitions of who people are have been overwhelmed by images on images, couched in diverse languages that cannot order self-reflection.

Thomas Luckmann

Although Thomas Luckmann[33] recognizes the importance of the media and advertising in creating a postmodern culture, he focuses on the process of de-institutionalization as it pushes people into the cultural markets found in the mass media. The basic function of any institution, Luckmann argues, is to provide a set of predetermined meanings for the perceived world and, simultaneously, to provide legitimation for these meanings. Religion, in particular, provides a shield of solidarity against any doubts, fears, and questions about ultimate meaning by giving and legitimating an ultimate meaning set. Yet, modern structural differentiation and specialization has, Luckmann contends, made the ultimate meanings of religion structurally unstable because individuals must confront a diverse array of secular tasks and obligations that carry alternative meanings. This structural instability has, in turn, resulted in the privatization of religion. This privatization of religion is, however, more than a retreat from secular structural forces; it is also a response to forces of the sacralization of subjectivity found in mass culture.

Because of the effects of structural differentiation, markets, and mass culture, consciousness within individuals is one of immediate sensations and emotions. As a consequence, consciousness

---

[33]Thomas Luckmann, "The New and the Old in Religion," in *Social Theory for a Changing Society*, eds. Pierre Bourdieu and James S. Coleman (Boulder, CO: Westview, 1991).

is unstable, making acceptance of general legitimating myths, symbols, and dogmas problematic. Yet, capitalist markets have turned this challenge into profitable business. The individual is now faced with a highly competitive market for ultimate meanings created by mass media, churches and sects, residual nineteenth-century secular ideologies, and substitute religious communities. The products of this market form a more or less systematically arranged meaning set that refers to minimal and intermediate meanings but rarely to ultimate meanings. Under these conditions, a meaning set can be taken up by an individual for a long or short period of time and combined with elements from other meaning sets. Thus, just as early capitalism and the structural forces that it unleashed undermined the integrative power of religion, so advanced capitalism creates a new, more postmodern diversity of commodified meaning sets that can be mass produced and consumed by individuals in search of cultural coherence that can stave off their anxieties and fears in a structurally differentiated and culturally fragmented social world.

Zygmunt Bauman

Like Luckmann, Zygmunt Bauman[34] examines the effects of de-institutionalization on meanings about self in chaotic, often random, and highly differentiated systems. Within these kinds of systems, identity formation consists of self-constitution with no reference point for evaluation or monitoring, no clear anchorage in place and time, and no lifelong and consistent project of self-formation. People thus experience a high degree of uncertainty about their identity, and as a consequence, Bauman argues, the only visible vehicle for identity formation is the body.

Thus, in postmodernity, body cultivation becomes an extremely important dynamic in the process of self-constitution. Because the body plays such an important role in constituting the postmodern self, uncertainty is highest around bodily concerns, such as health, physique, aging, and skin blemishes; these issues become causes of increased reflexivity, evaluation, and, thus, uncertainty.

Bauman, like Luckmann, argues that the absence of any firm and objective evaluative guide tends to create a demand for a substitute. These substitutes are symbolically created, as other people and groups are seen as "unguarded totemic poles which one can approach or abandon without applying for permission to enter or leave."[35] Individuals use these others as reference points and adopt the symbols of belonging to the other. The availability of the symbolic tokens depends on their visibility, which, in turn, depends on the use of the symbolic tokens to produce a satisfactory self-construction. In the end, the efficacy of these symbols rests on either expertise in some task or mass following.

Bauman also argues that accessibility of the tokens depends on an agent's resources and increasingly is understood as knowledge and information. So, for example, people might adopt the symbols associated with a specific professional athlete—wearing the same type of shoe or physically moving in the same defining manner—or individuals might assume all the outward symbols and cultural capital associated with a perceived group of computer wizards. The important issue for Bauman is that these symbols of group membership can be taken up

---

[34]Zygmunt Bauman, *Modernity and Ambivalence* (Ithaca, NY: Cornell University Press, 1991); *Intimations of Postmodernity* (London and New York: Routledge, 1992).

[35]Bauman, *Intimations of Postmodernity* (see note 34), p. 195.

or cast off without any commitment or punitive action because the individuals using the symbols have never been an interactive part of these groups' or celebrities' lives.

The need for these tokens results in "tribal politics," defined as self-constructing practices that are collectivized.[36] These tribes function as imagined communities and, unlike premodern communities, exist only in symbolic form through the shared commitments of their members. For example, a girl in rural North Carolina might pierce various body parts, wear mismatched clothing three sizes too large, have the music of Biohazard habitually running through her mind, and see herself as a member of the grunge or punk community but never once interact with group members. Or, an individual might develop a concern for the use of animals in laboratory experiments, talk about it to others, wear proclamations on T-shirts and bumper stickers, and attend an occasional rally, and thus, might perceive himself as a group member but not be part of any kind of social group or interaction network. These quasi groups function without the powers of inclusion and exclusion that earlier groups possessed; indeed, these "neo-tribes" are created only through the repetitive performance of symbolic rituals and exist only as long as the members perform the rituals.

Neo-tribes are thus formed through concepts rather than through face-to-face encounters in actual social groups. They exist as "imagined communities" through self-identification and persist solely because people use them as vehicles for self-definition and as "imaginary sediments." Because the persistence of these tribes depends on the affective allegiance of the members, self-identifying rituals become more extravagant and spectacular. Spectacular displays, such as body scarring or extreme or random violence, are necessary because in postmodernity, public attention is the true scarce resource on which self and other are based.

Conclusion

Since the beginnings of sociology, there has always been a critical approach to analyzing modernity and, later, postmodernity. This critical approach turned anti-science in the twentieth century, seeing science as part of the problem with modernity and, moreover, as not able to adequately conceptualize and explain postmodernity. More substantively, critical theories of modernity and postmodernity postulate particular problems inherent in industrial and post-industrial societies that have negative consequences for individuals. In the assumptions and postulates below, the nature of the criticism becomes clearly evident.

1. Modernity, as fueled by capitalism, industrialization, urbanization, and rise of the bureaucratic state systematically generates problematic conditions, including

   A. The exploitation of industrial labor in supposedly free markets by those owning and controlling the means of production

   B. The commodification of labor, which must sell itself as a commodity under unfavorable market conditions

   C. The spread of rational-legal domination and its effects on dehumanizing persons and controlling potentially emancipatory revolution by labor

---

[36]Ibid., pp. 198–199.

D. The spread of power and money as symbolic media into virtually all institutional domains, thereby decreasing the salience of emotions, traditions, and personal relations

E. The lack of weakened cultural systems to provide needed regulation, or the spread of anomie, in market-driven differentiation of divisions of labor

F. The lack of embedded ties in traditional groups as the number and multiplicity of group affiliations increases marginality and egoism of actors who trade a wider set of weak ties to groups for traditional and more meaningful ties to kin and community groups

G. The breakdown of community ties with urbanization and the conditions listed above

2. With post-industrialization comes the globalization of capitalism and the dramatic increase in communication and transportation technologies. These transformations create a postmodern condition that amplifies some of the pathologies of modernity, while generating new kinds of pathologies, including

A. The overaccumulation of capital and its rapid circulation around the globe, which in turn

1. Aggravates the problems of labor when capital can constantly be moved to lower priced labor anywhere in the world

2. Increases financial speculation in meta-markets that can collapse

3. Disrupts government's capacities to control the money supply, to manage interest rates, and to cope with unemployment and bankruptcies

4. Decreases government's capacity to control capitalists and key actors in economy

B. The spread of technologies for reproduction rather than production, creating a social world of images detached from material reality, which in turn increases

1. The commodification of cultural systems and their detachment from their group anchorage as they are sold on global commodities markets

2. The increasing prominence of culture and cultural images, creating signs that signify less and less material reality

3. The decline of a core self as elements of culture are purchased in markets and "tried on" for their effect on others

4. The further detachment of self from groups that can provide a material anchorage for people's identities

5. The growing incapacity for culture to provide stable meanings for persons and groups

3. With modernity and postmodernity, it becomes increasingly difficult to resolve pathologies and problems, especially those related to

A. Emancipation of those subject to the abuses of inequality

B. Challenging the bureaucratized state

C. Providing a cultural means for regulating conduct

D. Providing a stable source of anchorage of self and identity in cultures tied to groups

E. Sustaining local cultures and their meaning systems for groups

CHAPTER 11

Stage-Model Evolutionary Theorizing

A s sociology began to emerge in the nineteenth century as an explicit field of inquiry, notions of evolution were circulating inside of academia and among literate members of the general population. Just like the current century, the nineteenth century was an era of biology as the ascendant science, and Auguste Comte made the appeal for sociology to supplant biology at the top of his famous hierarchy of the sciences. For the functional theorists of this early era of sociology—beginning with Comte, moving through Spencer, and ending with Emile Durkheim (see Chapter 2)—evolution was conceptualized as the movement of societies from simple to complex forms, or as a process of increasing *differentiation* of the structure and culture of society. Differentiation was also a focus of Georg Simmel and George Herbert Mead, but they did not develop explicitly evolutionary approaches. Karl Marx had a developmental view of societal evolution from primitive communism through slavery and feudalism to capitalism and, at the end of history, communism, but his analysis was not couched within the conceptual framework of differentiation. Weber also had an analysis of societal evolution—although he would not have used this term—as increasing *rationalization* as rational-legal authority and systems of legitimation of ever-spreading bureaucratic forms of social organization were driving out traditional systems of organization. Weber did not think that rationalization had been inevitable, as most scholars had, but once it got started, rational-legal authority was such a powerful force that society would increasingly become a "steel enclosure" of rational-legal domination.

Evolutionary theorizing vanished from sociology during the first two decades of the twentieth century, but like functionalism in sociology, anthropologists kept evolutionary thinking about stages from simple to complex forms going for several decades—perhaps waiting for sociologists to return to this form of theorizing. And, just like the revival of functionalism in the 1950s brought back what had been considered a "dead" approach (i.e., functionalism), the 1960s witnessed a revival of evolutionary theorizing by both functionalisms and non-functionalists, and even some conflict theorists.[1]

---

[1]Not only did early and later functionalists, such as Talcott Parsons and Niklas Luhmann, develop evolutionary models, but so did critical theorist such as Jürgen Habermas (see last chapter) and conflict theorists such as Gerhard Lenski, who was also an ecological theorist. Thus, after a long period of lying dormant, stage models of differentiation reemerged and remain today.

For some, the emphasis on differentiation as the master process remained, whereas for others, analysis shifted to stages of societal evolution and the driving forces pushing societies toward more complexity. Unlike earlier evolutionary theories, these new theories were not ethnocentric, and so they gained much more purchase in the second half of the twentieth century and continue to be developed into the present century. Indeed, as the twenty-first century became, once again, the century of biology, evolutionary theorizing in sociology has grown dramatically, but in addition to models of societal evolution from simple to more complex sociocultural formations, some sociologists began to borrow ideas from evolutionary biology as it had penetrated some social sciences—as we will see in the next chapter. And so, evolutionary theorizing in the current century has expanded considerably beyond stage models of societal development. But we should begin with where sociology began and then see how, in the modern era, stage models of societal evolution have extended the ideas of the founding maters of the discipline. Then, we can turn to more explicitly biologically inspired evolutionary theories in sociology.

Early Stage Models of Societal Evolution

Functional Theories of Evolution

Comte's Early Theory

Auguste Comte, who gave sociology its name in 1830, argued that "ideas" and beliefs evolved in relation to societal transformations. He felt that the age of science has arrived and that he and all other would-be sociologists could now focus on sociocultural phenomena; in addition, he offered a very sparse view of societal evolution as a process of increasing differentiation.[2] His model was perhaps a simple outline of what Herbert Spencer and later Emile Durkheim would make more robust and detailed empirically and conceptually. For Comte, as societies differentiate, they immediately encounter problems of integrating the differentiated parts of society into a coherent whole (see Figure 2.1 on page 9). If these pressures cannot be met, then a society will exhibit increased potential for social pathologies—e.g., conflict, deviance, poor coordination. He argued that the only way to reintegrate a society is through three basic mechanisms: (1) mutual interdependence of differentiated system parts, (2) centralization of power and authority to control, coordinate, and regulate diverse system parts, and (3) common culture or symbols systems—norms, values, beliefs—that all members of a society would hold. Comte did not develop these ideas into an important evolutionary framework, but Herbert Spencer did.

Spencer's Robust Theory

Herbert Spencer's entire philosophical scheme, which he termed Synthetic Philosophy, was built around an evolutionary model of movement from simple, homogeneous structures to complex,

---

[2]Auguste Comte, *The Positive Philosophy of Auguste Comte*, condensed and translated by H. Martineau (London: George Bell and Sons, 1896, originally published in serial form between 1830 and 1842). See also his later, rather flawed work that has some relevance for his views on evolution: Auguste Comte, *System of Positive Philosophy*, four volumes (New York: Burt Franklin, 1875, originally published in serial form between 1851 and 1854).

differentiated structures.[3] This model was stated as a master law of the universe because it could be used to understand the social, ethnical, biotic, and physical worlds that, Spencer believed, were governed by the same forces. This was, to say the least, a rather grand approach to explanation, but Spencer turned it into the most complete and sophisticated stage model of societal evolution developed by any social scientist in the nineteenth century, but also in the early twentieth century. Spencer's approach, in particular, is noteworthy for the data that are used to illustrate various stages of evolution. Spencer, as a wealthy man, had hired professional scholars to assemble vast files of data on all types of societies well into the 1930s (long after Spencer's death with monies bequeathed to the project). He termed the many volumes from this collective effort, *Descriptive Sociology*,[4] and they constituted the data source for his analysis of distinctive stages of societal evolution. He termed these stages (1) simple societies without a head (or political leader) and (2) with head or political leaders; then he recorded their "compounding" of simple societies into successively more differentiated social formations along three (really four) great axes: production, reproduction, distribution, and regulation (see Table 2.1 on page 12). He used the rather awkward labels of *compound*, *double compound*, and *treble compound* (he probably would have added a quadruple compound if he had lived to see the post-industrial era). These stages correspond to the stages after simple hunter-gatherers and settled hunter-gatherers evolved to horticultural societies (compound), agrarian societies (doubly compound), and industrial societies (trebly compound). The descriptions hold up rather well in the contemporary era, but more important is the theory that Spencer developed to explain this movement of societies from simple to more complex forms. Figure 11.1 gives a visual representation that Spencer had in mind as he saw societies as moving from simple to ever-more complex and differentiated forms, although the descriptive detail of Spencer's analysis is not captured in the figure.

Spencer saw population growth as the initial force that pushed simple societies or hunter-gatherers out of their equilibrium. Population growth occurred when hunter-gatherers settled down, and as growth occurred, the larger number of individuals in the society generated selection pressures for higher levels of (1) economic production, (2) regulation through power and cultural symbols, (3) distribution of resources, information, and people, and (4) reproduction of new members and social units regulated by culture organizing their activities. As new structures are created to resolve these selection pressures, these new structures become differentiated from each other—thus increasing the overall level of differentiation of a society. But differentiation itself generates increased selection pressures for more diverse goods and services, for more regulation with power, authority, and culture, for expanded capacities to distribute goods, resources, information, and people across more territory composed of more diverse social units, and for reproduction of new types of structures and specialized personnel in these structures. Thus, once the ball gets rolling on differentiation, it feeds off itself, creating new kinds of problems of adaptation that generate their own selection pressures.

---

[3]Herbert Spencer, *The Principles of Sociology*, three volumes (New York: Appleton-Century-Crofts, 1895, originally published in serial form between 1874 and 1896). See the footnote 2 on p. 10 for Spencer's definition of the evolution of the universe.

[4]Herbert Spencer, *Descriptive Sociology, or Groups of Facts* was initiated in 1873 and finished after Spencer's death, with the last volume coming out in 1934. There were fourteen volumes in all. See my discussion in *Herbert Spencer: Toward a Renewed Appreciation* (Newbury Park, CA: Sage Publications, 1985). See also my and Alexandra Maryanski's review of the logic of descriptive sociology in "Sociology's Lost Human Relations Area Files," *Sociological Perspectives* 31 (1988): pp. 19–34.

Figure 11.1 Spencer's Stage Model of Societal Evolution

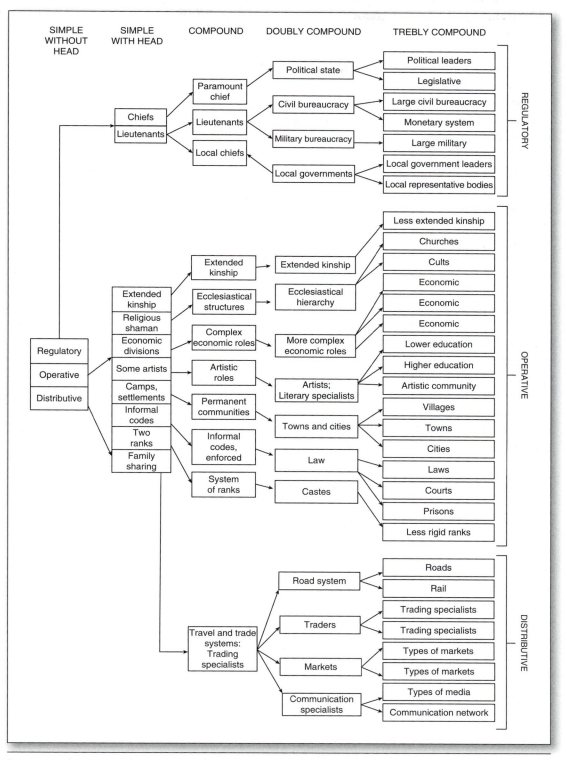

Source: Jonathan Turner, *The Emergence of Sociological Theory 7e,* SAGE Publications Inc., 2012

At any point, however, these selection pressures can overwhelm a society, causing it to dis-integrate or be conquered by a more powerful society, but conquest generally increases the level of differentiation and stratification in the victorious society as it absorbs conquered societies; these outcomes of conquest only ratchet up the selection pressures on a population—thus keeping the engine driving differentiation fueled up. Thus, societies become larger and more differentiated by the dynamics of population growth and conquest, and each new stage or phase of differentiation generates selection pressures that produce even more differentiation.

Like Marx, but with greater reverence for capitalism, Spencer had a somewhat utopian hope that as differentiation increased the use of markets for distributing people as labor, resources, goods, and services, differentiation in the modern industrial era would no longer be fed by war and conquest. For Spencer, use of coercive power only increased the centralization of power that, in turn, deprives the domestic economy of capital, while increasing inequalities, stratification, and tension that leads to the centralization of ever-more coercive force that, ironically, only serves to increase inequality, stratification, and domestic tension. And, once societies get locked into this more centralized and coercive form of regulation, the dynamic powers of markets are undone as an integrative force, while the over-concentration of coercive and administrative power comes to dominate efforts at integration, which in the long run have the effect of eventually destabilizing a society. When societ-ies concentrate power and use it in the geo-political sphere, they begin to stagnate because concen-trated power creates disincentive for free market development and productive innovations.

Thus, Spencer made some important breakthroughs in analyzing societal evolution: growth and differentiation always generate selection pressures on populations to create new kinds of produc-tive, reproductive, regulatory, and distributive structures, which ratchet up differentiation that can encourage more population growth. Once this process is initiated, it fuels itself and, moreover, aggravates adaptive problems when military conquest is driving differentiation. Societies that con-centrate power for conquest also generate increased inequalities that lead to internal societal inte-grative problems to go along with external threats from other societies. As a result, societies can face ever-increasing disintegrative pressures, which can cause de-evolution of societies to smaller and simpler forms or lead to the complete collapse of a society as a coherent form.

Durkheim's Theory of Differentiation-Integration

Emile Durkheim borrowed much from Spencer in his first great work, *The Division of Labor in Society*,[5] which analyses the causes and consequences of growth and differentiation, viewing popu-lation growth as creating a kind of Darwinian struggle by individuals and collective actors to find resource niches, thereby increasing the level of differentiation in a society. His main focus, how-ever, was not so much on evolution as on how a new basis of societal integration can—indeed, must—evolve with societal growth and differentiation. Like Comte, he saw the potential for pathologies when a new basis of integration for differentiated societies is not in place—pathologies such as *anomie* (lack of regulation by common cultural symbols), *egoism* (lack of integration of persons into social structures), inequality (or *the forced division of labor*), and *poor coordination* for lack of structural interdependencies. But, he also argued that these potential pathologies would disappear as the new bases of integration began to evolve—a picture much rosier than Spencer's.

---

[5]Emile Durkheim, *The Division of Labor in Society* (New York: Free Press, 1947, originally published in French in 1893).

How, then, was a new basis of integration to be achieved? For Durkheim, the new basis of integration would be achieved in several ways. As Comte had emphasized, members of a society must possess a common culture—language, norms, beliefs, values, and other symbol systems. Durkheim recognized that structural differentiation places people in somewhat different social worlds, and as a response, cultural values become more generalized so that they still have relevance to individuals and social units in diverse locations in the differentiated system. But, a highly generalized and abstract system of moral codes loses its capacity to regulate precisely the actions of actors because these codes, while being highly moral, are so abstract. For instance, if a moral code indicates that persons should "achieve" and "do well," such an abstract code does not tell persons *how* to achieve and *what* standards to invoke in measuring success. Hence, the code increases the potential for anomie, or a state of low regulation by culture.

To solve this problem, Durkheim implicitly argued that there are selection pressures to backfill abstract moral codes like value premises with more precise and domain-specific moral guidelines for how to realize the tenets of moral codes like the mandate to do well and achieve. Thus, these new beliefs or what is often termed *ideology* today, tell individuals *how* to "achieve" in diverse institutional contexts like kinship, economy, education, community, religion, sports, and all other broad spheres of social life.

Later, Durkheim increasingly realized that more than domain- and situation-specific ideologies are necessary for social solidarity among larger, differentiated populations. By the last years of the nineteenth century, he had begun to argue that any social unit, even a large and highly differentiated society, must have (a) symbols regulating members of social units' perceptions and actions, (b) objects (or totems) of "worship" symbolizing the social unit, and (c) emotion-arousing rituals directed at group totems and reaffirming the symbols marking the group and regulating its members' activities. For people to develop commitments to societies, then, they must hold common symbols marking the society—whether these be flags and other types of physical objects or songs, phrases, and other symbols denoting the collective social whole. This is why Durkheim became interested in totems among traditional, preliterate peoples because he felt that even in larger-scale and highly differentiated societies, members must "worship" the symbols and totems representing the society, thereby affirming their commitments to the social whole even as they pursue differentiated and diverse activities.

For Durkheim, structural interdependence must accompany differentiation. He assumed that such interdependence would naturally emerge, and so, he did not specify the mechanisms by which interdependence is achieved. If pushed, he might have emphasized markets as one mechanisms, and whatever other mechanisms are involved, he also would have stressed that there must be a common morality—enshrined in values, ideologies, and moral commitments to collective symbols—undergirding exchange and contracts—an idea similar to Comte's emphasis on common culture as an integrative mechanism. There is always a non-contractual morality for social relations among individuals and social units.

Durkheim emphasized that differentiation will place individuals in many different positions in diverse kinds of social structures in different institutional domains. Individuals can thus often feel isolated from social structures because they stand between so many diverse types, never feeling that they are fully part or integrated into any social structure. Here, again, individuals become morally integrated into diverse groups when they engage in ritual practices toward the symbols marking each group, and as these rituals arouse positive emotions, they generate a sense of being part of, and committed to, a social structure—thereby eliminating egoism even in complex systems where individuals move about different groups in a wide variety of contexts and domains (see Collins' model of interaction rituals in Figure 3.3 on page 49).

Finally, Durkheim indicated that inequality can be a disintegrative force in societies, if the distribution of rewards for efforts does not correspond to the differentiation of talents and abilities. But, he argued that this "forced division of labor" was only temporary and, eventually, selection pressures would work to reward people for their talents and abilities—obviously a conclusion that is a bit naïve.

Durkheim understood that the need for interdependence among differentiated structures did not necessarily produce these interdependencies. But, he did feel that there were selection pressures to increase interdependence, and if normative rules, often enshrined in law, can emerge and carry the general morality of a population, interdependencies could be forged that were both strong and moral, thereby increasing the efficiency of coordination among diversely situated actors.

Unlike Spencer or even Comte, Durkheim did not recognize the importance of power and authority as a force of social control, or at least he tended to underemphasize power and, instead, emphasize cultural bases of integration. In the preface to the second edition of his famous first major work, *The Division of Labor* in *Society*, Durkheim offered a somewhat weak but still intriguing way in which government could operate as an integrative force. He suggested that government should be democratic and that political parties should develop among major occupational groups in society. These occupational groups would include those at roughly similar locations in the division of labor, and thus because of the structural equivalence among their members, individuals would have common interests and exert pressures on government to further these interests. Thus, power would be connected to moral communities (built around occupational specializations) that, in turn, engage in political contests to fulfill the needs and interests of their members. Governmental power would be held in check, therefore, because it must respond to the demands of diverse clusters of occupations; the more government could adjudicate these interests, members of occupational groups would develop commitments to polity and thereby legitimate their right to use power.

Early Conflict Theoretic Explanations

In somewhat different ways, the German founders of sociology—Karl Marx, Max Weber, and Georg Simmel—all developed stage models of evolution, especially models of the transition to modern, capitalist societies. Marx viewed capitalism as simply the last stage before the end of evolutionary history when communism would liberate humankind; Weber did not see evolution as inevitable, but once the transition to modernity and rational-legal authority occurred, certain evolutionary dynamics were inevitable; and Simmel, who did not develop a model of evolution, still argued that the emergence of modernity had certain liberating effects (in contrast to Marx) and altered the basis of social integration. Thus, while not full-blown evolutionists, these conflict theorists had much to say about the evolutionary transition into modernity. Let me examine each of the models proposed by these theorists.

Marx's Stage Model

Among the three, Marx had the most developed of the stage models, viewing society as evolving from primitive communism (i.e., hunting and gathering) through slavery (advanced horticulture) and feudalism (agrarianism) and capitalism (industrialism) to the end of societal evolution with the arrival of communism.[6] The stages in his model are rather loose and really not intended to be robust because Marx was primarily concerned with the contradictions of capitalism as they would usher in communism. We saw Marx's theory of the conflict that would cause this transition in Chapter 3, and so, in this short section, I only was to emphasize Marx's ideas on the basis of integration of capitalist societies.

Marx argued that the basic substructure of society is the means of production, with all other institutional domains and their cultures being "mere" superstructures. This assertion is problematic and extreme, but it does suggest certain integrative dynamics. For Marx, those who own and control the means of production are able to usurp resources from those who do not own the means of production. In capitalism, this usurpation occurs through exploitation in which capitalists are able to extract surplus value inhering in the proletariat's labor, or the difference between what capitalists pay labor and the actual revenues they receive when selling the products of this labor in markets. Thus exploitation is defined as this difference between the price that commodities sell for in markets and the costs of labor and machine production to produce them.

With this surplus, capitalists are able to control societal superstructures, particularly the production of ideologies legitimating capitalists' forms of production and the actions of polity to enforce the interests of capitalists vis-à-vis labor. Marx's theory overestimated capitalists' control of ideologies and government, but in making the argument in the extreme, he nonetheless highlights three critical elements in sustaining any social system. As societies use new industrial technologies to organize production in more open and competitive markets, new forms of wealth are created and used to finance polity and the production of ideologies legitimating capitalist production and distribution. Integration is, therefore, achieved by (1) markets that create interdependencies among actors in the system, even if these are seen as exploitive, (2) consolidation of power to enforce these relations, and (3) ideologies that legitimate both patterns of interdependence created by markets and use of power by government. Marx assumed that those who did not benefit from this system of integration would mobilize for conflict, but his predictions go astray because he assumed incorrectly that those in lower classes could not exert pressures on governments that would mitigate exploitive relations of interdependence. And, he also overemphasized the capacities of elites to control government and the instruments of ideological production. Still, these mistakes aside, Marx does offer a conceptualization of the three prongs of integration in modern, capitalist, and market-driven societies. When phrased at this higher level of abstraction, Marx's model does not seem so different than either Spencer's or Durkheim's models.

---

[6]Karl Marx and Friedrich Engels, "The Communist Manifesto," *in Birth of the Communist Manifesto*, ed. D. J. Struik (New York: International Publishers, 1971).

Max Weber's Stage Model

For Weber, societies are built from actions that created organizations and systems of domination (stratification).[7] Like Marx, he saw conflict potential in societies because stratification always generates tensions between those who have wealth, prestige, and power, on the one side, and those who do not have these resources. Yet, unlike Marx, Weber recognized that the correlation among class (wealth from economy), party (political power), and status groups (rights for honor, deference, and prestige) are not always high, thus reducing polarization of people in societies. Still, the conflict potential remained and periodically erupted under the right historical circumstances (a) where the correlation among those high and low in class position, access to power, and rights to prestige is high, (b) where large discontinuities between high and low locations in systems of domination exist, and (c) where mobility across social strata is infrequent. Under these conditions, conflict can erupt and lead to the emergence of a new system of domination that sets into motion the potential for conflict in the future.

But, Weber also argued that, while the emergence of capitalism was not inevitable, once present, it changes the fundamental nature of society. Capitalism is built on means-ends rationality as not only a mechanisms for organizing activities in a society but also as an ideology legitimating the spread of bureaucracies into almost all institutional spheres—economic, political, religious, legal, etc. This rationality erodes away traditional forms of domination and makes people cogs in bureaucratic orders, mediated by money and labor markets. The result is for revolutionary potential to be dramatically reduced because rational-legal bureaucracies become a "steel cage" encapsulating people's activities and passions in virtually all institutional spheres, except perhaps kinship. Thus, the modern stage of societal evolution generates a new basis of organization of what Weber termed "legitimated orders" in societies: the spread of means-end rationality over other forms of domination, such as tradition and emotional commitments, that lead to the spread of bureaucratic forms of social organization, regulated by law and polity while being legitimated by ideologies of rationality. In such a world, it is difficult to even perceive inequalities as unfair and even more difficult to mobilize actors to pursue conflict against the system. There is, then, more stability in means-end rationality as a form of domination, even as this form of domination strips life of much of its passion and encloses people in structures that regulate through authority the actions of persons. Indeed, in contrast to Marx, Weber saw the end of history as rather stark and hardly liberating as bureaucracies increasingly constricted the options and actions of persons

Simmel's Stage Model

George Simmel viewed the transition into modernity in a more benign light than either Marx or Weber. Societies built around markets and interdependencies among ever-more groups and social structures that open up new freedoms.[8] Individuals have more options now to choose their affiliations, and they are no longer bound by old repressive traditions but by their own preferences. Individuals can use money to realize their preferences in markets on a scale never possible in precapitalist societies, even hunting and gathering. Individuals have the capacity to gain increased

---

[7]Max Weber, *Economy and Society* (Berkeley, CA: University of California Press, 1968), pp. 901–1158.

[8]Georg Simmel, *The Philosophy of Money*, trans. Tom Bottomore and David Frisby (Boston: Routledge, 1990).

value as they purchase goods and services in markets because such purchases are based upon the assumption that the money given up will provide enhanced value from the thing or service purchased in a market.

Thus, capitalism increased individualism, reduced embeddedness in ascriptive groups, and dramatically increased options to realize preferences. True, people are often marginal to many groups; they no longer can feel fully embedded in many group affiliations; and perhaps they feel somewhat isolated. Still, Simmel implied that when markets provide the principle mechanisms of societal integration, individuals achieve a greater sense of efficacy, which in turn leads them to legitimate the system regulated by law, markets, and polity. Integration is no longer so dependent up common culture as it is to the sense of freedom and choice that comes with markets. So, from Simmel's perspective, markets are liberating rather than exploitive, and rationality is not so restrictive because it is what drives the formation and spread of markets that open up new options for individuals to realize their unique needs and preferences.

The End of the Classical Era

The great early masters of sociology all began to die off at the very time that evolutionary theorizing was being rejected. Only Spencer had a robust theory of evolutionary stages, but the classical theorists were all concerned by the problems and pathologies, or lack thereof, that accompany the evolution of capitalism and modernity. For Marx, capitalism set the stage for the last great revolution, and in so doing, capitalism carried the seed for the sprouting of communism and its liberating potential. For Weber, capitalism destroyed passion, tradition, and non-rational forms of social relations and enclosed people in steel cages. For Simmel, capitalism possessed liberating potential. All of these arguments by Marx, Weber, and Simmel were perhaps overdrawn, but when coupled with the insights of Comte, Spencer, and Durkheim, they offer a view of key forces that are involved in societal evolution.

There are forces that drive evolution: processes revolving around population grown as it generates selection pressures for increased production and distribution. As societies become more complex and differentiated under these pressures, the basis of integration changes along several fronts. First, culture also differentiates between highly generalized moral tenants, on the one side, and beliefs, ideologies, and norms that fill the regulatory vacuum created when morality become so abstract in differentiated societies. Abstract moral codes allow for differentiation and can provide highly generalized moral imperatives, but they cannot supply specific moral guidelines for persons and social units operating in diverse domains. Only when societal-level values are incorporated into ideologies and norms in diverse institutional domains can abstract moral codes provide the necessary detail to regulate the actions of individuals and social units. Second, interdependencies as a mechanism of integration are increasingly mediated by markets and less by systems of authority, with the result that they increase individualism and allow persons and social units to pursue preferences somewhat independently from centers of power. Third, polity becomes more democratic and capable of absorbing conflicts of interest among actors located in different domains and at different places in the system of inequality.[9] Fourth, law and its

---

[9]Talcott Parsons, *Societies: Evolutionary and Comparative Perspectives* and *The System of Modern Societies* (Englewood Cliffs, NJ: Prentice Hall, 1966 and 1971, respectively).

capacity to adjudicate the law in courts become increasing important for regulating exchanges in markets and for defining the relations between polity and the population governed by polity.

These themes seemingly disappeared with the demise of evolutionary theorizing in sociology in the first half of the twentieth century but, in fact, they remained part of the debate in critical theoretical circles but equally important, they came back into sociology generally and evolutionary theorizing on stages of societal development when such theorizing reemerged in the 1960s.

Modern Stage Models of Societal Evolution

Without much warning, stage models of societal evolution suddenly reemerged in sociology by the mid-1960s. Not surprisingly, functional theorists like Talcott Parsons began to bring evolutionary ideas back into the renewed interest in evolutionary theorizing, but his efforts, which I will review later, were far less important than the work of Gerhard Lenski[10] who developed a stage theory of societal evolution emphasizing power, inequality, and potential conflict. This line of emphasis was more in tune with the times—the conflict-ridden 1960s. Conflict theorizing was reemerging in the United States in the post-McCarthy era, where Marx could once again be examined in public places, and Lenski's model was received much better than Parsons' because it did not carry functionalist trappings and, instead, focused on conflict dynamics systematically generated by the evolution of stratification systems. Later, in association with Gene Lenski and then, Patrick Nolan, this early approach was broadened to a full macro-level theory of social organization; more recently, Lenski himself reconfigured his theory to emphasize the ecological dynamics woven into the stage model of societal-level evolution. By the time that this revival of evolutionary theorizing occurred, most sociologists had long forgotten about Herbert Spencer's emphasis on the dynamics of power during societal evolution because his functionalism, like that of Parsons, would arouse suspicion in an era that wanted to talk about conflict without functionalist trappings. I will begin with Lenski's and his associates' analysis of societal evolution; then I will examine Parsons' stage model of evolution.

Gerhard Lenski's Theorizing on Societal Evolution

The Early Theory

The basic argument developed in *Power and Privilege: A Theory of Stratification* is that the *level of technology* determines, along with other factors, the *level of production* in a society. The higher is the level of technology in a society, the greater will be the level of economic production, and the higher is the level of production, the greater will be the amount of *economic surplus* in a society. Furthermore, as the level of economic surplus increases, the more it can be usurped by those consolidating power, thereby increasing inequality and privilege among those with this power. This basic set of dynamics is outlined in Figure 11.2.

The fundamental relationship among technology, production, economic surplus, and inequality in a society is mediated by a number of factors. One factor is environmental or ecological conditions, such as the level of resources in the available geographical space, as well as the

---

[10]Gerhard Lenski, *Power and Privilege: A Theory of Social Stratification* (New York: McGraw-Hill, reprinted by the University of North Carolina Press); Gerhard Lenski, Patrick Nolan, and Gene Lenski *Human Societies: An Introduction to Macrosociology*, 7th ed. (New York: McGraw-Hill, 1995). For the most recent edition, see Patrick Nolan and Gerhard Lenski, *Human Societies*, 12th ed. (Oxford University Press, 2012); Gerhard Lenski, *Ecological-Evolutionary Theory: Principles and Applications* (Boulder, CO: Paradigm Press, 2005).

Figure 11.2 Lenski's Basic Model of Conditions Generating Societal Inequality

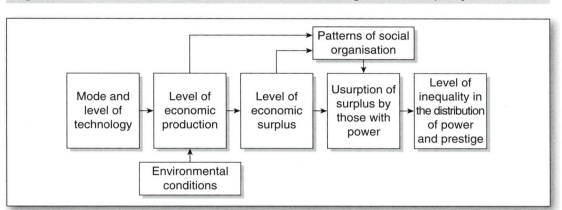

presence of other societies and the potential threats that they might pose. Another key factor is demographic, revolving around the size of a population and the profile of its characteristics (e.g., age, ethnicity, class locations, religious affiliation, etc.). Still another set of factors is the nature of social organization generated, in particularly the form of polity and its degree of consolidation of power, but also other institutional systems such as structure of kinship, religion, law, education, and science. Yet another is the geo-political situation of a society revolving around competition for resources and warfare with other societies. Still another is the value and ideological cultural systems that emerge and constrain patterns of social organization and action.

These additional factors are all labeled in Figure 11.3, but as the bold-faced arrows try to make clear, the primary factors in Lenski's model revolve around technology, production, surplus, consolidation of power, inequality, and system of stratification. What made this analysis appealing in the 1960s is that Lenski used a stage model of evolution to explain variations in the primary influences affecting the forces generating stratification. Thus, the lower is the level of technology, the lower will be the level of production in a society, and hence, the less will be the size of the productive surplus, if any, generated. And, without surplus, there is nothing to usurp by those consolidating power; as a consequence, degree of stratification in a society will be low. The history of human societies, then, has revolved around a series of basic stages during which the level of technology, production, and surplus have *all* increased. The stages proposed by Lenski are very similar to those developed by Herbert Spencer: hunting and gathering without a head; hunting and gathering with a head (and hence, beginnings of polity); simple and advanced horticultural (gardening without animal power); simple and advanced agrarian (farming using animal power); industrial (relying on inanimate sources of power). Within each of these stages, there are variations in the degree of development. For example, there are fishing variants for nomadic hunting and gathering, as well as herding variants for horticultural and agrarian societies. Moreover, there is a marine variant for agrarian societies. Still each stage and its variants is defined by its basic mode of technology that is used to gather resources and produce material products.

Lenski's analysis attempts to explain two facets of societal evolution. One is the same goal of earlier functional stage models: the growing complexity of societies by virtue increases in the level of technology and production that, in turn, affect the number of people who can be supported in a society and, hence, a society's size. But this relationship is mediated by the consolidation of power in polity or government and, in turn, the degree to which power is

Figure 11.3 Lenski's Model of Stratification

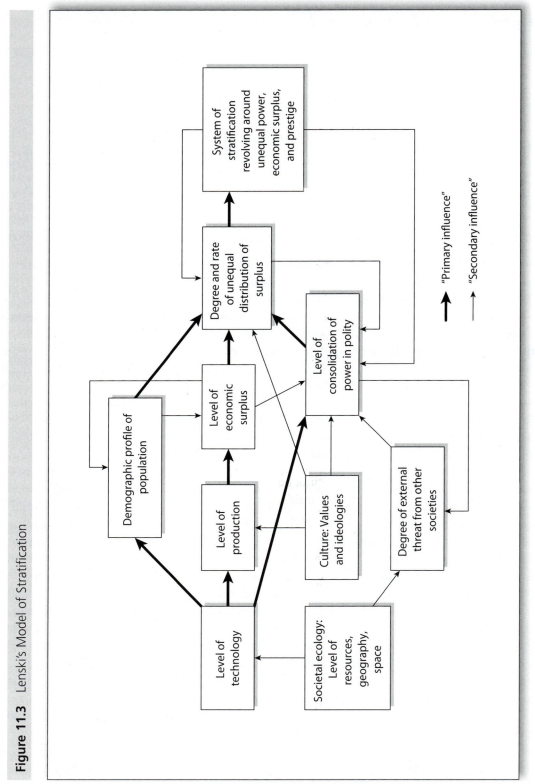

used to usurp productive surplus to sustain elite privilege. So, Lenski like all functional theorists before him sought to isolate the driving forces of evolutionary history—in his case, technology, production, and economic surplus (whereas functionalists like Spencer and Durkheim tended to emphasize increases in population size and rates of growth as what kick-starts the development of technologies and a productive capacities). These demographic forces are also part of Lenski's model, as laid out in Figure 11.3, but they are given somewhat less significance than in early functional models outlining the stages of societal evolution.

The second facet of Lenski's effort is to explain the evolution and operation of stratification systems in human societies, with stratification hypothesized to increase with the level of technology, production, and surplus. In a very real sense, data assembled on societies at different stages of development are intended to assess Lenski's theory of inequality and stratification—thus making this kind of evolutionary theorizing more in tune with the conflict theories that were emerging at the same time.

The hypothesized relationship among technology, production, surplus, and inequality is that as technology and production continued to grow, so would inequality and stratification. Yet, the actual findings across stages of societal development are more curvilinear. The hypothesized relationship holds up until the industrial stage. Thus, from hunting and gathering forward, stratification increases as technology and production generate ever-more surplus that historically has led to the consolidation of power in polity and the usurpation of surplus—thereby increasing the level of inequality in the stratification system. Going against this long-term evolutionary/historical trend, however, is a significant, though still rather modest, decrease in inequality in industrial societies. This reversal requires an explanation, and hence, Lenski introduces what he terms "secondary variables"—(1) democratization of power, (2) reliance on education and its extensions to the masses as an important criterion for resource distribution, and (3) changes in societal ideologies toward advocating more equality or at least equality of opportunity. These variables become more highly valenced in industrial societies, and the result is a reversal of the long-term historical trend toward ever-more inequality and stratification in human societies.

The influence of Lenski's analysis cannot be underestimated. He made stage-modeling of evolutionary sequences respectable again outside of functional analysis because he emphasized the forces—power, inequality, and stratification—that are at the core of the conflict-theory critique, which has been used to discredit functional theory in general and Talcott Parsons' particular version of functional and evolutionary theory. And, over the last five decades, Lenski himself has continued to refine the model of societal evolution, but equally, if not more importantly, a large number of theorists began to follow the path opened up by Lenski's *Power and Privilege*.

The More Recent Evolutionary Theory

As Lenski continued to theorize on evolution, he increasingly added more biological and ecological forces to his analysis. Working with his wife before her early death, and later with Patrick Nolan, Lenski began to include in his theory societal development more Darwinian theoretic ideas as well as ideas form the Modern Synthesis in biology—perhaps a good indicator of how much biological theorizing was beginning to influence the social sciences in the 1970s and 1980s (see next chapter).

Both biological and social evolution are, first, "based on records of experience that are preserved and transmitted from generation to generation in the form of coded systems of information" and, second, on "processes that involve random variation and selection" of those traits that promote adaptation to the environment.[11] Yet, there are some important differences between biological and social evolution. One is that, in organic evolution, the genes are the preservers of the informational codes, whereas in social evolution, cultural "symbol systems are the functional equivalents of the genetic alphabet."[12] Another difference revolves around the way that information is transmitted. In biological evolution, genetic information can be transmitted only through the reproduction of new organisms; moreover, diverse species cannot interbreed, and so, the transmission of information is limited to one species. In contrast, cultural information is more readily and broadly transmitted, moving from one type of society to another. The end result is that in biological evolution, speciation leads to ever-new patterns of differentiation and diversification, whereas in social evolution the movement of information across societal types "is likely to eventuate in ever fewer and less dissimilar societies than exist today."[13] A related difference is that in biological evolution, both simple and complex species can continue to exist in their respective resource niches, whereas in social evolution, simpler societal types tend to be extinguished by more complex types. Still another difference is that acquired traits can be transmitted through socialization, whereas in biological evolution, such Lamarckian processes do not occur. An outcome of this difference is that genetic change in biological evolution is comparatively slow (because natural selection has to sort out genes across many generations), whereas cultural evolution can be very rapid (because new traits can be created, learned, transmitted, and diffused within one generation).

These similarities and differences lead to the recognition that (a) human societies are part of the natural world and subject to selection forces from both their biophysical *and* sociocultural environments, (b) humans like any other animal are influenced by their genetic heritage, and (c) only humans are the creators of their cultural heritage or the informational codes that guide behavior and social organization. A given society, then, has social structural and cultural (symbolic) characteristics that, for analytical purposes, can be divided into (1) its population size and characteristics, (2) its culture or systems of symbols, particularly technologies, (3) its material products generated by the application of its technology to productive processes, (4) its organizational forms that structure activities, and (5) its institutional systems that combine (1) through (4) into systems addressing basic problems of survival and adaptation for individuals and the society as a whole. These five components of a society influence, while being influenced by other forces, (1) a society's biophysical environment, (2) its social environment of other societies and their respective cultures, (3) the genetic heritage of humans as a species, namely an evolved ape, and (4) the prior social and cultural characteristics of a society as these continue to influence its internal operation and its adaptation to the external environment.

In this more recent analysis, Lenski's earlier emphasis on technologies as the driving force of social evolution is retained, but the argument is recast into an evolutionary framework inspired by Darwin and the Modern Synthesis. As Lenski remarks, "It seems no exaggeration to say that advances in subsistence technology are functionally equivalent to adaptive changes in a population's gene pool; new energy resources and new materials enable populations to do things that they could not do before."[14]

---

[11]Lenski, Nolan, and Lenski, *Human Societies*, p. 75 (see note 10).

[12]Ibid.

[13]Ibid., 75–76.

[14]Gerhard Lenski, "Societal Taxonomies: Mapping the Social Universe," *Annual Review of Sociology* 20 (1994): p. 23.

Social evolution is a cumulative process in the sense that new technologies proving more adaptive to a society alter the pattern of social organization, generally toward larger and more complex forms of organization. Two basic forces drive change in human societies: (1) innovation where new information and social structural patterns are created, whether by chance or conscious intent, and (2) extinction where old cultural and structural patterns are abandoned. Innovations in sociocultural evolution cause more rapid change than forces in biological evolution, because (a) humans have conscious capacities to develop new informational codes; (b) humans have "needs and desires" that are potentially "limitless" and, under certain conditions, drive them to make new discoveries as old needs are satisfied and new ones emerge; (c) humans can adopt the information of other societies through diffusion; (d) humans can force another society to adopt their informational codes through conquest and repression of older cultural and structural patterns, especially when larger and more complex societies conquer or co-opt smaller and less complex ones; (e) humans can institutionalize innovation in such structural forms as science, thereby creating a set of cultural codes and social structures specifically geared to constant innovation; and (f) humans can create complex interconnections among systems of information that force changes in other elements as changes in another occur.

Yet, Lenski, Nolan, and Lenski stress that there are also forces operating to sustain continuity in the cultural systems that guide the organization of a population. One force for continuity is *socialization*, in which older patterns are transmitted to each new generation. Another force is *ideology*, which preserves cultural systems and guides the transmission of culture from one generation to another. Still another force is the *systemic nature* of human sociocultural systems, which resist change in one element because so many other elements will be forced to change (although, as noted earlier, once change in one element does occur, it has a cascading effect and actually accelerates change). Another force is *vested interests*, especially of the powerful in stratified societies who have the power to suppress innovations when changes threaten status quo interests. Yet another force is *inertia*, where past practices appear to promote adaptation and sufficient satisfaction for individuals, leading them to resist adopting new practices whose impact cannot be fully known.

Yet, despite these forces promoting continuity, the long-term historical record confirms that societal evolution has involved change, fueled by technological innovations, toward larger and more complex societies. Societies vary, of course, in their rates of innovation; these rates vary because of several important forces. First, the amount of information already possessed by a society greatly influences its capacity to create and adopt new information. Second, the size of a population is another important factor because larger populations have more individuals who hold ideas and who can potentially generate new ideas. Third, the stability and nature of a society's environment, both social and biophysical, is another force of change; the more the environment changes, the more likely a society is to be innovative or adopt the innovations of other societies. Fourth, the nature of the innovations per se is a very significant factor; some innovations are fundamental and pave the way for additional innovations (for example, the discovery of metallurgy or new sources of energy stimulated even more innovations). And fifth, the ideology of a society greatly circumscribes the creation or adoption of innovations; powerful and conservative ideologies make it difficult for individuals to be innovative, while discouraging the diffusion of innovations from other societies.

Over the long course of societal development, however, productive technologies are the most important driving force of evolution. In the end, technological innovations can overcome the forces promoting continuity, even the ideologies and the vested interests of the powerful. The reason for this significance of technology is that those societies that can better gather, produce, and distribute resources will generate an economic surplus that can support a larger population and its differentiation into new organizational forms and institutional systems. Eventually, their technologies diffuse to other societies, and particularly so when larger, more complex societies conquer, co-opt, or out-compete smaller and less complex societies. Thus, a kind of group selection operates in the history of human societies, as more powerful societies (with better technologies, productive capacities, and organizational forms) impose their cultural systems and structural patterns on others through conquest, provide models and incentives for less developed societies to adopt their cultural and structural systems, or take the resources on which less developed societies depend for their survival. These last points echo Herbert Spencer's argument that survival of the fittest operates at the group level where the better organized society will prevail in war and in economic competition over the less organized. Indeed, selection processes have favored an emerging world system of societies.

Talcott Parsons' Stage Model of Evolution

Partly in response to intense criticisms that functional analysis cannot explain change in social systems, Talcott Parsons developed an evolutionary model of societal change. Such a model did not silence the critics because the dynamics of power, stratification, and conflict were not sufficiently prominent in this theory. Despite these criticisms, Parsons' theory helped bring stage-model evolutionary theorizing back into sociology after nearly a fifty-year absence, and so, it is worth examining this theory here.

I will focus mostly on the first of the two slim volumes where this theory was outlined, *Societies: Evolutionary and Comparative Perspectives*, and then just briefly summarize the key ideas in the second volume, *The System of Modern Societies*.[15] Parsons theory begins with his general conception of the four action systems.

The Four Action Systems

As I reviewed in Chapter 2, Parsons began to conceptualize the social universe as composed of four action systems (see pages 18–23 and Table 2.2 on page 19): *cultural, social, personality*, and *organismic* (later termed *behavioral*). Each of these systems corresponded to one of the four functional requisites of action in general, with organismic action system meeting needs for *adaptation*, personality system needs for *goal attainment*, social meeting needs for *integration* of all action systems, and cultural system meeting needs for *latency* (tension management and pattern maintenance). Like all functional theories, such as those developed by Herbert Spencer and Emile Durkheim, Parsons argued that long-term societal *evolution has been a process of differentiation*, and in his eyes, this differentiation revolved around, first of all, differentiation *among* these action systems and, then, differentiation *within* these systems, particularly the cultural, social, and personality. That is, personality, social, and cultural systems began to differentiate from the organismic system and then from each other, and subsequent evolution revolved around increasing differentiation of

---

[15]See note 9 for references to Parsons' key works on evolution.

the social, cultural, and personality action systems, particularly social systems. In many ways, Parsons was positing a kind of "mechanical solidarity" in Emile Durkheim's terms because, in simple societies, the personality, social, and cultural systems are not differentiated from each other and are regulated by common cultural systems (see pages 13–14). At the same time, Parsons was also drawing from Herbert Spencer who saw the biological, social, psychological, and ethnical systems as evolving according the his law of evolution from homogeneous masses to ever-more heterogeneity (see pages 9–13 and footnote 2 on page 10) forms.

Parsons also argued that this kind of differentiation generated, again a la Durkheim, integrative problems, but as these are resolved by new forms of culture and new units in the social system, societies became more adaptive. There was, then, a kind of *adaptive upgrading*, in Parsons' terms, during the evolution from simple to complex because more complex systems have multiple ways to adapt and adjust to environmental contingencies.

Stages of Societal Evolution

Parsons' model is outlined in Figure 11.4. He posited, as had Spencer, two types of "primitive societies" (low and advanced), two types of intermediate societies (archaic and advanced), and finally, a transition to modern societies. These correspond roughly to Lenski's conception of hunting and gathering (nomadic and settled), horticultural, agrarian, and industrial/post-industrial.

One key dynamic in the transitions from one type of societal formation to another revolves around development of an earlier stage of evolution to a critical threshold point of differentiation in particular social structures and cultural forms; once this threshold was reached, it then becomes possible for further evolution or differentiation among and within the four action systems. For example, in Parsons' view, industrial societies could not evolve, nor could truly advanced agrarian societies evolve, without the evolution of a system of laws that contained elements of universalism (or equal application to all types of actors). Thus, until this system of law evolved in the Roman civil codes, societies could not reach the necessary threshold to evolve more complexity.

Key Elements in Stages of Evolution

For Parsons, each stage of evolution involves the emergence of several key elements that, when all present, allow a society to reach the threshold for evolution to the next stage. Let me briefly highlight these elements for the stages delineated in Figure 11.4.

Low Primitive Stage. The basic components of the simplest society are a means of *symbolic communication, kinship, religion,* and *technology*. For Parsons, symbolic communication revolves around "constitutive symbolism," which can denote and represent others, territories, oneself, lineages, and other properties of the social world. This kind of symbolism, in turn, enables members of a population to develop rules and regulations guiding interaction, in two senses: first, rules and regulations that allow interactions to occur and, second, that regulate and control these interactions. In turn, such regulated interactions facilitate the formation of key institutional activities, such as marriage and kinship, economic activity, and religious practices; in turn, these activities increase the degree of differentiation among social structures

Figure 11.4   Parsons' Image of Societal Evolution Up to Modernity

Primitive Societies		Intermediate Societies		Transition to Modern Societies
Low	*Advanced*	*Archaic*	*Advanced*	
Cultural System Differentiation	**Cultural System Differentiation**	**Cultural System Differentiation**	**Cultural System Differentiation**	**Key Cultural System Changes**
Symbolic communication and religious beliefs about – magic – supernatural forces – powers of ancestors Hunting-gathering technologies and conceptions of territories Normative regulation of – marriage – economic roles – kin roles – relations between age/sex categories	Religious beliefs begin to legitimate – power and polity – property – inequality and – stratification – control of territories Normative systems elaborate and regulate – systems of lineages – more complex divisions of labor – emerging administrative structures of polity – settlements and communities Expanded technologies	Written language system that – expands symbol systems, including technological, religious, political, historical norms and emerging laws – allows for increased differentiation between and within social and cultural systems – allows for increased structural differentiation in social system	Expansion of writing leading to – coherent set of quasi-codified religious beliefs – accumulation of knowledge and technology – histories and stable traditions – written contracts in expanded economy and emerging markets – more codified sets of more universalistic laws in emerging	Universalistic and contract law Beliefs about capitalism New technologies using inanimate and fossil fuel sources of energy Ideologies emphasizing rights of persons and political democracy Sense of societal community, unified by common culture and sustained by commitments to this culture
Social System Differentiation	**Social System Differentiation**	**Social System Differentiation**	**Social System Differentiation**	**Key Social System Changes**
Kinship units (nuclear) Band Economic and kin divisions of labor	Settlements and communities Lineages and linkages among nuclear kin units Hierarchies of power in emerging polity Emerging stratification system Expanded economic and kin divisions of labor Emerging religious structures	Larger, more permanent settlements Centralized polity and expanded administrative functions Control of larger territories by polity and organized coercion Expanded religious structures	Increased differentiation among polity, kinship, religion Initial differentiation of legal system Expansion of markets and market relations among social structures Increasing use of money and credit markets Full institutionalization of contracts	Emergence of democractic polity Expansion of positivistic and universalistic legal system Expansion of free, profit oriented markets using money and credit Ascendance of polity over religion as agent of social control Legitimation of polity by law and more secular legal codes Expansion of educational system and access to citizenry to this system Institutionalization of science and innovation

and the stocks of symbols in culture, while enabling individuals to develop more unique personalities.

In low, primitive societies, kinship is the principle unit of social organization in the social system. Such kinships systems reveal incest rules and marriage rules, with (nuclear) kin units of mother, father, and children revealing very little differentiation from each other. The only differentiation in these low, primitive societies is between age and sex categories.

Advanced Primitive Societies. With the level of development outlined above, it becomes possible for a more complex primitive system to evolve. The social system begins to differentiate into clans within the larger kinship system; these begin to appropriate territories and to create notions of property; and as property is acquired, inequalities and stratification begin to evolve. Stratification, however, generates integrative problems that require legitimization, and religion becomes the principle integrative mechanism, with religious beliefs emphasizing the right of those with resources to horde wealth. As religion provides this "integrative function," it becomes more complex and differentiated structurally (with distinctive religious personnel) and culturally (with legitimating beliefs about supernatural forces granting power and privilege).

Inequalities in property and the maintenance of these inequalities also stimulate the evolution of polity, or the consolidation and centralization of power around chiefs of the wealthiest (in terms of property) lineages in clans. While still rudimentary, kin-based incumbents in the emerging polity govern territories, carry out the chief's work, and form a military system to sustain order or to conquer more territory. Thus, as societies move between settled hunter-gatherers into horticulture, they reveal more cultural and social structural complexity.

At the cultural level, they have more complex communication codes, technologies, religious beliefs, and legitimating ideologies; at the structural level, they evidence more complex and differentiated systems of kinship (lineages and clans), stratification, religion, and polity (forming an incipient bureaucracy for administration and warfare). With this cultural and structural base, societies can evolve into a more intermediate stage of societal development, composed to two sub-stages, the archaic and advanced.

The Archaic Stage. The key invention marking this stage is the invention of writing, which enables the cultural system to expand and differentiate. Symbolism is now freed from human memory and from face-to-face interaction. Indeed, symbolism is no longer tied to time and space, and this feature of communication allows for the efficient accumulation of knowledge, for the recording of history, for the preservation of customs and traditions, and for the development of systematic and more complex systems of religious beliefs. It now becomes ever-more possible for generations to build up knowledge and for innovations to accumulate; and as this accumulation occurs, culture becomes increasingly autonomous and differentiated from all other action systems.

Literacy is, of course, not universal in archaic societies; rather, it is confined to a relatively few positions, primarily in religious and political structures. Yet, as literacy comes to dominate religion and the administrative structures of the developing polity, these become further differentiated from kinship and, hence, more autonomous as institutional domains. Moreover, particularly in the administrative system of polity, differentiation will increase, enabling it to expand its influence and control, with the king legitimated, and considered almost "sacred," by the power of religious beliefs.

Yet, even as polity and its administrative structure expand and differentiate, it is not a full civil bureaucracy because recruitment and promotion in the system are still highly ascriptive, tied to kin units and religious affiliation (and perhaps other criteria such as ethnicity). Still, the growth and differentiation of this administrative structure increases the capacity of government to mobilize and coordinate activities, especially with respect to war-making, public works, taxation and redistribution of resources. In expanding its activities, polity dramatically increases the adaptive capacity of a society to its environment and, in so doing, sets the stage for a more advanced intermediate stage.

Advanced Intermediate Societies. In more advanced intermediate societies, increased differentiation among polity, religion, and kinship occurs; and polity continues to differentiate internally as ever-more power is concentrated and resources are extracted through taxation to support the elaboration of the administrative structure. In turn, stratification increases, and the class system differentiates to some degree. These large changes in societies come with the increasing secular content of law, thereby differentiating it from religion even further.

But, more importantly, a more universalistic legal system (i.e., equal application of law to all) begins to emerge, which in turn gives the economy a more autonomous base, while insulating it from the continued ascription evident in polity and religion. Law and universalism in economic affairs encourages the development of money as the dominant medium of exchange, the expansion of markets that begin to differentiate to meet ever-more diverse demand, the increased velocity of trade and commerce within and, increasingly, between societies, and the institutionalization in law of binding contracts on economic actors. These kinds of transformations are only possible when the economy is isolated from the ascription still prevalent in polity, religion, and kinship. But, once law becomes more universalistic in the economic sphere and encourages the development of markets using money and credit, as well as contracts, the level of differentiation within a society will increase. Indeed, markets, money, contracts, and universalistic are differentiating machines, and this differentiation increases the differentiation among psychological action system (in terms of individuals' demands and preferences in markets), the cultural system composed of laws and other symbol systems that can be codified and written down, and social systems of more complex relations among diverse actors not only in the economy but in other institutional domains as well.

The Transition to the Modern System of Societies. Modernity grows out of this cultural, structural, and psychological base of advanced agrarian societies. Economies operating in profit-seeking markets create incentives for increased production that eventually results in the development of industrial technologies harnessed to capitalism and the cultural ideology of capitalism. Universalistic laws and contracts in the economy provide a template for the same types of transactions within and among other institutional domains, eventually paving the way for movements toward political democracy and the decline of ascription in many institutional domains. The consolidation of power in polity and the expansion of culture eventually leads to what Parsons somewhat vaguely defined at the *societal community* or a sense of a population that they represent a culturally unified territorial unit regulated by polity; and once this sense of what today might be termed "nationalism" emerges, this sociocultural base, coupled with common currencies, more dynamic markets, and universalistic laws increase the likelihood of political democracy, which Parsons saw as the last element of societal evolution.

Without going into more detail, we can see the thrust of Parsons' analysis. It is very functional in that it emphasizes differentiation among and within action systems, particularly personality, culture, and social action systems (each of which meets a fundamental functional need or requisite). And, it seeks to outline the sequence of key transformations that pushed society along a number of stages during the course of societal evolution toward the current post-industrial form. For Parsons, certain events had to occur before other elements in societies could evolve, and thus, each stage of evolution has been preceded by transformations that reach a critical threshold point that allows for, and indeed often pushes for, new kinds of social and cultural systems. Thus, Parsons' theory, unlike many other stage models, does not see a master force driving evolution; rather, there is a general increase in complexity or differentiation among and within the four action systems, but at different stages of societal development, somewhat different sociocultural forces and formations were historically necessary for movement to the next stage in societal evolution.

Conclusion

Stage-model theorizing is not dominant, compared to other approaches examined in this book, but it is probably the most enduring approach—along with functionalism. It began with the founding and naming of the discipline and, except for a four-decade hiatus in the early twentieth century, it has been an important way of explaining the social universe. Moreover, the image of evolution as a process of differentiation has remained vibrant in other theoretical perspectives, as diverse as functionalism and critical theories of modernity, and it is a key component of more general theories of macrostructures that are not specifically evolutionary.

Moreover, conflict theories, especially world systems theories, are often couched in evolutionary terms, with the world system of societies seen as evolving from geo-political empires to world-level capitalism and, then, as many argue, to world-level socialism. There is an inherent appeal of stage models because they seek to tell us where societies have been historically, and often, where they are going into the future.

Increasingly, more explicit biological and bio-ecological ideas are slipping into stage-model theorizing, although the approach remains distinctive for the reasons listed by Lenski about what makes social evolution different than biological evolution.[16] This infiltration of biological ideas into stage models is only one indicator of a more general effort to introduce biology back into sociology. As we will see in the next chapter, this rapprochement between biology and sociology may resurrect Comte's view of sociology as arising out of biology and, eventually, informing biology, but many sociologists remain not only skeptical but quite hostile to any use of biological ideas in sociology, which is perhaps a good way to end a review of sociological theory by examining in the next chapter the relation between biology and sociology because this is where sociology began. Chapter 12 thus summarizes the key approaches in a small but growing turn in sociology to biology. For the present, let me conclude with a list of key assumptions and postulates in stage-model evolutionary theorizing.

---

[16]For another analysis of the limits of biological reasoning and concepts in sociological analysis, see Jonathan H. Turner and Alexandra Maryanski, "The Limitations of Evolutionary Theory from Biology in Explaining Sociocultural Evolution," *Sociologica* 3 (2008): pp. 1–38.

1. Societies have, over the long run, evolved toward more complexity in, or differentiation of, their structures and cultures.

2. This evolution can be characterized as a series of stages, whether a dichotomy distinguishing premodern with modern societies or a specification of distinct stages, including the following:

   A. Hunting and gathering societies without head

   B. More settled hunting and gathering societies, with a political leader or head

   C. Simple horticulture or gardening with wood, bone, and stone tools and only human power and kin-based polity (with fishing and herding variants)

   D. Advanced horticultural with more advanced tools, animal power, and increasingly a state-based polity (with fishing and herding variants)

   E. Simple agrarian, using the plow and animal power, with a monarchy as center of power but also with religion as a potential center of power

   F. Advanced agrarian, using animal, water, and wind power, governed by a monarchy and feudal lords on manorial estates, and with religion becoming a large and powerful actor

   G. Industrial, using fossil fuels in economic activity, increasingly open and free markets for distribution, a bureaucratized state for organization of polity, and with some decline in religion as a base of political power

   H. Post-industrial, or use of both fossil and inanimate sources of energy, increasingly dynamic and global markets, democratic polity, and some separation of religion and state

3. No one society lasts sufficiently long to have gone through all of these stages, but a society at one stage will, over time, be likely to evolve into the next stage through internal differentiation or differentiation imposed by more advanced societies in the environment.

4. For movement from one stage to another, basic problems of integration—coordination, control, and regulation—of increasingly differentiated institutional domains and actors in these domains must be managed through a number of mechanisms:

   A. Markets for distributing goods, resources, people, and information

   B. Patterns of structural interdependence, often mediated by markets but also by law and administrative structures of the state

   C. Legal rules and courts for adjudicating the rules, with enforcement provided by agencies in the bureaucratized state

5. For support of larger populations and their differentiation, productive technologies must keep pace with this growth and differentiation if a society is to evolve to the next stage.

6. For regulation of the larger and more differentiated population, an increasingly large and bureaucratized state must evolve to supplement mechanisms 4A-C listed above.

CHAPTER 12

Biologically Inspired Evolutionary Theorizing

tage-model theories of evolution, outlined in the last chapter, first emerged before the revolution in biology inspired by Charles Darwin's *On the Origins of Species*. Still, as was evident in Emile Durkheim's analysis of the division of labor and, later, in ecological theories (see Chapter 4), biological ideas had begun to creep into sociology by the end of the nineteenth century. In Darwin's analysis of the process of speciation, he emphasized the process of *natural selection* in which variations in the phenotypes (and underlying genotypes) among members of a species would be "selected" if they enhanced *fitness*, or the capacity of a species to reproduce itself. But, Darwin did not know the mechanisms by which variations are created, even thought he had Gregor Mendel's short monograph in his library, nor did he understand the importance of mutations as a source of variation on which selection could work. Indeed, by the 1920s, many were predicting the demise of Darwin because many did not see the connection among what became known as the forces of evolution: natural selection, mutations, gene flow, and genetic drift (see Table 12.1 for definitions of each force). In fact, the new understandings of genetics were at first seen to surpass Darwin's theory, but in the end, the four forces of evolution were combined to build what is often called the Modern Synthesis in biology. As this synthesis was used to explain the biotic universe, some began to believe that understanding the dynamics of biology could be used to explain at least some of the processes of the social world. Beginning in the 1960s, explicitly biological ideas began to enter the social sciences, offering an entirely new way to understand the social world.

Table 12.1 The Forces of Evolution

1. **Natural Selection**: The process whereby environmental conditions select on those phenotypes (and underlying genotypes) that promote fitness of members of a species and, thereby, pass on their genes to offspring.
2. **Mutations**: Random changes in the information on genes along chromosomes that alter the phenotypes of organisms.
3. **Gene Flow**: The movement of genes from one population to another, across ecological space, thereby changing the distribution of genes in the gene pool of a species.
4. **Genetic Drift**: Random changes in the distribution of genes among species that become ecologically isolated from each other that, over time, can lead to speciation, especially if selection on phenotypes is not high for one or more of the isolated members of a species.

New Ideas From Biology[1]

Two key ideas that emerged with the Modern Synthesis were (1) greater understanding of the mechanisms of variation among individuals and (2) distributions of genes in populations of organisms, including humans. Let me briefly summarize these.

The Genetics of the Individual

Gregor Mendel[2] used the term *merkmals* for what we now call *genes*, but the basic ideas are the same: genes are the basic units of inheritance that hold the information necessary to reproduce life forms across generations. Differences in the characteristics of individuals result from the information on discrete genes, bundled into *chromosomes*, that provide a vast fund of possible variations. This information is termed the *genotype* of an organism, and its expression in the physical features and, later, the behavioral propensity of organisms is called the *phenotype*. Natural selection works on the phenotype, and as it does so, it determines which genetic material is going to be preserved in a species, whose phenotypes or bodies constitute a vessel in which the genes will be stored. Eventually, early efforts to bring the ideas of genetics into the social sciences saw phenotypes of humans as "survivor machines" for the genes that relentlessly seek to stay alive by producing more fit survival machines that can reproduce and keep the information stored in genes "alive." Those variants of phenotypes, and their underlying genotypes, that promote fitness or the capacity to reproduce will survive whereas those that do not promote fitness will eventually disappear. Thus, natural selection selects on those phenotypes that are best fit to survive and reproduce; in so doing, some variants or *alleles* of genes persist and some are selected out.

The Genetics of Populations

While natural selection works on phenotypes and the underlying genes housed in individual phenotypes, it is populations that evolve. What is actually evolving is a cluster of genes, residing in their survivor machines or phenotypes because, in the end, organisms come and go, but it is the information in genes that can have a certain immortality if successive generations of phenotypes housing these genes are fit and can reproduce. For, what they pass on are their genes, not their bodies that die and wither away.

As this idea of what is actually evolving spread, the notion of *gene pool* was introduced.[3] The concept of gene pool shifts analysis away from individuals to the sum total of genes and

---

[1]This section is coauthored with Alexandra Maryanski.

[2]Gregor Mendel, "Versuche über pflanzen-hybriden," translated into English in the *Journal of the Rural Horticulture Society* 26 (1901), originally published in 1865.

[3]Although the term *genetics* was coined by William Bateson in 1906 as the basic construct to describe individual heredity and variation, the term *gene pool* was coined by Dobzhansky in 1950 and became the fundamental construct of population genetics. See Theodosius Dobzhansky, "Mendelian Populations and Their Evolution," *American Naturalist* 14 (1950): pp. 401–418. For further readings on the history of genetics, see Theodosius Dobzhansky, *Genetics and the Origin of Species*, 3rd rev. ed. (New York: Columbia University Press, 1951) and *Mankind Evolving* (New York: Bantam, 1962). See also Mark B. Adams, "From 'Gene Fund' to 'Gene Pool': On the Evolution of Evolutionary Language," *History of Biology* 3 (1979): pp. 241–285 and "The Founding of Population Genetics: Contributions of the Chetvevikov School 1924–1934," *Journal of the History of Biology* 1 (1968): pp. 23–39; Alfred Sturtevant, *A History of Genetics* (New York: Harper & Row, 1965); and James Crow, "Population Genetics History: A Personal View," *Annual Review of Genetics* 21 (1987): pp. 1–22.

the variations contained in alleles. Thus, a species of organisms, such as humans, can be conceptualized as the sum total of the information in its gene pool.

The shift to the analysis of pools of genes increasingly intrigued biological thinkers to consider the implications of these ideas for populations of humans and, soon thereafter, to the behaviors and organization of populations of humans. Could biology explain some of the dynamics of behavior and social organization of humans? If the answer were yes, then sociology could become a subfield within biology—causing Auguste Comte to turn over in his grave and to make many contemporary sociologists contemptuous of any effort to bring biology into sociology.

The Codification of Sociolobiology

Fitness and Evolution

R. A. Fisher in his *The Genetical Theory of Natural Selection*[4] was the first to document that mutations could not account for evolution. Until Fisher, many thought—as I mentioned earlier—that mutations and other forces of variation could explain the evolution of species, but in fact, Fisher documented that mechanisms of variation alone cannot account for the emergence and evolution of species. With respect to mutations, which were thought to obviate the need for natural selection as an explanatory tool, Fished demonstrated that most mutations are harmful and do not promote what he termed *fitness*, or as I have noted earlier, the ability of members of a species to reproduce themselves. Without something that selects on variation, evolution of species cannot occur; for it is in their capacity to promote fitness that allows genes to survive, and new genes or alleles arising from mutations to survive by virtue of producing more fit phenotypes. The notion of "fitness" as a general concept was very old, emerging before Darwin in the works, for example, of Herbert Spencer and Thomas Malthus, but this particular terminology caught on and became central to understanding how biology was able to enter sociology and the social sciences more generally.

Group and Individual Selection

Another idea that had existed in sociology but was eventually introduced into biology was the idea of *group selection*. That is, selection is not so much on the phenotypes of individuals but the organizational structures of the groups in which they live. Thus, groups as much as bodies can become a kind of "survivor machine" for bodily phenotypes that, in turn, house and protect genes. When Spencer examined the evolution of societies through warfare, he was positing in essence that societies evolve by a kind of selection process inherent in warfare.[5] More fit societies win wars, thus sustaining their populations and often incorporating those populations that they have defeated. Since his focus was on societies and not on individuals, this kind of group-selectionist argument makes considerable

---

[4]R. A. Fisher, *The Genetical Theory of Natural Selection* (Oxford: Oxford University Press, 1930).

[5]Herbert Spencer, *The Principles of Sociology* (New York: Appleton-Century-Crofts, 1895, originally published in serial form, beginning in 1874 and ending in 1896).

sense—at least to sociologists. But to biologists, the dogma that selection only works on individual phenotypes, while the population as a whole evolves, argued against the notion of group selection. And it was in this reaction against those who viewed group selection as a key evolutionary force that sociobiology was born.

Thus, *sociobiology* emerged as a reaction against group-selectionist arguments.[6] In making this argument, earlier pioneers of sociobiology like George C. Williams[7] went even further, claiming that what is important is *genic selection*. Genes are only temporarily housed in bodies or phenotypes that promote survival and reproduction, or fitness. Whatever their consequences for groupness, it is genes that are ultimately selected to stay in the gene pool. Particular genes and alleles may promote behaviors that promote groupness, but it must be remembered that it is the gene that is driving the show; and if groups promote survival, it is the genes that have promoted the necessary phenotypical behaviors among individuals for group formation that are the driving force and ultimately the unit that is selected for reproduction. Thus, the fitness of groups is the result of the total of behaviors— say, for reciprocity, affiliation, support of kin, etc.—are driven by genes not the group. This argument became dogma for several decades, and only recently have some sociobiologists reconsidered its merits.

Key Behaviors Driven by Genes: Inclusive Fitness, Kin Selection, and Reciprocal Altruism

W. D. Hamilton took Williams' ideas a step further by introducing the notion of inclusive fitness.[8] This concept was introduced to account for the propensity of individuals to support, cooperate, and help kin. Natural selection, he argued, had produced *kin selection* because by cooperating with each other over strangers with whom they do not share genes, humans are more likely to pass on their genes. And, the more genes kindred share, the greater is this propensity to help and support kin because, in doing so, their common genes are more likely to remain in the gene pool. This idea makes sense if genes are considered the driving force of behaviors promoting fitness. Thus, families are a mechanism by which genes, through blind natural selection, have pushed for behaviors that allow those sharing genes to keep them in the gene pool. Self-sacrifice is not, then, altruist; rather, it is a selfish strategy of family members to maximize the number of their genes that stay in the gene pool.

---

[6]V. C. Wynne-Edwards, *Evolution through Group Selection* (Oxford: Blackwell, 1986) and *Animal Dispersion in Relation to Social Behavior* (New York: Hafner, 1962). For a review of the controversy surrounding group selection arguments, see David Sloan Wilson, "The Group Selection Controversy: History and Current Status," *Annual Review of Ecological Systems* 14 (1983): pp. 159–187.

[7]George C. Williams, *Adaptation and Natural Selection: A Critique of Some Current Evolutionary Thought* (Princeton, NJ: Princeton University Press, 1966). For his defense of reductionism away from the group level, see "A Defense of Reductionism in Evolutionary Biology," in *Oxford Surveys in Evolutionary Biology 2*, eds. R. Dawkins and M. Ridley (Oxford: Oxford University Press, 1985), pp. 1–27.

[8]W. D. Hamilton, "The Evolution of Altruistic Behavior," *American Naturalist* 97 (1963): pp. 354–356; "The Genetical Theory of Social Behavior I and II," *Journal of Theoretical Biology* 7 (1964): pp. 1–52; "Innate Social Aptitudes of Man: An Approach from Evolutionary Genetics," in *Biosocial Anthropology*, ed. R. Fox (New York: Wiley, 1984), pp. 135–155; "Geometry for the Selfish Herd," *Journal of Theoretical Biology* 31 (1971): pp. 295–311.

Of course, this assertion produced the question: Why would individuals ever be altruistic toward those not sharing genes? Robert Trivers[9] answered by positing the concept of *reciprocal altruism* in which he argued that in helping nonkin, individuals are likely to have their altruism reciprocated and, hence, increase their fitness by keeping their genes in the gene pool. So, once again, something as universal as the need to reciprocate is seen as a selfish strategy to maximize fitness among those offering assistance to others; in being able to call upon the help of others in the future, fitness is enhanced.

This kind of argument led Richard Dawkins write his famous book, *The Selfish Gene*.[10] Genes are copy machines that are driven to reproduce themselves, and they have hit upon the solution of housing themselves in bodies or phenotypes; even when groups are added to the body as a survival machine, we must remember just what—genes—is pushing for this kind of additional layer of protection so that the genes and their alleles can remain in the gene pool. The essence of Dawkins' argument is captured in this quote:[11]

> What weird machines of self-preservation would the millennia bring forth.... They (replicators) did not die out, for they are past masters of the survival arts.... Now they swarm in huge colonies, safe inside gigantic lumbering robots, sealed off from the outside world, communicating with it by tortuous indirect routes, manipulating it by remote control. They are in you and me; they created us, body and mind; and their preservation is the ultimate rationale for our existence. They have come a long way, those replicators. Now they go by the name of *genes*, and we are their survival machines.

Dawkins, however, did not stop here. He recognized that once cultural and social structures emerged in the organization of human societies, another type of survival machine is created. He offered the notion of a "meme pool" as the sociocultural equivalent of gene pool in which culture also drives the behaviors of individuals and their construction of social structures. There is, perhaps, a kind of co-evolution between the meme and gene pools once societies are built up by humans. Many sociobiologists were not willing to make this concession, however, and it is for these reason that sociobiology was received so unfavorably by sociologists. Still, the rejection was not universal because some sociologists took up the cause.

Pierre van den Berghe[12] was one of the first prominent sociologists to pursue sociobiology as a theoretical explanation. He adopted Hamilton's notion of kin selection to describe why the percentage of common genes explains how close relatives will be to each other in terms of love, affection, cooperation, and mutual aid. The percentage of genes held in common determines their self-interest in helping each other in order to keep their common genes in the gene pool.

---

[9]Robert L. Trivers, "The Evolution of Reciprocal Altruism," *Quarterly Review of Biology* 46 (4, 1971), pp. 35–57; "Parental Investment and Sexual Selection," in *Sexual Selection and the Descent of Man, 1871–1971*, ed. B. Campbell (Chicago: Aldine, 1972); and "Parent-Offspring Conflict," *American Zoologist* 14 (1974), pp. 249–264.

[10]Richard Dawkins, *The Selfish Gene* (Oxford: Oxford University Press, 1976).

[11]Ibid., p. 21.

[12]Pierre van den Berghe and David Barash, "Inclusive Fitness and Family Structure," *American Anthropologist* 79 (1977), pp. 809–823; van den Berghe, "Bridging the Paradigms," *Society* 15 (1977–1978), pp. 42–49; *The Ethnic Phenomenon* (New York: Elsevier, 1981) and *Human Family Systems* (Prospect Heights, IL: Waveland, 1990).

He also accepted Trivers argument about reciprocal altruism, arguing that reciprocity greatly increases cooperation beyond nepotism and allows for larger societies beyond simple kinship. More original was his assertion that coercion or the mobilization of capacities for power is also means for expanding social structures beyond kinship and reciprocity. Coercion increases fitness of those able to coerce, but it also increases the capacity to organize larger societies that, as survivor machines for the whole society, increase the fitness of larger numbers of persons beyond those with power. And, sociologists should not consider this solely a sociocultural process; the selfish genes have a hand in driving individuals to use coercion in order to create bigger survivor machines.

Perhaps one of van den Berghe's most important contributions comes in the area of the dynamics of ethnicity. He argues that, historically, larger kin groups (composed of lineages) began organizing a larger breeding population, and from these larger kin groups came even more extension of sense of shared origins. He termed these larger subpopulations *ethnys*, which are much larger than a cluster of kinship circles but more like an ethnic population that shares not only distinctive phenotypes but culture and history as well. Thus, an ethny is an adaptive strategy driven by genes to enhance people who share common characteristics, such as skin color or an eye fold beyond kinship because an ethny creates bonds of obligations among those sharing cultural characteristics; in this way, these bonds enhance the fitness of ethnic subpopulations, even when they do not share very many common genes. The pull of fellow ethnics is more than sociocultural then. It is a biological drive of genes that natural selection selected upon to promote the fitness of larger numbers of individuals, and this drives causes people to cooperate with fellow members of their ethny. The pull of ethnicity is thus partly to be explained by genic selection.

These kinds of arguments became very persuasive in biology where culture, social organization, and capacities for agency using complex minds did not intrude in analysis—as is the case for insects. But, for sociologists, the arguments seem to represent an effort to explain sociological topics with a list of assumptions that were highly suspicious, including the following:

1. Organisms are the survivor machines for what really drives evolution: genes blindly seeking to reproduce themselves and remain in the gene pool of a population.

2. The phenotypes of organisms, and the behavioral propensities of organisms, can thus be seen as an adaptive strategy ultimately in response to pressures from genes.

3. Thus, universal behaviors—self-interest, altruism, reciprocal altruism, kin selection, inclusive fitness—and social structures can been seen as a result of genic selection, to be explained by selection processes working on the relentless pressure of genes to remain in the gene pool.

4. Since social structures of all sorts are built from the capacities of humans to engage in these behaviors, there are biological underpinings to all sociocultural phenomena.

There is a significant number of prominent sociologists who have adopted at least some of the ideas of sociobiology. More recently, however, the basic ideas of sociobiology have entered the social sciences through another approach: evolutionary psychology.

Evolutionary Psychology

Sociobiology was the beachhead of an invasion into the social sciences by biology, but over recent decades, evolutionary psychology has gained considerably more influence in the social sciences than sociobiology, especially in sociology. Evolutionary psychology accepts most of the tenets of sociobiology, such as behaviors evolved to maximize the fitness of humans, but inserts the operation of the human brain explicitly into the theory. Natural selection, as it worked on hominin and human phenotypes and the underlying genotypes, has rewired the brain by creating a series of specialized brain modules during the Pleistocene—the more immediate period of evolution of late hominins and early humans. These modules are responsible for many key behaviors that, in the past, solved recurrent problems in human's ancestral environments.

Evolutionary psychology operates under a number of key assumptions:

1. The brain is an information-processing device that has evolved like any other trait in organism.

2. The brain and the adaptive mechanisms that it reveals evolved by natural selection.

3. The various neural mechanisms of the brain are specialized for solving problems generated by selection pressures in human's and hominins' evolutionary past.

4. The human mind, then, is a stone-age mind because its specialized mechanisms for processing information, perception, and universal behaviors evolved during the Pleistocene.

5. Most contents and processes of the brain are unconscious, and mental problems that appear easy to solve are actually difficult problems that are solved unconsciously by modules of neurons that have evolved to solve adaptive problems during the course of the evolution of late hominins and early humans.

6. The psychology of humans, then, consists of many specialized mechanism wired into distinctive modules of neurons that are sensitive to different classes of information and external inputs and that combine to produce human behavior, and by implication, patterns of interaction and even social structures and their cultures.

For example, an evolutionary psychologists might argue that human speech is a psychological mechanism that evolved by selecting on the association cortices, such as the inferior parietal lobe, that give humans and higher primates the capacity for language facility, followed by selection on relatively discrete areas of the brain (Broca's area) and surrounding tissues for speech production and Wernicke's area for speech comprehension and uploading of meanings into the brain's processes information. Moreover, there are modules along the fissure separating the parietal lobe regulating muscle movements and the frontal cortex that gives humans (but not the great apes) the ability to produce articulated words in speech. Such speech capacities evolved to solve problems of communication and social bonding among humans, and this line of argument might not be controversial because the modules can be found in the brain. Similarly, the evolution of human emotional capacities is lodged in modules in subcortical areas of the brain. Some subcortical areas like those generating *anger* and *fear*, which date back to the evolution of reptiles, are generated in a discrete module labeled the *amydala*, but other emotions are not so easily isolated in discrete modules. However, evolutionary psychologists still predict that the modules will be found with more research.

Other topics are potentially more controversial. Evolutionary psychologists suggest that, for instance, there are incest avoidance mechanisms (which is probably true, but where is the brain module for this?), as well as mechanisms for cheater detection, sex-specific preferences, reciprocity, kin selection, altruism, reciprocal altruism, inclusive fitness, alliance tracking, and other universal human behaviors. For evolutionary psychologists, the more universal a behavior is, the more likely is this behavior regulated by neurological mechanisms situated in modules of the human brain. These modules evolved because they enhanced fitness of hominins and then humans during the Pleistocene.

These basic features of evolutionary psychology have been adopted by a small but growing number of sociologists and used to explain human behaviors, often reported in the sociological literature as rates of particular kinds of behaviors.[13] For example, there is a universal behavioral propensity for crime, and especially violent crime rates, to be committed by males, increasing during puberty, and then, with age, declining dramatically. Sociobiologists sought to explain this universal pattern, and evolutionary psychologists have added characterizations of the mechanisms by which this behavior is produced. Such explanations become "just-so" stories outlining what occurred in the distant past to generate brain modules (rarely specified) that produce particular patterns of behavior, like rates of crime and violent crime among adolescent males. For example, part of the just-so story begins with men's need and desire to gain access to women (so as to pass on their genes), and young men are particularly driven to do so. They are thus more likely to take risks and incur costs in competition with other males to gain access to females. To ensure that such would be the case, natural selection created a module (not clearly specified except for mention of those parts of the brain responsible for the production of the hormone testosterone). This module evolved long before individuals had much property and a criminal justice system existed, but men still seek resources and status so as to impress females with their qualities and, thereby, maximize their reproductive success. In modern societies, young males have fewer resources than older males, with the result that they seek resources through crime. The story is much more nuanced than this, and it even adds interesting details. For example, smaller men, contrary to what we might think, will tend to be more aggressive and violent because they have to compensate for the lack of size and thus must gain status and resources to attract females—hence, they are more likely to commit violent crimes to do so.

Other arguments can be developed along these lines. Sociobiologists have argued that males and females develop somewhat different strategies to maximize their reproductive fitness. For instance, since women produce relatively few eggs in their lifetimes and must make heavy investments in offspring (since they, rather than men, must bear and breastfeed them), whereas as males generate millions of sperm daily. Thus, women have a vested interest in ensuring that they hook

---

[13]For example, see essays in J. Barkow, Leda Cosmides, and John Tooby, eds., *The Adapted Mind: Evolutionary Psychology and the Generation of Culture* (New York: Oxford University Press, 1992); Rosemary L. Hopcroft, *Sociology: A Biosocial Introduction* (Boulder, CO: Paradigm Press, 2010); Martin Daily and Margo Wilson, *Homocide* (New York: De Gruyter, 1988); Satoshi Kanazawa and Mary C. Still, "Why Men Commit Crimes (and Why They Desist)," *Sociological Perspectives* 18 (2000): pp. 434–447; Christine Horne, "Values and Evolutionary Psychology," *Sociological Perspectives* 22 (2004): pp. 477–493.

up with males who can provide resources and who can, thereby, protect to their women's eggs, whereas males maximize their reproductive fitness by being promiscuous and spreading their sperm to as many females as possible. Thus, males will tend to be more promiscuous than women because of biologically driven strategies for maximizing fitness. Evolutionary psychology adds to this scenario the notion that males possess evolved mechanisms in their brains that drive them to limit female partners' access to other males. For example, males will generally become more *reflexively jealous* (from an emotional module) when female infidelity occurs and are more likely to push for restrictive norms on female sexuality in order to ensure that female offspring carry their genes rather than those of another male. These norms can change, however, when women have resources independently of their male sexual partners because, now, they do not need the resources provided by males and thus are likely to resist male control and demand more permissive sexual norms. They are, again, more nuanced versions of this story, but the plot line of the just-so story is clear.

One problematic issue of these "explanations" by just-so stories is that there are almost always *ad hoc*. One could construct a just-so story for empirical regularities in behavior that are just the opposite of those illustrated above. The assumptions of evolutionary psychology, as it has incorporated the arguments of sociobiologists, are so general that it is easy to develop a story—or an explanation—of almost any behavior regularity. All that is necessary is to hypothesize a module in the brain that evolved to produce a behavior that; to develop a scenario of why selection generated this module, or just-so story; and then to indicate the ways that the behaviors generated by this module enhances fitness. But these stories are not only *ad hoc*, there are generally *post hoc*, although some have sought to be more predictive. They are post hoc and ad hoc, without providing firm evidence about, first of all, the existence of the module and, second, data supporting the just so story and assertions of fitness enhancement. Yet, evolutionary psychologists seem undaunted by these criticisms and, in fact, are highly confident that their approach can explain more than standard social science practices, which tend to assume that biology has very little influence on human behavior, interaction, and social organization.

Cross-Species Comparisons

Other sociologists have developed theoretical approaches that compare humans with other species. Here, the goal is to highlight particular questions in the social sciences and to seek answers by comparing humans and their patterns of social organization with other species. These cross-species comparisons may, or may not, also include ideas from sociobiology or evolutionary psychology, but these are not so much emphasized. The basic idea is to provide answers to questions by comparing human behavior propensities and patterns of social organization to those of other species, sometimes species that are closely related to humans biologically and, at other times, to species that are very distant to humans.

Richard Machalek's Approach

Richard Machalek has applied modern evolutionary theory to traditional sociological problems.[14] Machalek would like to see a truly comparative sociology or one that crosses

---

[14]Richard Machalek, "Why Are Large Societies Rare?" *Advances in Human Ecology* 1 (1992): pp. 33–64.

species lines. His approach is to search for the foundations and development of *sociality* wherever it is found, in both human and nonhuman species. By identifying the elementary forms of social life among human and nonhuman organisms, information can be gleaned about how the organizational features among species are assembled. In this effort to create a comparative sociology, Machalek outlines a four-step protocol for conducting a sociological analysis of generic social forms "with a priority on sociality, not the organism."

1. Identify and describe a social form that is distributed across two or more species lines.

2. Identify the "design problems" that might constrain the evolution of this social form. In other words, what prerequisites are necessary for a particular social form to come into existence?

3. Identify the processes that generate a social form.

4. Identify those benefits and beneficiaries of a social form that will help explain the persistence and proliferation of certain social forms over other forms.

In applying this protocol, Machalek focused on the evolution of macro societies, a social form that first appeared in human social evolution about 5,000 years ago. He asked this: What makes human macro societies possible? Machalek suggests that we cannot just look at agrarian and industrial societies to answer this question, but rather, we must subordinate the study of human macro-level societies to the study of macro societies as a general social form. If we take a cross-species comparative approach, it is evident that macro sociality is rare and exists in only two taxonomic orders: insects and human primates.

Machalek describes a macro society as a society with hundreds of millions of members with distinct social classes and a complex division of labor. Among social insects, this social form is very old, but in humans, it is very recent, beginning about 5,000 years ago with the emergence of agrarian societies. Obviously, humans and insects are remote species, separated by at least 600 million years of divergent evolution; hence, they cannot be compared by individual biological characteristics. Indeed, humans and insects are separated by major anatomical differences that include "six orders of magnitude in brain size," and so, intelligence did not play a role in the evolution of insect macro societies. Instead, insect and human macro-societal social forms must be compared strictly for their "social structural design" features in what appears to be a case of convergent evolution.

In considering the fundamental similarities between the organization of human and insect macro societies, Machalek maintains that "whatever the species, all social organisms confront the same basic problems of organizational design and regulation if they are to succeed in evolving a macro society."[15] When looked at this way, the existence of this social form in two such distinctive and biologically remote taxa allows us to address such questions as this: What constraints must be surmounted before a species can evolve a macro society?

Machalek suggests that macro societies are rare because the evolution of this social form requires successful solutions to a series of difficult and complex problems. He suggests that only insects and humans have managed to push aside or overcome (1) organismic constraints, (2) ecological

---

[15]Ibid., p. 35.

constraints, (3) cost-benefit constraints, and (4) sociological constraints. Each of these will be briefly examined.

Organismic Constraints

In detailing the organismic constraints that must be overcome before complex cooperative behavior can evolve, Machalek highlights the morphology of a species as an important factor that can either promote or inhibit the ability of a species to evolve a macro society. For example, aquatic social species such as whales, who are extremely intelligent and who clearly enjoy a "social life," are hopelessly constrained by their enormous "body plans," a constraint that makes it difficult for them to engage in "diverse forms of productive behavior."[16] And, when a body plan constrains the variety of cooperative behaviors possible, it "also constrains the evolution of a complex and extensive division of labor."[17]

Ecological Constraints

In addition to organismic constraints, the ecological niche of a species sets limits on both the population size and complexity of a society. An ecosystem's physical properties can vary in the number of predators, competition for resources like food and shelter, diversity of other species, and mortality rates because of disease. All these can become factors in limiting population size for a given species. Social insects are more likely to find a habitat with ample resources to support their macro societies because they are very small creatures.

Cost-Benefit Constraints

In addition to organismic and ecological constraints, the evolution of a macro society will depend on economic factors or various "costs and benefits" that accompany any macro society. Although the evolution of a macro society would seem to be beneficial to any social species, a society with complex and extensive cooperation has both costs and benefits. Using the logic of cost-benefit analysis, a particular evolved trait can be analyzed for the ratio of its costs to benefits. Among social insects like ants, costs (which include such problems as social parasitism where alien species expropriate labor or food from unsuspecting ants) do not exceed benefits. This is because social insects greatly benefit from a complex division of labor that allows them to compensate for the small size of each individual "and thus increase their ergonomic efficiency and effectiveness."[18]

Sociological Constraints

Of all the constraints, this one is the most important. Even if all other constraints are overcome, the evolution of a macro society requires a unique form of social interaction that is rare

---

[16]Ibid., p. 42.

[17]Ibid.

[18]Ibid., p. 44.

in nature and beyond the capacity of most organisms. Essentially, an organism must overcome three large sociological problems to evolve a macro society:[19]

1. The individuals must be able to engage in impersonal cooperation.

2. The labor of members must be divided among distinct social categories.

3. The division of labor among members must be integrated and coordinated.

In considering these critical design problems that must be surmounted before a macro society can evolve, we should ask why it is that only the social insects and humans have been able to generate a rare and complex form of sociality. If we turn to other social species for clues, we find that the fundamental mechanism underlying social organization in most animals is kinship or genetic relatedness. Machalek argues that kinship bonds effectively restrict the number of individuals within a particular cooperative group, making it very difficult for most species to evolve a macro society. Machalek notes that the general principle that links kinship to social behavior among animals can be stated as follows: "The greater the degree of genetic relatedness among individuals, the higher the probability that they will interact cooperatively."[20] In other words, natural selection has seemingly favored social species with the basic capacity to distinguish individual kin from nonkin, thereby making kinship networks possible. Thus, kinship connections based on individual recognition of relatives are the basis for social cooperation for most social species.

In social insects, however, kin are distinguished from nonkin largely through remote chemical communication, for there is no evidence that "blood relatives" recognize each other as individuals. Thus, in ant societies, members interact with five or six types of ants—not millions of individual ants. Ants treat each other as members of distinct categories or castes. In turn, social categories or castes are occupationally specialized, allowing task specialization (that is, foraging, brood tending, nest repair, defense, and so on) and leading to a complex division of labor. Caste types are recognized by olfactory cues, the dominant mechanism behind the organization of ants. Machalek notes that humans often link a complex division of labor to human intelligence, culture, and technological development, but this social form among insects clearly exists outside the range of human intelligence.

In contrast, despite selection for language and culture, human societies were small and based on face-to-face individualized kinship relations for most of human evolutionary history. Yet, in agrarian times, full-blown hierarchical stratification evolved, leading to the question: How were humans able to escape the constraining influences of personalized kinship relations and their highly evolved capacity for individual recognition? Following Machalek:[21]

Humans have evolved macro societies because they are empowered by culture to form highly cooperative patterns of behavior with "anonymous others." Thus, for the social insects, a state of permanent personal anonymity enables them to form large, complex

---

[19]Ibid., p. 45.

[20]Ibid., p. 46.

[21]Ibid., p. 47.

societies comprising purely impersonal cooperation among members of different castes. Humans, on the other hand, are capable of forming cooperative social systems based either upon personal relationship or impersonal status-role attributes.

Thus, chemical communication allows insects to convert individuals into social types, whereas humans employ *cognitive culture* and socially constructed typifications. This capacity allows humans to interact cooperatively, not as individuals but as personal strangers, dividing individuals into types of social categories. Machalek believes that impersonal cooperation lies at the foundation of macro sociality. Social insects and humans have used different but still analogous strategies to achieve the capacity for close cooperation among anonymous others, thereby facilitating the evolution of macro society. In addition, this impersonality specifies and limits the rights and obligations between (or among) parties to an interaction, for as Machalek notes, status-role constructs are the human analogue to the chemical and tactile typification processes among social insects. Essentially, status-role constructs allow humans to ignore the unique and distinctive qualities of persons, thereby increasing the economy of a cooperative interaction. Unlike social insects, however, humans can also move between personal and impersonal attributes in organizing their social lives.

In sum, then, only insects and humans have been able to evolve a system of macro sociality, primarily because of the design problems in creating macro societies. Machalek emphasizes that sociologists have long struggled to understand the elementary forms of social behavior, but this quest has been limited because of a general reluctance by sociologists to expand their perspective to include inquiry into nonhuman social species. It is important, Machalek argues, to see how particular social traits are spread across species. The ability to research questions such as the emergence of a complex division of labor and why it is found in only a few societies can help us discover how it evolved in human societies. In addition, if we compare sociality forms across species by consequences, the adaptive value of sociality as a response to ecological challenges can be better understood. Finally, beginning with the social form and then selecting for observation those species in which that form appears would also allow us to better understand the emergent properties of social systems, the adaptive value and processes that generate particular social forms, and the essential design features that might represent a solution to common problems facing diverse species.

Alexandra Maryanski's Approach

In recent years, Alexandra Maryanski, in conjunction with sometime collaborator Jonathan Turner, has approached the question of human nature by examining the social network ties of humans' closest living relatives, the apes.[22] As is well known, humans share well over 98 percent of their genetic material with chimpanzees (*Pan*); indeed, chimpanzees might be closer

---

[22]Alexandra Maryanski, "The Last Ancestor: An Ecological Network Model on the Origins of Human Sociality," *Advances in Human Ecology*, ed. L. Freese, vol. 1 (1992), pp. 1–32; Alexandra Maryanski and Jonathan Turner, *The Social Cage* (Stanford, CA: Stanford University Press, 1992) and Alexandra Maryanski, "African Ape Social Structure: Is There Strength in Weak Ties?" *Social Networks* 9 (1987): pp. 191–215. For the most recent statement of this argument, see Jonathan H. Turner and Alexandra Maryanski, *On the Origins of Societies by Natural Selection* (Boulder, CO: Paradigm Press, 2008).

to humans than they are to gorillas (*Gorilla*). And both chimpanzees and gorillas, who are African apes, are certainly closer to humans than they are to orangutans (*Pongo*) or gibbons (*Hylobates*), the other two genera who are Asian apes. In fact, humans and chimpanzees came from the same ancestral primate that lived only about five million years ago, according to the latest fossil and molecular data.

Long-term field studies have documented that primates are highly intelligent, slow to mature, undergo a long period of socialization, and live a long time. The majority of primates are organized into year-round societies that require the integration of a wide variety of age and sex classes, not just adult males and females. In addition, primates have clear-cut social bonding patterns that vary widely among the 187 species of primates.

Using a historical comparative technique, which is termed *cladistic analysis* in biology, Maryanski began by examining the data on social relations among present-day great-ape genera—that is, chimpanzees, gorillas, gibbons, and orangutans. Following this procedure, Maryanski first identified a limited group of entities—in this case one crucial property of ape social structure, the strength of social bonds between and among age and sex classes in all ape genera—to see if there were structural regularities in the patterning of relations. If phyletically close species living in different environments reveal characteristic traits in common, then it can be assumed that their Last Common Ancestor (LCA) also had similar relational features. For this exercise, Maryanski undertook a comprehensive review of bonding propensities for apes living under natural field conditions in an effort to profile their social network structures, with the goal of uncovering a blueprint of the LCA population to present-day apes and humans.

To assess the validity of these relational patterns, she followed the normal procedures of cladistic analysis by including an *outgroup lineage*—a sample of Old World monkey social networks—for comparison to the networks of apes. She also subjected her data set to two fundamental assumptions associated with this comparative technique: (1) the *Relatedness Hypothesis*, which indirectly assesses whether or not the shared patterns of social relations are caused by chance and (2) the *Regularity Hypothesis*, which indirectly assesses whether the modifications from the ancestral to descendant forms evidence a systematic bias and are not randomly acquired. Both hypotheses provided strong empirical support for her reconstruction of the ancestral patterns of organization among hominoid (that is, apes and humans).

Her analysis led to a striking conclusion: Like the contemporary apes that are phyletically closest to humans, the LCA population evidenced a fluid organizational structure, consisting of a relatively low level of sociality and a lack of intergenerational continuity in groups over time.

The proximal reasons for this structure are a combination of several forces that are still found in all living ape social networks: (a) a systematic bias toward female (and usually male) transfer from the natal unit at puberty, which is the opposite trend from monkeys where only males transfer and females stay to form intergenerational matrilines in monkey troops; (b) a promiscuous mating pattern that makes paternity difficult to know (the gibbon being the exception); and (c) an abundance of weak social ties among most adults. In addition, the modifications from the LCA social structure suggested that after descendants separated from the ancestral population, the future trend in hominoid evolution involved selection pressures for heightened sociality, seemingly to increase hominoid survival and reproductive success.

Indeed, it is an established fact in the fossil record that about 18 to 10 million years ago, a huge number of the many species of apes underwent a dramatic decline and extinction, just when species of monkeys suddenly proliferated and, according to the fossil record, moved into the former ape niches, perhaps because monkeys developed a competitive, dietary edge over apes. Whatever the explanation, the fossil record confirms that, when ape niches were being usurped by monkeys, apes began to undergo anatomical modifications in order to marginal niches in the arboreal habitat. These adaptations revolved around a peculiar locomotion pattern that involves hand-over-hand movement in the trees through space along with other novel skeletal features that characterize the anatomy of both apes and humans today. Currently, monkeys remain the dominant primates, and apes are a distinct tiny minority; moreover, with the exception of humans, the few remaining nonhuman hominoids—that is, chimpanzee, gorilla, orangutan, and gibbon are now considered "evolutionary failures" and "evolutionary leftovers" because of their small numbers and specialized and restricted niches.

The significance of this finding is important for thinking about human nature. If humans' closest relatives reveal a tendency for relatively weak social ties, then humans are also likely to have this social tendency as part of their genetic coding. What, however, is meant by weak and fluid ties? Maryanski confirmed in her review of the data that monkeys have many strong ties, especially among females who live in high-density matrifocal networks. In monkey societies, males disperse at puberty to other groups, whereas females remain behind, forming as many as four generations of strongly tied matrilines (composed of great-grandmothers, grandmothers, mothers, sisters, aunts, cousins, and daughters). These extended female bonds provide intergenerational continuity and are the backbone of most monkey societies. In contrast, females in ape societies evidence the rare pattern of dispersal where, at puberty, females leave their natal community forever. In addition, males in ape societies (with the exception of the chimpanzee) also depart their natal communities, migrating to a new community. Thus, with both sexes dispersing at puberty, most kinship ties are broken, intergenerational continuity is lost, and the result is a relatively fluid social structure with adult individuals moving about as a shifting collection of individuals within a larger regional population.

In Asia, adult orangutans are nearly solitary, rarely interacting with others. A mother with her dependent young is the only stable social unit. In Africa, chimpanzees and gorillas are more socially inclined, with gorillas living together peacefully in small groups, but individuals are so self-contained that it is uncommon to observe any overt social interactions between adults. Among humans' closest relatives, the common chimpanzee, adult females are also self-contained, spending most of their days traveling about alone with their dependent offspring. Adult chimpanzee males, in contrast, are relatively more social and are likely to have a few individual friendships with other males because, unlike females who come from outside in the regional population and are hence strangers to each other, chimpanzee males have grown up in this larger regional community. A mother and son also form strong ties. But, except for mother and her young offspring, there are no stable groupings in chimpanzee societies. Thus, chimpanzee males are still highly individualistic and self-reliant, preferring to move about independently in space within a large and fluid regional population.

Thus, if humans' closest African ape relatives evidence behavioral propensities for individualism, autonomy, mobility, and weak social ties, Maryanski argues that these genetically coded propensities are probably part of human nature as well. Indeed, if we examine the societal type within which humans as a species evolved—that is, hunting and gathering—it is clear that it approximates the pattern among the great apes, especially African apes: There is considerable mobility within a larger home range of bands; there is a high degree of individualism and personal autonomy; and except for married couples, relatively loose and fluid social ties are evident. At a biological level, then, Maryanski argues that humans might not have the powerful biological urges for great sociality and collectivist-style social bonding that sociologists, and indeed social philosophy in general, frequently impute to our nature.

In collaborative work with Jonathan Turner, Maryanski has described the implications in a review of the stages of societal development. Hunting and gathering is the stage of evolution in which basic human biological coding evolved. In these societies of small societies, wandering bands within a territory evidence rather loose and fluid social ties among their members, high individual autonomy, self-reliance, and mobility from band to band. Yet, as human populations grew in size and were forced to adopt first horticulture and then agriculture to sustain themselves, they settled down to cultivate land, and in the process, they caged themselves in sociocultural forms that violated basic needs for freedom, some degree of individual autonomy, and fluid ties within a larger community of local groups.

Thus, sociocultural evolution began to override the basic nature of humans. As Maryanski and Turner conclude, market-driven systems of the present industrial and post-industrial era are, despite their many obvious problems, closer than horticulture and agrarianism to the original societal type in which humans evolved biologically, at least in this sense: They offer more choices; they allow and indeed encourage individualism; they are structured in ways that make most social ties fluid and transitory; and they limit strong ties beyond family for many. Maryanski and Turner note that, for many sociologists of the past and today, the very features of human behavior required by market-driven societies are viewed as pathologies that violate humans' basic nature. For Maryanski and Turner, societal evolution has, since the hunting and gathering era, just begun once again to create conditions more compatible with humans' basic hominoid nature as an evolved ape.

Although many of these conclusions are obviously somewhat speculative, the point of Maryanski's analysis is clear: If we use evolutionary approaches from biology, such as cladistic analysis and cross-species comparison with humans' close biological relatives, we can make informed inferences about human nature. Then, we can use these inferences to determine whether sociocultural evolution has been compatible or incompatible with humans' primate legacy. From this analysis, it is possible to examine basic institutional systems, such as kinship, polity, religion, and economy to determine how and why they evolved in the first societal type—that is, hunting and gathering—and how they have interacted with humans' basic nature as an evolved ape during the various stages of societal development.

The operating assumptions of Maryanski's approach should perhaps be highlighted, in closing:

1. Humans' closest ape cousins can serve as a distant mirror in which to see the Last Common Ancestor (LCA) to humans and the great apes.

2. By performing cladistic analysis and seeing the traits that humans' primate cousins possess, particularly their network structures, it becomes possible to discern what the LCA's patterns of organization were.

3. This ancestor was virtually solitary, with few strong social ties beyond those of mothers and their offspring, and these ties were likely broken when offspring moved to new communities at puberty.

4. Present-day humans must have some of these bio-programmers in their genes, and so, humans may not be as social as is often assumed.

5. This conclusion forces that sociology reconsider some of its biases about the nature of humans and the basis of human societies, since the common ancestor of humans and the great apes was not social, had no permanent group structures, and indeed, did not have a kinship system beyond a mother and her immature offspring. If such is the case, evolutionary analysis can perhaps indicate how these limitations of humans' primate heritage were mitigated so that present-day humans can forge strong ties in groups. These changes from the ancestor form should be evident by comparing the brains of the great apes with the human brain, but without the restrictive assumptions of evolutionary psychology with its emphasis on modules.

Making Evolutionary Theorizing More Darwinian, More Biological

As is evident, Darwinian-inspired theoretical approaches are highly diverse. Sociobiology and evolutionary psychology are closely linked, but outside this theoretical line, Darwinian approaches are diverse. Perhaps the most promising are those approaches that are comparative, examining humans and their societies with an eye to where they converge with, or diverge from, the societies of other species. Machalek's comparative approach looks for the design problems that natural selection had to overcome to produce macro societies; in isolating these problems, he hits upon key social forces in organizing large-scale patterns of social organization in general. In many ways, his analysis confirms the insights of the fist functional sociologists who all recognized that evolution generates macro societies through differentiation and new modes of integration—whether this society be composed of insects or humans. Indeed, Herbert Spencer's emphasis on *superorganic systems* as the subject matter argues for a sociology that studies all animals and life forms that form societies composed of organisms.

Maryanski's approach takes theorizing back to an issue that has always been prominent in theorizing: human nature. But, her approach liberates analysis from excessive speculation about the needs and drives of humans because it uses cladistic analysis to look back in time to the features of the last common ancestor to apes and humans. In so doing, inferences about human nature are tied to data from the networks of primates to reconstruct the nature of sociality among those species of hominins from which all humans have descended. The picture that emerges of humans' distant ancestors—individualistic, mobile, promiscuous, and weak-tie animals that do not form permanent groupings—is very different than the popular image among both sociologists and the lay public of humans as group oriented and collectivistic. No doubt, evolution has made humans more social than the last common ancestor to apes and humans, and compared to apes as well. But, natural selection does not typically wipe away older traits; rather, it adds new traits onto existing ones, with the result that humans are individualistic and weak-tie animals on whom natural selection has laid down a patina of sociality. There is, in many ways, a conflict in human neuroanatomy between individualism and collectivism that has large consequences for how humans behave, interact, and organize.

The fact that these Darwinian-inspired approaches address traditional sociological questions argues for their persistence in sociology, even as they come under criticisms by those who do not think biological dynamics are necessary in developing sociological theories. Still, even in the face of persistent criticisms, this line of evolutionary sociology is not likely to go away. It is not, as some have claimed a fad, but a pervasive effort to develop a more interdisciplinary sociology—one that recognizes that humans are animals and, hence, have evolved like all other animals, thereby making biological forces relevant in sociological theorizing.

Conclusion

For many sociologists, the revival of evolutionary theorizing in their stage models of societal evolution or in their adoption of key ideas from the Modern Synthesis in evolutionary theory has not been a good thing. These critics had hoped that evolutionary theorizing—whatever its guise—would simply stay dead, but this is only wishful thinking. As I tried to point out, some notion of stages is useful not only as history about how human societies have evolved over the last 200,000 year, the data assembled in tracing the stages of this history are also critical to assessing the plausibility of all macro-level theorizing. It is also wishful thinking that more Darwinian-inspired ideas could stay out of the social sciences because both biologists and then psychologist, and even economists, have brought them back into the social sciences. These are all high-prestige fields compared to sociology, and if they bring the ideas back, then sociologists had better be prepared to deal with them. Rather than reject biologically oriented theorizing, sociologists should bend it to our purposes. Rather than be threatened, as so many are, sociologists should view the revival of biology in sociology as an opportunity to do some new and interesting theorizing and research that does not make the mistakes so evident in sociobiology and evolutionary psychology. Sociologists thus need to demonstrate where biological theorizing can be useful and supplement traditional sociological explanation and where biological reasoning is not useful. In this way, sociology will not make the same mistake as it did at the beginning of the twentieth century by throwing "the body out with the bathwater."

Index

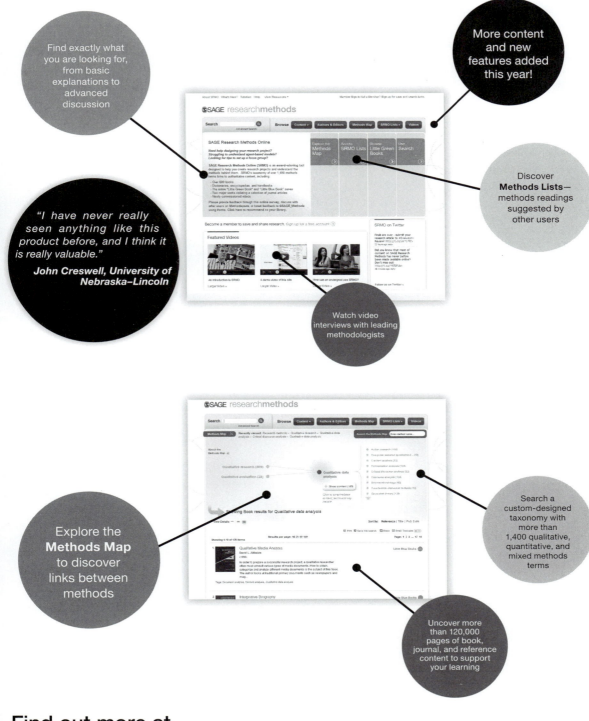

SAGE researchmethods

The essential online tool for researchers from the world's leading methods publisher

Find exactly what you are looking for, from basic explanations to advanced discussion

More content and new features added this year!

"I have never really seen anything like this product before, and I think it is really valuable."

John Creswell, University of Nebraska–Lincoln

Discover **Methods Lists**— methods readings suggested by other users

Watch video interviews with leading methodologists

Explore the **Methods Map** to discover links between methods

Search a custom-designed taxonomy with more than 1,400 qualitative, quantitative, and mixed methods terms

Uncover more than 120,000 pages of book, journal, and reference content to support your learning

Find out more at
www.sageresearchmethods.com